BEST BIRDWATCH

North-East ENGLAND

by
Brian Unwin

with
additional material from Ian Kerr

Illustrations by Richard Allen

BUCKINGHAM PRESS LTD

in
association
with

SWAROVSKI
OPTIK

Published in 2012 by:

Buckingham Press Ltd, 55 Thorpe Park Road, Peterborough

Cambridgeshire PE3 6LJ, United Kingdom

Tel/fax: 01733 561 739

e-mail: buck.press@btinternet.com

www.buckinghampress.co.uk

© Buckingham Press Ltd 2012

ISBN 978-0-9569876-2-4

ISSN 0144-364 X

Editor: David Cromack

Design and maps: Hilary Cromack

Publisher: Hilary Cromack

About the author: After enjoying a long and distinguished career as a newspaper journalist in North-East England, **Brian Unwin** became the local correspondent for The Press Association and in later years contributed news and features to birdwatching magazines and national newspapers. In his spare time he was an enthusiastic birder and helped to form the Durham Bird Club. His death in 2011 robbed the local birdwatching community of an enthusiastic and hardworking contributor but much of his knowledge is preserved in this book, which he laboured to complete despite the seriousness of his illness.

The publishers are grateful to **John Miles** (author of *Best Birdwatching Sites: The Solway* for contributing accounts for Slaley Forest and Derwent Reservoir and to **Ian Kerr** (author of *The Birds of Holy Island*) for his reports on Lindisfarne NNR, Holy Island and a number of other sites, plus the introductory chapters, bird checklist and site access details, to enable this book to be completed. Another of Brian's friends, **Bob Coursey**, made a valuable contribution to proof-reading the final draft.

About the artist: Richard Allen is a freelance wildlife artist and illustrator based in Essex whose work appears in a number of authoritative fieldguides. To see more of his work visit: www.richardallenillustrator.com

Cover: An array of the wildfowl and seabird species that can be seen along the North-East coastline.

Buckingham Press Ltd is registered in England and Wales, no 0533739.
Registered office: 55 Thorpe Park Road, Peterborough PE3 6LJ.

Printed and bound in Great Britain by: Berforts Information Press, Eynsham, Oxford, UK.

CONTENTS

Featured sites in Cleveland

Featured sites in County Durham

CONTENTS

Featured sites in Northumberland

A LAND OF CONTRASTS is a lazy travel writer's cliché that is deployed freely for many parts of the globe, but it is a perfectly appropriate description for the region that encompasses Cleveland, County Durham and Northumberland.

As you explore the pages of this book, written with so much passion and enthusiasm by Brian Unwin, you'll quickly come to appreciate the broad diversity of habitats on offer.

Those of you who enjoy walking peacefully in wild places will be spoilt for choice because Brian tramped many miles to mark out birding trails throughout the upland dales of County Durham and Northumberland. He's also picked out the best places to explore in the vast forested areas of Kielder, Hamsterley and other sites, so if you like to escape the crowds head for the hills.

Naturally the world-famous seabird sites such as the Farne Islands, Coquet Island and Lindisfarne are included in the book, but the coastline of the region has so many other delights to offer, particularly during the periods of spring and autumn migration. Keen-eyed local observers have recorded many rarities, so who knows what you might find yourself?

Even the urbanised areas that were once blighted by coal mining and industrial development are now reverting to nature, so there are exciting birdwatching opportunities from the Scottish border right down to the River Tees.

As a company which is dedicated to providing genuine benefits to the larger birdwatching community, Swarovski Optik is particularly pleased to support this latest addition to a celebrated series of Buckingham Press site guides. As you will read elsewhere, author Brian Unwin sadly died before seeing his book in print, but thanks to the dedication of his family and friends, his words are now available to inspire us all for years to come. Enjoy.

Peter Antoniou
Country Manager UK & Eire
Swarovski Optik UK

SWAROVSKI
OPTIK

THIS BOOK was written by Brian Unwin under the most difficult of circumstances. Brian, an old work colleague and birding friend for more than 30 years, became ill with cancer in 2008 just as he was starting writing up the birding sites of a region of which he had an astounding knowledge. The fact that he was able to largely complete the job gives a measure of his tremendous courage and dedication.

Born the son of a miner in Horden, County Durham, in 1945, he developed an early passion for the natural world from his mother, a farmer's daughter. He acquired his early birdwatching skills in the nearby local wooded denes and on family visits to the Durham moors. As one write-up shows, he had already got to grips with typical upland stream species, Common Sandpipers, Dippers and Grey Wagtails, before he had his first rudimentary pair of binoculars.

Professionally, Brian was a journalist on the North-East's two morning newspapers, *The Journal* and *The Northern Echo*, before becoming the regional reporter for the national news agency, the Press Association. In that role he was the first journalist to be allowed through the police cordon into Lockerbie, devastated by the exploded Pan-Am jet which crashed on the small Scottish town. His graphic account, dictated on his mobile phone as he walked the shattered streets, instantly went around the world.

Brian also cannily managed to arrange a sabbatical with the Royal Navy in the South Atlantic – complete with scope and binoculars, of course – just before the Argentine invasion of the Falklands. On his return he was in much demand by the media as a local expert on that part of the world.

Locally, he was the driving force in setting up the Durham Bird Club and organised the first meeting of local birders which led to its formation. The attention he focussed on Washington, while fighting to save a local pond, was also instrumental in persuading the Wildfowl and Wetlands Trust to establish its major centre in the new town.

Though Durham was his first love, he also birdwatched throughout the North-East, as well as enjoying trips to America, Japan, Sri Lanka, just about every region of Britain and many parts of Europe.

For the last 20 years of his career Brian was a freelance writer, specialising in wildlife, particularly birds, and working mainly for national newspapers, magazines and turning his skilled hand and experience to the rapidly developing world of websites. His association with *The Northern Echo* continued with his weekly and much-appreciated *Birdwatch* column until shortly before his death.

As he worked on the book his health continued to deteriorate and he spent long periods in hospital for major surgery. I remember regularly visiting him in the Royal Victoria Infirmary, Newcastle, and finding him compiling 'still to do' lists. On return home to convalesce he went straight back to work.

However, an indication of just how ill he had become was in 2009 when he was unable to get along to see Britain's first Eastern Crowned Warbler, even though it was just three miles from his home at Whitburn, Sunderland.

INTRODUCTION

During 2011, to ease the pressure he was then feeling and knowing that his time was limited, Brian asked me to help with a few site write-ups from my home county of Northumberland. These included St Mary's Island, Tynemouth, North Shields fish quay, Whittle Dene reservoirs and the Bamburgh and Stag Rocks area. I also provided the site account for Lindisfarne and Holy Island, a bit of a busman's holiday as my own book for that migration hotspot is now in its third edition.

Brian's dearest wish was to see this book completed and with the support of his wife, Jennifer, and children, Barry and Beverley, he worked right until his death at the early age of 66 just after Christmas 2011. I know that even in his final days he continued to make notes on things which still needed to be sorted out and points to be checked.

After his death, Jennifer and David Cromack of Buckingham Press invited me to finish the job on Brian's behalf. I was delighted to do so. My job was, essentially, tying up loose ends, doing a bit of editing and proof-reading and providing the introductory sections and sorting out our long and impressive regional bird list.

This book is, therefore, a tribute to a very fine birder and old friend whose courage during his long illness impressed everyone who knew him. Brian's work should ensure that visitors can enjoy not just the many birding hotspots of the North-East but also the quieter corners, particularly the Durham dales and moors, which, I suspect, were really his favourites.

Enjoy your visits!

Ian Kerr
Newcastle upon Tyne July 2012

ACKNOWLEDGEMENTS

DURING the research and writing of the site accounts, Brian received help and advice from many local birdwatchers. Unfortunately, he didn't get around to listing their names before his illness brought the job to a standstill. In the circumstances, the publishers can only express their thanks and gratitude to everyone he did consult and apologise for the fact that their contributions are not acknowledged in the usual way.

Brian did leave a list of organisations, particularly local bird clubs, whose data from annual reports, bulletins and other publications was used to help to compile the bird lists for the sites. Other organisations helped with details of breeding species, the occurrences of rarities and other information which has helped to make the site accounts so comprehensive.

These organisations included: British Birds Rarities Committee, Durham Bird Club, Durham Wildlife Trust, Easington District Council, Industry Nature Conservation Association, National Trust, Natural England, Northern Kites and Friends of Red Kites, Northumberland National Park, Northumberland & Tyneside Bird Club, Northumberland Wildlife Trust, Northumbrian Water, Royal Society for the Protection of Birds, Teesmouth Bird Club and Wildfowl and Wetlands Trust.

ACKNOWLEDGEMENTS

Brian's family wish to publicly express heartfelt thanks to Mr Daya Karat, Upper Gastro Intestinal Surgeon and his team on Ward 36 at the Newcastle Royal Victoria Infirmary, who saved his life in October 2009, enabling Brian two more years to work on his book.

PUBLISHER'S PERSONAL TRIBUTE

MY ASSOCIATION with Brian Unwin was both a professional relationship and friendship conducted almost exclusively by telephone and e-mail for a period of more than 25 years because we lived more than 150 miles apart.

When I was appointed as editor of Peterborough-based *Bird Watching* magazine in 1988 I felt it was important to create a team of freelance contributors with birding and ornithological credentials that far outstripped my own. Brian's position as the Press Association's North-East England regional correspondent was a guarantee that he was a proven journalistic talent and throughout our long working relationship he proved this repeatedly with a string of important news stories, as well as news-based and travel features and detailed obituaries of the great and good within the birding community.

When Brian expressed an interest in writing a guide for his beloved North-East England for Buckingham Press, I jumped at the chance to add this particular volume to the growing stable of *Best Birdwatching Sites* books.

Sadly he was unable to complete the manuscript before he died in December 2011. At the funeral the vicar told a very touching story about how Brian met his wife Jennifer and on their first date declared that his ambition was to write a book ....now thanks to the sterling efforts of his close friend and fellow journalist Ian Kerr, who has filled in the missing gaps, the promise has been fulfilled.

All of us associated with *Best Birdwatching Sites: North-East England* believe the depth of detail and passion that Brian brought to the writing will be obvious to every reader and that the book will become a fitting memento to his dedicated efforts on behalf of all birdwatchers. Brian's twin passions of finding vagrants and exploring undiscovered corners of the vast hinterland of the Durham Dales shine out from so many of the site accounts that I'm sure you'll be inspired to visit them yourself. Put the book to the test and we are sure you will agree that this is the 'guide of choice' for anyone visiting sites in Cleveland, County Durham or Northumberland.

David Cromack
Publisher, Buckingham Press

COMPRISING the counties of Cleveland, County Durham, Tyne and Wear and Northumberland, this is a region of very sharp contrasts, ranging from old industrial areas to spectacular coasts and seabird colonies, broad farmland, huge forests and vast tracts of high and very peaceful moorlands.

North to south, the region stretches 110 miles from the Scottish border, just beyond Berwick-up-Tweed, to Saltburn south of the River Tees and some 60 miles from North Sea coast to the border with Cumbria.

Cleveland was founded on steel and chemicals, Tyne and Wear on shipbuilding and heavy engineering and Durham and much of Northumberland on the once-mighty coal industry. Not much you might think at first glance to appeal to birds – but you'd be wrong. Much of the old industry has vanished and been replaced by the new and this has left a legacy that birds in their thousands are only too happy to exploit.

Some of the wetlands of the region are an industrial legacy while others, particularly around the Tees, are the remnants of a once-vast marshland and saltings most of which was swallowed up by development. The superb RSPB reserve at Saltholme in Cleveland shows what can be achieved with old 'brown field' sites.

Many of Durham's wetlands and, particularly, those at places like Cresswell Pond on the Northumberland coast, result from centuries of mining subsidence. The newer bird-rich wetlands at Druridge, Chevington, Hauxley and Maiden's Hall are the result of imaginative restoration after more recent opencast mining. That work is still going on and those areas just get better and better as nature takes over.

Coastal attractions are provided, particularly in Northumberland, by some of England's longest, broadest and finest beaches and the huge seabird colonies of the Farne Islands and Coquet Island.

Much of the hinterland throughout the region is dominated by lowland farming. Further west, the dales of the region reach upwards into the Pennines and Cheviot Hills, some of the quietest places left in Britain. Their solitude always seems to come as a very pleasant surprise to visitors from the South-East and more crowded parts of Britain. Recently a birder from Kent told me: "We walked all day in the Cheviots and never saw a soul. We could have been the only folk left in the world."

Other upland areas are dominated by vast forests, including Kielder, reputedly Britain's largest man-made forest surrounding its largest man-made lake. Other huge forests blanket sections of the uplands at Hamsterley, Harwood and Kidland.

All of these very different areas have their own birding attractions, as a glance through this book will show.

BIRD COUNTY DESIGNATIONS

Though Cleveland, which is centred on the Teesside urban area, ceased to exist as a local government county in 1996 it has been retained as a bird recording area by the British Trust for Ornithology, RSPB and the Association of County Recorders. Accordingly, we have retained it as a geographical entity within the book.

Tyne & Wear, which was abolished as a county in 1986, now consists of the cities of Newcastle and Sunderland and the metropolitan boroughs of South Tyneside, North Tyneside and Gateshead.

Bird records for these areas are now submitted either to the Durham or Northumberland county recorders depending on the location of the site where a bird was seen, with the River Tyne the dividing line for most of the region. For the purposes of this book, the publishers have assigned sites within the boroughs to either Durham or Northumberland to stay consistent with this bird recording policy.

VISITING THE NORTH-EAST – SOME PRACTICAL POINTS

Though there are alternative methods of seeing North-East England, the vast majority of birders are likely to be travelling by car with the obvious flexibility it provides for making the most of any visit.

The eastern half of the region has a very good road network but it should be borne in mind that this is a busy urban area, particularly around Cleveland, Hartlepool, Sunderland and Tyneside.

The A1M through Durham, which continues northwards as the A1 through Northumberland, is very busy at most times. However, it does act as a handy dividing line with areas to the west, except for the main A66 and A69 routes to Cumbria, being much quieter and more pleasant, particularly for visitors from more crowded regions.

Many minor country roads, particularly in western areas, are just that – often single-tracked with passing places where, obviously, care must be taken and courtesy exercised. Many roads across moorland are narrow and unfenced and sheep, which shepherds insist have an uncanny talent for thinking up new ways of suicide, just love to sit on, either to absorb warmth in cool weather or to cool off on hot days. Trying to watch for Red Grouse, Curlews and Wheatears while you're on the move is definitely not recommended!

Parking is not much of a problem, even at busy sites on the coast. Most towns and villages have pay & display systems but elsewhere parking is plentiful and often free. Care should be taken not to block field gates, and other accesses and narrow lanes to maintain good relations with farmers and others who have to earn their living from the land.

PUBLIC TRANSPORT AND DISABLED ACCESS

Rail links from London and other major centres to Darlington, Durham, Newcastle and Berwick are very good. Local train services link Newcastle with Sunderland, Hartlepool and Middlesbrough and westwards to Carlisle.

The Tyne and Wear Metro is a very efficient service and operates fast and very frequent services between Newcastle and Sunderland and from the city to North Shields, Tynemouth, Whitley Bay and Newcastle Airport, all areas containing some very good local birding sites, as the book shows.

Bus services in the major conurbations are generally good but in more rural and remote areas they are often few and far between. At the time of writing, some services are being threatened with closure altogether because of spending cuts by the local councils which provide their subsidies. But it is still possible to use buses to reach many sites in this book by carefully planning your journey.

By the very nature of some sites, disabled access can be limited. Again, those with access for wheelchairs are detailed in the site write-up and in the section at the back of this publication. If you have any doubt,s it would be best to contact the relevant site management bodies or local tourist authorities.

ACCOMMODATION, FOOD AND TOILETS

Finding accommodation in the North-East is usually not a problem but please bear in mind that some areas, particularly the Northumberland coast, attract large numbers of holidaymakers right through from spring to autumn and things can be busy at peak periods. For example, it would be unwise to turn up unprepared at a birding hotspot such as Holy Island during the October school holidays (also the peak time for migration) and expect to find a bed for the night. Time spent in preparation, as my military friends always tell me, is never wasted!

There is a range of accommodation to suit all budgets from expensive hotels to bed and breakfast and self-catering in cottages or caravans. Contacting local tourism offices is the quickest and simplest way, particularly as most keep lists of available accommodation in their areas. Contact details are included in many write-ups.

There in no shortage of places to eat around the region, again something to suit all pockets. Many hotels, pubs and restaurants take pride in using local ingredients, particularly meat and fish, for which the region is famed. Craster kippers, for example, have a world-wide reputation and the region seems to have lots of Rick Stein 'Food Heroes.'

In country areas and smaller towns and villages, evening meals tend to be served early. Away from cities and larger centres, if you turn up expecting to be fed after 9pm you could have difficulties. Again, planning ahead is wise and at busy times, particularly during school and bank holidays, booking is recommended.

The region's main reserves all have good toilet facilities and all towns and most villages have their public facilities. However, many of the more remote birding areas do not. An attempt has been made to deal with this issue in the Key Points sections for each site.

NORTH-EAST ENGLAND has a huge diversity of other creatures ranging in size from grey seals down to butterflies, moths and a myriad of other insects, so there are plenty of other reasons for the natural history enthusiast to visit the region.

Mammals including foxes, badgers, stoats, weasels and a full range of voles, shrews and mice are widespread but there are special species which are always worth making that extra bit of effort to encounter.

Grey seals are particularly numerous and are very easy to find, particularly along the Northumberland coast, because of their huge breeding colony on the Farne Islands. A highlight of any autumn visit is a trip out to the islands during their breeding season (see Farne Islands section).

Mainland rocky outcrops often attract basking parties of seals. The sandbars off the Heugh, Holy Island, can hold many hundreds at low tide in summer and autumn, their rising and falling voices (I like to think of it as singing) often baffling first-time visitors. Common seals are usually confined to southern areas with parties regularly congregating on the mud-banks at Greatham Creek.

Another special animal is the otter, which now has healthy and growing populations along every river, with individuals regularly seen even in busy urban areas along the Tyne. Though normally nocturnal, they do show regularly during the day, particularly at the chain of waters along Druridge Bay. It's really a question of luck, patience and being in the right place at the right time.

Roe deer are common, not just in the woodland and forested areas, but often on urban fringes. They also frequent moorland and other places without any tree cover. Visitors are often amazed to see a small herd on Holy Island where they have bred successfully since 2008.

The really special mammal, but sadly now largely confined to Northumberland, is red squirrel. The county is one of England's last strongholds with good populations in both large conifer forests, isolated moorland shelter belts and some hanging on in deciduous and mixed woodlands.

Grey squirrels have advanced right through Cleveland and Durham into south Northumberland where a rearguard action is taking place against them. Fortunately, they don't seem to like conifer forests, so hopefully the embattled native squirrels can remain safe from competition and disease.

Though the region doesn't have as many butterfly species (an average of around 40 per year) as southern England, it does have its own specialities. These include northern brown argus at sites in County Durham, including Bishop Middleham quarry (the country's only recent Bee-eater nesting site).

Brown argus has its northern outpost in Cleveland, where sites include Cowpen Bewley Country Park. Similarly, White-letter hairstreak is at its northern limit, with sites including the Lower Derwent Valley. Small pearl-bordered fritillaries can be found on moorland areas. Holly blue and speckled wood are recent arrivals from further south, so the picture is one of constant change. See www.northeast-butterflies.org.uk for up-to-date information.

So far more then 1,280 moth species have been recorded. But with 22 new species found in 2010 and ten more in 2011, obviously many more are still to be discovered. If you're into moths don't forget to bring your trap and you might just add to the region's tally. www.nemoths.co.uk and www northumberlandmoths.org are useful websites.

Most ponds, marshes and waterways support good populations of dragonflies and damselflies with amphibians including great crested newts. Grass snakes tend to reach their northern limit in Durham but adders are widespread on our moorlands.

The region has its flora hotspots, too. Two of them, Upper Teesdale and Lindisfarne, are of international importance. The Moor House-Upper Teesdale NNR around Cow Green Reservoir is famed for its assemblage of rare Arctic-alpine plants, a relic of the last Ice Age. It is the only site in England to see the incredibly bright blue flowers of the spring gentian. It also has bird's eye primrose and mountain pansy.

Three species of lady's mantle found in Upper Teesdale grow nowhere else in Britain. The valleys below this wonderful upland area are rich in globeflower (site office 01833 622 374)

At Lindisfarne NNR, the Snook area of Holy Island is particularly important. Apart from the full range of northern coastal plants, the island has ten species of orchid, including coralroot and frog orchid. It also has its own unique orchid, the recently-discovered Lindisfarne helleborine, which attracts botanists from around the world.

Other special species include creeping willow, seaside centaury, grass of Parnassus, butterwort and round-leaved wintergreen (site office 01289 381470).

I hope that this very brief summary convinces you that a visit can produce very much more than the birds for which the region is so special.

SEAWATCHING ALONG THE NORTH-EAST COAST

WITH WELL OVER 100 miles of coastline Cleveland, Durham, Tyne and Wear and Northumberland can provide some exhilarating seawatching, some of it in truly magnificent scenic surroundings. Much of the north Northumberland coast is officially designated as an Area of Outstanding Natural Beauty.

Of course, weather conditions play a major part in the success or otherwise of seawatching and a general rule is 'The worse the weather, the better the birding.' That means that you have to be prepared for anything the elements can fling at you. In the right conditions, i.e. with winds from the east or north and perhaps accompanied by heavy rain, you'll probably find plenty of knowledgeable local company at prime sites.

TOP SEAWATCHING TIPS

• The best times are usually April-May for spring passage and August-November for the really exciting stuff. But good birds can turn up virtually at any time, so don't be put off at other times of year if conditions look right.

• Keep a close eye on local weather forecasts, particularly wind directions as they are absolutely crucial to movements at sea. Easterly and northerly winds, allied with low pressure systems and rain, usually produce the best passages.

• Wrap up warmly, and remember that waterproofs are one of the essential bits of kit for seawatching, even during summer, particularly along such an exposed coastline.

• You'll struggle with identification without a telescope as many birds can be flying past at a great distance.

• Identify stationary features such as buoys or flags to help describe the positions of passing birds. The coast has a thriving inshore fishing industry for crabs and lobsters and its lines of pots – locally called creels – are marked with coloured flags: 'Sooty passing double black flag NOW!' is the kind of thing you are likely to hear from knowledgeable locals.

• High tide when birds are nearer the coast can often be the most productive periods for seawatching. Early mornings and the couple of hours before dusk can often be productive, but in the right weather conditions birds can pass at any time.

• Don't be shy about calling out birds when you spot one moving. Other watchers present will appreciate it and reciprocate. Many eyes make for better birding!

• Always expect the unexpected by paying close attention to passing common species, including gulls and Fulmars, as part of 'getting your eye in' on size, colour and flight action or 'jizz' in birding parlance.

• Keep your notebook handy and if passage is heavy count what you are seeing. Please don't just assume someone else will be passing on sightings to the local county recorder.

KEY SEAWATCHING SITES

Anywhere along the coast can produce some good spells of seawatching when conditions are right. But there are a number of localities which thrust out into the North Sea and which, year after year, produce the real goodies and the highest counts. Mobile phones mean that many local seawatchers now keep in close contact to ensure that some rare species can be logged from a number of sites as they move along the coast.

The prime sea-watching sites are listed here from south to north and further details and maps are included in the various site accounts.

South Gare

This site at the mouth of the Tees gives tremendous views to the south. As most heavy passage off the north east coast involves birds moving northwards, birders here can often be the first to realise that something good is happening. Watching from your car is possible in the worst of the weather. Please don't under any circumstances go beyond the 'No entry' signs as this can be extremely dangerous in storms.

Hartlepool Headland

Year after year the headland produces good seabird counts and many rarities. But you could have a happy dilemma! During migration seasons it's such a prime site you could be torn between watching the sea and seeking out migrants making their first landfall.

Whitburn

It's the prime site on the Durham coast and local birders have built up a very impressive list of rarities. A seawatching hide is managed by the National Trust. Keys cost £12, so for a one-off visit it won't be worthwhile. Further details from NT at nearby Souter Lighthouse (0191-5290909 or www.nationaltrust.org./souter-lighthouse.

St Mary's Island

A public hide is available on the seaward side of the lighthouse and provides excellent views, both to the north and south. This very popular site has produced a multitude of good records including a Northumberland record passage of Storm Petrels.

Church Point, Newbiggin

This exposed headland is Northumberland's prime seawatching site. The term 'exposed' says it all. There is no shelter from the elements except a tiny brick building capable of holding a couple of folk at a squeeze although caravans on the point can at least provide a windbreak. But the rewards during heavy passage can more than compensate.

Snab Point

Just a mile north of Newbiggin at the southern end of Druridge Bay, the point has a small car park high above the sea. In the worst of weather it's possible to sea-watch without even getting out of your vehicle. There's a larger car park a few yards to the south. A thick screen of bushes on its north side gives plenty of shelter from northerly winds.

Hauxley

The Northumberland Wildlife Trust reserve has a seawatching hide looking out towards Coquet Island, the UK's main site for Roseate Terns. During really bad weather many birds pass between the mainland and island. At other times they tend to be deflected out to sea by the island.

Newton Point

Another headland without shelter which can provide good seawatching in the right conditions. Between April-September on days when no obvious passage is underway large numbers of terns from local colonies are usually offshore.

Emmanuel Head

This exposed easterly point of Holy Island with its 200-year-old white navigation pyramid provides some very good watching, particularly during heavy passages of shearwaters, skuas and, particularly from October onwards, of Little Auks when influxes occur. The pyramid gives some shelter and has two handy benches.

SPECIES WHICH CAN BE EXPECTED

Below are listed the main seabird species which can be expected but obviously some are rarer than others. Not included are geese, ducks, divers, grebes, Cormorants, Shags, waders, regular gull and tern species which also occur offshore but not only during periods of good sea passage. The usual months for sightings appear in brackets.

- Fulmar (February-September). Common and usually involved in heavy passage in late summer and autumn. Some return to sit around colonies during fine periods in winter. Occasional 'blue' phase birds are seen and, on one occasion, a pure white individual.
- Cory's Shearwater (September-November). Scarce but usually an annual visitor
- Great Shearwater (September-October). Rare occasional visitor.
- Sooty Shearwater (August-September). Usually uncommon but numbers vary considerably and occasional large influxes occur.
- Manx Shearwater (April-May and August-October). Locally common, usually passing in good numbers, particularly during latter period.
- Balearic Shearwater (August-September). Scarce but a few are seen in most years.
- Storm Petrel (July-September). Sightings are scarce from land but occasionally occur. The regular presence of birds in local waters has been shown by tape-luring for ringing during summer.

• Gannet (late February-November, occasional birds in winter). Common because of fishing movements from Bass Rock colony but with large numbers, sometimes thousands per day, involved in spring and autumn movements

• Pomarine Skua (August-November). Usually uncommon but influxes can occur. Occasional birds have appeared in winter.

• Arctic Skua (April- May and August-November). Uncommon during spring passage but much more plentiful in late summer and autumn. Rare in winter.

• Long-tailed Skua (August-October). Uncommon in most years.

• Great Skua (April-May and August-November). Usually uncommon but regular in small numbers.

• Sabine's Gull (August-November). Uncommon but fairly regular during heavy passages of Kittiwakes and other species.

• Kittiwake (April-November). Common during periods of heavy passage but also regularly offshore from local breeding colonies.

• Little Gull (July-October). Usually uncommon but increasing numbers have appeared in recent years. Occasional winter records.

• Black Tern (July-October). Scarce but sometimes associated with Kittiwake and Little Gull movements.

• Guillemot (March-November). Common during heavy passage. Many with young are also offshore in summer from local breeding colonies. A few remain offshore in winter.

• Razorbill (March-November). Locally common but not as numerous as Guillemot. Again numbers are obscured by presence of local breeders.

• Little Auk (October-March). Uncommon in most years but occasional influxes, some huge, can occur after north westerly Atlantic gales push birds into the North Sea. A staggering 28,000 in a day has been recorded from the Farne Islands.

• Puffin (March-November). Uncommon during passage but many thousands are offshore during the breeding season.

Other species on the north east list which have occurred during heavy passages include Fea's/Zino's Petrel, Macaronesian Shearwater, Leach's Petrel and White-winged Black Tern. All are very rare but keep a good look-out, you might just be lucky!

HERE is a typical layout of the site guide pages. Once familiar with the layout, you will be able to extract the information you need quickly and painlessly.

Title of site. Sites are listed in alphabetical order and numbered.

Key points: Opening times, terrain, suitability for wheelchair users and other useful tips. ALWAYS check opening times with the site managers before you visit.

Target birds and the likelihood of seeing them: Lists the species for which the reserve is most noted. The percentage figure gives a rough idea – based on the author's experiences at the site – of how likely you are to see the target species, provided you visit the site at the correct time and stay for a reasonable amount of time. Where you see 'winter raptors (25%)' this means that you have a 25% chance of seeing each species of raptor at the site.

Other possible species: A guide to some of the commoner species you are likely to see, season-by-season, though space does not allow 100 per cent to be covered. Under the *Occasional birds* sub-heading you will find a list of rarer species which are not recorded enough to be included in the Target Birds section.

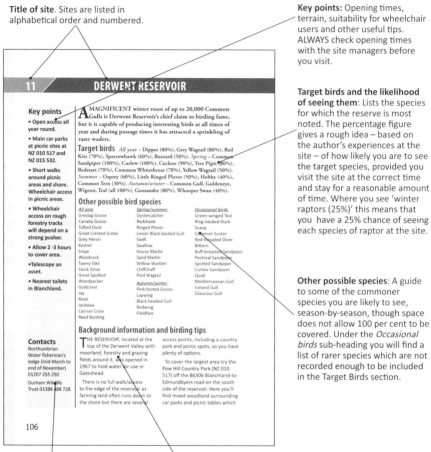

Useful contacts: Phone numbers to confirm access details etc.

Background information: Generally, this section will take you through the walk, with details of the birds that you might see and handy tips to help you see them. It might contain more information on points which have been briefly mentioned in previous sections, e.g. more extensive bird lists, more detailed information about terrain etc.

Best time of year to visit. There may be things to see at other times of year but this season is likely to produce the best results.

Relevant OS Landranger map number

Grid reference(s) of parking area(s) giving easiest access to site.

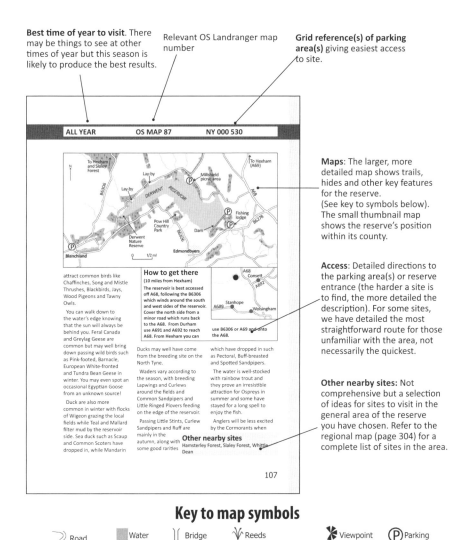

Maps: The larger, more detailed map shows trails, hides and other key features for the reserve. (See key to symbols below). The small thumbnail map shows the reserve's position within its county.

Access: Detailed directions to the parking area(s) or reserve entrance (the harder a site is to find, the more detailed the description). For some sites, we have detailed the most straightforward route for those unfamiliar with the area, not necessarily the quickest.

Other nearby sites: Not comprehensive but a selection of ideas for sites to visit in the general area of the reserve you have chosen. Refer to the regional map (page 304) for a complete list of sites in the area.

ALL YEAR   OS MAP 87   NY 000 530

attract common birds like Chaffinches, Song and Mistle Thrushes, Blackbirds, Jays, Wood Pigeons and Tawny Owls.

You can walk down to the water's edge knowing that the sun will always be behind you. Feral Canada and Greylag Geese are common but may well bring down passing wild birds such as Pink-footed, Barnacle, European White-fronted and Tundra Bean Geese in winter. You may even spot an occasional Egyptian Goose from an unknown source!

Duck are also more common in winter with flocks of Wigeon grazing the local fields while Teal and Mallard filter mud by the reservoir side. Sea duck such as Scaup and Common Scoters have dropped in, while Mandarin

How to get there
(10 miles from Hexham)
The reservoir is best accessed off A68, following the B6306 which winds around the south and west sides of the reservoir. Cover the north side from a minor road which runs back to the A68. From Durham use A691 and A692 to reach A68. From Hexham you can use B6306 or A69 and onto the A68.

Ducks may well have come from the breeding site on the North Tyne.

Waders vary according to the season, with breeding Lapwings and Curlews around the fields and Common Sandpipers and Little Ringed Plovers feeding on the edge of the reservoir.

Passing Little Stints, Curlew Sandpipers and Ruff are mainly in the autumn, along with some good rarities

which have dropped in such as Pectoral, Buff-breasted and Spotted Sandpipers.

The water is well-stocked with rainbow trout and they prove an irresistible attraction for Ospreys in summer and some have stayed for a long spell to enjoy the fish.

Anglers will be less excited by the Cormorants when

Other nearby sites
Hamsterley Forest, Slaley Forest, Whittle Dean

107

Key to map symbols

- Road
- Track
- Footpath
- Water
- Trees
- Mud
-)(Bridge
- Lighthouse
- Marsh
- Reeds
- Conifer forest
- Broadleaf woodland
- Viewpoint
- Scale (miles)
- Train station
- (P) Parking

THE AIM of this chapter is to give a brief overview of what birds are normally around during each month and the best spots to see them.

JANUARY

MANY BIRDERS like to be out bright and early to get their annual lists off to a flying start, though in a region where Scottish influences are strong and old-fashioned New Year celebrations are still big, it doesn't apply to everyone! New Year bird-races are popular and some keen characters can clock up as many as 125 species, starting with Tawny Owl before dawn.

Coastal areas are always the most productive with large concentrations of waders and wildfowl and flocks of gulls in harbours and local ponds. Inland, things are normally quiet, with most species concentrated around reservoirs.

January is excellent for the prime sites of Lindisfarne and Druridge Bay in Northumberland, the reservoirs of Durham and for the many pools and coastal hotspots around Cleveland. Normally around 3,000 Brent Geese are at Lindisfarne, the only British wintering ground of the pale-bellied Svalbard race, while in recent winters several hundred Barnacle Geese have remained around Budle Bay.

The area also teems with Shelducks, Wigeon, Golden and Grey Plovers, Lapwings, Knot, Curlews, Bar-tailed Godwits and Dunlin. Offshore are hundreds of Eiders and smaller numbers of Long-tailed Ducks, Common Scoters, Red-breasted Mergansers, Shags and Cormorants. It's also by far the best regional site for Pintails and Red-necked and Slavonian Grebes.

Druridge Bay has large numbers of Pink-footed, Greylag and Canada Geese, Wigeon, Teal and other duck, including the occasional Smew. Herds of Whooper Swans are regular and one or two Bitterns are usually present but always extremely elusive.

The Durham reservoirs at Derwent, Hurworth Burn and Crookfoot also hold large numbers of wildfowl and one or two Smew. Similarly, in Cleveland the Tees estuary, Greatham Creek and the various ponds at RSPB Saltholme and neighbouring sites prove a magnet for wintering wildfowl and waders.

The entire coastline is usually good for flocks of smaller wintering species, including Skylarks, Linnets and Twite and variable numbers of Snow Buntings. Birders should always be alert for brief glimpses of their predators as Hen Harriers, Merlins and Peregrines are also drawn to coastal areas. Rough coastal ground also usually has a few Short-eared Owls, though their numbers vary considerable from year to year.

Harbours at Seahouses, Amble, Blyth, the Tyne estuary, Sunderland, Hartlepool and theTees estuary all hold large concentrations of regular gulls, always worth checking carefully for 'white-winged' Arctic species. Iceland and Glaucous Gulls are fairly regular visitors, particularly after north westerly Atlantic gales.

FEBRUARY

EVERYTHING said about January birds and sites still applies. All of the wintering species remain and the same sites are all worth further visits, particularly if some have been missed. During the month, geese and ducks can become restless and start to move around. There can be a small but steady decline with some Brent Geese leaving Lindisfarne for Denmark, the other wintering area of the Svalbard race, and skeins of Pinkfeet drifting northwards into eastern Scotland.

Some Black-headed Gulls moult into breeding plumage and it is noticeable that Shags are beginning to get breeding crests. Late in the month the first signs of seabird migration are underway. Herring and Great Black-backed Gulls are moving north as are first lines of Gannets beating steadily northwards to claim the best breeding sites on the Bass Rock in the Firth of Forth.

On fine days, Fulmars are back on breeding cliffs at Holy Island, Howick, Dunstanburgh, Tynemouth and South Shields and the first Kittiwakes are back offshore after spending the winter out in the Atlantic.

If the weather is fine Robins, Mistle and Song Thrushes and Blackbirds can be tempted into song. On farmland a few Skylarks are usually starting to sing and on rough and marginal land Lapwings can begin to display. Sudden changes in the weather can stop all that in its tracks.

MARCH

THIS IS THE great change-over month: days are lengthening and numbers of many wintering species decline as spring arrival begins. Wildfowl and waders numbers drop as birds move off northwards, leaving the mudflats and coastal ponds noticeably quiet.

Many common resident species are now in full voice. The North-East is lucky in still having good populations of farmland species, including Lapwings and Skylarks. Lapwings are now in full, rolling display on both lowland pasture and on moor-edge fields. The reserves at Saltholme and Druridge Bay has provided new habitat for healthy local breeding populations while even a small area such as Holy Island provides up to 30 pairs.

Another species which has crashed in Britain, Black Grouse, still has thriving populations in upper Teesdale and upper Weardale and neighbouring areas of south-west Northumberland and males are now normally in full and bizarre display. Few regional birders can resist a visit to the best lekking site at Langdon Beck.

Another regional speciality, Goshawk, is also in full aerial display over prime forest sites such as Kielder, Harwood and Hamsterley. The trick is to find a good vantage spot – and then be patient.

By mid-month the first early migrants arrive, usually along the coast. Little groups of Sand Martins seek insect hatches over rivers and ponds and early Wheatears flash white as they flit along the beaches and coastal fields. Others arrive overland, flying up the Pennines to rocky moorland breeding areas.

Ring Ouzels are now an uncommon species in England, so it is always thrilling to hear newly-arrived males in song in the upper reaches of the Durham dales and upstream from Alwinton in Coquetdale. From mid-March onwards Chiffchaffs are singing in woodland throughout the region.

On the coast the first Sandwich Terns arrive and thousands of Puffins and other auks gather excitedly around breeding colonies at Coquet Island and the Farne Islands.

APRIL

THE ARRIVAL of migrants continues apace, ranging from Ospreys which are usually back at breeding sites around Kielder Reservoir down to the first Swallows, House Martins, Willow Warblers, Blackcaps, Garden Warblers, Lesser and Common Whitethroats, Grasshopper and Sedge Warblers. They are followed late in the month by Wood Warblers in local hotspots, including Allen Banks, and Reed Warblers around pools at Druridge Bay, their most northerly local breeding site.

Redstarts occupy woodland and Cuckoos move into upland areas. Spotted Flycatchers take up territories across a wide range of habitats while Pied Flycatchers arrive in oak woodlands in the dales and higher valleys.

By the end of the month thousands of Arctic and Common Terns have arrived, followed by the first Roseate Terns at Coquet Island. Little Terns have colonies at Crimdon, Long Nanny Burn and Lindisfarne. Coastal ponds prove attractive to passage waders including Ruff, Greenshanks and Black-tailed Godwits.

Moorlands are back to life after winter's silence with displaying waders and thousands of Skylarks and Meadow Pipits. Teesdale, Weardale and Allendale all have particularly high concentrations of Lapwings, Curlews and Snipe, all a joy to see and hear at this stage.

MAY

THE BREEDING SEASON is now in full swing and the arrival of late migrants continues. It is also the period along the coast which usually provides a few rarities such as Wrynecks, Red-backed Shrikes, Subalpine Warblers, Bluethroats, Black Redstarts, White and Blue-headed Wagtails and Ortolan Buntings. This leads to many local birders putting in time at migration hotspots including Hartlepool Headland, Whitburn, St Mary's Island, Bamburgh and Holy Island, particularly when easterly or northerly weather and rain provides 'fall' conditions.

During May when local birds are already breeding another run of Wheatears takes place along the coast. Birds of the Greenland race can often be prominent, with Holy Island producing regular records of parties lingering for a few days. Some have involved as many as 100 birds.

New waves of passage waders also occur. Large numbers of Golden and Ringed Plovers, Sanderlings and Dunlin which have wintered further south move through the region with big concentrations at areas that include Seal Sands and Lindisfarne.

JUNE

THIS IS THE month to take in breeding seabirds. Kittiwake colonies at South Shields, Tynemouth, inland at Newcastle Quayside, and further north along the Northumberland coast are in full raucous action. The mainland tern colonies at Crimdon, Long Nanny Burn and Lindisfarne are noisy but the real jewels are the Farne Islands and Coquet Island. With almost 100,000 pairs of seabirds in situ, they are 'must see' localities for every birder.

Whenever I take first-time visitors to the Farnes they are always staggered by the experience of walking through tern colonies (even if the Arctics have a nasty habit of pecking heads hard enough to draw blood) and of seeing thousands of Puffins and Guillemots and hundreds of Razorbills going about their business. To be able to stand next to the nests of Eiders, Cormorant and Shags is for them an unforgettable experience.

Though landing is not permitted on Coquet Island, boat trips from Amble allow visitors very close views all of its breeding birds, including its rare Roseate Terns, at their main UK colony.

Other coastal areas are now rather quiet, though annually small numbers of non-breeding waders remain, including a couple of hundred Bar-tailed Godwits at Lindisfarne, though Oystercatchers, Redshanks and Turnstones are spread thinly.

June is also a good time to see Avocets at their nesting site alongside the busy main road at Greatham Creek. This colony probably provided the springboard for breeding in Durham in 2008 and in Northumberland for the first time at Cresswell Pond in 2011.

Inland attractions are breeding Ospreys at Kielder and the opportunity to listen for Nightjars at Slaley Forest, one of their few regular sites in the region.

For those interested in botany, June is the best month for the region's flora such as ten species of orchids on Holy Island, including the unique Lindisfarne Helleborine.

JULY

THOUGH THE breeding season is just about over, there is still time to visit the seabird colonies if you missed out last month. Very soon auks will start dispersing to sea, while terns and their young have already begun to wander the coast.

Return wader passage gets underway. By mid-month the first returning Grey Plovers, Knot and Bar-tailed Godwits are on the coast. These very early birds are probably failed breeders which departed early from the Arctic. For a short period these Knot and godwits in their brick-red breeding plumages and Grey Plovers, resplendent in silvery grey and black, really stand out among the small numbers of drab non-breeding waders which have summered.

Return passage also begins to involve Whimbrels, moving overhead with their far-carrying calls, and Common Sandpipers down from their breeding sites on upland rivers and streams. Large numbers of Oystercatchers, Curlews and Redshanks which have bred locally are prominent at this stage.

Smaller species are also on the move with passage involving good numbers of Sedge and Willow Warblers, often joined by a few Grasshopper Warblers, Wheatears and Spotted Flycatchers.

AUGUST

THE COAST really is the place to be at this stage of high summer. Return wader passage is now in full swing with many thousands of birds on the move. Someone once told me: "If you get a good bird in August it's usually a wader," and that certainly holds true. The prospect of American Golden Plover, Little and Temminck's Stints and Pectoral Sandpiper among the more usual waders all adds excitement to regular checks on coastal ponds.

Off-shore, Arctic Skuas, usually joined by a few Great Skuas, target the dispersing terns.

Raptor species remain prominent in NE England and you'll have a good chance of seeing Peregrine at any coastal location during the winter.

Thousands of Sandwich, Common and Arctic Terns congregate at favoured areas like Druridge Bay, Newbiggin, the Tyne Estuary and Seal Sands, providing a challenge to pick out accompanying Roseate Terns.

These gatherings and off-shore feeding parties of Kittiwakes often pull in more uncommon species including Little Gulls and Black Terns and the occasional early Sabine's Gull.

In most years large numbers of Manx Shearwaters start to appear, often passing over adult Guillemots and Razorbills on the sea with half-grown chicks.

SEPTEMBER

SUDDENLY it can really feel like autumn, particular during spells of northerly and easterly wind and heavy rain. September usually marks the arrival of sought-after eastern migrants, including Yellow-browed and Barred Warblers, meaning that in good migration weather every isolated bush and bit of cover in areas such as Holy Island, Bamburgh, Newton, Druridge Bay, St Mary's, South Shields, Whitburn, Hartlepool and around the Tees estuary are painstakingly checked by hopeful birders.

Other rarities which have been found at this stage are Wrynecks, Red-backed Shrikes and Pallas's Warblers. More regular autumn migrants, including Redstarts, Whinchats, Wheatears, Pied Flycatchers and Lesser Redpolls, can also occur in good numbers.

Terns remain numerous, wader numbers continue to build and the first passage wildfowl appear. Pale-bellied Brent Geese start to arrive back at Lindisfarne, large numbers of Pinkfeet are on the move and the first skeins of Barnacle Geese beat southwards along the coast, most en route to their main wintering grounds on the Solway. The mudflats of Lindisfarne and the pastures and ponds of Druridge Bay act as staging posts.

Towards the end of the month the first light influxes of northern thrushes give a hint of what is to come.

OCTOBER

FOR MANY folk this month is the climax of their birding year. Autumn migration peaks and few birders can resist the usual hotspots. Expect to find company on your visits but many pairs of eyes mean that most goodies are found and news travels fast!

Thousands of Blackbirds, Fieldfares, Song Thrushes and Redwings from Scandinavia and Russia flood in, usually accompanied by a few Ring Ouzels and large numbers of small common migrants such as Goldcrests, Robins, Chaffinches, Bramblings and Siskins.

With them come the real stars, with October marking the main period for Firecrests and Yellow-browed Warblers and the occasional Pallas's and Dusky Warblers, Red-breasted Flycatchers and Great Grey Shrikes. Year after year, Holy Island proves the epicentre for Yellow-browed Warblers, sometimes with up to ten present in a day.

Concentration on Siberian and other eastern 'gems' tends to distract from other arrivals.

Wader and wildfowl numbers continue to mount as huge numbers of Wigeons, Teal and Mallards cross the North Sea accompanied by Shovelers, Pochards and Tufted Ducks.

Huge flocks of Golden Plovers, Lapwings, Dunlins, Curlews and Redshanks are all moving into winter quarters. Small numbers of Short-eared Owls and a few Long-eared Owls also arrive from the north and east, usually arriving low and tired over the coast as they are mobbed by squadrons of gulls.

NOVEMBER

NOVEMBER USED to be considered the start of winter but now for birders it is really just an extension of autumn as migrants continue to arrive. Despite shorter hours of daylight, in recent years the first half of the month has proved excellent for rarities, including more Yellow-browed Warblers and the occasional Pallas's Warbler and Dusky Warbler as well as challenging northern and eastern races of Chiffchaffs and 'mega' regional species such as Red-flanked Bluetail. All this means is that attention remains focussed on coastal areas when weather conditions over Scandinavia promise further departures.

Passage of northern thrushes continues at a reduced pace as birds either move south-westwards through the region or settle in large flocks to rove local farmland before the winter sets in. Movements of migrant geese, ducks and waders continue, many passing to winter further south while others settle into winter quarters along the coast or inland at lakes and reservoirs.

DECEMBER

MOST SPECIES are settled in for winter and the month usually proves a mirror image of January. It's a period when most birders remain concentrated on the coast as swan, goose, duck and wader numbers reach their late peak.

The pale-bellied Brent Geese and Pintails are always a big mid-winter draw at Lindisfarne as are Barnacle Geese around Budle Bay. Large numbers of Pink-footed Geese are now settled around Druridge Bay, occasionally pulling in European White-fronted and Tundra Bean Geese. Don't forget your scope!

Coastal waters hold large numbers of Common Scoters with the chance of a few Velvet Scoters and the odd Surf Scoter. Long-tailed Ducks, Slavonian and Red-necked Grebes all increase, particularly between Bamburgh and Holy Island, and it's quite possible to see all three species of regular divers on a day's outing.

On coastal grassland and in rough marshy areas inland, Short-eared Owls settle in and usually stay as long as vole populations hold up and the region escapes heavy snow.

Inland waters usually hold small numbers of geese and duck and special winter species such as Smew. In direct contrast, inland areas away from reservoirs, villages or farmsteads, are usually quiet. However, there are some exceptions. Prestwick Carr, near Newcastle Airport, attracts concentrations of Short-eared Owls in good influx years and usually holds another winter prize, Great Grey Shrike. Harwood Forest is another fairly regular site for this most sought-after species.

CLEVELAND SITES

Parts of Cleveland's industrial past remain intact, but species such as Avocet and Little Egret are finding life on the new wetlands much to their liking.

Key points

• Headland car park off Middlegate (between Town Square and St Hilda's) at NZ 528 337. Parking space also near seawatch point at NZ 533 338.

• Jackson's Landing car park at NZ 513 332. Park for Old Cemetery at NZ 509 350 and West View Cemetery in vicinity of NZ 495 351.

• Toilet block (disabled access) by seawatch point at NZ 533 338. Further toilets, with disabled access and also baby-changing facilities, at Town Square's west end.

Contacts

Hartlepool Tourist Information
01429 869 706

One of the North-East's most urban birding sites is also among its most productive – depending on the season and prevailing weather. As well as providing some of the best seawatching along Britain's east coast, the Headland can score superbly when wet, misty conditions during April-early June or August-October ground many migrants and make the Headland's few sheltered places worth checking closely.

Target birds

October to March – **Mediterranean Gull (70%), Great Northern Diver (30%), Iceland Gull (30%), Black-throated Diver (20%), Red-necked Grebe (20%), Glaucous Gull (20%), Little Auk (20%).** *July to October* – **Sooty Shearwater, (60%), Balearic Shearwater (40%), Pomarine Skua (40%), Roseate Tern (40%), Black Redstart (40%), Yellow-browed Warbler (40%), Long-tailed Skua (30%), Sabine's Gull (30%), Wryneck (30%), Icterine Warbler (30%), Barred Warbler (30%), Pallas's Warbler (30%), Red-breasted Flycatcher (30%), Firecrest (30%), Greenish Warbler (20%), Red-backed Shrike (20%).**

Other possible bird species

All year
Eider
Common Scoter
Red-throated Diver
Fulmar
Gannet
Sparrowhawk
Kestrel
Oystercatcher
Familiar gulls
Kittiwake
Guillemot
Common garden birds
Pied Wagtail

March to June
Sea passage/onshore/flyover
Manx Shearwater
Common waders
Purple Sandpiper
Whimbrel
Arctic and Great Skuas
Little, Sandwich and Common Terns
Razorbill
Puffin
Swift

Hirundines

Parks/gardens etc
Meadow Pipit
Grey Wagtail
Redstart
Whinchat
Wheatear
Ring Ouzel
Lesser Whitethroat
Common warblers
Spotted Flycatcher
Pied Flycatcher

July to October
Sea passage/onshore/flyover
Pink-footed Goose
Barnacle Goose (passage mainly during Sept 25 – Oct 10)
Brent Goose
Scaup
Long-tailed Duck
Velvet Scoter
Red-breasted Merganser
Goosander
Common diving ducks
Manx Shearwater

Shag
Common waders
Whimbrel
Arctic Skua
Great Skua
Little Gull
Black
Sandwich, Common and Arctic Terns
Razorbill
Skylark
Swift
Hirundines

Parks/gardens etc
Long-eared Owl
Short-eared Owl
Meadow Pipit
Grey Wagtail
Redstart
Whinchat
Stonechat
Wheatear
Ring Ouzel
Fieldfare
Redwing
Common warblers
Goldcrest

Spotted and Pied Flycatchers
Brambling
Siskin
Lesser Redpoll
Reed Bunting
Late October to February
Sea passage/onshore/flyover
Whooper Swan
Pink-footed Goose

Brent Goose
Shelduck
Wigeon
Scaup
Long-tailed Duck
Velvet Scoter
Goldeneye
Red-breasted Merganser
Great Crested Grebe

Slavonian Grebe
Storm-petrels
Shag
Common waders
Purple Sandpiper
Woodcock
Curlew
Snow Bunting

Background information and birding tips

A TALE OF TWO THRUSHES would be an appropriate title for an account of Hartlepool Headland's birding significance. Massive endorsement of its potential came when a Dusky Thrush from eastern Siberia – only the second for Britain – turned up in December, 1959, for a ten week stay.

Fifty years later a Black-throated Thrush – also of Siberian origin and a county 'first' – was discovered near the harbour in April, 2010. Throughout the intervening decades, Hartlepool maintained a high profile on the UK birding scene and continues to do so.

Ironically, being heavily built-up helps: in mist and rain, migrants take refuge in the few small parks and gardens which simplifies finding them. An indication of the scale of such 'falls' came on October 10, 2010, when ringers caught 379 birds, including 120 Goldcrests. They were most likely just a fraction of the total on the Headland.

The Dusky Thrush hung about the rugby pitch, just inland from the main seawatching point on the southern edge of the Town Moor. The bushes fringing that little recreational complex – the first cover for migrants arriving from the north-east – kept on making ornithological history: the Pallas's Warbler in October 1962 was only the seventh for Britain; the first of two Paddyfield Warblers

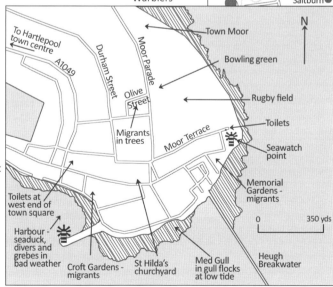

Key points

• **Key birding area between watchpoint and harbour (less than half-a-mile). Allow three hours to check all sites during a big 'fall'.**

• **Small parks always open. Virtually all birding is from paved or tarmac surfaces suitable for wheelchair use.**

• **Verrill's fish and chip shop at Town Square. More shops and pubs nearby.**

(September 1969 and October 1984) was just the third for Britain and the first for England.

Across the Headland by the harbour is a further open space with small parks much-visited by migrants. Thrush Nightingale and Marsh, Booted, Greenish, Arctic and Hume's Warblers are among rarities recorded there.

More regular but still scarce passage visitors include Icterine, Barred, Pallas's and Yellow-browed Warblers plus Wryneck, Bluethroat, Firecrest, Red-breasted Flycatcher and Red-backed Shrike. Even the churchyard of 12th century St Hilda's, with old gravestones providing the only cover, plays a part; Richard's Pipit and Great Grey Shrike are among species it has hosted.

This area's main section used to be Borough Hall Gardens but after a £1.6m project replaced its lawns, shrubs and flower beds with granite block paving, it was re-named Town Square in 2006.

Teesmouth Bird Club pleas saved the migrant-attracting big sycamore across Middlegate from the Borough Hall but not the equally significant trees by Verrill's fish and chip shop (a favourite haunt of hungry visiting birders).

Fortunately the project didn't affect the

bushes and flower beds of Croft Gardens and a hedge-rimmed putting green to the south. Spring 2010's Black-throated Thrush and a Woodchat Shrike that autumn confirmed their continuing potential.

Changes to the bowling green/tennis courts complex visited by the famous Dusky Thrush of 1959-60 have seen the green on Marine Crescent's seaward side turned into a children's playground, while the courts have been adapted for other sporting activities. However, the perimeter shrubbery remains, so this area (other past rarities include Thrush Nightingale and Subalpine and Dusky Warblers) still has pulling power.

Nearby sites include Olive Street, with trees which have held Icterine, Greenish and Yellow-browed Warblers. Another, known to birders as the 'Doctor's Garden', is a private plot at the Friar Terrace/Durham Street junction. Surrounded by high walls, it's a perfect migrant hideaway and if something really special is there, arrangements may be made for birders to enter the neighbouring allotment to look discreetly over the party wall. Britain's third White-throated Robin was here in June 2011.

Similarly, birders are sometimes allowed into the secluded garden behind St Mary's RC Church beside the Cosmopolitan pub at the Durham Street and Middlegate junction. However, there's no permanent procedure in either case, so access shouldn't be taken for granted.

A post-2000 development impacting directly on Headland birding was Hartlepool Council's eviction of the bird club from the former Heugh Gun Battery's observation tower which it rented for seawatching after the military strongpoint's closure in 1956. The council intends to restore the site to its original state as a tourist attraction.

Seawatching continues outdoors as birders

How to get there

Turn off A19 at Sheraton crossroads (12 miles north of Middlesbrough/16 miles south of Sunderland) on to A179 to Hartlepool. At junction with A1086 (third roundabout after four miles), continue straight ahead on to A1049. Harbour area, with parking immediately west of prominent St Hilda's Church, is 2.5 miles further on.

For seawatching point, watch for obvious road fork more than a quarter-mile beyond A1049's junction with A1048 (from town centre). Go left into Durham Street, which leads to a T-junction, with St Hilda's immediately ahead. Turn left into Church Close (edge of churchyard) and keep straight on to lighthouse.

From Teesmouth's marshes, take A178 north into Hartlepool town centre, then at main street's west end, turn right (signposted Headland) into A179 Marina Way (passing big retail outlets). At third roundabout, turn on to A1048 – which after half-a-mile becomes the A1049 and continues to harbour area as above.

Jackson's Landing lies E of A179 Marina Way dual carriageway,

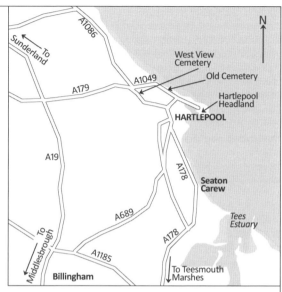

its position indicated by the tall masts of HMS Trincomalee, part of Hartlepool's Historic Quay tourist attraction. Free car park on dock's north side is between first two roundabouts north from town centre.

For Old Cemetery, turn off A1049 into Thorpe Street (second left after junction with A1048 or, if driving from Headland, second right after junction with Durham Street). Then turn left immediately into Old Cemetery Road which leads to site. West View Cemetery is off West View Road, the final section of A1049 before its junction with the A1068 and A179.

Public transport: Regular bus service between Hartlepool town centre and Headland. Hartlepool has bus links with all other North East centres and rail links with Newcastle, Sunderland, Stockton, Middlesbrough and Darlington.

monitor passage from the next-door lighthouse compound. The good news is that the ever-resourceful TBC plans to build a new two-storey observatory with a lift for disabled users beside the redundant lighthouse Probably available to all birders, not just TBC members, due to the likely funding arrangements, it could be in operation by 2015 if the club achieves its goals.

Enthusiasm for Headland seawatching has been fuelled by numerous landmark events, such as September 2006's Wilson's Storm-petrel – the first recorded off Britain's east coast during a land-based sea-watch.

That maintained the standard set by records of off-beat rarities such as Little Shearwater (September, 1984 and 1990, and July, 2000) and Bridled Tern (August, 1988). Also notable was the Pallid Swift seen near the seawatching point in October, 1999.

Many memorable incidents involved exceptional numbers of more regular passage visitors, eg: September 7, 1991's unprecedented three-figure count of Long-tailed Skuas; October 9, 1992's four-figure Pomarine Skua movement; and September 22, 2002's 1,914 Sooty Shearwaters (another local record high).

A sustained northerly blow in late autumn or winter can spark spectacular Little Auk movements – 8,500-plus over two days in January 1995 stands out. Scarcer species such as Balearic Shearwater and Sabine's Gull are likely each autumn and there is always hope of appearances by less frequently occurring Cory's and Great Shearwaters, Leach's Storm-petrel and Grey Phalarope.

Mediterranean Gull, a regular winter visitor since the mid-1950s, is liable to be encountered at low tide along the rocky foreshore between the lighthouse and the harbour.

Iceland and Glaucous Gulls are possible too, along with typical waders, while scarcer sea duck, diver and grebe species may be in the harbour in stormy weather. In calm conditions, the latter can be off the north-western end of the promenade, which runs for more than half a mile beyond the Town Moor.

Birders visiting the Headland may also benefit from calling at the following nearby sites at certain times of year:

Old Cemetery (NZ 510 310)
OVERLOOKING the shore, the Old Cemetery and adjoining small Old Jewish Cemetery offer minimal cover for migrants. Nevertheless the site accommodated Britain's earliest-ever autumn Booted Warbler on August 10, 2004 – a remarkable follow-up to

the country's first spring Booted on the Outer Headland on June 7, 1992.

Other outstanding visitors include Rustic Bunting in September 2000 and Dusky Warbler in October 2010, plus two notable flyovers – an Alpine Swift in June 2002 and a Purple Heron in June 2006.

There have been several Black Redstart records, including a singing male in March 2006. More promising is the shrubbery flanking adjacent Old Cemetery Road: scarcities have included Red-breasted Flycatcher, Red-backed Shrike and Icterine, Greenish and Yellow-browed Warblers.

West View Cemetery (NZ 495 350)
ONLY HALF-A-MILE from the sea and a green oasis in Hartlepool's increasingly built-up north-west, this was the location of the Tees-Tyne coast's first Yellow-browed Warbler in October 1962.

It hasn't produced much since, possibly due to insufficient coverage as thorough checking of its avenues of mature trees takes time. However, in recent years Pallas's and Yellow-browed Warblers have occurred, with Barred and Greenish Warblers nearby.

Jackson's Landing (NZ 515 331)
BESIDE HARTLEPOOL'S main tourist draw, the Historic Quay, and close to the town centre, this dock can be quite birdless at times. However, in winter it may be graced by a Black-throated or Great Northern Diver; at least once since 2000 both were present along with a Red-throated Diver.

Red-necked Grebe is a further occasional visitor and a few Red-breasted Mergansers are there most winters. Rooftop gull flocks may include Mediterranean, Iceland or Glaucous. It's certainly worth at least a quick look if passing during November-March.

THIS COASTAL strip is in a class of its own for so many reasons. The Cleveland Way winds by awesome precipices, with Hunt Cliff, east of Saltburn, rising to more than 300ft and the Boulby stretch's highest point almost twice that. Below ground in Boulby potash mine, astrophysicists conduct experiments searching for Dark Matter, while on the surface birders often experience eureka moments of their own, especially at migration times.

Target birds *Autumn passage* – Sooty Shearwater (60%), Pomarine Skua (40%), Yellow-browed Warbler (40%), Richard's Pipit, Pallas's Warbler, Red-breasted Flycatcher (all 30%), Hobby (20%). *Spring and autumn passage* – Ring Ouzel (60%), Marsh Harrier (20%), Osprey (20%), Dotterel (10%). *Autumn to spring* – Black Redstart (40%). *Winter* – Lapland Bunting (40%), Peregrine (30%).

Other possible bird species

<u>All year</u>
Red-legged Partridge
Grey Partridge
Little Grebe
Fulmar
Gannet
Cormorant
Sparrowhawk
Kestrel
Moorhen
Lapwing
Kittiwake
Familiar gulls
Guillemot
Common farmland birds
Little Owl
Skylark
Meadow Pipit
Rock Pipit
Grey Wagtail
Pied Wagtail
Stonechat
Yellowhammer
Reed Bunting

<u>Spring/summer</u>
Whimbrel
Curlew
Sandwich Tern
Razorbill
Swift
Hirundines

Tree Pipit
Yellow Wagtail
Redstart
Whinchat
Wheatear
Grasshopper Warbler
Summer warblers

<u>Autumn</u>
Pink-footed Goose
Barnacle Goose
Brent Goose
Wigeon
Teal
Common Scoter
Velvet Scoter
Manx Shearwater
Jack Snipe
Woodcock
Whimbrel
Curlew
Turnstone
Arctic Skua
Great Skua
Little Gull
Sandwich Tern
Common Tern
Long-eared Owl
Short-eared Owl
Swift
Hirundines
Tree Pipit

Redstart
Whinchat
Wheatear
Fieldfare
Redwing
Common warblers
Goldcrest
Spotted Flycatcher
Pied Flycatcher
Brambling
Siskin
Lesser Redpoll

<u>Winter</u>
Eider
Long-tailed Duck
Common Scoter
Velvet Scoter
Goldeneye
Red-breasted Merganser
Red-throated Diver
Merlin
Oystercatcher
Knot
Sanderling
Purple Sandpiper
Dunlin
Curlew
Redshank
Turnstone
Twite
Snow Bunting

Key points

• Pay & display car parks: Saltburn seafront, near Skelton Beck; Staithes Bank Top, leading to old village.

• Free car park at Skinningrove sea front. No parking at harbour.

• Cleveland Way from Saltburn to Skinningrove and back (seven miles) takes up to four hours.

• Skinningrove to Staithes is longer, but minor roads to Hummersea and Upton Farms, Boulby and Cowbar make access easier.

• Steep climbs include steps behind Saltburn's Ship Inn; path from shore to cliffs at Cattersty Gill.

Contacts

Saltburn Tourist Info: 01287 622 422

Tees Valley WT 01287 636 382

33

Key points

- **Only coastal path suitable for wheelchair users.**

- **Stout footwear essential: take waterproof and warm clothing.**

- **Public toilets at Saltburn car park near Ship Inn; Staithes (by Bank Top car park and also by harbour).**

- **Pubs, shops and eating places at Saltburn and Staithes.**

Background information and birding tips

BIRDING ALONG Teesside's most easterly and loftiest coastal stretch requires stamina and dedication. Migrant potential is strung out along eight miles of coast and some sites are a good half-hour's trek, or more, from the nearest road.

The knack of being in the right places at ideal times is a further asset as passage birds here tend to move on quickly. For instance, trees at Hummersea Farm amount to a veritable oasis to migrants grounded on the largely open clifftop farmland between Skinningrove and Staithes. The site has clocked up several Red-breasted Flycatchers as well as even more Yellow-browed Warblers.

The potential of the Saltburn-Staithes strip came strongly during 1985-90, with autumn appearances by White-tailed Eagle, Alpine Swift, Olive-backed Pipit and Greenish Warbler at Boulby Cliffs and a winter Ivory Gull at Saltburn.

Other outstanding records include a White-billed Diver (Staithes, February 1996), Little Swift (Boulby, May 1998) and Desert Wheatear (Boulby, November 2000 and Loftus 2011). The following September a Red-flanked Bluetail and Dusky Warbler put the spotlight on Cattersty Gill, the Tees Valley Wildlife Trust reserve near Skinningrove.

The area's outstanding array of unusual birds includes Great Reed Warbler (Hummersea Farm), Short-toed Lark (Cowbar), Hume's Warbler (Skinningrove) and Dusky Warbler (Hunley Hall Golf Course, Brotton). Hummersea scored in 2004, with a male Red-footed Falcon and a Pallid Swift, while this coastline's third Dusky Warbler in five autumns was at Boulby in October, 2005.

An adult Bonaparte's Gull (Saltburn, November 2006) and a Red-rumped Swallow (Boulby, April 2007), Subalpine Warbler (near Brotton, May 2008), female Red-footed Falcon at Saltburn and a Rustic Bunting at Hummersea in the autumn all kept the rarity pot boiling.

Of scarce visitors, Yellow-browed Warbler stands out, with Hummersea Farm's sycamores among the most favoured sites. There was a double-figure total between Saltburn and Boulby in October, 2005, when an unprecedented 1,000-plus occurred nationally.

Richard's Pipit is another near-regular, sighting, often involving a bird on the move, attracting attention with its loud 'shreeep' flight call. Wrynecks don't turn up so frequently, but a widespread arrival on Britain's east coast can mean several are present. Such an influx in autumn 2008 resulted in five in the Warsett Hill/Hunley Hall Golf Course area and another at Boulby.

Migrants take refuge regularly in bushes on the slope at the golf course's southern end. Other promising spots can be reached via paths leading from there to the cliffs to the north.

Black Redstarts appear in numbers periodically; during late October, 2004, at least three were at Boulby and up to four by Skinningrove jetty. Meanwhile Corncrake, Siberian Stonechat, Firecrest, Red-breasted Flycatcher, Golden Oriole, Red-backed Shrike and Marsh, Icterine, Barred and Pallas's

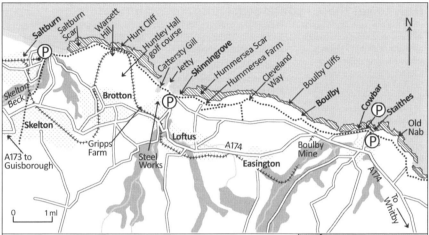

How to get there

(Saltburn is 12 miles E of Middlesbrough)

All birding locations reached via A174, which runs from the A19 at Middlesbrough towards Saltburn-by-the-Sea and onto Whitby, North Yorkshire (about 20 miles). Access details to the individual sites (from west to east):

For Saltburn – Hunt Cliff (NZ 682 219):

At A174 roundabout junction with A1085 to Marske-by-the-Sea) take unclassified road into Saltburn centre and then descend sharply to promenade. Fork right at bottom and enter pay-and-display car park on right (opposite Ship Inn).
Take steps behind Ship Inn to the Cleveland Way, which climbs steadily to the top of Hunt Cliff, more than a mile to the east.

For Huntley Hall Golf Course, Brotton (NZ 693 205):

Driving eastwards on A174, turn left at roundabout into Skelton Road towards west end of Brotton's High Street. After about a mile, soon after going under a railway bridge, turn left into minor road to Saltburn (Saltburn Road), turning right after a short distance into St Margaret's Way (signpost Hunley Hall).

For Skinningrove (NZ 713 200):

Between Brotton and Loftus the A174 dips steeply to cross a wooded gulley running northwards towards the sea. If driving from the west turn left (signposted Skinningrove and the Tom Leonard Mining Museum) soon after a sharp left hand bend at the foot of Brotton Bank. Alternatively, drivers from the east turn right at the bottom of Loftus Bank.

This road (Mill Lane) continues into the village, but when it bears right, you go straight on to the free car park from which seawatching is possible in bad weather.

For Cattersty Gill Nature Reserve (NZ 707 206):

This Tees Valley Wildlife Trust site is most quickly reached from

Skinningrove seafront car park. Walk north-westwards along the shore to beyond the jetty, then take the steep path up the cliffs at the back of Cattersty Sands. Turn right onto Cleveland Way, then left after about 50 yards into the reserve via a kissing gate. A longer alternative which avoids that cliff climb is to use the public footpath running north-east from Brotton Road, starting at NZ 695 198.

For Hummersea Farm

(NZ 723 197):

Turn off A174 in High Street, Loftus, into narrow North Road which becomes Hummersea Lane from the edge of this small market town. After climbing for almost a mile, keep straight

35

How to get there - continued:

on at the top, passing in quick succession, a right turn (which connects with A174) then a left one (going downhill to Skinningrove). It is a short descent to the farm, where there's only room for three or four cars, so park with consideration.

The lane bends sharply to pass the farm, then from a gate becomes an unsurfaced track heading towards the higher cliffs to the east. After about 250 yards a path branches off to the left to join the Cleveland Way. It also leads to a long, steep flight of steps down to the shore – which should be walked with care (some steps may be missing).

For Upton Farm (NZ 738 193):
The farm is almost 1.5 miles east along the road from the aforementioned T-junction in Hummersea Lane and just south of Hummersea Farm. It is an access point to a Boulby Cliffs stretch of the Cleveland Way rather than a birding site. Park on north side of the minor road, just east of the farm and

walk to the coastal path (almost half-a-mile to the north) via a public footpath across the fields.

Boulby Village (NZ 760 191):
Park on the verge after turning into the village at the foot of Boulby Bank and then walk NW on the Cleveland Way – which coincides with the road on the seaward side of the houses.

After 300 yards the Cleveland Way turns sharply inland to steeply climb Rockhole Hill, but it may also be worth continuing straight on along a clifftop path for about 200 yards as it leads to a site with sycamores and bushes where migrants occur. On returning to the Cleveland Way, carry on up Rockhole Hill to scan scrub in a hollow.

For Cowbar (NZ 780 189):
The Cowbar turn-off from A174 is about four miles east of Loftus and a mile west of Staithes; it is also just over 300 yards east of the junction with the minor road passing Boulby village and leading to Upton Farm and Hummersea Lane. Only permit-holders can drive all the

way to the harbour (one mile), but there's a visitors' car park 0.75 miles along the lane. Verge parking is also possible on some sections of lane before this. Seawatching can be carried out from near the car park.

For Staithes (NZ 783 190):
The A174 dips to cross Easington Beck and the well-signposted turning into Staithes Lane, leading to the historic harbour area, is at the top of the eastern bank. A pay-and-display car park is on the right just past the Captain Cook Inn and reached from a road into a small industrial estate. Don't drive down to cobbled High Street and harbour area as there's nowhere to park. Church Street, rising from the harbour front, links with the Cleveland Way which leads, after three-quarters of a mile to Old Nab.

Public transport: Bus services from Middlesbrough stop at Saltburn, Brotton, Skinningrove, Loftus and Staithes. Also, trains from Middlesbrough link Saltburn with rest of North-East rail network.

Warblers have all been logged along this coast since 1999.

Fields around Staithes held the UK's biggest Shore Lark presence outside Norfolk in late 2002/early 2003. The flock near Old Nab headland, just into Yorkshire, peaked at 26 in December and up to 15 were in fields in Cleveland's Cowbar/Boulby area during March - April.

Lapland Bunting is a more regular winter visitor in small numbers, so 12 at Cowbar (2008) and ten in 2004, were above average. As for Snow Buntings, 80-plus were in fields just east of Staithes in mid-November, 2007

and 70 at Cowbar a year later.

Given suitable tail winds, hundreds of birds of a wide range of species – including Swifts, hirundines, pipits, wagtails and finches – fly along the cliffs in spring and autumn. Significant numbers of Wheatears and Ring Ouzels may be grounded, particularly in springtime, and large scale arrivals of Blackbirds, Fieldfares and Redwings can occur during mid to late autumn.

The White-tailed Eagle of 1985 and recent Red-footed Falcons head an enviable list of raptor species reported over the past three decades. Hen and Montagu's Harriers and Rough-legged Buzzard have occurred on passage and the Saltburn-Skinningrove stretch produced three sightings in each of the nationally-significant September movements of Honey Buzzards in 2000 and 2008.

Marsh Harrier has become a regular visitor; records usually involve single birds, but in August, 2007, an advancing fog bank caused five – four of them together – to fly in off the sea at Hummersea and then continue inland.

Merlins, which nest on the relatively near North York Moors, hunt along the coastal strip from autumn into springtime, while Peregrines are most likely over that period too.

Many waders – Oystercatcher, Knot, Curlew, Redshank and Turnstone – feed along the rocky foreshore at low tide in winter, particularly below Hunt Cliff, but birders wishing to enjoy this spectacle should always check tide times; with no escape routes up the cliffs, there's a danger of being trapped by incoming waves.

Also, leave Saltburn on the falling tide and be back there at least three hours before the next high water. Another sensible policy is to not go too far east – ie around the headland – so that Saltburn disappears from view.

Above the cliffs there's less scope for waders, though Dotterels have appeared with some regularity in fields at Boulby and Cowbar in both spring and autumn since 2000.

Woodcock and, now and again, Jack Snipe appear on clifftops later in the autumn. Cattersty Pond, half-a-mile inland, has been graced by Long-tailed Duck, Black-throated Diver and, more recently, Little Egret – a species which has also been recorded in flight along the coast.

Onshore winds, particularly during August-November, result in seabird and wildfowl movements but there are few suitable observation points, Hunt Cliff and Boulby Cliffs being too high for successful watching. Old Nab, east of Staithes, offers the best scope; Cory's Shearwater, 500-plus Sooty Shearwaters in a day and Leach's Storm-petrel are among memorable events since 2000.

Skinningrove, although not much above the waves, can be productive too; species recorded include Grey Phalarope, Pomarine and Long-tailed Skuas and Sabine's Gull.

Kittiwakes nest on Cowbar Nab's sheer face and there's seawatching potential from the cliff base. Back in Staithes, Church Street, rising from the harbour front, links with the Cleveland Way which leads, after three-quarters of a mile to Old Nab, an outstanding, but exposed, seawatching point. Snow Bunting flocks haunt Cliff Farm's fields by the path in winter and 20-plus Shore Larks were there during 2002/03.

Divers, grebes and sea duck may be on the sea off Saltburn in winter. Glaucous Gulls are seen occasionally and there have been more frequent Mediterranean Gull appearances, while periods of passage have led to Grey Phalarope and Pomarine Skua sightings.

Seabird colonies at Hunt Cliff (the more watchable site) and Boulby cliffs involve mainly Kittiwakes, but 2008's total of 3,840 pairs was a third of the mid-1990s level. The *Cleveland Bird Report* for 2008 shows that the two sites held 205 pairs of Fulmars, 51 of Cormorants and 500 of Herring Gulls, while Boulby's small Razorbill colony continued to thrive, with about 23 pairs.

Warsett Hill, rising above Hunt Cliff, is a likely spot for Wheatears and Ring Ouzels at passage times. Paths to it branch from the Cleveland Way (both to the west and east of Hunt Cliff).

Key points

• Sailing club car park (signposted on A171) at NZ 741 126. East end car park at NZ 756 127. No parking charges.

• Allow two hours to walk round reservoir (almost three miles). Main birding potential is along nature reserve stretch.

• Bog House Lane section (SW corner) is very swampy with insufficient duckboard. Unsuitable for wheelchairs.

• Hide (with unlocked, sliding door) reached by path from sailing club car park. Wheelchair-accessible and comfortable.

Contacts

North Yorks Moors National Park
01439 770 657

THE NORTH-EAST'S moorland reservoirs generally aren't richly endowed with birds, but Scaling Dam is different. With a species list of 200-plus, around 70 per cent of which are recorded annually, it ranks among the region's most productive inland waters at any altitude. Waterfowl and waders are particularly prominent, but you can also expect raptor sightings and a wide variety of woodland birds.

Target birds *All year* – Merlin (30%), Peregrine (30%). *Spring/ autumn passage* – Garganey, Black-necked Grebe, Marsh Harrier, Osprey (all 20%). *Breeding season* – Little Ringed Plover (80%), Cuckoo (60%). *Late autumn/winter* – Willow Tit (80%), Bullfinch (80%), Whooper Swan (40%), Mediterranean Gull (40%), Kingfisher (30%), Water Pipit (30%), Hen Harrier (20%), Raven (20%), Rough-legged Buzzard (10%).

Other possible bird species

All year	Pied Wagtail	Swift
Common waterfowl	Dipper	Hirundines
Shelduck	Mistle Thrush	Yellow Wagtail
Teal	Coal Tit	White Wagtail
Tufted Duck	Goldfinch	Whinchat
Red Grouse	Linnet	Wheatear
Grey Partridge	Lesser Redpoll	Lesser Whitethroat
Little Grebe	Yellowhammer	Whitethroat
Cormorant	Reed Bunting	Garden Warbler
Grey Heron		Blackcap
Sparrowhawk	*Spring to early autumn*	Chiffchaff
Kestrel	Great Crested Grebe	Willow Warbler.
Golden Plover	Oystercatcher	
Lapwing	Ringed Plover	*Late autumn/winter*
Snipe	Little Stint	Pink-footed Goose
Woodcock	Curlew Sandpiper	Wigeon
Curlew	Dunlin	Gadwall
Redshank	Ruff	Pintail
Regular gulls	Black-tailed Godwit	Scaup
Common farmland/ woodland birds	Whimbrel	Goldeneye
Stock Dove	Spotted Redshank	Goosander
Green Woodpecker	Greenshank	Common Buzzard
Meadow Pipit	Green and Common Sandpipers	Winter thrushes
	Little Gull	Brambling
		Siskin

Background information and birding tips

SCALING DAM, which lies on the Yorkshire side of the county boundary, proved attractive to birds from the time of its construction in the late 1950s and its success has grown in recent years. You can expect the richest bird prospects during spring and autumn passage periods and winter time.

The 105-acre (42ha) Northumbrian Water site began with distinct advantages over the region's other upland reservoirs, being just 590ft (180m) above sea level and only four miles from the coast, which improves the chances of appearances by migrants.

The shallow 20-acre (8ha) south-west corner is a nature reserve, so no angling and yachting is permitted there. A further boost for birds came with the reservoir's water supply role ending in 1995.

Eventually water level management was passed to the Scaling Dam Wildlife Advisory Group, which represents nature conservation and relevant recreational interests.

Lowering the water levels has made this a more reliable site for spring and autumn passage waders, with 20-plus species per year likely.

Little and Temminck's Stints, Pectoral and Curlew Sandpipers, Ruff, Jack Snipe, Black-tailed Godwit, Whimbrel, Green Sandpiper, Spotted Redshank and Greenshank have all occurred since 2003.

Little Ringed Plovers

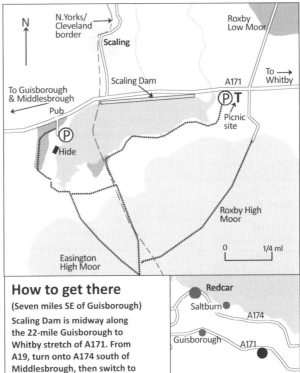

How to get there

(Seven miles SE of Guisborough)

Scaling Dam is midway along the 22-mile Guisborough to Whitby stretch of A171. From A19, turn onto A174 south of Middlesbrough, then switch to A172 at third junction and go left on to A171 after two miles (follow signs to Whitby).

Public transport: Arriva bus service 93 and X93

(Middlesbrough - Scarborough via Guisborough and Whitby), stops at The Grapes Inn. Reduced service in winter.

have become regular breeders, along with Common Sandpipers and Oystercatchers. There is also the possibility of occasional appearances by normally coastal species such as Grey Plover, Knot, Sanderling and Turnstone.

Rarities have appeared throughout the reservoir's history – from Wilson's Phalarope in the mid-1960s and Terek Sandpiper (Britain's seventh) in 1971 to Black Stork in 2008.

Further unusual species on its list include Green-winged Teal, Great White Egret, Spoonbill, Montagu's Harrier, Red-footed Falcon, Common Crane, Avocet,

39

Key points

• **Visitor Centre near sailing club car park includes toilets (not open in winter). Toilet block at east end car park (National Park-established) is open 24 hours all year (advertised as disabled accessible).**

• **Meals/accommodation at Grapes Inn (disabled access), just east along A171 from turning into sailing club car park. Tel: 01287 640 461**

Kentish Plover, Red-necked Phalarope, Ring-billed Gull and White-winged Black Tern.

Distinguished as a raptor viewpoint, Scaling Dam is among the region's most promising places for Hen Harrier. Though occurring less frequently than in the past, there are still annual appearances over adjacent moorland, some just passing through, others lingering for a period.

October to January have been the most productive months since 2000, but there have also been February, May, August and September records. Any over Easington High Moor or Roxy High Moor, to the south, may be visible from the hide, a big plus on cold days. They may be seen also over Roxby Low Moor and Liverton Moor – north of the A171 and not viewable from the hide.

There's a chance you might see Marsh Harriers and Ospreys on passage. In the former's case, 2008 was particularly outstanding with at least 12 during late July-early September, including three on a single day. Sometimes an Osprey sticks around for a while, especially in late summer, and can be seen fishing at the reservoir.

Occasional Honey Buzzards and Hobbies may pass through too, while Red Kites and Rough-legged Buzzards show up in winter. Common Buzzards, Merlins and Peregrines may be seen over

a wider spread of the year; Short-eared Owls and Ravens are further possibilities.

Scaling Dam – nowhere deeper than 30ft (9m) – attracts a wide waterfowl assortment. Feral Greylags dominate but Canada Geese, Wigeon, Teal, Mallards, Tufted Ducks and Goldeneyes all occur in reasonable numbers.

Gadwall, Pintail, Shovelers and Goosanders tend to be only thinly represented and little has been seen of Pochard in recent years. Garganey appears on passage only very occasionally.

Whooper Swans – typically fewer than 20 – occur on passage but usually don't stay long. Pink-footed Geese skeins pass over but few are seen at ground level.

Sometimes Barnacle Geese drop in during their Svalbard to Solway Firth migration and the odd Bean and White-fronted Goose crops up also. The winter of 2011-2012 was exceptional, with good numbers of both species during a big influx into North-East England.

Proximity to the coast influences irregular visits by Scaup, Long-tailed Ducks, Common Scoters and Red-breasted Mergansers. Other maritime waterfowl recorded include Red-throated and Black-throated Divers and Red-necked and Slavonian Grebes.

More recent Black-necked Grebe passage appearances have been in late summer/early autumn but they are possible in springtime too.

Of scarcer gulls, Mediterranean is the most reported species (mainly August-March). Yellow-legged and Glaucous Gulls have been recorded, while Little Gulls may visit on spring and autumn passage when there's also a chance of Black and Arctic Terns.

Grey Heron are here year-round but Little Egret remains a rare sight. Rock Pipit, a nearby coastal resident, is seen occasionally and winter-visiting Water Pipit with some regularity. Grey and Pied Wagtails are breeding species and Yellow and White Wagtails are spring passage possibilities. Kingfisher may flash into view in winter.

The nature reserve includes conifer plantations, birch and rowan woodland, hawthorn scrub and sheep pastures between the reservoir's western edge and Bog House Lane, which runs south from the A171 and on to Easington High Moor.

Woodcock, Green Woodpecker, Willow Tit and Bullfinch are among woodland species that may be encountered; the latter two are star attractions at the winter feeding station by the hide.

Scaling is a reliable site for Cuckoos in spring and summer. Willow Warbler is the most numerous of summer-visiting songbirds, with Lesser and Common Whitethroats, Garden Warblers, Blackcaps and Chiffchaffs also present.

Redwings, Bramblings, Siskins and Lesser Redpolls can be anticipated in winter.

There is no access to the reserve's woodland but its birds can be viewed from the hide, the footpath between the car park and Bog House Lane and from the lane itself (Great Grey Shrike has been seen from there).

The lane links with several paths crossing the Red Grouse-occupied moorland and is part of the route around the reservoir. Obviously, paths to the south provide opportunities for closer scrutiny of the moors than from the hide, though lacking its shelter on cold days.

The site's varied list of waders includes Little Ringed Plovers, which now breed regularly.

Key points

- Little walking from roadside watchpoints. It's possible to watch from your car.

- Uneven surfaces difficult for wheelchair use.

- Pull-off points at The Chevrons road sign and on either side of bridge over Sleddale Beck.

- View eastern ridge from Percy Cross Rigg road verge.

- View Raven Gill from lay-by at top of Sand Hill Bank which descends to village's east end.

- Nearest facilities at Cleveland Inn, Commondale (two miles east).

- Public toilets at Commondale (near inn). Toilets at Kildale railway station have RADAR disabled access.

MOORLAND is in short supply in Teesside's 230 square miles, which is packed with more than half a million people and considerable industry. However, the North York Moors National Park fragment protruding into the borough of Redcar and East Cleveland has birding potential that far exceeds its modest acreage. Particularly from late autumn to early spring, Sleddale is one of the North-East's more reliable raptor-watching sites.

Target birds
All year – Buzzard (60%), Merlin (30%). *Late spring/early autumn* – Marsh Harrier (10%), Osprey on passage (10%). *Late autumn to early spring* – Peregrine (40%), Rough-legged Buzzard (30%), Red Kite (20%), Hen Harrier (20%), Goshawk (10%), Raven (10%).

Other possible bird species

All year		
Sparrowhawk	Linnet	House Martin
Kestrel	Lesser Redpoll	Meadow Pipit
Red Grouse	Crossbill	Grey Wagtail
Red-legged Partridge	Reed Bunting	Pied Wagtail
Grey Partridge	*Spring to early autumn*	Whinchat
Dipper	Golden Plover	Wheatear
Common woodland/	Lapwing	Willow Warbler
farmland birds	Snipe	*Late autumn/winter*
Stonechat	Curlew	Pink-footed Goose
Mistle Thrush	Cuckoo	(passage skeins
Coal Tit	Skylark	overhead)
Siskin	Swift	Fieldfare
	Swallow	Redwing

Background information and birding tips

EVEN BEFORE 2010, Sleddale/Commondale was the North-East's likeliest area for Rough-legged Buzzard sightings. While not appearing annually, there had been occurrences in five of the winters between 2000 and late 2009.

Usually reports involved one or two birds and that pattern was repeated in early 2010 but it became a quite exceptional year thanks to events in the autumn.

Hopes were raised by a surge of Rough-legged Buzzard arrivals, mainly between Yorkshire and Essex, in mid-October. Sleddale's first of the influx wasn't reported until the 20th but the number increased to four by the month's final days.

In addition, Hen Harriers, Merlins and Peregrines displayed their aerial skills and Buzzards (up to eight), Sparrowhawks and Kestrels were also present. As if that was not more than enough to satisfy the many birders who travelled to enjoy the spectacle, a Great Grey Shrike attempted to

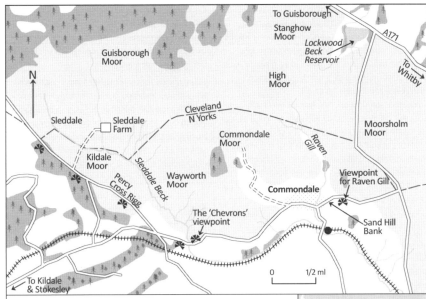

How to get there

(Approx 12 miles SE of Middlesbrough)

Main approach is via A171 Middlesbrough to Whitby road, which rises steeply to moors three miles SE of Guisborough. Take first right (signpost Castleton) after another mile and immediately beyond Lockwood Beck Reservoir (on right). After almost three miles over moors, turn right to Commondale (one mile).

Continue for another mile-and-a-half to Chevrons watchpoint on descent to bridge over Sleddale Beck. If preferring the Percy Cross Rigg watchpoints, continue for half mile and turn right at crossroads.

Public transport:
Middlesbrough-Whitby trains stop at Commondale station (no disabled facilities) – two mile walk to Chevrons watchpoint — see www.northyorkstravel.info

In summer, a go-everywhere ramblers' Moors Bus Service operates from Middlesbrough (daily during school holidays).

steal the show, sometimes perching just yards from assembled watchers.

Though on a larger scale, this wasn't an entirely new experience for Sleddale. The 2010 'raptorfest, as the Teesmouth Bird Club website dubbed it, was short-lived

as the Rough-legs left during November's first half, but a juvenile discovered in January 2008 remained for two months.

It was well-watched too and other raptors logged over the period included an adult Rough-leg (just one

day), Hen Harrier, Merlin and Peregrine. Some birders were able to observe the juvenile feeding, unusually, on snails. This involved dropping them from heights of up to 20m to break their shells and then, after picking off any remaining shell fragments, eating them on the wing. However, seeing Rough-legged Buzzard at Sleddale isn't as easy as such occasions might suggest. Individuals can range extensively over the moors, so watchers may have to wait several hours for just a brief appearance – and it mightn't turn up at all.

Weather, of course, is a key factor in the success or otherwise of a visit; the ideal at Sleddale is a fine clear day with some cloud (raptors stand out better with some cumulus in the background) and not too much or too little wind, preferably from the south-west. It's a waste of time to go there in wet or misty conditions and don't even think about it when snow and ice prevail as you may end up stranded on an exposed moorland road.

As for where to watch, there are pull-offs along the Commondale-Kildale road on either side of the bridge over Sleddale Beck. One popular spot is known as The Chevrons, referring to a road sign indicating the coming steep descent to the beck. It offers the most panoramic view up Sleddale but, unfortunately, it's on a bend. However, traffic is usually very light and, with care, it's possible to drive on and off the verge safely.

There are further verge parking possibilities at the foot of the hill but the problem with watching from there is that the lie of the land causes raptors drifting south-eastwards over Wayworth Moor to go out of sight when at their closest.

Another option is to watch from Percy Cross Rigg road, which runs along Sleddale's western ridge after branching from the Commondale-Kildale road at the top of the hill on the beck's western side. There are several verge parking points along this narrow cul-de-sac and they are fine for scanning the Sleddale Farm area and the eastern ridge but some parts of the dale are out of sight.

Also worth checking is Raven Gill, north of

Commondale village (Rough-leg sightings there in October 2010). This can be viewed from a Commondale road lay-by at the top of Sand Hill Bank, which descends to the village's eastern end.

Sleddale's raptor potential isn't confined to late autumn and winter. Marsh Harrier and Osprey are possible on spring and early autumn passage, Red Kite has occurred during both these periods and Goshawk in spring. Merlin is possible in every season, Buzzard increasingly so and Peregrine can be anticipated over much of the year too.

As for other types of birds, Red Grouse occurs widely over the moors, with particularly close views possible along Percy Cross Rigg. Stonechat used to be there too but probably not since the recent colder winters. During the 2010 'raptorfest', Snow Bunting was seen along that road and Richard's Pipit and up to five Ravens were reported near Sleddale Farm. A few Twite were noted in the area too.

Sleddale's position provides a suitable access and departure point for day-flying migrants crossing the North York Moors. Skylarks, Meadow Pipits, Pied Wagtails and thrushes have been noted following this route.

With spring's approach, Golden Plovers, Lapwings, Snipe and Curlews can be expected and from mid-March early Wheatear and Ring Ouzel appearances are likely, the latter sometimes in autumn too. Wheatear remains a scarce nesting species in Sleddale but Ring Ouzel is not known to have bred since 1987 (although pairs have since been seen).

Grey Wagtail and Dipper can be anticipated on moorland streams and in winter a Fieldfare flock may be in pastures where Percy Cross Rigg road joins the Commondale-Kildale road. Siskins, Lesser Redpolls and maybe a Crossbill party are possible in nearby conifer plantations.

THE TEES ESTUARY'S eastern side has developed so heavily since 1829, when Middlebrough was just a farmstead with 40 people, that birding potential is restricted to the three-mile coastal strip between the rivermouth and Redcar. However, surviving estuarine and marsh habitats continue to support many wetland birds and the area has significant migrant-pulling power.

Target birds
Autumn passage – Barnacle Goose (50%), Pomarine Skua, Black Redstart, Yellow-browed Warbler (all 40%), Wryneck (30%), Barred Warbler (30%), Garganey, Long-tailed Skua, Sabine's Gull, Icterine, Greenish and Pallas's Warblers, Firecrest, Red-breasted Flycatcher, Red-backed Shrike (all 20%).

Late autumn/ winter – Mediterranean Gull, (60%), Great Northern Diver, Merlin, Water Rail, Little Auk (all 40%), Black-throated Diver (30%), Red-necked Grebe (30%), Slavonian Grebe, Bittern, Grey Phalarope (all 20%).

Spring passage – Garganey, Little Ringed Plover, Black Redstart (all 30%), Marsh Harrier, Osprey, Temminck's Stint, Wryneck, Icterine Warbler, Firecrest, Red-backed Shrike (all 20%), Bluethroat (10%).

Summer/early autumn - Roseate Tern (60%).

Other possible bird species

All year
Mute Swan
Canada Goose
Shelduck
Tufted Duck
Eider
Grey Partridge
Little Grebe
Fulmar
Gannet
Grey Heron
Sparrowhawk
Kestrel
Oystercatcher
Ringed Plover
Lapwing
Dunlin
Snipe
Curlew
Redshank
Familiar gulls
Stock Dove
Skylark

Meadow Pipit
Pied Wagtail
Linnet
Reed Bunting

Spring passage/summer
Ruff
Black-tailed Godwit
Whimbrel
Green Sandpiper
Wood Sandpiper
Common Sandpiper
Lesser Black-backed Gull
Sandwich Tern
Common Tern
Little Tern
Black Tern
Auks
Swift
Hirundines
Yellow Wagtail
White Wagtail
Redstart
Whinchat

Wheatear
Ring Ouzel
Grasshopper Warbler
Sedge Warbler
Reed Warbler
Lesser Whitethroat
Whitethroat
Garden Warbler
Blackcap
Chiffchaff
Willow Warbler
Spotted Flycatcher
Pied Flycatcher

Autumn
Whooper Swan
Pink-footed Goose
Brent Goose
Wigeon
Teal
Pochard
Long-tailed Duck
Common Scoter
Velvet Scoter

Key points

• Main car parking near Gare End at NZ 557 277.

• Use various pull-off points along approach road.

• Do not venture onto exposed parts of Gare End in stormy weather or with a heavy incoming swell on a rising tide.

• Take care walking over blast furnace slag as it is very uneven.

• Nearest toilets three miles away on Redcar sea front – near boating lake in Majuba Road; Tourist Info (at junction of West Terrace and Esplanade) and in Moore Street, (near Lifeboat Station).

• Wheelchair hire available at Tourist Info (01642 471 921, e-mail: redcar_tic @ redcar-cleveland. gov.uk)

45

Goldeneye	Long-eared Owl	Velvet Scoter	Purple Sandpiper
Red-breasted Merganser	Short-eared Owl	Goldeneye	Jack Snipe
Red-throated Diver	Grey Wagtail	Red-breasted Merganser	Bar-tailed Godwit
Manx Shearwater	Redstart	Goosander	Turnstone
Golden Plover	Whinchat	Red-throated Diver	Short-eared Owl
Grey Plover	Wheatear	Great Crested Grebe	Kingfisher
Knot	Ring Ouzel	Shag	Rock Pipit
Little Stint	Winter thrushes	Golden Plover	Water Pipit
Curlew Sandpiper	Migrant warblers	Grey Plover	Stonechat
Ruff	Goldcrest	Knot	
Woodcock	Spotted Flycatcher	Sanderling	
Black-tailed Godwit	Pied Flycatcher		
Whimbrel	Brambling		
Spotted Redshank	Siskin		
Greenshank	Lapland Bunting		
Green Sandpiper	*Late autumn/*		
Wood Sandpiper	*winter*		
Turnstone	Wigeon		
Arctic Skua	Gadwall		
Great Skua	Teal		
Little Gull	Shoveler		
Sandwich Tern	Pochard		
Common Tern	Scaup		
Arctic Tern	Long-tailed Duck		
Auks	Common Scoter		

1. South Gare (NZ 551 277)

PROTRUDING invitingly into Tees Bay, the huge breakwater of South Gare must be a welcome sight to desperate migrants in murky weather.

The mouth of the Tees was very different in 1861 when a storm killed 60 seamen and wrecked 50 boats. This led to a decision to build breakwaters, starting with South Gare, with five million tons of blast furnace slag and 18,000 tons of cement going into the two-and-a-half-mile structure.

Most of this lies under the road along which visitors now drive to reach Gare End, the wave-pounded outermost stretch.

This huge structure really does pull in migrants. Its species list of more than 300 includes Europe's second Cliff Swallow (1988) and mouth-watering rarities including Black Kite, Pallid Swift, European Roller, Short-toed Lark, Richard's and Red-throated Pipits, Desert Wheatear, Subalpine, Greenish and Radde's Warblers, Arctic Redpoll, Common Rosefinch, Ortolan and Rustic and Little Buntings.

The places harbouring migrants are alongside the two miles of road leading to Gare End. Some are barely noticeable to the casual passers-by, being no more than a few bushes or modest scrub. What they can offer is indicated by the following lists of species since 2000:

Contacts
Check date of annual autumn one-day closures of South Gare Road for maintenance 01642 877 200.

Tea Bushes – Bluethroat, Greenish and Pallas's Warbers, Red-backed Shrike.

Gulley – Long-eared Owl, Icterine, Barred, Pallas's and Yellow-browed Warblers, Firecrest.

Bomb Hole – Roller, Wryneck, Bluethroat, Black Redstart, Greenish and Yellow-browed Warblers, Red-breasted Flycatcher, Red-backed Shrike.

Paddy's Hole – Wryneck, Marsh, Subalpine, Barred, Pallas's, Yellow-browed, Radde's and Wood Warblers, Red-breasted Flycatcher, Little Bunting.

Cabin Rocks – Roller, Wryneck, Short-toed Lark, Black Redstart, Pallas's Warbler, Great Grey Shrike, Rose-coloured Starling.

Shrike Bushes – Roller, Golden Oriole, 'Desert' Lesser Whitethroat, Marsh and Yellow-browed Warblers, Firecrest, Bearded Tit, Red-backed and Great Grey Shrikes.

An elder and willow clump with a tangle of brambles, the Shrike Bushes provide a refuge for migrants moving from sparser cover to the north.

Nearer Gare End, Cabin Rocks can be equally productive despite its apparent barrenness. Reminiscent of a solidified volcanic lava flow, but really consisting of blast furnace slag in a sandy hollow, Paddy's Hole is a small harbour.

Cabin Rocks can attract early Wheatears from mid-March while in late April-early May there can be 100-plus Greenland Wheatears present.

Early September 'falls' of migrants can provide Wryneck, Icterine and Greenish Warblers, Red-breasted Flycatcher and Red-backed Shrike as well as numerous Redstarts, Whinchats, Wheatears, Lesser and Common Whitethroats, Garden Warblers, Blackcaps, Willow Warblers and Spotted and Pied Flycatchers.

It can also attract incoming northern thrushes. In winter Snow and Lapland Buntings are often present. Unfortunately, Shore Lark, which used to occur regularly, has become rare.

South Gare presents a possible route for migrant raptors trying to avoid passing over the Teesside conurbation or the bay. Black Kite, Honey Buzzard, Marsh and Hen Harriers, Osprey and Hobby have been reported in spring or autumn since 2000.

Peregrines have increased their local presence, birds sometimes perching on top of the steelworks' largest gasholder.

A Great Snipe on rough ground between the road and the sea in September 2008 was Teesmouth's first since 1976 – a fine addition to South Gare's impressive wader list which includes the area's famous 1996 Great Knot (see Seal Sands section) and also Avocet, Kentish Plover, Temminck's Stint and White-rumped, Baird's, Pectoral and Spotted Sandpipers.

Routine waders include Grey Plovers, Knot, Sanderlings and Bar-tailed Godwits and occasionally Little Stints, Curlew Sandpipers and Whimbrels. Spotted Redshanks, Greenshanks and Green, Wood and Common Sandpipers occur sometimes on the Blast Furnace Pools across the road from the steelworks.

South Gare's extensive bird list is boosted by seawatching, particularly from July until late November. Strong winds from the north-east spark the most exciting passages but care must be taken. The safest place is the road's most northerly point where seawatching from a car means comfort and shelter.

Despite No Entry signs, some seawatchers venture to Gare End, which in rough weather is extremely risky – I remember how a wave swept a birding friend to his death in the early 1960s.

Sabine's Gulls and Pomarine and Long-tailed

Skuas are good autumn prospects, all three having been recorded since 2000. Sabine's Gulls aren't confined to stormy weather but can turn up in tern flocks or with Kittiwakes roosting on the sea at dusk. There's an even stronger chance that close scrutiny of late summer tern assemblies will be rewarded by a few Roseate Terns.

 Wildfowl, including Whooper Swans and Pink-footed, Barnacle and Brent Geese are possible during mid to late autumn seawatches.

 Little Auks pass during late autumn and winter storms, though numbers are usually well below those seen from the region's headlands. Calm winter weather can provide opportunities to 'scope Black-throated and Great Northern Divers, Red-necked and Slavonian Grebes and Glaucous and Iceland Gulls. There's also a fair chance of Grey

How to get there

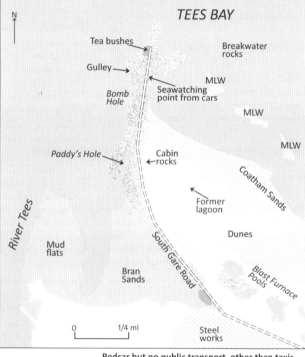

(Four miles from Middlesbrough)

Approach South Gare from A19. Leave it just over two miles south of the River Tees Flyover, turning onto A174 heading east to Redcar. Ignore the left turn onto A1053 after about eight miles but at a second roundabout turn left onto A1042 to Redcar.

This ends after two miles at traffic lights at the junction with the A1085 from Middlesbrough. Go straight ahead into the north end of Kirkleatham Lane leading to Redcar seafront but after a quarter of a mile, before a railway bridge, turn left at a small roundabout (signposted to Warrenby).

For three-quarters of a mile this passes through a rather run-down area and has a 'road to nowhere' look but it's actually the South Gare Road, the last two miles following the line of the breakwater.

Though narrow, it has passing places and there are pull-off points to park while checking off-road sites. There is more extensive roadside parking when you reach Gare End.

Public transport: Good bus and rail services to Redcar but no public transport, other than taxis, to South Gare (three miles). Closest bus stop is near Coatham roundabout where road to South Gare starts. Services X3 and X4 (Middlesbrough – Redcar – Loftus), Service 22 (Middlesbrough – Redcar – Saltburn) and Service 81 (Stokesley – Guisborough – Redcar) stop there.

2. Coatham Marsh (NZ 587 250)

THE SALTMARSHES east of Teesmouth were the scene of a futile last stand during William the Conqueror's ruthless Harrying of the North in 1069.

Almost a thousand year later, the vestiges of the once huge wilderness makes up part of this 134-acre reserve managed by the Tees Valley Wildlife Trust and today's harriers are birds of prey rather than Normans.

Divided by the Middlesbrough-Saltburn railway, the reserve separates the seaside resort of Redcar from the steelworks to the west. Its southern section was once a refuse tip but has been landscaped to provide grassy hillocks to soften the appearance of the steelworks.

During this process, the Long and Round Lakes were created. These, along with a scrape on the

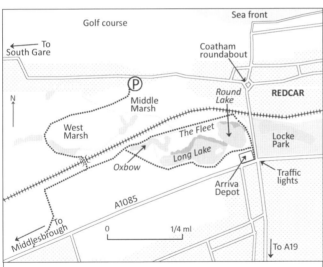

How to get there

Follow same route as for South Gare except for final directions. After turning left from Coatham roundabout (signposted to Warrenby) at north end of Kirkleatham Lane, head west for about 600 yards. Straight after the road crosses a disused railway, turn left into the small car park at the reserve's northern access.

Public transport: The better access for bus-users is in Kirkleatham Lane just north of the traffic lights at the A1085/A1042 junction as services from Middlesbrough (X3, X4 and 22) and Stokesley/Guisborough (81) stop at Coatham roundabout at the end of the lane.

north side, mean the reserve is usually well flooded but with plenty of mud for waders.

It's yet another Teesmouth site with a big reputation for rarities on its 200-plus species list. They include the fifth Bufflehead for Britain, a first-summer male in 1994, which might or might not have been a true vagrant.

More regular New World waterfowl have included Blue-winged and Green-winged Teal and Ring-necked Ducks. American waders include White-rumped, Baird's and Pectoral Sandpipers and Wilson's Phalarope. They join an impressive wader list also featuring Black-winged Stilt, Avocet, Stone Curlew, Temminck's Stint and Red-necked Phalarope.

Varied habitats give scope for a wide range of marshbirds, with Phragmites reed specialists taking advantage. These include Savi's Warblers, Cetti's Warblers (new colonists to the North-East) and Teesmouth's third Great Reed Warbler and a Marsh Warbler. Sedge and Reed Warblers and Whitethroat are regular breeders and Bearded Tits, another regional rarity, have occurred.

It is also the area's most reliable site for wintering Bitterns, while Spotted Crakes occasionally occur.

Common Crane is another spectacular migrant which has provided the occasional spring highlight, particularly when an astonishing 24 arrived off the sea at Redcar in mid-March 2004. Almost exactly four years later four circled the reserve and steelworks.

Garganey can occur in both spring and autumn, sometimes coinciding with passage waders such as Little Stint, Ruff, Black-tailed Godwit, Spotted Redshank, Greenshank and Green, Wood and Common Sandpipers.

In winter, the occasional Smew and Goosander can appear on the lake among the commoner species, while other maritime species that may take refuge include Scaup, Long-tailed Duck, Common and Velvet Scoters and Red-breasted Merganser. Red-necked and Slavonian Grebes and Red-throated and Black-throated Divers have also been recorded.

Key points (Coatham Marsh)

• Wheelchair hire available at Tourist Information.

Contact

Tees Valley Wildlife Trust 01287 636 383.

E-mail info@ teeswildlife.org www.teeswildlife.org

3. Locke Park, Redcar (NZ 59 24)

THE FIRST five Black-billed Cuckoos recorded in Britain between 1932 and 1967 were found dead or dying in west coast locations after crossing the Atlantic. The sixth was made of sterner stuff and was still in good shape when it reached this splendid park in 1975 and ended up in a mist net during Blackbird ringing.

While undoubtedly the biggest occasion in the park's birding history, it was by no means the only pulse-racing moment as a local Thrush Nightingale was only the eighth for Britain and an Olive-backed Pipit the 20th.

The park covers 25 acres with avenues of trees and numerous shrub clumps bordering its paths and central lake. A stream flows out into Coatham Marsh.

Many of the trees are

Key points (Locke Park)

• Free parking at park entrance in Corporation Road at NZ 595 247.

• Extensive paths network around park – good for wheelchair users.

Key points
(Locke Park)

- Allow plenty of time when migrants are about.

- Nearest toilets half-a-mile away on Redcar sea front (see South Gare key points).

- Wheelchair hire available at Tourist Information office (see South Gare key points).

sycamores, with huge populations of aphids attracting many small migrants along with the common resident species. Yellow-browed Warblers are very regular with more than 50 recorded between late September and mid-November since the 1950s along with a couple of Pallas's Warblers.

Other autumn rarities and scarcities have included Night Heron, Barred, Greenish and Dusky Warblers and Little Bunting. Bluethroat and Hawfinch have been springtime visitors. Wryneck, Icterine Warbler, Firecrest, Red-breasted Flycatcher, Red-backed Shrike and Rustic Bunting have occurred in both seasons.

Their presence usually coincides with larger scale appearances by species such as Redstart, Lesser Whitethroat, Garden Warbler, Blackcap, Chiffchaff, Willow Warbler and Spotted and Pied Flycatchers.

Water Rails and Kingfishers occur in winter – in icy conditions the former can be anticipated along the outflow stream from the lake. Occasionally Scaup, Long-tailed Ducks, Goldeneyes, Smew and Goosanders turn up on the lake.

How to get there

Same as for South Gare and Coatham Marsh except for final directions.

If approaching Redcar from A1042, on reaching traffic lights at junction with A1085, turn right into Corporation Road and park entrance is on left after 200 yards.

Alternatively, if approaching on A1085 from Middlesbrough, go straight ahead into Corporation Road at the lights.

Public transport: Redcar rail station half-a-mile east of park. Bus services X3, X4 (Middlesbrough-Loftus), Service 22 (Middlesbrough-Saltburn) and Service 81 (Stokesley/Guisborough – Redcar) stop near Coatham roundabout at top of Kirkleatham Lane at park's west end.

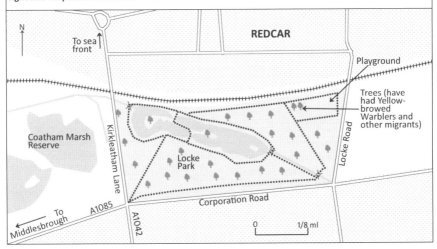

RIVER-MOUTH expanses of sand for gulls, terns and waders and dunes with cover for grounded migrants make the northernmost section of the Tees's western fringes a place of great potential for visiting birdwatchers. These areas, plus a salt-marsh remnant and a grazed freshwater marsh, are part of the 771-acre Seaton Dunes and Common SSSI, part of Teesmouth National Nature Reserve and of the Teesmouth and Cleveland Coast Special Protection Area.

Target birds

Autumn passage – Barnacle Goose (50%), Black Redstart (40%), Yellow-browed Warbler (40%), Wryneck, Barred Warbler, Pallas's Warbler (all 30%), Sabine's Gull, Icterine and Greenish Warblers, Red-backed Shrike (all 10%).

Late autumn/ winter – Short-eared Owl (70%), Snow Bunting (70%), Merlin, Mediterranean Gull, Twite (all 60%), Iceland and Glaucous Gulls, Barn Owl (all 40%), Great Northern Diver (30%), Red-necked Grebe (20%).

Spring passage – Black Redstart (40%), Icterine Warbler (20%), Red-backed Shrike (20%).

Summer/early autumn – Little Tern (70%), Roseate Tern (50%).

Other possible bird species

All year
Greylag Goose
Canada Goose
Shelduck
Gadwall
Mallard
Eider
Grey Partridge
Fulmar
Gannet
Cormorant
Grey Heron
Sparrowhawk
Kestrel
Moorhen
Coot
Oystercatcher
Ringed Plover
Lapwing
Snipe
Redshank
Turnstone
Familiar gulls
Common farmland birds
Stock Dove
Skylark
Meadow Pipit
Pied Wagtail
Stonechat

Linnet

Spring passage
Black-tailed Godwit
Wood Sandpiper
Water Pipit
Redstart
Whinchat
Wheatear
Ring Ouzel
Fieldfare
Redwing
Lesser Whitethroat
Chiffchaff
Willow Warbler
Goldcrest
Spotted Flycatcher
Pied Flycatcher

Late March - August
Lesser Black-backed Gull
Sandwich Tern
Common Tern
Swift
Hirundines
Yellow Wagtail
Grasshopper Warbler
Sedge Warbler
Whitethroat
Yellowhammer
Reed Bunting

Autumn passage
Whooper Swan
Pink-footed Goose
Knot
Little Stint
Curlew Sandpiper
Dunlin
Woodcock
Whimbrel
Arctic Skua
Great Skua
Little Gull
Sandwich Tern
Common Tern
Arctic Tern
Redstart
Whinchat
Wheatear
Ring Ouzel
Blackbird
Fieldfare
Song Thrush
Redwing
Lesser Whitethroat
Whitethroat
Chiffchaff
Willow Warbler
Goldcrest
Spotted Flycatcher

Pied Flycatcher
Chaffinch
Brambling

Late autumn/winter
Brent Goose
Wigeon
Teal
Long-tailed Duck
Common Scoter
Goldeneye
Red-breasted Merganser
Red-throated Diver
Great Crested Grebe
Water Rail
Golden Plover
Grey Plover
Knot
Sanderling
Purple Sandpiper
Dunlin
Jack Snipe
Bar-tailed Godwit
Curlew
Turnstone
Rock Pipit
Snow Bunting

Background information and birding tips

THIS IS ANOTHER area now much more industrialised than when I began birding 50 years ago and was awestruck by the never-repeated sight of 1,000 Snow Buntings in stubble west of the A178 between Seaton Carew and Graythorp. Those fields are now an industrial estate and a golf driving range.

Another section was swallowed up by Hartlepool nuclear power station. The rest, the triangle from Seaton Carew and Seal Sands, bordered by the A178 to the west and the sea to the east, is superficially the same and its chief birding components are:

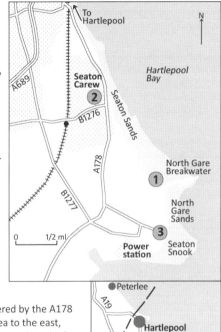

Key points
(North Gare)

• Car park half-a-mile east of A178 at NZ 533 282.

• If using short footpath across golf course take care to avoid disrupting play.

• Quarter mile walk to breakwater along a stony path. Expect to walk at least half-a-mile through dunes to check sea buckthorn for migrants.

• Wheelchair-users restricted to the surfaced roadway across Seaton Common

• Do not venture on to breakwater's outer section in stormy weather or if there's a heavy incoming swell on a rising tide.

• Nearest toilets at Seaton Carew's south end (by clock tower at bus stop off A178).

1. North Gare/Seaton Common (NZ 533 282)

THE ROUGH GRASSLAND stretching towards the sea from the A178 may not look too inspiring but Seaton Common has a distinguished birding past, present and, hopefully, future.

One way of visiting is to use the unclassified road signposted to North Gare and marked by two tall stone columns. It leads half a mile to the car park on the western edge of Seaton Carew golf course.

The track provides views of mud-fringed pools and channels not visible, except in flood conditions, from the A178. They can hold spring passage Garganey and sometimes Barnacle Geese in autumn.

53

Little Egret sightings are increasing as the species has become more established. Great White Egret and Purple Heron (still regional rarities) as well as Spoonbills have been recorded, as have Cranes.

A Wilson's Phalarope in January 2005 was remarkable, being Britain's first winter record. Buff-breasted and Pectoral Sandpipers have also occurred. More typical waders such as Black-tailed Godwits (up to 70 have been present) regularly occur.

The pools have also proved a popular local site for spring Temminck's Stints and Wood Sandpipers. Other rarities on the local list include Quail, White-winged Black Tern, Red-rumped Swallow, Water Pipits and Scandinavian Rock Pipits.

Raptors include passing Honey Buzzards, Marsh and Hen Harriers, Rough-legged Buzzards, Ospreys and Hobbies. Merlins and Peregrines can be anticipated in winter when flocks of Golden Plovers and Lapwings provide prey potential for the latter.

The North Gare bushes are a broad sea buckthorn belt sheltering the golf course's eastern flank. They're an obvious refuge for grounded migrants which have included a couple of 'megas,' a Hume's Leaf Warbler in November 2000 and Red-eyed Vireo in October 1991.

There have also been spring and autumn Hoopoe, Bluethroat and Red-backed Shrike. Other migrants have included Wryneck, Firecrest and Marsh, Pallas's and Yellow-

How to get there

(Two miles from Hartlepool)

From Seal Sands roundabout (A1185/ A178 junction), drive N for three miles to turn right onto surfaced roadway (half-mile) over Seaton Common to North Gare car park. The signpost is not prominent, so look for tall stone columns on either side of the roadway entrance. It comes half-a-mile along A178 after a large roundabout at the entrance to Hartlepool Nuclear Power Station (on right), with the B1277 to Hartlepool on left.

If travelling south from Hartlepool, take A178 to Seaton Carew, after which the North

Gare car park turning is the first on the left after three-quarters of a mile of driving alongside Seaton Common.

Public transport: Regular Hartlepool-Port Clarence bus

service along A178 (bus stop for North Gare). Newcastle to Middlesbrough trains stop at Hartlepool and Seaton Carew. Tourist Info, 01429 869 706; Traveline 0870 608 2608.

browed Warblers. Open areas always attract Wheatears while Black Redstarts favour the area around the tank traps and other Second World War relics near the breakwater.

Snow Buntings can sometimes be found in dune slacks in winter, often moving between this site and the South Gare. Shore Larks and Lapland Buntings have been found but are rare. Typical shorebirds, including Sanderling, can be prominent in winter on North Gare beaches, with Turnstones and possibly Purple Sandpipers at the breakwater.

This exposed pier can be dangerous during on-shore winds but during fine weather can provide a handy scanning spot for skuas and terns in late summer and for divers, grebes and sea-duck in winter. Its most impressive rarity was an adult Franklin's Gull, third for Britain, in July 1977. If in this area in late September or early October, it's another place to watch out for Barnacle Geese migrating from Svalbard to the Solway Firth.

Contacts
Teesmouth NNR Site Manager 01429 853 325.

Field Centre 01429 264 912.

2. Seaton Carew (NZ 527 294)

DUSKY WARBLER is no longer a British rarity but it was in 1981 when many regional birders discovered Holy Trinity churchyard, tucked away behind the southern end of the resort's sea-front. The Siberian stray in the churchyard sycamores was only the 30th for Britain and put the place on the birding map.

Seaton Carew was again a site of birder pilgrimage in September 1994 when a Paddyfield Warbler (Britain's 25th) was found in bushes on a landscaped former industrial site, while at the same time the churchyard held an Icterine Warbler, two Yellow-browed Warblers and a lively supporting cast of Blackcaps, Chiffchaffs, Goldcrests and Spotted and Pied Flycatchers.

I mention those occasions as reminders that the churchyard should not be overlooked as birders pass to other better-known local hotspots. It may get fewer birding headlines but it still has potential.

Yellow-browed Warblers have been recorded in at least four autumns since 2000 and Siberian Stonechat and Ortolan Bunting are among other rare or scarce visitors on its list. Regular checks in suitable weather between September and November can be productive.

One way to include the churchyard in coverage is to start from Seaton Carew's southern beach car park. You can then cross the A178 into Church Street

Key points
(Seaton Carew)

• Large car park (NZ 527 294) at south end of Seaton Carew sea front.

• To reach churchyard walk to A178, cross it and go down Church Street.

• OK for wheelchair users except in dunes and on golf course.

• Toilets at bus stop (below clock tower).

• Newburn Outfall, half-a-mile north of Seaton Carew at NZ 518 318 just before A178, is always worth checking. Road bears left from seafront to cross railway (over Newburn Bridge) to continue to Hartlepool town centre.

to Holy Trinity. After that you can walk along the edge of the sea buckthorn between the golf course and the dunes to North Gare, and then continue to the Zinc Works Road bushes, Seaton Common and Seaton Snook.

The footpath on the golf course's west side offers an alternative return route. It means being distant from your car for much of the time but for those who enjoy a lengthy walk, there's much ground to cover and the possibility of a wide range of species.

How to get there

(Three miles from Hartlepool)

From Hartlepool town centre take A178 to Seaton Carew. The car park access road is at the very southern end of the resort, straight after the off-road bus stop and prominent clock tower on the left.

From Seal Sands roundabout (A1185/A178 junction) to the south, drive north on A178 for almost four miles, then immediately on reaching Seaton Carew take the first right turning (just before the bus stop and clock tower on the right).

Public transport: Regular bus services from Hartlepool. Also Newcastle - Middlesbrough trains stop at Hartlepool and Seaton Carew.

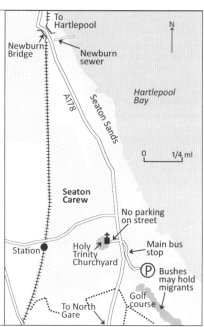

3. Seaton Snook/Zinc Works Road (NZ 53 26)

Key points
(Seaton Snook)

• Park on eastern end of ZWR (NZ 534 274), 0.75 miles east of A178 to check nearby bushes and Seaton Snook.

• Lay-bys along road provide viewpoints for Seaton Common.

KNOWLEDGE of tide times is essential to get the best from visits to this sandy area where the Seaton-on-Tees Channel (as Greatham Creek's outer stretch is now officially known) joins the main river. For many years birders have called these sands Seaton Snook, the name which features on Natural England's map of the reserve, though for some reason the OS Explorer map places Seaton Snook in the middle of Seaton Common!

The best time to visit is between half and high tide as waders, gulls and terns arrive to roost.

Hundreds of terns gather during July-September. Though mainly Common, Sandwich and Arctic Terns, sometimes the odd Roseate Tern may be present and on some occasions as many as 30 have appeared.

A few Little Terns may also be there and Black Terns are regularly pulled in, with groups of up to 25 having been recorded. Caspian Tern and the famous Farne Island Lesser Crested Tern made May, June and July appearances in four years between1984-1995.

The Snook's rarest waders so far

have been Broad-billed Sandpiper and the famous Teesmouth Great Knot in autumn, 1996. More recent attractions include a White-rumped Sandpiper in August 2002 and two in late July-early August 2006.

Ringed and Grey Plovers, Knot, Dunlin and Bar-tailed Godwits are the typical visiting species and Little Stints, Curlew Sandpipers and Whimbrels can occasionally be found.

With many Little Gulls visiting inshore waters in late summer and early autumn some may join the gull roosts. Mediterranean, Ring-billed and Sabine's Gulls have also been recorded.

The Snook's lack of cover makes it unattractive to passerines but the area did produce one of only two Pied Wheatears ever

recorded between the Tyne and Flamborough Head. The only small songbird attracting birders regularly to this section of the estuary is Twite, flocks of which feed among areas of Salicornia in the wetter areas.

Snook-bound birders can approach via the Zinc Works Road (ZWR) which branches from the A178 about 300 yards south of the turn-off to the North Gare car park. Verges near the eastern end (wide enough for parking without blocking industrial traffic) are half-a-mile nearer the Snook than the North Gare car park.

From ZWR's end, a short track leads through a break in the dunes to a sandy beach on the west side of the rivermouth. For Seaton Snook, turn right and

Key points

- View Seal Sands and Seaton on Tees Channel from beside wartime pillbox on power station's east side.

- Nearest toilets at Seaton Carew's south end (by clock tower at bus stop off A178).

- Bushes where migrants can occur north of ZWR's end can be viewed from dunes or public path (runs north from ZWR to North Gare path).

How to get there

(Three miles from Hartlepool)

Directions are the same as for Seaton Common/North Gare – except that the signposted turning for ZWR is 300 yards south along the A178 from the turning to the North Gare car park and 0.25 miles north of the roundabout at the power station access road junction.

Public transport: Regular Hartlepool-Port Clarence bus service along A178 (bus stop for ZWR). Newcastle to Middlesbrough trains stop at Hartlepool and Seaton Carew. Tourist Info, 01429 869 706; Traveline 0870 608 2608.

Map labels: A178; Seaton Common; P; North Gare Sands; N; TEESMOUTH; Zinc Works Road; Landfill site viewable from Zinc Works Road (good for gulls); Scattered bushes good for migrants; Zinc works; Nuclear power station; Seaton Snook; 0 – 1/4 ml; Seaton on Tees Channel

Key points

• **No wheelchair access to Seaton Snook (soft sand) but there's no problem viewing Seaton Common or landfill site from ZWR.**

• **Be aware security patrols near power station may challenge birders, especially at dusk. Relations are cordial but it helps if you can show Wildlife Trust or RSPB membership card.**

walk for around a quarter-of-a-mile over the sand until roosting birds come into view

Between the south side of the ZWR west end and the nuclear power station access road is an area of scattered scrub and young trees. Behind the dunes, north of the ZWR's east end, are small pools and more bushes. Each of these areas has birding potential.

These areas have attracted rarities including Hoopoe and Bluethroat and even a Serin, a very rare bird in the North-East. A fly-over Alpine Swift was another attracti

The ZWR bushes produce migrants consistently in autumn with Wryneck, Firecrest, Ortolan Bunting and Barred, Greenish, Pallas's and Yellow-browed Warblers among species recorded since 2000. Recent spring sightings include a Red-backed Shrike and Wood Warbler as well as commoner Redstarts, Lesser Whitethroats and Pied Flycatchers.

Meanwhile, the scrub that has become established on the south side of ZWR provides breeding habitat for Grasshopper and Sedge Warblers and Common Whitethroats.

Winter Short-eared Owls hunting over Seaton Common can be watched from the ZWR, while towards dusk Barn Owls have also delighted birders. Little Egret, Merlin, Water Rail, Jack Snipe, Woodcock, Kingfisher and Stonechat are among other species recorded in the ZWR vicinity since the start of 2008.

There's also gull-watching potential at a landfill site across the A178 from its junction with the ZWR. Mediterranean, Iceland, Glaucous and Yellow-legged have all

The Seaton Snook gull roost attracts a range of species, including Mediterranean Gull.

A QUALIFICATION for 'birding hotspot' status could be a site with a first sighting for Britain. Teesmouth, a place where nature and commerce live side-by-side, earns its accolade thanks to the next best thing, a spate of 'seconds for Britain', plus many other crowd-pullers among the thousands of migratory birds which visit each year.

Target birds
All Year – **Peregrine (40%)**, **Water Rail (30%)**. *Spring to autumn* – **Avocet (70%)**, **Little Egret (60%)**, **Garganey**, **Spoonbill**, **Black Tern (all 40%)**, **Marsh Harrier (30%)**, **Black-necked Grebe (20%)**, **Hobby (20%)**. *Winter* – **Merlin (30%)**.

Other possible bird species

All year
Mute Swan
Greylag Goose
Canada Goose
Gadwall
Shoveler
Tufted Duck
Red-legged Partridge
Grey Partridge
Grey Heron
Sparrowhawk
Kestrel
Moorhen
Coot
Lapwing
Curlew
Redshank
Familiar gulls
Common woodland and farmland birds
Stock Dove
Little Owl
Tawny Owl
Great Spotted Woodpecker
Skylark
Meadow Pipit
Grey Wagtail
Pied Wagtail
Mistle Thrush
Long-tailed Tit
Coal Tit
Treecreeper
Jay
Goldfinch
Linnet
Bullfinch
Yellowhammer

Reed Bunting

Spring to early autumn
Shelduck
Oystercatcher
Ringed Plover
Knot
Little Stint
Dunlin
Ruff
Black-tailed Godwit
Spotted Redshank
Greenshank
Green Sandpiper
Wood Sandpiper

Common Sandpiper
Common Tern
Cuckoo
Swift
Hirundines
Yellow Wagtail
Whinchat
Wheatear
Sedge Warbler
Reed Warbler
Whitethroat
Chiffchaff
Willow Warbler

Late autumn/winter
Whooper Swan
Pink-footed Goose
Barnacle Goose
Wigeon
Teal
Pintail
Pochard
Goldeneye
Golden Plover
Snipe
Green Sandpiper
Fieldfare
Redwing

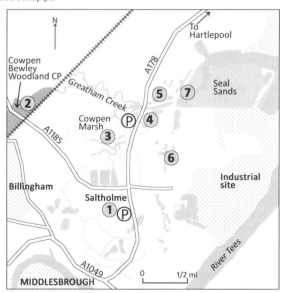

Background information and birding tips

TEESSIDE'S industrial image is so powerful that it's hard to imagine it in medieval times when 40 square miles of inter-tidal mud and marsh surrounded the river mouth. Now only fragments remain.

This precious habitat came under increasing pressure with the opening of the world's first public railway between Stockton and Darlington in 1825 which accelerated the Industrial Revolution with the development of the steel and, later, the chemicals industries.

Amazingly, it remains a place where nature prospers and thanks to guarantees over the future of key sites, habitat enhancement and public access, the estuary remains a prime birding location.

Historically, the group of key birding sites here have been referred to as the North Tees Marshes though that is incorrect geographically. The Tees curves northwards on its final stage to the sea, so all locations in this sector are to the west or, mainly, south-west of the surviving principal estuarine habitat, Seal Sands.

Outstanding places on the former Durham side of the rivermouth include:

1. Saltholme RSPB Nature Reserve (NZ 506 231)

WHATEVER ELSE the Teesside Urban Development Corporation achieved, it deserves credit for sowing seeds which silenced the complaint of local birders: "Why do we have to travel to other UK regions to visit a flagship RSPB wetland reserve?"

This project began in 2002 on land formerly owned by ICI and the reserve eventually opened in 2009 following completion of its £4m Discovery Centre and visitor complex.

Just a shade early, an adult Glaucous-winged Gull arrived at New Year 2008-09, the second British record of this America Pacific species, followed in April by two Whiskered Terns.

Long before its creation the area had already pulled in Britain's second Long-toed Stint in 1982, as well as Montagu's Harrier, Semi-palmated, White-rumped, Baird's, Broad-billed, Buff-breasted, Marsh and Spotted Sandpipers, Lesser Yellowlegs, Wilson's Phalarope, Bonaparte's Gull and Caspian Tern.

On the western side of the 1,000-acre reserve, Haverton Hole has an impressive background too, having attracted Glossy Ibis, Penduline Tit and singing Savi's and Great Reed Warblers. Now a watchpoint reached by the reserve's paths system overlooks not only Haverton Hole, but also the adjacent North West Reedbeds and, to the south, another large reed-fringed pool created from abandoned allotments.

New wetlands have been created, including the lake at the Discovery Centre and Paddy's Pool with another large hide overlooking a tern island. Management of extensive grassland has quickly helped breeding birds with big increases in Lapwings from five to 50 pairs and Redshanks, from one to 13 pairs.

Yellow Wagtail, now a comparatively scarce species in the North-East, has also benefited. In winter, many thousands of Golden Plovers and Lapwings use the reserve area, often attracting Peregrines.

The hides with a range of shutter heights are very

Contacts

Saltholme Reserve Discovery Centre, 01642 546 625.

Stockton Tourist Information, 01642 528 130.

Teesmouth Bird Club Secretary: Chris Sharp, 20 Auckland Way, Hartlepool, TS26 0AN (01429 865 163).

birder-friendly (not always the case) for everyone from the very young to wheelchair users.

Discovery Centre features include a viewing gallery by the lake, CCTV coverage of live action around the reserve, exhibitions and an education centre including an outdoor wetland boardwalk where children can learn about pond-life.

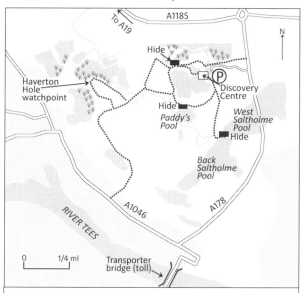

Key points (Saltholme)

• **Open daily, except Dec 25 (10am-5pm – April 1 to Sept 30); 10am-4pm – Oct 1 to March 31).**

• **Free entry for RSPB members and non-members arriving by bus, pedal cycle or on foot; car park charge for non-members.**

• **Five miles (8km) of firm-surfaced paths.**

• **Cycleway across reserve from High Clarence Community Farm.**

• **Paths, hides and Discovery Centre all wheelchair accessible.**

• **Hides with seating designed for three-deep viewing.**

• **Centre includes shop, toilets and lift to first floor café.**

How to get there

(3 miles E of Billingham)

Saltholme is west of A178 between Hartlepool and Port Clarence. Its entrance is about 300 yards south of Seal Sands roundabout, from which the A1185 connects with the A19 at Wolviston (four miles to the north-west).

The reserve can also be reached from the A19 via A1046 (junction just north of A19 Tees flyover bridge) which connects with southern end of A178 at Port Clarence, 1.5 miles south of the reserve entrance.

Public transport: Half-hourly Stagecoach No 1 (Hartlepool-Middlesbrough) buses stop on A178 near reserve entrance. This service is handy for anyone arriving by train at Hartlepool and Middlesbrough stations.

Stockton-Port Clarence services stop on A1046 near south end of walk/cycleway which starts from near the Community Farm at High Clarence. This is reached via Holly Terrace from the A1046 where two Stockton-Port Clarence bus services (run by Compass Royston) stop: the 555 running on the hour from Stand 24 in Stockton town centre; and the 589 on the half-hour from Stand 12.

2. Cowpen Bewley Woodland Country Park (NZ 47 25)

FOLLOWING the Stockton Borough Council's planting of 300,000 trees since 1990 the park has added a significant new dimension to the local wildlife scene. It now provides extensive habitat for a range of birds that is represented thinly around or absent totally from the nearby marshes.

I'm not just talking about woodland birds, either; regularly the park's lake hosts winter gatherings of Goosanders, which are comparatively scarce visitors to the estuary.

Occupying both sides of the A1185 to the west of the Hartlepoool-Billingham railway, the park also boasts managed grassland, hedgerows and several ponds and three streams. Two small hills with viewpoints and seating provide useful spots for raptor watching (Honey Buzzards were noted over the park during the significant movement of September 2008 and Marsh Harrier passed in the spring).

Around 100 bird species have been recorded in the park, with the section to the north of the A1185 generally more productive. Significant for the

Key points
(Cowpen Bewley CP)

• **Open all year. Car park access in summer 9am-9pm; winter 9am-4pm.**

• **Activity Centre (including shop and toilets) open Sundays (10am-4pm) plus Mon and Fri during school summer holidays).**

• **All paths wheelchair accessible.**

• **Site includes uncovered picnic area and children's play area.**

How to get there

(3 miles NE of Billingham town centre)

The Country Park's signposted entrance is 1.25 miles east along A1185 Seal Sands Road from the roundabout at the junction with the A19 slip road and A689 to Hartlepool at Wolviston. Look for turning where A1185 starts to rise towards the bridge over the railway.

From the other direction, it is two miles north-west of the A1185/A178 junction at the Seal Sands roundabout.

Public transport: Take Bus Service 91 from Middlesbrough to Low Grange or Service 52 from Middlesbrough, Stockton, Norton or Billingham to Low Grange Avenue. From the stop at Bewley Infants School, cross Wolviston Back Lane, to enter the park section south of the A1185. A ten-minute walk brings you to the Activity Centre.

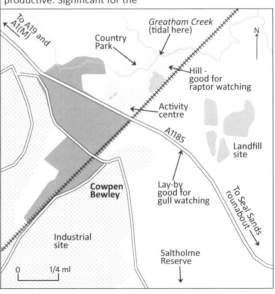

Contacts

Activity Centre,
Cowpen Bewley
Woodland Park, Seal
Sands Link Road,
Billingham TS23 3NF.
Tel: 01642 371 633.

estuary's immediate vicinity are species such as Green Woodpecker, Coal Tit, Treecreeper, Jay, Tree Sparrow and Bullfinch. Some of these are among the 20 species – Great Spotted Woodpecker, Long-tailed Tit, Brambling and Yellowhammer are among the others – that visit the park's feeding station particularly during the year's first and final quarters.

Summer visitors recorded include Grasshopper and Sedge Warblers, Lesser Whitethroats, with Cuckoos, Redstarts and Spotted Flycatchers also possible on spring and autumn passage. In winter, the park's alder trees hold feeding flocks of Siskins and Lesser Redpolls, sometimes joined by a few of the scarcer Common Redpolls.

Hawthorn berry crops attract Fieldfares and Redwings and, during irruptions years, the occasional Waxwing party. Linnet flocks can be targeted by Merlins, while Short-eared Owls can be seen hunting over the grassland. Barn Owls maybe on show too.

The park's north side includes upper reaches of Greatham Creek and its tributary Cowbridge Beck, which are tidal. The mud at low tide attracts waders, with Ruff and Green and Common Sandpipers, even the occasional Sanderling, among species recorded.

A routine range of waterfowl on the main lake are joined occasionally by scarcer species like Red-crested Pochard and Red-necked Grebe. Kingfisher and Water Rail occur, the latter particularly on the smaller water. Also, it's one of Teesside's growing number of places that have logged Little Egret.

The occasional Little Gull and Common Tern are seen over the main lake. Mediterranean Gulls turn up also, no doubt as a result of the landfill site nearby at the back of Cowpen Marsh.

3. Cowpen Marsh (NZ 50 24)

THE MARSH is a rather sad relic of past centuries when the estuary was vast and its network of channels allowed the tide to daily flood the area. It has SSSI status due mainly to its range of plants, including sea club-rush, grey club-rush, brackish water-crowfoot and sea rush.

Like other local sites, it has enjoyed a notable run of rare and unusual birds over the years including Terek, Sharp-tailed and Pectoral Sandpipers, Temminck's Stint and Lesser Yellowlegs. The 2009-10 Glaucous-

How to get there

(5 miles NE of Billingham town centre)

Cowpen Marsh is west of A178 between Greatham Creek Bridge and the A1185 Seal Sands roundabout to the south.

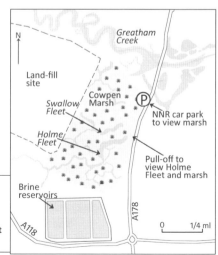

Key points
(Cowpen Marsh)

• **No access to marsh. View from Teesmouth NNR car park or from higher grass embankment south of Greatham Creek Bridge.**

• **To view Holme Fleet, use a grassy track leading to a raised area. Look for obvious opening in roadside fenceline 0.25 mile south of the NNR car park. Wheelchair access is possible.**

• **When leaving take care not to pull out into fast-approaching traffic.**

• **Nearest toilets at Saltholme Reserve and Seaton Carew.**

winged Gull was among the huge gathering of commoner gulls attracted here by local waste dumping.

It has to be said, however, that the marsh isn't consistently productive. It's the sort of place that's always worth checking out on a quiet day but often there may be nothing more than the Common Terns nesting on raft islands on Holme Fleet.

Surprises are possible, like in April 2004 when a birder on such a speculative visit flushed a Corncrake from along the track between the A178 and the viewpoint.

Garganey, Black-necked Grebe, Spoonbill and Little and Great White Egrets have all occurred since 2000 and its versatility has been further illustrated by sightings of Honey Buzzard, Marsh and Montagu's Harriers and Hobby passing through at migration times.

4. Greatham Creek (NZ 510 254)

SENSATIONAL birding events regularly occur at Teesmouth but Britain's first Short-billed Dowitcher at Greatham Creek stands out in particular.

This American mega had already attracted crowds in Aberdeenshire before moving south where during its month-long stay it attracted thousands of birders, causing parking problems along the extremely busy A178.

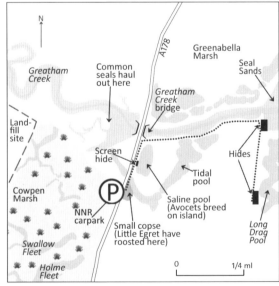

Things have improved and visitors now have the Teesmouth National Nature Reserve car park just south of the creek, which consists of a tidal channel with extensive areas of saltings. It also has adjacent saline lagoons to the north and south.

This parking is very useful in spring to visit the nearby Avocet colony on the saline lagoon created south-east of the bridge in 1999 by the Industry and Nature Conservation Association with funding from Natural England and Northumbrian Water Environmental Trust.

The site is managed by Saudi Basic Industries Corporation, further evidence of how local industry and conservation are in tune. Two pairs raised young in 2008, rising to 18-20 pairs by 2011.

A nearby Natural England display board gives information about the NNR, the southern section of which consists mainly

of Seal Sand's tidal mudflats. The hide overlooking these mudflats is reached by walking eastwards along the top of Greatham Creek's southern bank. The narrow path is well fenced on either side.

After 200 yards it passes the north end of the tidal pool which often holds waders and ducks and during spring and summer period yet more Avocets and often Little Egrets, another rapidly increasing species in the region. Back in 1995 it attracted an adult Ross's Gull.

In summer Common Terns are regularly present from the colony on the saline lagoon island. Little Ringed Plover, Little Stint, Curlew Sandpiper, Black-tailed Godwit, Spotted Redshank and Greenshank are among regular passage waders and Buff-breasted Sandpiper is among rarer species which have been recorded. In winter, Greatham Creek often attracts Twite.

5. Greenabella Marsh (NZ 513 256)

GREENABELLA MARSH is an extensive area of saltmarsh and rough grassland to the north of Greatham Creek and east of the A178 Tees Road. It includes ICI's No 5 Brinefield and has a hide provided by Huntsman Tioxide.

The area is excellent for wildfowl, waders, terns and, in winter, small birds such as Twite, Goldfinches and Linnets. Common Terns breed on the artificial islands. The marsh has an impressive list of rare and scarce birds, including Britain's second Short-billed Dowitcher,

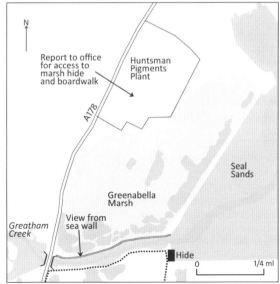

65

Pacific Golden Plover and Semi-palmated Sandpiper.

It is regarded as an important winter feeding area and high tide roost site for waders, notably Ringed Plovers, Knot, Dunlin, Curlews and Redshanks.

During spring and autumn migration it is well used by wildfowl such as Wigeon, Teal and waders such as Black-tailed Godwits, Greenshanks and Green, Wood and Common Sandpipers. It is also a regular winter site for Short-eared Owls, Merlins and the occasional Peregrine.

Greenabella Marsh is most safely accessed by parking in the Teesmouth National Nature Reserve car park and walking north over the A178 Greatham Creek bridge and down on to the northern sea wall of the creek. This gives extensive views out over the marsh.

The sea wall eventually leads to Seal Sands and good views over the mudflats can be obtained from here. The route leads to the hide.

The Great Knot visited Greenabella during its stay, detailed under Seal Sands, and on one occasion an adult male Red-footed Falcon hunted from one of the posts out on the marsh.

6. (The) Long Drag (NZ 516 245)

THE LONG DRAG is a rough track which stretches more than a mile along the former western wall of the Seal Sands NNR. Three hundred yards south of Greatham Creek another Natural England hide overlooks a 12-acre pool.

Immediately south is a 25-acre reedbed which has produced Bearded Tits almost annually since the mid-1990s but without any indication of breeding. This spot has had a fine run of birds over the years, including Kentish Plover, Terek Sandpiper and Teesmouth's first Laughing Gull in 1981.

Dotterel, American Golden Plover, plus Sharp-tailed, Baird's and Broad-billed Sandpipers have provided further highlights as have Golden Oriole and Great Spotted Cuckoo. There have been September and October records of

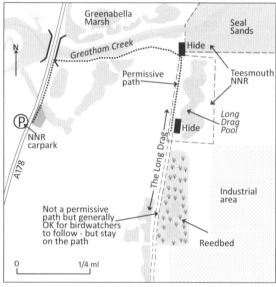

Richard's Pipit, Yellow-browed Warbler and Red-backed Shrike.

In spring it's a likely spot for early Wheatears and Ring Ouzels and in May 2009 two Red-rumped Swallows appeared. Savi's Warblers nested here in 1994.

With its extensive reedbed, this is among Teesmouth's better spots for Marsh Harrier on spring or autumn passage. Hen Harrier is a very occasional winter possibility. The area has also produced migrant Bittern and Great White Egret reports.

7. Seal Sands (NZ 530 260)

FIRST-TIME visitors to the Seal Sands hide are often impressed by the extent of the spread of water or mud (at low tide) ahead of them until they realize that it's the only surviving fragment of this precious estuarine habitat.

The hide is sited at the bottom left-hand corner of the sands, which up to the 1970s covered 1,000 acres and extended more than a mile further south.

The 1960s North Sea oil boom swallowed up two thirds of those mudflats. The square mile of rich feeding grounds for wildfowl and waders to the south was filled in to produce land for an oil terminal and petrochemical plants. Frustratingly, much of the former mudflats remains as rough grassland.

The remaining 350 acres forms the southern section of the National Nature Reserve established in 1995. Britain's second Great Knot spent three weeks in the estuary in 1996 and was nick-named the "Great Dot" as it was often so distant. However, with a telescope, sessions there can be very satisfying with a wide variety of waders on show in autumn and winter. It is the region's best spot for wintering Black-tailed Godwits.

Winter waterfowl on show – liable to be much closer at high tide – can include sizeable Goldeneye and Red-breasted Merganser gatherings, plus the occasional Smew, as well as scarcer divers and grebes. After long-term relative scarcity, more Brent Geese have appeared in recent times.

Common seals move up Greatham Creek to haul out and rest on the mudbanks at the bridge carrying the A178. When there you can view them from a distance of only 50 metres.

DURHAM SITES

Many of the upland streams in the Durham Dales are likely
to provide views of Dippers or Grey Wagtails.

BACKSTONE BANK WOOD is a prime location for birders heading into the hills to seek some of the region's most delightful summer visitors. The first tributary valley on Weardale's north side as you head up the dale well deserves its place in the North Pennines Area of Outstanding Natural Beauty, particularly because of the semi-ancient woodlands spread across its eastern flank.

Target birds
Spring/early summer – Pied Flycatcher (70%), Redstart (60%), Spotted Flycatcher (60%), Wood Warbler (40%), Tree Pipit (30%), Osprey (20%). *All year* – Buzzard (70%), Marsh Tit (50%).

Other possible bird species

Spring/early summer		
Mute Swan	Familiar gulls	Song Thrush
Mallard	Common farmland and	Mistle Thrush
Tufted Duck	woodland birds	Blackcap
Goosander	Stock Dove	Garden Warbler
Great Crested Grebe	Cuckoo	Whitethroat
Cormorant	Tawny Owl	Chiffchaff
Grey Heron	Swift	Willow Warbler
Sparrowhawk	Green Woodpecker	Goldcrest
Kestrel	Great Spotted	Long-tailed Tit
Moorhen	Woodpecker	Coal Tit
Coot	Sky Lark	Nuthatch
Oystercatcher	Sand Martin	Treecreeper
Lapwing	Swallow	Jay
Woodcock	House Martin	Goldfinch
Curlew	Meadow Pipit	Siskin
Redshank	Grey Wagtail	Linnet
Common Sandpiper	Pied Wagtail	Lesser Redpoll
	Dipper	Bullfinch

Background information and birding tips

TUNSTALL RESERVOIR, a 50 acre (20ha) lake created by the beck's damming in 1879, is the valley's most striking map feature, but it is the wooded slope rising from its eastern bank to Wolsingham North Moor, that is most productive for birders.

Backstone Bank has a history of coppice management – rotational timber removal enabling trees to re-grow from stumps – dating back to at least the 16th Century.

Now an SSSI, its more acidic soil areas are dominated by sessile oak, while ash and wych elm flourish in lime-rich ground sections.

This is ideal territory for the summer-visiting dales quartet – Redstart, Wood Warbler, Pied Flycatcher and, in more open areas, Tree Pipit. Sadly, the national decline all four have suffered since the 1980s has affected this area, so nowadays

Key points

• Open access at all times.

• Official Tunstall Reservoir car park at NZ 064 413. Roadside parking at W end of dam at NZ 064 407. If walking from Wolsingham, park at Waskerley Beck picnic site(NZ 075 376).

• Reservoir circuit about two miles – allow at least three hours. From Wolsingham, you could cover up to ten miles so allow at least seven hours.

• Baal Hill Wood terrain uneven and path slippery. Two boggy stretches at northern end of path through Backstone Bank Wood.

Contacts
Tunstall Reservoir – Northumbrian Water 0870 240 3549.

How to get there

(Approx 15 miles W of Durham).

From Durham City take A690 to Crook (11 miles) where it becomes the A689 for a further five miles to Wolsingham. From Consett on A68 head W from A689 junction roundabout south of Tow Law.

For Tunstall Reservoir continue through Wolsingham centre then, just after a small park on the left, turn right onto minor road (signposted To Swimming Pool and Tunstall Reservoir). After three miles park on roadside by reservoir dam.

 Alternatively, continue half-a-mile to reservoir car park. Walk back to dam to cross to Backstone Bank Wood's south end.

For bus users walking from Wolsingham, start from where B6296 reaches town's northern edge. Four hundred yards beyond the Waskerley Beck bridge and on the town's northern edge, take first left (unclassified road leading to the Holywood luxury housing estate).

After about 200 yards, you come

to Holywell Farm after which a public footpath branches to the right to head north to Baal Hill House Farm. This continues up the east side of the Waskerley Beck Valley for two miles to Backstone Bank and Tunstall Reservoir.

If you wish to visit Baal Hill Wood, take waymarked path

branching left round south side of Baal Hill House Farm.

there is much less certainty about encountering Tree Pipits and Wood Warblers than in past decades.

 Your success or failure can

be influenced by the timing of visits, both in terms of the chosen spring period and the hour of the day. Backstone Bank, more than 700ft above

sea level, doesn't hurry into its spring cycle. Even well into April the woodland can show minimal tree foliage, oak and ash being ever-cautious about bursting into leaf too soon – which can restrict bird activity.

The best results 'window' is quite narrow: visit before late April and you'll be ahead of summer visitors such as Wood Warblers and Spotted Flycatchers; leave it too far after mid-May and there are problems finding birds in the fast-spreading leaf canopy.

As for the time of day, the full glory of the dawn chorus cannot be over-emphasised. While singing continues through the day, it is especially intense around daybreak.

Early-arriving birders have the pick of the limited parking places and can look forward to undisturbed woodland. From mid-morning on fine weekends family groups tramping noisily around the reservoir circuit can render the wood's lower part virtually birdless.

I prefer parking along the road near the reservoir dam's west end as this is closest to Backstone Bank's more bird-rich southern end. This is equally convenient for making a quick return to the car if just visiting the wood rather than walking all around the reservoir.

To reach the wood from there take the broad track along the dam top leading to Backstone Bank Farm. Strolling over the dam can be among the circuit's more rewarding sections outside the wood.

My finest dam moment came in June, 1984, when an Osprey was summering locally. I was in the middle when it flew up the valley, passing quite close before wheeling back and forth across the broadest part of the reservoir. As Scotland's population has grown since then, the odds in favour of a passage Osprey calling at Tunstall have risen too.

Oystercatcher, Common Sandpiper and Grey Wagtail are the species seen most regularly from the dam during spring/early summer, along with the occasional female Goosander with ducklings.

Goosanders, incidentally, used to occur in substantial numbers at Tunstall outside the breeding season. There were record-setting September roosts of up to 89 during 1974-76 but increases in angling, particularly from boats, brought an end to that sequence.

At the dam's eastern end the track rises into the wood. As it bends to continue to the farm, a display board about the SSSI marks the start of a path branching off northwards above the reservoir shore.

Soon you will realise why an early May visit is best; the trees are well spaced and the shrub understorey spread thinly, so with the leaf canopy not much advanced, pinpointing a Redstart or a Pied Flycatcher singing some distance from the path is achievable.

Green and Great Spotted Woodpeckers, Blackcap, Chiffchaff, Willow Warbler, Marsh Tit, Nuthatch, Treecreeper and

Key points

• **Path over fields may be muddy in places. Unsuitable for wheelchairs.**

• **Portaloo-type public toilets at official reservoir car park. Also public toilets in park off A689 W of Wolsingham centre.**

• **Pubs, restaurant, fast food outlet and a few shops at Wolsingham.**

• **Durham Dales Centre facilities at Stanhope, seven miles to W, include toilets, shops, café and Tourist Information (01388 527 650) with pubs and more shops in main street.**

Bullfinch are among further likely species. A visit deeper into May should add later-arriving Garden Warblers and Spotted Flycatchers to the list.

If on an evening visit – maybe while en route to nearby Hamsterley Forest to seek Nightjars – you may see a Woodcock's roding flight or catch a glimpse of a Tawny Owl. The wood's other wildlife includes the slow worm (it's one of the few places in North-East England where I've seen this legless lizard).

After a footbridge over a stream, the path leads through conifer-dominated Backhouse Wood where Siskins nest. Eventually it links with a track across the reservoir's narrow top end, a nature reserve due to its expanse of the nationally scarce thread rush *Juncus filiformis*.

Watch out here for Great Crested Grebes (attempts to nest can be thwarted by fluctuating water levels), Grey Herons, Tufted Ducks, Moorhens and Redshanks. Goldfinches may twitter atop trees between the reserve and Tunstall House Farm, where Swallows and House Martins are usually prominent.

The farm is at the head of the valley's solitary road which forms the circuit's last section. It leads back to the reservoir car park on a headland half way along the reservoir's west edge and the dam's west end car park.

Finally, I should stress Backstone Bank isn't beyond the reach of birders relying on public transport. They, together with car-borne birders keen for a much longer trek, can walk there from Wolsingham via paths along the valley's eastern side.

A mile north of Wolsingham this route passes the Durham Wildlife Trust's Baal Hill Wood. There's a link to a waymarked trail circling its southern end. This 38-acre (15.5ha) reserve – owned by the Bishop of Durham back in the 14th Century – is undergoing improvement work, including the removal of non-native trees. The aim is to establish more open birch/oak woodland; it will be interesting to see how dales speciality birds respond to this habitat enhancement.

As with Backstone Bank, in past times it was coppiced to provide timber for producing charcoal needed for ore smelting. In case you're wondering, this explains the wood's curious name, "Baal" being a local term for this traditional activity apparently.

After Baal Hill House Farm the path presses on northwards for two miles to Backstone Bank Farm, where you join the track leading down to the woodland walk.

Between the two farms the path crosses large open pastures and the all-round view boosts the chances of seeing a Buzzard drifting over the valley. Also, you may see a Cuckoo as along the valley slope you're closer to the moorland from which its evocative calls sound.

To return by a different route, from Tunstall's dam head south along the road for a mile, leaving it at Bishop Oak for paths following the Waskerley Beck all the way to the Wolsingham picnic site near the B6296 crossing of this stream. It's a pleasant alternative and if you haven't already caught up with Dipper there's a reasonable prospect of doing so during these final two miles.

DESPITE their upland location and the inevitable disturbance from angling and water sports, the three reservoirs in Baldersdale have been welcome additions to Durham's range of birding sites. The potential for productive birding is broadened by extensive surrounding moorland and the unimproved meadow habitats of Hannah Hauxley's celebrated farm. With the Pennine Way crossing the dale and a footpath extending west across the moors into Cumbria, there are opportunities for even wider exploration.

Target birds
All year – Black Grouse (70%), Kingfisher (50%), Merlin (40%), Peregrine (40%). *Spring/early autumn* – Osprey (30%). *Spring/summer* – Lesser Redpoll (90%), Yellow Wagtail (60%), Sedge Warbler (50%). *Late autumn/winter* – Whooper Swan (50%), Short-eared Owl (50%), Hen Harrier (30%), Rough-legged Buzzard (20%).

Other possible bird species

All year
Greylag Goose
Canada Goose
Wigeon
Mallard
Tufted Duck
Red Grouse
Grey Partridge
Cormorant
Grey Heron
Sparrowhawk
Buzzard
Kestrel
Moorhen
Coot
Black-headed Gull
Stock Dove
Common woodland birds

Common farmland birds
Dipper
Mistle Thrush

Spring/ summer
Oystercatcher
Ringed Plover
Golden Plover
Snipe
Woodcock
Curlew
Redshank
Common Sandpiper
Lesser Black-backed Gull
Cuckoo
Sky Lark
Sand Martin
Swallow

House Martin
Meadow Pipit
Grey Wagtail
Pied Wagtail
Whinchat
Wheatear
Willow Warbler
Linnet
Lesser Redpoll
Reed Bunting

Autumn/ winter
Teal
Goldeneye
Goosander
Common Gull
Fieldfare
Redwing

Background information and birding tips

COUNTY DURHAM, not well endowed with large freshwater bodies, gained five more reservoirs, together with the rest of Yorkshire's former Startforth Rural District, in the 1974 local government boundary changes, with three of them lying in Baldersdale.

Yellow Wagtail, an increasingly scarce species in the area, has occurred regularly in spring and summer along the walk I'm about to describe.

While this walk could start equally from the Balderhead Dam, I've tended to use the small car park near Clove Lodge

Key points

• Open access at all times.

• Car parks at Clove Lodge; Balder Head; both ends of Hury Reservoir dam; north end of Blackton Reservoir dam; and both ends of Balderhead Reservoir dam.

• Firm surfaces for walking and wheelchairs.

• Allow 90 mins to walk from Clove Lodge to Hannah's Meadow via Blackton Reservoir and back.

• Shoreline paths of all three reservoirs each about a mile long (an hour each).

• Balder Head car park good for watching over Hunderthwaite Moor for raptors and also wildfowl, gulls and waders at reservoir's west end.

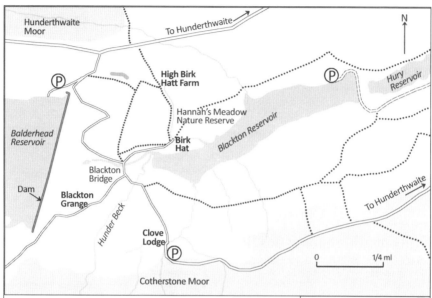

How to get there

(Approx eight miles NW of Barnard Castle).

From Bishop Auckland head for Staindrop on A688 or via A68 from junction 58 of A1(M), joining A688 at West Auckland (13 miles).

At Staindrop, turn right on B6279 Teesdale road, then after seven miles turn right on to B6278 to descend (one mile) to Eggleston. Bear left at bottom of hill on to B6282 (the B6278 goes straight on) then after just 300 yards turn left on B6281 to cross River Tees.

Turn left straight after Eggleston

Bridge onto minor road to Romaldkirk to join B6277. Just south of village turn right on minor road to Balderhead Reservoir with car park at road's end. To reach south side of Hury and Blackton Reservoirs, turn left 1.5 miles past Hunderthwaite village. Below Hury dam, head west to car park at end of road near Clove Lodge.

From west, leave A66 at Bowes, joining A67 to Barnard Castle, but quickly turning left on to minor road to Cotherstone (four miles). Join B6277 but at village's north end turn left onto minor road heading up dale.

On approaching Hury Reservoir,

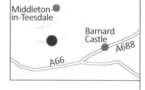

road forks; left takes you further up south side of dale, right links up with north side road.

Public transport: Bus services 95/96 stop at Cotherstone and Romaldkirk en route to Middleton-in-Teesdale from Barnard Castle – which has bus links with Darlington, Durham and Bishop Auckland.

at the dale's south side road end. This is partly because of the close-up views of waders along the way; Oystercatchers perhaps

on the roadside boundary wall of Hury Reservoir, then Lapwing, Snipe, Curlew and Redshank along the northern edge of Cotherstone Moor.

Red Grouse may be on show there too.

Also, I enjoy walking the short Pennine Way section that heads north from Clove

Lodge and through the nature reserve at Blackton Reservoir's western end. This is at the very middle of the 268-mile walking route and comes after a stretch over miles of open moorland. Any birder tackling it and approaching from the south couldn't fail to be uplifted by the sudden increase in species evident at this point.

Willow Warblers and Chaffinches are likely to be singing in the patch of planted saplings and shrubs at Clove Lodge. From the mature copse behind this farmhouse/B&B, listen to the voices of Blackbirds, Song and Mistle Thrushes.

On reaching the gate opening on the track down to the reservoir in early June 2008, I had a splendid close-up view of a pair of Lesser Redpolls foraging about the ground so intently they ignored me totally.

The subsequent descent to the nature reserve is where I have found Yellow Wagtails regularly, often calling from the flanking dry stone wall or in the meadows on either side.

Sadly, there was no sign of any when I checked in 2008, possibly a reflection of the previous summer's persistent wet weather which must have had particular impact on such ground-nesters.

While the long-term downward trend of this species doesn't inspire great confidence, I hope for a comeback, as it has always been a chief highlight of this walk.

There are others, however, such as a Common Sandpiper, which could be calling anxiously upstream of the bridge over the Hunder Beck just before it flows into the reservoir. Watch out also for Kingfishers, which operate along this stream, though they can be anticipated equally in the nature reserve's more tranquil waters.

While severe weather can lead to Black Grouse moving down from the fells to feed on birch here in winter, they can occur at other times. In mid-May 2006 I found a fine male in the adjacent grounds of what was then the YHA Hostel – but more of that later.

Often the rhythmic flight calls of Lesser Redpolls are the dominant sound as the track approaches the Blackton Bridge over the channel flowing into the reservoir from the towering earth dam of its much bigger Balderhead neighbour.

In some summers, considerably more varied and erratic flows of sound from waterside shrubs indicates Sedge Warbler presence. Movement in the rushes by the channel may betray a Tufted Duck family that has taken refuge – or perhaps one of Durham's few Wigeon broods.

The track turns away from the reservoir at Low Birk Hat, former home of Hannah Hauxwell, famous since the 1973 ITV documentary *Too Long a Winter*. It focused on her running an 80-acre farm single-handed, without electricity, gas or running water – on an income of just £280 a year.

The legendary daleswoman, who celebrated her 82nd birthday on August 1, 2008, sold the farm in 1987. Books and DVDs about her life continue to inspire people internationally.

Now her old home is much spruced-up after years of dilapidation, but the traditional hay meadows certainly haven't changed. A Site of Special Scientific Interest, they're preserved as Hannah's Meadow Nature Reserve, managed

Key points

• Toilets at Hury and Balderhead Reservoir dams.

• Hide at W end of Blackton Reservoir by Birk Hat House.

• Pub facilities at Romaldkirk and Cotherstone. Shops and toilets at Middleton-in-Teesdale.

Contacts

Barnard Castle Tourist Information (01833 690 909).

by the Durham Wildlife Trust. As a youngster in the 1930s, she must have heard Corncrakes calling from the lush vegetation; with the habitat so well maintained, there has to be a flicker of hope that one day they may do so again.

Meanwhile Goldfinches twitter from the telegraph wires now linking Low Birk Hat to the modern world and Meadow Pipits perform song flights into the ragged robin-rich grassland. These and the nearby calls of displaying Lapwings and Curlews form the background sound as you proceed uphill to High Birk Hat Farm, where a left turn brings you onto a path leading to Balderhead Dam's north end.

After crossing the dam turn left onto a path that descends to pass the former YHA hostel, which was bought by First Ascent, a leadership and team performance development company in 2007. Now it is the four-star Blackton Grange training centre and self-catering farmhouse.

The public footpath through its 11-acre grounds provides an ideal opportunity to check out some of the best bird habitat in the upper dale, including an area of juniper bushes where I saw the Black Grouse in 2006.

This path joins the Pennine Way between the Hunder Beck Bridge and Blackton Bridge. So turn right to return to the Clove Lodge car park.

Alternatively, if you started from the Balderhead Dam car park, you may wish to walk the few hundred yards up towards Clove Lodge to look for Yellow Wagtail. You would then retrace your steps to return to the dam via Blackton Bridge and High Birk Hat.

Canada Geese are the most prominent wildfowl on the three reservoirs or adjacent farmland at any time of year. First recorded as recently as 1945, they took awhile to become established, with no more than 38 reported during 1975-80. Subsequent breeding success is indicated by counts exceeding 200 becoming the norm since the late 1990s.

Smaller numbers of Greylag Geese are present throughout the year and between October and March there's always a possibility of a few Whooper Swans, though the species lingers less frequently these days

In the 1960s, Mallard was the most numerous duck on these waters, with Hury alone holding 882 one winter, but numbers have been considerably lower in recent times. Counting other species present – usually limited to Wigeon, Teal, Tufted Duck, Goldeneye and maybe Goosander – doesn't take long either.

The large winter roosts of Black-headed and Common Gulls present a greater challenge, as their late afternoon arrivals allow little time for assessing numbers or sifting through the massed assembly for the possible presence of any unusual species.

Fieldfare flocks frequent the dale's lower pastures while higher up Black Grouse is always an attractive prospect. The best viewpoint for the latter is Balder Head car park which offers fine views over Hunderthwaite Moor as well as the west end of the uppermost reservoir.

Birds of prey are a further incentive to carry out a sustained watch; regular visits and much patience may be rewarded by the occasional Hen Harrier or, if it happens to be a winter of above-average numbers nationally, a Rough-legged Buzzard.

As Scotland's Osprey population grows, more pass through the North-East. Luck plays a strong part inevitably, but with three reservoirs offering feeding potential, the dale is one of the likelier places for connecting with this skilled fish-catcher during spring and autumn passage periods.

MOST BRITISH birders didn't know the village of Bishop Middleham existed until 2002 when a pair of Bee-eaters nested in a disused quarry and drew 22,000 visitors to the site. Inevitably, the Bee-eaters didn't return, but various locations around the village are now gaining recognition for their wetland and farmland bird attractions.

Target birds
All Year – Willow Tit (60%), Corn Bunting (60%), Kingfisher (50%), Tree Sparrow (50%), Peregrine (40%), Water Rail (30%). *Spring/summer/autumn* – Little Ringed Plover (70%), Yellow Wagtail (70%), Little Egret (50%), Garganey (40%), Black Tern (40%), Marsh Harrier (30%), Black-necked Grebe, Hobby (20%). *Winter* – Merlin (30%).

Other possible bird species

All year		
Mute Swan	Meadow Pipit	Common Tern
Greylag Goose	Grey Wagtail	Cuckoo
Canada Goose	Pied Wagtail	Swift
Gadwall	Mistle Thrush	Sand Martin
Mallard	Long-tailed Tit	Swallow
Shoveler	Coal Tit	House Martin
Tufted Duck	Treecreeper	Whinchat
Red-legged Partridge	Jay	Wheatear
Grey Partridge	Goldfinch	Sedge Warbler
Cormorant	Linnet	Blackcap
Grey Heron	Bullfinch	Garden Warbler
Sparrowhawk	Yellowhammer	Whitethroat
Kestrel	Reed Bunting	Chiffchaff
Moorhen	*Spring/ summer/early*	Willow Warbler
Coot	*autumn*	*Late autumn/ winter*
Lapwing	Shelduck	Whooper Swan
Curlew	Oystercatcher	Pink-footed Goose
Redshank	Ringed Plover	Barnacle Goose
Familiar gulls	Knot	Wigeon
Common woodland	Little Stint	Teal
and farmland birds	Dunlin	Pintail
Stock Dove	Ruff	Pochard
Little Owl	Black-tailed Godwit	Goldeneye
Tawny Owl	Spotted Redshank	Golden Plover
Great Spotted	Greenshank	Snipe
Woodpecker	Green Sandpiper	Green Sandpiper
Skylark	Wood Sandpiper	Fieldfare
	Common Sandpiper	Redwing

Background information and birding tips

THE UNEXPECTED arrival of a pair of Bee-eaters which managed to raise three young – the species' first UK breeding since two out of three pairs succeeded in Sussex in 1955 –

Key points

• Park to view Stonybeck Lake at NZ 338 316; Castle Lake (NZ 328 313); quarry reserve (NZ 331 324).

• Open access at all times.

• No Wheelchair access to hide but some areas are accessible.

• 1.5 mile walk around Castle Lake and return to village green. Allow three hours. Follow instructions on display boards.

• Key needed to access public hide at NZ 328 307. Details from Durham Bird Club.

• Two pubs and small café in village. Full motorway services at J61 of A1(M).

Contacts
Tourist Information: (0191 384 3720)

How to get there

(Approx 10 miles from Durham)

Village lies E of A1 (M) motorway between Junctions 60 and 61. Access from minor road (Stonybeck Lane) running W from A177 Durham City – Sedgefield road, which links to both Junctions.

From J60, take A689 for two miles and just before Sedgefield, turn left on to A177 and drive N. After half a mile you pass the Hardwick Hall Hotel on your left; continue for two miles, taking first left to Bishop Middleham.

From J61, go on to A688 Bishop Auckland road then, after 1.5 miles, turn left at T-junction roundabout on to A177. After a mile cross over motorway but stay on A177. After passing the Hare and Hounds pub at a crossroads, travel 1.5 miles and turn right for Bishop Middleham.

You're now in Stonybeck Lane. After 600 yards check Stonybeck Lake on right after a downhill stretch and bend. After another 600 yards, take first left into village and at bottom turn left into Church Street.

Park on grass and path to Castle Lake – reserve starts at steel gate leading into farmyard on south side of green.

To visit quarry reserve, from Church Street drive north and uphill until, after 600 yards, you reach Stonybeck Lane. Don't go right or left but straight on into a narrow country lane. After 600 yards there's a small parking area on left and a signpost points to path leading into reserve on right.

Public transport: Bus service links between Bishop Middleham and Durham City, Sedgefield and Bishop Auckland.

aroused much public interest in 2002 and viewing arrangements, well organised by the RSPB and Durham Wildlife Trust, enabled 22,000 people to enjoy the birds.

The Bee-eaters were probably Bishop Middleham's most distinguished visitors since poet Samuel Taylor Coleridge came to stay with farmer George Hutchinson in 1801. Officially there to do some research in Durham Cathedral's Dean and Chapter Library, the poet's real reason was his passion for George's sister, Sara, who was the inspiration behind the poem Love.

Castle Lake hasn't a Coleridge connection

but does have impressive medieval history links. It became established in a depression of the former 70-acre deer park overlooked by the fortified manor house after which it is named. Now earthworks are the only surviving trace of what was said to be a favourite residence of Bishops of Durham during the 13th Century.

Potentially Durham's top spot for wildfowl and wading birds has become a nature reserve thanks to an agreement between the local farmer and the Durham Bird Club under the government-sponsored Countryside Stewardship Scheme.

A hide overlooking most of the lake and continuing habitat improvement work by club volunteers should progressively enhance what can be seen from it. The DBC team, headed by Conservation Officer John Olley, responsible for the achievements so far deserve considerable credit.

The lake attracted particular attention in 2007 when a White Stork lingered in the spring and one to three Little Egrets, a Pectoral Sandpiper and a Wilson's Phalarope provided August and September highlights. Up to five Little Egrets during August - October 2008 underlined how this location is being visited increasingly by this colonising species; it is also one of the furthest inland to have produced records so far.

Several 2008 flyover reports – including a Spoonbill in March, three Marsh Harriers in August and a Honey Buzzard in September – indicated the value of being there, even if nothing particularly unusual happens to be on the lake.

A satisfyingly wide range of waterfowl can be expected, some in regionally significant numbers. Scarcer species, like Pintail, Garganey and Scaup, can occur too; in January 2004 up to 24 Bewick's Swans spent a couple of days there.

Spring and particularly autumn lay on a selection of typical passage waders, plus occasional rarities, along with other migrating marshbirds such as Black Tern (up to nine in May 2008) and Yellow Wagtail. Peregrines may be hunting over the area all year with Merlins in autumn and winter.

The lake is also one of the Bishop Middleham wetlands where the vivid colours of Kingfisher flash. With so many hirundines often over the lake, it is worth watching for a marauding Hobby.

To minimise disturbance, display boards and notices ask birders circling the lake to keep just inside the crumbling stone wall marking the boundary of the old deer park. While this means restricted fields of view, it's possible to see all sections of the lake from various points, but a telescope is essential.

The hide, high on the lake's west bank and just south of the sewage works, is a big boost to coverage, especially after midday when it's sunny.

However, I recommend a circuit following the boundary wall to see a variety of birds on adjacent farmland. Also, there is access to a network of public footpaths through about four square miles of countryside between the motorway and the A177. It leads to other waters, wooded areas and the scrub-lined banks of the River Skerne, a Tees tributary that is little more than a stream at this point

South of Castle Lake, across a water channel flowing from under the motorway, is a large flat pasture that is often flooded; scanning it with a telescope can be rewarding. A pool just outside the old deer park boundary wall's eastern extremity sometimes holds wildfowl and waders.

Further east there is a small lake close to Carr Wood. While there tends to be few birds on the water, Whitethroats, Garden Warblers, Chiffchaffs and Willow Warblers sing in surrounding scrub and Sedge Warblers and Reed Buntings in the waterside vegetation.

Nearby, the Skerne's course is a haunt for Water Rail and Kingfisher. One spot worth checking is the bridge carrying the path over it, just north of the lake, which provides an opportunity to look up and down a particularly overgrown stretch.

In midsummer I've seen Willow Tits with fledged young in flanking hawthorns; habitat loss may have contributed to this species' alarming decline elsewhere in the country but, with accommodation still available in the Bishop Middleham area, this is one place where it retains a foothold.

Similar thoughts arise over several farmland species. An abiding memory of 2002's huge birder influx was that many went away delighted at having seen not only Bee-eaters but also Tree Sparrows and Corn Buntings.

With local farmers involved in Countryside Stewardship Schemes, it isn't just coincidence that Bishop Middleham is a major Corn Bunting stronghold. A DBC survey found 15 territorial males – about 20 per cent of County Durham's total – on Farnless Farm (scene of the 2002 Bee-eater public viewing sessions).

Also present were Grey Partridges (eight pairs), Lapwings (12), Yellow Wagtails (ten), Tree Sparrows (six), Linnets (ten) and Yellowhammers (six). A Turtle Dove was present for almost a fortnight in late spring 2006.

Immediately north-west of Farnless Farm is Bishop Middleham Quarry reserve managed by Durham Wildlife Trust in partnership with Natural England and an internationally important SSSI for 34 years before the shock Bee-eater discovery. Mature woods occupy the 25-acre site's southern end, but the rest is magnesian limestone grassland, with almost a bare rock floor in places.

This is the realm of special plants like dark red helleborine, bee orchid, moonwort, blue moor grass, autumn gentian, fairy flax and common rock-rose. It is equally famous for associated butterflies – northern brown argus, ringlet, small heath and large, small and dingy skippers among them – and moths. Summer bird potential includes a Sand Martin colony in one quarry face.

South of Farnless Farm is Stonybeck Lake, by the lane from the A177 to the village. This long-term expanse of flooded farmland depression is, at the time of writing, making a quiet comeback after drying up for a while.

Previously it had a good run, with outstanding visitors during 2000-2005 including County Durham's first Lesser Scaup as well as Black-necked Grebe, Little Egret, Smew, Temminck's Stint and Mediterranean Gull.

Only time will tell whether it will return to that standard but John Olley and his DBC colleagues are optimistic. Talks have taken place with Stuart and Daphne Anderson at the farm with a view to future habitat improvement work.

Meanwhile on stopping on the roadside to check the lake you may just think you're hallucinating. However, you haven't switched mentally to the American prairies – that really is a herd of bison in an enclosure between the lake and the farm.

Having welcomed thousands on to their land to see Bee-eaters, the Andersons hope to establish a permanent visitor attraction which also includes red deer and elk.

ENCOUNTERS with unusual birds of prey in County Durham's uplands tend to be haphazard and, unfortunately, far too infrequent considering the extensive habitat potential. One exception, north of Eggleston in Upper Teesdale, is a series of ridges which regularly attract raptors. And these can be viewed easily from roadsides or public footpaths. The location is the source of a significant proportion of the winter records of several scarce species since the 1970s.

Target birds
Winter – Buzzard (90%), Red Kite (60%), Peregrine (60%), Raven (60%), Merlin (40%), Short-eared Owl (40%), Hen Harrier (30%), Rough-legged Buzzard (10%).

Other possible bird species

Winter
(bb = Blackton Beck only; me = Middle End only; lc = Langleydale Common only)

Greylag Goose
Red Grouse
Grey Partridge
Pheasant
Sparrowhawk
Kestrel
Stock Dove

Woodpigeon
Collared Dove (bb)
Green Woodpecker (bb)
Great Spotted Woodpecker (bb)
Wren
Robin
Blackbird (bb)
Fieldfare
Redwing (bb)
Mistle Thrush
Blue Tit (bb)

Great Tit (bb
Coal Tit (bb)
Jay (bb)
Starling
Chaffinch
Brambling (bb)
Greenfinch (bb)
Goldfinch (bb)
Siskin
Lesser Redpoll (bb)
Crossbill (me)
Snow Bunting (lc)

Background information and birding tips

WEATHER is such a crucial factor in the outcome of raptor watching at this location that there may be just a handful of days between late October and early March when prospects for a successful visit are good.

If rain or snow is forecast for the North Pennines don't even think about it and even visits on dry days will be wasted if the cloud base is below 1,500ft because the ridges will be obscured. A fine clear day may seem promising but an absence of wind tends, in my experience, to mean fewer, if any, raptors flying. They seem equally reluctant to take to the air during gales.

With the ridges mostly west facing, a moderate to fresh blow from the direction of the Atlantic is best. As it's usually easier to spot high-flying raptors against cloud, overcast conditions aren't a problem as long as the base is well above the hilltops and the cover is not so thick that the daylight is diminished. There have also been days that seemed ideal, yet I've seen very little. When it comes to raptor-watching, luck, to some extent, figures in the equation.

Key points

• Blackton Beck raptor viewpoint is half mile up track from B6278 by a gate next to a sheep wash marked on map (NZ 002 254).

• At Middle End, if there's no immediate activity visible, try walking at least to beck ford three-quarters of a mile along track.

• Moorcock and Three Tuns pubs and public toilet at Eggleston. Shops and toilets at Middleton-in-Teesdale (four miles NW).

How to get there

(Approx seven miles NW of Barnard Castle)

Head for Staindrop on A688 between Barnard Castle and Bishop Auckland. At Staindrop, turn right onto B6279 Teesdale road*, then after seven miles turn right onto B6278 to descend (one mile) to Eggleston. At the foot of the hill (Folly Bank) and just past a small petrol station, keep right to continue on B6278 towards Stanhope. As you leave Eggleston on B6278 road you pass the Moorcock pub on the right, then there's a series of three bends; Blackton Beck path starts by the two cottages just after the third.

Middle End is 2.5 miles N of Blackton Beck path start. The B6278 rises for almost a mile and at top of hill there's a cattle grid before open moorland (worth stopping there to check for raptors over ridge on right). Continue north for 1.5 miles, then turn left onto minor road to Middleton-in-Teesdale, passing Middle End Farm after a quarter of a mile. Just past farm, the path up Great Eggleshope Beck valley starts on right.

This site can also be reached from A66 trans-Pennine road between A1 and M6. From west, leave A66 at Bowes, joining A67 to Barnard Castle, but quickly turning left on to minor road to Cotherstone (four miles). At Cotherstone, you join B6277 for two miles to reach Romaldkirk, where you turn right onto a minor road to Eggleston. After half-a-mile turn right on to B6281 to cross traffic light-controlled narrow Eggleston Bridge over the Tees. From bridge, turn right onto B6282 then after 300 yards left on to B6278 into Eggleston village (after that same as above).

Driving on A66 from E, turn right 12 miles W of Scotch Corner A1 junction on to B6277 to Barnard Castle (two miles) but stay on it for four more miles to Cotherstone (remaining directions as from west).

*A potentially interesting diversion along Staindrop-Eggleston road is to turn right off B6279 at Kinninvie on to a minor road. After a mile-and-a-half, turn left at junction with B6282 to head W along S edge of Langleydale Common (watch for raptors). After two-and-a-half miles, turn right to re-join B6278 at the top of Folly Bank to descend to Eggleston.

Public transport: 95/96 buses call at Eggleston from Barnard Castle - which has regular links (Services 75/76) to Darlington. Timetables from Tourist Information (01833 690 909), at Barnard Castle (seven miles SE).

Timing is a more controllable factor. In the Eggleston area I've had some of my more memorable experiences in late afternoon.

That's because the birds have a tendency to congregate over the Blackton Beck valley ridges prior to roosting. On October 29, 2007, for instance, I saw a Red Kite, a ringtail Hen Harrier, two Buzzards and a Peregrine during the last 90 minutes of daylight; at one point they were all in the air together.

Once in the 1990s I watched a Rough-legged Buzzard drifting south along the White Hill - Middle End ridge towards me. As it switched to the ridge to the east of the B6278, I drove to Blackton Beck and – due to the bird making slow progress – was able to reach the regular watchpoint on foot as it appeared over the valley's north side.

Though the light was fading, its generally pale appearance meant it stood out magnificently as it glided low over the dark heather, passing within 200 yards of me.

You may have to wait a while to enjoy something like that. Rough-legged Buzzard isn't a regular North East winter visitor; I haven't seen one in Upper Teesdale since the turn of the century, so that's why I've placed just 10% likelihood on the species in the Target Birds list.

However, when there is an above-average autumn influx, one or two could well venture into the west of Durham – and, if so, the chances of sightings at Blackton Beck and Middle End will be much stronger.

Common Buzzard and Kestrel are the only species you're likely to see on every visit. However, Red Kite has graced skies around Eggleston increasingly since the re-introduction scheme in the Lower Derwent valley, more than 20 miles to the north-east. Prospects of Peregrine appearances have improved but sadly, thanks to illegal persecution, Hen Harriers show up very irregularly.

On the way to Eggleston from Staindrop, it's well worth diverting from the B6279 at Kinninvie to continue the journey via the B6282 running along the southern edge of Langleydale Common. Having seen Short-eared Owl in the past, it's become my regular route and now and again there are rewards. In November, 2007, for instance, a sudden halt because of two Snow Buntings on the roadside was followed by a flurry of activity as a Lapwing flock took off to avoid both a Red Kite and a Merlin.

Blackton's greater habitat diversity includes deciduous trees along the roadside where Bramblings are present some winters. Also, I've seen flocks of up to 400 Fieldfares fly in to roost in the more extensive woodland higher up from the road. Trees by the cottages at the start of the path often have much tit and finch activity. I've seen Great Spotted Woodpecker there too and noted Green Woodpecker in woods on the south side of the beck.

While watching for raptors by the sheep wash, there are opportunities to see Red Grouse on the heathery slopes rising to the ridges to the north, east and south, while typical grating calls reveal the presence of Grey Partridges in the sheep pasture sloping away to the west.

Occasionally small skeins of Greylag Geese pass over and Ravens appeared above the valley twice during my visits in the final quarter of 2007.

Ravens can also appear at Middle End and though at the start of the path up the Great Eggleshope valley you're a few hundred yards from the conifer plantation to the north of the farm, it's still possible, through a telescope, to have reasonable views of any Siskins or Crossbills in the tree-tops. Wrens and Robins are likely to be seen around the bare fields; one November day I well remember one of each vigorously mobbing a Buzzard perched on a dry stone wall.

Key points

- For the site SW of Hill End, park at NZ 006 349.

- More parking where the B6278 crosses Bollihope Burn (NY 987 352).

- Open access at all times.

- Paths can be muddy and unsuitable for wheelchair users away from parking areas.

- Allow at least two hours to cover upstream site.

- Durham Dales Centre facilities at Stanhope, include toilets, shops, café and Tourist Information (tel 0300 262 626).

- Other facilities at Frosterley.

SPRING MAY TAKE a long time to become established in the North-East but it's not unusual for County Durham's earliest summer visitors to appear in this moorland valley, where snow patches in high shaded corners can linger into April. Wheatears and Ring Ouzels may be present by mid-March if the weather is unseasonably mild and, with upland breeding waders displaying all around, a burnside stroll can be an ideal way of getting rid of winter blues.

Target birds (*not before April)

Grey Wagtail (90%), Dipper (90%), Wheatear (90%), Ring Ouzel (90%), *Common Sandpiper (80%), Woodcock (50%), Buzzard (40%), Black Grouse (30%), Merlin (30%), Peregrine (20%).

Other possible bird species

Spring/summer (* not before April)		
Red Grouse	Snipe	Pied Wagtail
Red-legged Partridge	Curlew	Wren
Grey Partridge	Redshank	Robin
Pheasant	Black-headed Gull	Blackbird
Sparrowhawk	Common Gull	Fieldfare
Kestrel	Lesser Black-backed Gull	Song Thrush
Oystercatcher	Stock Dove	Mistle Thrush
Golden Plover	Skylark	*Willow Warbler
Lapwing	*Sand Martin	Starling
	*Swallow	Lesser Redpoll
	Meadow Pipit	

Background information and birding tips

SOME OF THE species listed for this site are lumped together as "common woodland birds" elsewhere in the book. They're listed individually here because the location is mostly heather moorland and their presence is somewhat unusual. It's part of the reason why the Bollihope Valley has always fascinated me.

I first became acquainted with the upper reaches of this River Wear tributary as a boy. At two points the burn runs by roadside disused quarries and both have been popular unofficial picnic sites since the 1950s. My tendency on such family outings was to wander off to explore people-free places and during these mini-expeditions I became familiar with Common Sandpiper, Grey Wagtail, Dipper, Wheatear and Ring Ouzel long before I acquired my first binoculars.

The more easterly site is where the minor road from Frosterley crosses the Bollihope Burn after going downhill from the hamlet of Hill End. If it's a fine weekend you won't miss it as scores of cars may be parked there and an ice cream van could be doing a roaring trade. I note the latest

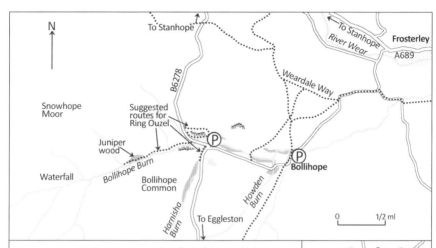

How to get there

(Approx 20 miles W of Durham)

From Durham City, drive SW for 11 miles on A690 to Crook where it becomes the A689. Head W for eight miles.

At Frosterley, just beyond the bend past the village centre car park, turn left onto minor road crossing River Wear and rising to Hill End.

First disused quarry site is a mile SW of Hill End by burn road crossing. For upstream disused quarry site, continue W for just over a mile to junction with B6278. Turn right then after an almost immediate sharp bend, park on verge.

Public transport: Regular bus services from Durham City (change at Crook) and Bishop Auckland to Stanhope via

Frosterley but you'll have to walk from there to the Bollihope sites.

Explorer Map features a parking symbol on this spot so now, after all these decades, it may even be an official picnic site.

Fortunately most people don't stray far from their cars, so it's still possible to find birds here. Ring Ouzels may be along the top of the quarry face furthest from the picnic area, while Wheatears tend to show on the conical spoil heaps opposite, if they haven't been disturbed.

Once you're well downstream from where children are paddling or throwing stones at floating sticks, Dippers and Grey Wagtails are likely to be encountered. For the best results, try to be there well ahead of the picnickers.

However, the other site a further mile-and-a-half upstream is more productive in my experience. It's where

the B6278 crosses the burn, four miles south of Stanhope, and is then joined by the minor road from Frosterley. There are always significantly fewer people here.

Also, there are more options to venture into quiet places, with disused quarries on either side, a tributary burn with its own hidden gill and the Bollihope itself winding more than two miles down from its starting point on the

85

slopes of Outberry Plain, 2,144ft above sea level.

Most years, however, I don't have to take a step from my car for my first Ring Ouzel. A careful scan of the top of the quarry face to the north or adjacent thinly-grassed banksides invariably locates that stunning combination of a white breast crescent emboldened by the blackness of the rest of the male's plumage.

If none can be found there, look in the quarry on the south side of the road but tread cautiously; a flushed Ring Ouzel here often flies half-a-mile or more, so relocating it may take some time.

If it's sufficiently early in the morning, I've found a Wheatear between the road and the burn. Generally, however, I see my first lone male, or a pair if the spring's a little more advanced, on a flattish area by the burn nearly half-a-mile upstream from the road bridge.

Maps don't show a public footpath along the burnside, but a clear track has become established due to so many people walking there over the past half century. Clearly most don't stroll further than the Wheatear site as the track peters out soon afterwards.

However, there are dividends for birders who keep going. First a rocky outcrop rises from the south side of the burn and the few weatherbeaten trees huddled there can provide a surprise. Considering there isn't a hint of a bush between here and a conifer plantation nearly two miles downstream, the presence of the Blue Tit I came across here once was most unexpected.

Blackbirds, Song Thrushes, Willow Warblers and Chaffinches have cropped up at this unlikely mid-moor outpost over the years. More appropriately, Fieldfares seeking a roost site sometimes drop in, and, inevitably, a Ring Ouzel perches regularly on the tree-tops.

A mile upstream from the road bridge, there's a fenced-off few acres of scattered junipers. Wrens and Mistle Thrushes aren't out of place there but the Robin in full song is surely going to struggle to find a mate in this isolated upland oasis. This is another regular spot for Ring Ouzel, while just to the west there's a rocky slope where Wheatears can be prominent.

Lapwings and Curlews are the most high profile waders in late March, but it's unusual not to see pairs of Oystercatchers and Redshanks. Sooner or later a Golden Plover's mournful cry and the 'drumming' of a displaying Snipe waft from higher up the fellside.

One species I never anticipated on Bollihope's open moorland was Woodcock but in three out of five recent springs I have flushed these secretive birds, so circumstances must have changed.

Normally Red Grouse aren't seen along the burn, not when people are around anyway, but a scan of the moor rising to the south should detect at least a few.

While Black Grouse can't be guaranteed, I've seen occasional males in March, so it's not out of the question. Also, there are prospects of this iconic species being better represented in future, thanks to habitat improvements to boost the North Pennines population.

As for birds of prey, Kestrel remains the only species of which one can be fairly certain. However, Buzzards soar into view more often than in the past, no doubt a reflection of its general eastern England expansion.

There's a reasonable chance of a Merlin too, especially if sufficient time is allowed; my sightings/visits ratio is about one in three. Also, while I've never seen Peregrine in this area in springtime, I wouldn't rule out the possibility of one appearing.

HAVING escaped the threat of coal mining waste being dumped, East Durham's denes, the narrow, sinuous ravines created at the end of the Ice Age by the action of glacial melt water flows, now enjoy National Nature Reserve (NNR) status. The area covers more than 500 acres strung out over four miles and since 1985 it has been a Site of Special Scientific Interest, a Special Area of Conservation – and a fabulously scenic place to seek woodland birds.

Target birds

All year – Nuthatch (90%), Green Woodpecker (70%), Grey Wagtail (70%), Marsh Tit (60%). *Spring/early summer* – Spotted Flycatcher (60%), Redstart (20%), Tree Pipit (10%), Wood Warbler (10%). *Winter* – Brambling (60%), Siskin (60%), Lesser Redpoll (30%), Common Crossbill (20%).

Other possible bird species

All year			Goldfinch
Mallard	Great Spotted	Coal Tit	Bullfinch
Sparrowhawk	Woodpecker	Blue Tit	*Spring/summer*
Kestrel	Wren	Great Tit	Garden Warbler
Pheasant	Dunnock	Treecreeper	Blackcap
Moorhen	Robin	Jay	Chiffchaff
Woodcock	Blackbird	Magpie	Willow Warbler
Stock Dove	Song Thrush	Jackdaw	*Winter*
Woodpigeon	Mistle Thrush	Rook	Redwing
Tawny Owl	Goldcrest	Carrion Crow	Fieldfare
	Long-tailed Tit	Chaffinch	

Background information and birding tips

DON'T EXPECT exceptional birds in Castle Eden Dene, just a range of routine woodland-dwellers in extraordinary settings. Some unusual species have been recorded – but with protracted gaps between occurrences.

The sixth White's Thrush for Britain was recorded in January 1872, but it was almost 119 years before the site held further *British Birds* rarities – 16 Parrot Crossbills in larches near the Oakerside Dene Lodge entrance from mid-December 1990 until early March 1991.

The few hundred yards from Oakerside Dene Lodge down to Castle Bridge over the burn at the gorge bottom is always promising. From that bridge, the eastbound dene floor path rises between avenues of lofty conifers, with a spread of lanky larches sloping down to the burn.

This was a classic spot for red squirrels before their local extinction some time during the 1990s but at least there's still plenty of bird activity.

Goldcrests, Long-tailed and Coal Tits, Treecreepers, Jays, Goldfinches and Siskins are on show regularly, with Lesser

Key points

• **Main access:** Oakerside Dene Lodge (NZ 428 394); Castle Eden Village (NZ 428 385); Blunt's Plantation/Bede Way, Peterlee (NZ 432 401); A1086/ Horden (NZ 448 405).

• **Open access at all times. No admission charge.**

• **Small car park (approx 15 cars) at Oakerside. Big one (NZ 429 408) in Peterlee town centre for Blunt's Plantation.**

• **Parking also by St James's Church, Castle Eden but avoid blocking driveways.**

Contacts

Natural England, Oakerside Dene Lodge, Stanhope Chase, Peterlee SR8 1NJ. 0191 586 0004

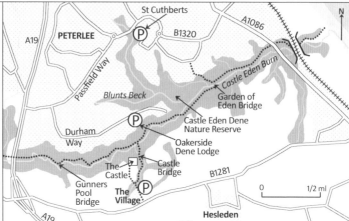

How to get there

(Approx 12 miles S of Sunderland)

This section of the NNR lies between A19 and the A1086 coast road (from Easington Village to Hartlepool). The A19 passes the dene's west end about 12 miles S of Sunderland.

For Natural England's Oakerside Dene Lodge base turn from A19's southbound carriageway into Passfield Way (the first left along a straight after the B1320 turning to Peterlee town centre).

Once into Passfield Way, take first right into Durham Way, then the tenth right turn into Stanhope Chase and Natural England base and public car park. There are signposts to it from Passfield Way. You can't turn directly into Passfield Way if driving north on A19 from Teesside.

For Castle Eden entrance, turn off dual carriageway at junction with A181 (from Durham City) which, after crossing over A19, becomes the B1281 that continues east to join the A1086 coast road at Blackhall. Southbound drivers on A19 turn left immediately after it passes the dene, then at the slip road's end turn left on to B128l. Northbound drivers take slip road to A181, then turn right to cross dual carriageway beyond which the road becomes the B1281.

After a mile, take first left into The Village with terraced housing on either side. At end of cul-de-sac are access to the dene and also the gated entrance to The Castle's drive (which leads to a further path heading west along the dene's southern edge). Park near St James's Church, taking care not to block any driveways.

Access from the A1086 is simpler: the gate lies between the villages of Horden and Blackhall about four miles from A1086 junction with A19 (there's off-road parking space for about eight cars) but watch for fast-moving traffic when leaving. This is a useful entrance for public transport-users as buses between Hartlepool and Easington/Horden/Peterlee stop within a few hundred yards, either side of the gate.

Public transport: Peterlee has bus links with Durham City, Hartlepool, Newcastle and Sunderland.

Redpolls and Crossbills as occasional bonuses.

However, the larch – an introduced species – is not one of the trees defining the dene's distinct character.

Ash and wych elm, which dominate the woodland canopy, with yew prominent in the understory, are relics of the great forest that formed across Britain after the Ice Age's end.

The dene holds the UK's most extensive northerly native occurrence of yew so it is fitting the species contributed to its name.

More than a thousand years ago Saxons called it "Yoden" meaning Yew Dene - which metamorphosed over the following centuries into Eden.

The main dene floor path from Castle Bridge east to Garden of Eden Bridge (about a mile) passes through the central dene's most impressive scenery. Features include the Seven Chambers' long stretch of sheer limestone cliffs and further on the Devil's Lapstone, a cottage-sized boulder that plunged down in a landslide so long ago that now mature trees grow precariously out of the rock.

Also growing from it – and in many other places along the way – is the strap-like hartstongue fern, which doesn't occur widely in the region. This reflects the dene's own moist, humid microclimate, sheltered from cold east and north winds.

Plants – there are 450 species – and insects are the basis of the dene's high conservation status. As for insects, "exceptionally diverse" is how the SSSI citation describes its population, which includes many national and regional rarities, such as the elm-feeding moth, Blomer's rivulet.

Though just two miles from the sea, the central dene has a Pennine dales feel, with sometimes birds to match. Grey Wagtails are liable to be along the burn and it's not unknown for Wood Warbler song to resound from path-side beech trees.

Along the dene's upper fringes I have recorded spring passage Tree Pipits in suitable open woodland very occasionally and Redstarts more frequently.

Back on the central dene floor, Green and Great Spotted Woodpeckers, Marsh Tits and Nuthatches can be expected all year. Spotted Flycatchers –much scarcer than in the past – are still possible from late spring, though hard to find once the trees are heavily in leaf.

There's a choice of ways into the dene if entering from Castle Eden village off the B1281 to Blackhall. The turn-off passes between terraced housing then leads to St James's Church and gates at the start of the drive to The Castle, an 18th Century mansion.

Just beyond those gates, on the right, is the western extremity of the main dene floor path that winds through the gorge for almost three miles from the stretch of the A1086 between Horden and Blackhall.

Alternatively, continue along the drive towards The Castle and when it finally bears right towards the mansion, there's kissing gate access to the dene; to the left is a trail leading deeper into its west end, to the right a track linking with the main path down to Castle Bridge.

The driveway has particular potential in winter when Bramblings may be feeding on beechmast on adjoining parkland, with Redwings and perhaps a

Key points

- At A1086 Horden entrance there's off-road space for eight cars. Bend restricts visibility of northbound traffic so exit with care.

- Public toilets at Oakerside Dene Lodge open Monday-Friday. Also in Peterlee town centre near Tourist Office (tel 0191 586 4450).

- Kissing gates at entrances limit wheelchairs and push chairs.

- Paths muddy in wet weather and icy during cold spells. Sections that are steep, narrow and edged by precipes are probably best-avoided by people with mobility difficulties. Trees over paths can be a problem too.

Key points

- More than 12 miles of paths – allow a full day to tackle all of it.

- Circular walks from the Oakerside or Castle Eden entrances (three or four miles) will take two-to-three hours.

- Castle Eden Inn (in Stockton Road between B1281 and village's southern link with A19).

- Nearest pubs to the Oakerside entrance are The Oaklands off Durham Way and The Black Bull just off the A19 at Old Shotton (reached from Passfield Way).

- More pubs and a range of shops including an Asda supermarket in town centre.

few Fieldfares foraging about the grassland.

Originally The Castle was the seat of the Burdon family, which influenced this area significantly over 150 years. After being incorporated into the estate in 1790, the dene became a glorious wilderness garden, which the Burdons opened to the public – for a small charge – in 1850.

The paths network now maintained by Natural England (which manages the dene in partnership with Peterlee Town, Easington District and Durham County Councils) follows the pattern established by the family. It includes two outstanding circular routes, scenic as well as bird-rich, which are most easily tackled from the Castle Eden Village or Oakerside Dene Lodge entrances.

One leads to the dene's most awesome place, Gunner's Pool Bridge (formerly on maps as Devil's Bridge), high above the gorge's narrowest section. The view to the east is what catches the eye – or for those comfortable about looking down, the burn gushing between cliffs just yards apart, 60ft below.

At the end of the long, cold 1962-63 winter I saw – flying downstream – the only Dipper I've ever come across in East Durham. More than 130 years after the Burdons installed the bridge in 1877, metalwork corrosion led to

doubt about its future but Natural England's £100,000 restoration project saw it safely back in use during summer 2009.

This bridge is best approached via the path along the dene's southern edge from The Castle (accessed from the kissing gate at the north end of the parkland drive or by taking the first right from the main path between Castle Bridge and the Castle Eden Village entrance).

Crossing Gunner's Pool Bridge brings you to a path along the top of the dene's north side; turn right, then take the right fork leading steeply down to the dene bottom. From there a trail passing the west end's most breathtaking cliff stretches links with the main path at Castle Bridge.

The other notable route is Miss Mary's Walk, a favourite stroll of a Burdon dynasty daughter. From Castle Eden Village, go on to the main dene path (rather than The Castle Drive) then branch right as you descend to Castle Bridge. If starting from Oakerside, it's the only left turn between Castle Bridge and The Village.

The walk heads east, through impressive yew stands, for a mile before descending Craggy Bank to rejoin the main path just west of Garden of Eden Bridge. If you've walked from the A1086 entrance, that junction provides a starting point for tackling the route in the opposite direction.

FOR DECADES Crimdon's wildlife significance was eclipsed by its role as the Durham coalfield's seaside playground. Now birds, including breeding Little Terns, rather than beauty queens are what makes headlines at one of only two stretches of Easington Rural District shore that were not buried under several feet of pit waste. This is a site that needs more coverage and could provide lots of rewards in autumn and spring passage times.

Target birds
Early spring – Wheatear (50%). *Summer* – Little Tern (100%); Little Gull (60%); Roseate Tern (40%). *Autumn* – Barred Warbler (30%), Richard's Pipit (20%). *Winter* – Sanderling (90%), Red-throated Diver (80%), Great Crested Grebe (80%), Red-breasted Merganser (80%) Snow Bunting (60%), Great Northern Diver (40%), Red-necked Grebe (40%), Mediterranean Gull (40%), Black-throated Diver (20%). *All year* - Stonechat (80%).

Other possible bird species

All year	Arctic Tern	Redstart
Cormorant	Hirundines	Whinchat
Sparrowhawk	White Wagtail	Ring Ouzel
Kestrel	Whinchat	Fieldfare
Oystercatcher	Grasshopper Warbler	Redwing
Ringed Plover	Sedge Warbler	Blackcap
Familiar gulls	Lesser Whitethroat	Garden Warbler
Common woodland birds	Whitethroat	Chiffchaff
Great Spotted	Blackcap	Goldcrest
Woodpecker	Chiffchaff	Pied Flycatcher
Skylark	Willow Warbler	Brambling
Meadow Pipit	*Autumn*	Siskin
Pied Wagtail	*Pink-footed Goose	*Winter*
Goldfinch	*Barnacle Goose	Knot
Linnet	*Brent Goose	Dunlin
Yellowhammer	*Wigeon	Bar-tailed Godwit
Reed Bunting	*Teal	Curlew
Spring/summer	*Common Scoter	Redshank
* Whimbrel	*Goldeneye	Turnstone
Arctic Skua	Woodcock	Grey Wagtail
Sandwich Tern	Short-eared Owl	
Common Tern	Black Redstart	* = usually seen at sea on passage.

Background information and birding tips

IN 1965 CRIMDON was a most unlikely future contender for a *Best Birdwatching Sites* slot – especially with more than 50,000 people gathered there on August Bank Holiday Mondays.

Many were in the dene to see which representative of local pit

Key points

- Crimdon cliff-top parking at NZ 483 373. Also coin-operated toilet there.

- Open access at all times.

- The Coastal path is wheelchair friendly.

- Dene Mouth is half a mile from cliff-top car park; path through dene is approximately the same; and Hart Warren path just under a mile.

- Soft sand in denemouth and dunes, surfaced path through dene.

- Nearest main shopping centre at Hartlepool.

Contacts
Tourist Information:
0191 586 4450
(Peterlee)

01429 869 706
(Hartlepool)

villages would be crowned the 30th annual Miss Crimdon by Manny Shinwell, the 80-year-old Easington Labour MP whose votes, legend had it, were weighed rather than counted. The rest, if not at the cliff-top funfair, were sunbathing or splashing in the sea under the watchful eyes of a lifeguard team that included local boxing hero Maurice Cullen, the new British lightweight champion.

While families still enjoy bracing breaks by the North Sea, most man-made features of this location's Lido heyday have gone. Apart from the grass on the dene floor being kept short, there is a more natural appearance these days.

The summer assets being flaunted are nationally scarce plants such as burnt-tip orchid at Hart Warren and Britain's second rarest breeding seabird in the denemouth.

As with any Little Tern colony, this one has had its low points. In 1998 the colony was the country's second most successful site – until one of Hartlepool's more despicable residents looted 27 clutches of eggs. He was labelled "selfish and wicked" when this and other serious egg collecting offences brought him to the town's Magistrates Court 12 months later.

The terns deserted the site for a few seasons but on returning did not take long to become as well established as

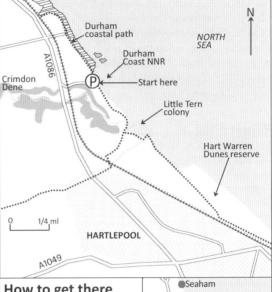

How to get there

(Approx two miles N of Hartlepool).

From Hartlepool, head N on A1086 to Blackhall. After a mile there's a long downhill stretch as road crosses Crimdon Dene, over which there's also a big railway viaduct. Just before road starts to go up dene's north side, turn right on to minor road running under viaduct. This road (featuring some of Britain's fiercest anti-speed bumps, so take care), leads to a cliff-top car park.

If travelling from N, turn off A19 via first slip road south of Peterlee on to B1281 (an extension of A181 from Durham City) to Blackhall,

turning right on to A1086. Just after closed Seagull pub to south of that village, road descends to cross Crimdon Dene. Turn left at bottom on to minor road to cliff-top car park.

Public transport: Hartlepool-Blackhall bus services stop at Crimdon. Also regular town services between West View Road (near start of path to Hart Warren) and Hartlepool centre and Headland.

such constantly vulnerable species can be. Their 2007 performance, for instance,

was particularly outstanding, with 47 pairs rearing about 105 young – around twice the usual output and possibly a best-on-record for northern England. Their resilience was underlined in 2008 when, despite heavy early season Kestrel, fox and hedgehog predation of chicks and eggs, 55 pairs had reared 67 chicks by the second week of August.

Seasonal warden Trevor Stephenson noted a distinct change in behaviour in 2008. No longer were adults lingering on the beach; they were simply flying in with fish and returning to sea straight after feeding youngsters.

On visiting the site in early July, I was surprised that no more than eight adults were present at any one time but there was a steady flow of adults between sea and colony.

Could this have been a tactical switch to make the colony less conspicuous to predators after the early season losses? Whatever it was, their eventual productivity far exceeded expectations after the predation setback.

Over the course of a year, Crimdon has much more to offer birders than Little Terns. Indeed, they aren't the only bird species to have contributed to its Special Protection Area qualification. Comparatively substantial wader numbers along the shore include Ringed Plover, Knot and Redshank, while Sanderling may be particularly numerous, with counts as high as 300.

Red-throated Divers, Great Crested Grebes and Red-breasted Mergansers are regular in inshore waters, while Great Northern Diver, Red-necked Grebe, Grey Phalarope, Mediterranean Gull and Little Auk are among scarcer species recorded during November – March.

In winter the stony denemouth beach and nearby dunes host at least a few Snow Buntings – exceptionally up to 30 – Twite is

a further possibility and very occasionally there's a Shore Lark.

Stonechats are there all year; in summertime it's not unusual to see a pair perched on tern colony security fenceposts. The arrival of March brings prospects of an early Wheatear and as spring advances maybe a White Wagtail too.

Patches of scrub, isolated bushes and the odd stunted sycamore in the denemouth/dunes area are the sort of places where grounded passage birds might be expected during murky weather.

However, when such 'falls' of migrants occur, birdwatchers tend to make for Hartlepool Headland and North Gare area to the south or Whitburn/Marsden and Dawdon Blast Beach to the north.

In the process Crimdon is overlooked consistently. The handful of autumn passage reports from between Hart Warren and Blackhall Rocks since year 2000 – including a couple of Richard's Pipits, a Black Redstart, a Barred Warbler and a Red-breasted Flycatcher – suggests that anyone making a point of working this area regularly could be well rewarded.

When the likes of Pallas's and Yellow-browed Warblers are being found at other, no better-positioned, locations between Tees and Tyne in October, there would seem to be a strong chance that a thorough working of Crimdon would have similar results.

Equally, sightings now and again of Pomarine and Long-tailed Skuas and Roseate Tern during summer and autumn months raise the prospect that watching from the cliffs north of the denemouth could scoop at least a reasonable share of the awesome range of seabirds that pass Hartlepool Headland just three miles down the coast during June-November.

Key points

• Park in cul-de-sac (NZ 266 377) on south side of old River Wear bridge (reached from B6300) and by Croxdale Hall drive entrance.

• Open access at all times.

• Paths inside grounds all accessible to wheelchair users.

• Visits to house by appointment only (Tuesday and Wednesday, May to second Wednesday in July, 11am - 1pm).

• Walk covers about four miles (allow at least three hours – more if waiting for Hawfinch to show).

• More extensive facilities in Durham City three miles to north.

Contacts

Tourist Information
0191 384 372.

DESPITE A LONG HISTORY of interesting bird reports, it is only since the nationwide Hawfinch influx of 2005/06 that Croxdale has had the coverage it deserves. The presence of up to 12 Hawfinches at the Hall made the location very popular and led to nearby places being checked regularly. Now the area is a priority winter venue for many birders – and it's not bad in spring either.

Target birds *Autumn/winter* – **Goosander** (70%), **Water Rail** (50%), **Hawfinch** (40%), **Lesser Spotted Woodpecker** (20%). *All year* – **Dipper** (80%), **Willow Tit** (70%), **Kingfisher** (60%). *Spring/summer* – **Reed Warbler** (60%).

Other possible bird species

All year	Goldcrest	Sand Martin
Greylag Goose	Long-tailed Tit	Swallow
Grey Heron	Coal Tit	House Martin
Sparrowhawk	Nuthatch	Sedge Warbler
Kestrel	Treecreeper	Blackcap
Common woodland,	Jay	Garden Warbler
farmland and wetland	Goldfinch	Whitethroat
birds	Linnet	Chiffchaff
Tawny Owl	Bullfinch	Willow Warbler
Kingfisher	Yellowhammer	
Green Woodpecker	Reed Bunting	*Winter*
Great Spotted	*Spring/summer*	Goldeneye
Woodpecker	Swift	Fieldfare
Dipper	Skylark	Redwing
Mistle Thrush	Grey Wagtail	Siskin
		Crossbill

Background information and birding tips

THE ACTION starts from the word go at this location. On parking in the cul-de-sac on the south side of the Wear, don't make an immediate beeline for the hall but walk back on to the bridge to look downstream towards the nearby A167 crossing.

If the river's in full spate, which is often the case in winter, the surge of water squeezing under the A167 bridge is awesome. However, focus mainly on any areas of slack water or exposed rocks along the edges; a Dipper could well be lurking as this is the most easterly point in Durham to produce regular records of this species.

There may be a Goosander or two on the calmer waters just beyond the A167 or perhaps a Kingfisher perched on an overhanging branch. Sometimes all three can be in view.

Only then do you start the half-mile walk along the rather stately drive leading to the country mansion. It sits on the crest of a spur of land thrusting into the river valley, but is partly hidden

How to get there

(Approx four miles S of Durham).

From Durham City head S on A167. A mile after leaving the city outskirts, turn right on to B6300 to Brandon then quickly left into a cul-de-sac road. Croxdale Hall's drive entrance is on the left across the River Wear bridge. Park on the roadside.

If approaching from S on A1(M), leave it at J61 to head W on A688 towards Bishop Auckland. After three miles and at second roundabout (large pub on right), turn right on to A167 to Durham. After three miles, the road descends to cross the River Wear just after a further roundabout.

Immediately after crossing the river turn left onto B6300 to Brandon (remaining directions as from north).

Public transport: Regular bus services from Durham City to Bishop Auckland stop at Croxdale.

DURHAM CITY

N

A177

Shincliffe

Houghall

A177

Watch/listen for Water Rail in winter/Reed Warbler in summer

Low Butterby Farm

A167

Low Butterby ponds

River Wear

Main start of walk

Other walk start point

Watch from E side of chapel for Hawfinch on treetops to N or in Hall grounds W of chapel

B6300

Croxdale Hall

P

P

Sunderland Bridge

Watch for Goosander Kingfisher Grey Wagtail or Dipper from bridge

Croxdale

B6288

0   1/2 ml

by the mature woodland on the slopes to the west and north. Take your time along here too as flocks of tits and their associates could be working through the trees by the drive.

Very occasionally a small Hawfinch party has been spotted in one of the surrounding parkland's trees. Redwings and other thrushes may be foraging about the parkland's floor in autumn and winter.

Eventually the drive crosses a cattle grid before rising through woodland to the hall. If you haven't already seen

a Nuthatch, your account should open here. This woodland supports one of the best concentrations of this species in the county.

The same goes for Great Spotted Woodpeckers and very occasionally there are Lesser Spotted Woodpecker moving with tits through these tree-tops. Finding this secretive rarity is really hard, however; even the low 20 per cent rating I've given the possibility is rather optimistic. Near the top of the hill there's a junction with the left turn going to Low Butterby. In winter, however, most birders

Durham

A690

Wolsingham

A1M

Bishop Auckland

A68

A688

prefer to keep that option for later and instead keep on the main track curving right for the final approach to the hall.

Inside the curve is a stand of tall beeches, rising from a flattish area due north of the hall's grounds; they look just right for Hawfinches. However, it is unusual for these shy birds to let anyone

95

get close to the foot of any tree in which they're perched.

Generally the place where most succeed is by the old chapel on the east side of the hall. This is reached by following the drive – now just an unsurfaced track – past the hall to where it bends around the east end of the chapel grounds. From there look back west towards the hall grounds; obviously the chapel blocks part of the view but not the tree-tops where Hawfinches show. Even better, they're also liable to appear in the much closer trees on the chapel's north side.

When I say 'they' that tends to mean no more than two Hawfinches nowadays. The sevens and eights and 12 reported in early 2006 were not repeated during the next two winters.

Waiting can take hours, quite possibly even more than one visit, so patience is required. Such exercises are best conducted on bright days with little or no wind. Some birders have scored by arriving at daybreak and watching out for treetops appearances, when the birds attempt to catch the first rays of the winter sun

The waiting is far from a tedious exercise as Great Spotted Woodpeckers, Nuthatches, Treecreepers and parties of tits and more routine finches, including Siskins, are constantly active.

Also, Lesser Spotted Woodpeckers have been seen in those trees by the chapel. If it does take a long while, there's additionally time to contemplate the local architecture and history. The 12th Century chapel is a Grade I listed building; so is the hall, which was originally a Tudor-style mansion dating from the 17th Century.

When the urge for a scene change occurs, it's worth continuing along the track, which after the chapel swings north-eastwards, with Fieldfares and Redwings likely to be on the farmland on either side. Eventually, after more than half a mile it reaches Croxdale Wood House; Hawfinches can occur in trees there.

It is also a reliable spot for Bullfinches and I've come across large tit flocks, which are always worth checking.

Turn left, via a stile just past Croxdale Wood House, to descend via a muddy path through the trees to link with the track to Low Butterby Farm on the Wear flood plain. There the focus is on a series of swampy ox-bow pools, remnants of a man-made change to the river's course in the early 19th Century.

The most northerly, almost out-of-sight from the farm track, has open water, which in winter can be occupied by a few Goldeneyes; its neighbour, directly by the farm track, has much established willow, birch and alder growth.

At the latter there's another waiting game to be played; watching for movement that might reveal a Water Rail lurking in the thick marsh vegetation. In summer, by the next, more open pool to the south a singing Reed Warbler may break cover eventually.

Willow Tit is another of Low Butterby's specialities – either in the trees established in the marsh or along the edge of the conifer wood on the other side of the farm track. During winter months the conifers may hold a large Siskin flock too.

Often I find myself here in the approach to sunset in December or January, so then there's really only time to trek the 1.5 miles back to the parking place. If it's earlier, however, there's a further opportunity to try for Hawfinch at Croxdale Hall driveway.

NOW RECOVERING from decades of coal waste pollution, Dawdon Blast Beach is a site in transition and holds the promise of becoming a prominent bird migration watchpoint, even though its potential didn't come to light until the end of the 20th Century.

Target birds
All year – Stonechat (80%), Tree Sparrow* (70%). *Spring* – Grasshopper Warbler* (40%), Lesser Whitethroat* (40%). * = most likely in Hawthorn Dene area. *Late summer* – Little Gull (90%), Manx Shearwater (80%), Roseate Tern (60%). *Autumn* – Sooty Shearwater (60%), Barnacle Goose (40%), Black Redstart (40%), Yellow-browed Warbler (40%), Pomarine Skua, Richard's Pipit, Pallas's Warbler (all 30%). *Autumn/winter* – Mediterranean Gull (60%), Great Northern Diver (50%), Snow Bunting (50%), Lapland Bunting (40%), Twite (40%), Black-throated Diver (30%), Little Auk (30%).

Other possible bird species

All year
Eider
Grey Partridge
Fulmar
Cormorant
Sparrowhawk
Kestrel
Familiar gulls
Kittiwake
Green Woodpecker
Great Spotted Woodpecker
Skylark
Mistle Thrush
Long-tailed Tit
Coal Tit
Marsh Tit
Nuthatch
Jay
Goldfinch
Linnet
Bullfinch
Yellowhammer
Reed Bunting

Spring
Hirundines
Redstart

Whinchat
Wheatear
Ring Ouzel
Whitethroat
Chiffchaff
Willow Warbler

Summer/early autumn
Whimbrel
Arctic Skua
Great Skua
SandwichTern
Common Tern
Arctic Tern
Guillemot
Razorbill
Puffin

Autumn
Whooper Swan
Pink-footed Goose
Brent Goose
Shelduck
Wigeon
Teal
Common Scoter
Velvet Scoter
Goldeneye
Red-breasted Merganser

Red-throated Diver
Great Crested Grebe
Gannet
Oystercatcher
Jack Snipe
Woodcock
Curlew
Arctic Skua
Great Skua
Short-eared Owl
Redstart
Wheatear
Ring Ouzel
Fieldfare
Redwing
Blackcap
Garden Warbler
Chiffchaff
Goldcrest
Brambling
Siskin

Winter
Red-breasted Merganser
Red-throated Diver
Great Crested Grebe

Key points
• Open access at all times.

• Dawdon Blast Beach parking at NZ 436 482 and NZ 436 479

• For Hawthorn Dene, park on roadside (not in front of bungalow by dene entrance) at NZ 425 459.

• For Seaham Dene use car park/picnic site at NZ423 508.

• Walk to Hawthorn Denemouth is two miles but can be extended into dene. Allow at least three hours.

• Durham Coast Path is firm and flat and suitable for wheelchair users.

Contacts
Tourist Information
0191 586 4450.

How to get there

(Approx 9 miles south of Sunderland)

Turn off A19 six miles south of Sunderland onto A182 to Seaham Harbour. After reaching new Dawdon Business Park on left, turn right just after third roundabout onto an access road to the Nose's Point cliff-top car parks.

Hawthorn Dene is accessed from half a mile along minor road running east from Hawthorn village's north end. Village is reached by minor roads east from B1432 running between Seaham and Easington, where there are links to A19.

Public transport: **Bus services link Seaham with Sunderland and Peterlee. Local trains between Sunderland and Hartlepool stop at Seaham.**

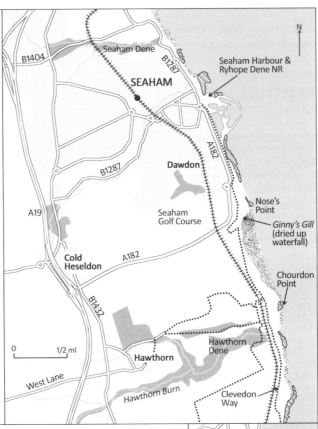

Background information and birding tips

AFTER ALMOST a century of waste-tipping, Dawdon Blast Beach looked so unearthly that, famously, it was used for the opening sequence of the 1992 outer space movie *Alien 3*.

When I first set eyes on Dawdon Colliery in the 1980s, its coal preparation plant towered above Nose's Point at the northern end. The beach's was weirdly multi-coloured – every imaginable shade of dark brown, patches of sickly grey-white and a section of sulphurous yellow.

Mining debris protruded from this almighty mess, over which hung an unpleasant chemical odour.

But my attention switched quickly to redeeming features. On the upper beach was a football pitch-length expanse of birch scrub. Hawthorn, blackthorn and elder were established on rock falls at the foot of the cliffs. In other places there were muddy pools and even a couple of reedbeds. This developed because the waste dumped into the shallow bay between Nose's Point and Chourdon Point, a mile to the south, had raised the beach's level enough to hold back the waves.

"Ideal for holding migrants arriving during misty, wet weather …" was my immediate thought and I was proved right over subsequent years as increased checking led to a bird list which included Long-eared Owl, Ring Ouzel, Black Redstart, Siberian Stonechat, Barred, Pallas's and Yellow-browed Warblers, Firecrest, Red-breasted Flycatcher and Great Grey Shrike.

Among seabird highlights were late summer gatherings of up to 400-plus Little Gulls on the shore and the occasional Roseate Tern family lingering in the early stage of its autumn passage.

Tipping waste directly into the sea had already stopped before Durham's remaining coastal mines closed during 1991-93. With no new material being added, the sea began to bite into the waste accumulation along the eight miles of shore from Seaham Harbour to Blackhall Rocks.

Then the £10-million Turning the Tide project, half-funded by the Millennium Commission, began. While the sea proceeded with its long-term cleaning of the shore, the project tackled industrial eyesores along the cliffs and created the Durham Coast Path.

The coastline is expected to be clear of pit waste by 2020; in Dawdon Blast Beach's case, the erosion rate has been measured at six metres per year. By 2008 there was no trace of the birch scrub that used to be a welcome first refuge for freshly-arrived Goldcrests and next to disappear will be the pools, reedbeds and bushes at the foot of the cliffs.

This doesn't mean a productive birding site is doomed. I prefer to think it is entering an intriguing new phase with exciting possibilities. In murky autumn weather, migrants will continue to drop into any readily available cover.

Due to future erosion this could be restricted eventually to the two breaks in the cliffs – Ginny's Gill, a dried-up waterfall at the north end, and a gulley half a mile to the south will definitely be worth checking when conditions are right.

Meanwhile the clifftop scrub and mainly open grassland further inland, with hawthorn and gorse clumps, will shelter migrants. Also, the grassland is just the sort of place where a Richard's Pipit might be found; three were recorded there in October, 2003.

Expect migrants in the mouth of Hawthorn Dene at this walk's southern end. Pallas's and Yellow-browed Warblers have occurred in trees and shrubs fringing the magnesian limestone grassland just west of the railway, but remember that success depends on finding new arrivals before they can disperse into adjacent mature woodland. Diminishing or no leaf cover makes late autumn and winter one of the better times for birding in this Durham Wildlife Trust reserve.

Hawthorn Dene is on a smaller scale and with a less complex paths system than Castle Eden Dene to the south, but its woodland species range is broadly similar.

One local speciality is Tree Sparrow; just

> ### Key points
>
> • **Steep steps into Hawthorn Dene ravine and descent to Hawthorn Hive at denemouth. Some ravine paths are muddy in places.**
>
> • **Modern shopping centre as well as pubs at Seaham Harbour sea front.**

beyond the gate at the entrance from the minor road east of Hawthorn village, there are usually some in the tall hedge by the farm buildings on the right.

Spring visits are worthwhile too. Blackcaps and Chiffchaffs mingle their voices with the mature woodland's resident songsters, while Willow Warblers and Whitethroats can be heard around the fringes. A patch of thick cover in the dene-mouth area can be the source of a Lesser Whitethroat's chattering outbursts.

Spring passage Pied Flycatchers and Redstarts make brief occasional appearances. Just south of the dene mouth, Beacon Hill (the Durham coast's highest point at 280ft) is a regular spot for passage Wheatears; I've found the odd Ring Ouzel there, too.

This Durham Coast Path stretch is a pleasure at any time of year. Stonechats are on show in every season, Whitethroats sing from the scrubby patches in spring and summer when a Grasshopper Warbler might be reeling.

Fulmars patrol the cliffs and seem likely to nest in future. Sometimes a Green Woodpecker from Hawthorn Dene ventures along the cliffs on an ant quest.

A mid-autumn stroll can be invigorated by the sight of Barnacle Geese that have strayed south while crossing from Norway, while a Twite party or a Lapland Bunting might warm a chilly winter outing.

The Seaham-Hawthorn coast offers the best seawatching potential between the long-established observation points at Hartlepool Headland and Whitburn on South Tyneside.

This is underlined by reports of the likes of Black-throated Diver, Cory's and Sooty Shearwaters and Pomarine and Long-tailed Skuas in recent years.

While July to November is the North-East's main season for this activity, divers are likely to be passing or on the sea throughout the winter and spectacular Little Auk movements can occur then too.

Seaham Denemouth car park (NZ 425 504), north of the harbour, and Chourdon Point are the long-term main sites for seawatchers. However, further sprucing-up of the seafront area completed in 2008 made Nose's Point an attractive extra option.

As well as car parking spaces close to the cliffs – useful for wet weather watches – the promontory's new art/education structures, including seating and a wall providing shelter from cold north-westerlies, amount to fine surroundings for viewing passage.

Seaham Dene & Hall (NZ 418 505) is another local patch, this time to the north of Seaham, with some good woodlands which can attract tired migrants coming in off the North Sea during spring and autumn. The hall is now one of the region's leading hotels.

The best road access is via the A1018 coastal route south from Sunderland, then at Ryhope switch to the B1287 to the hotel area and dene.

UPPER TEESDALE is much more than a huge Pennine moorland wilderness. Some of County Durham's most splendid deciduous woodlands flank the river and its tributaries in lower reaches of the dale, providing habitat for a rich bird array. This site at Barnard Castle covers one of the finest stretches.

Target birds *Spring/summer* – Pied Flycatcher (80%), Redstart (70%), Spotted Flycatcher (60%), Marsh Tit (50%), Kingfisher (40%), Tree Pipit (30%), Wood Warbler (30%), Lesser Spotted Woodpecker (10%).

Other possible bird species

All year
Canada Goose
Wigeon
Mallard
Tufted Duck
Goosander
Grey Partridge
Grey Heron
Sparrowhawk
Buzzard
Kestrel
Moorhen
Coot
Oystercatcher
Lapwing
Woodcock
Curlew
Common Sandpiper

Familiar gulls
Common farmland/
woodland birds
Stock Dove
Little Owl
Tawny Owl
Green Woodpecker
Great Spotted
Woodpecker
Skylark
Meadow Pipit
Grey Wagtail
Pied Wagtail
Dipper
Mistle Thrush
Goldcrest
Long-tailed Tit
Coal Tit

Nuthatch
Treecreeper
Greenfinch
Goldfinch
Siskin
Bullfinch

Spring/summer
Cuckoo
Swift
Sand Martin
Swallow
House Martin
Blackcap
Garden Warbler
Whitethroat
Chiffchaff
Willow Warbler

Background information and birding tips

BARNARD CASTLE is, undeniably, more famous for historical, literary and royal connections than birds. It all began with the actual fortress dating from the late 11th Century – which became the property of Richard, Duke of Gloucester, eleven years before his controversial crowning as Richard III.

Birdwise, there's much to enjoy along the Teesdale Way for many miles both up and downstream and along paths that follow tributary becks flowing through their own wooded valleys. The longest of these follows Deepdale Beck from its Tees confluence, a little way above the A67 bridge, to the edge of the Pennine fells three miles to the west.

While many readers will be happy to walk the full length and back, I'm splitting it into two sections to focus on the eastern and western ends.

Key points

• For eastern entrance park on river side of B6277 just south of the White Swan pub in Barnard Castle (NZ 048 164) or in small car park north of bridge.

• For west end, park on verge of Cotherstone-to-Bowes minor road (NY 995 167) near track leading to Low Crag Farm. It's about a mile from road to start of wood.

• Deepdale Wood stretches for three miles from Barnard Castle. Leave at least five hours for return trip.

Contacts

Tourist Information: Barnard Castle, 01833 641 001; email: tourism@ teesdale.gov.uk

How to get there

(Approx 15 miles W of Darlington)

Barnard Castle lies north of A66 trans-Pennine route. For Deepdale's eastern end, turn off A66 onto B6277 to drive north for two miles to Barnard Castle. Park on riverside just before White Swan pub.

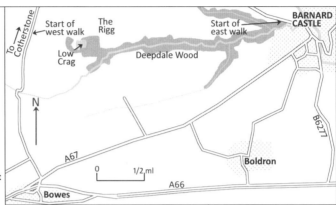

From the east, the B6277 turn-off is 13 miles NW of its Scotch Corner junction with A1. From the west, B6277 turn-off is 38 miles along A66 from J40 of the M6 at Penrith, Cumbria.

If entering Deepdale's west end, leave A66 at Bowes (17 miles NW of Scotch Corner, 13 miles E of Brough) to turn onto A67 which leads to Barnard Castle. However, after less than 200 yards and as the rising A67 bears right, turn left on to the minor road north to Cotherstone.

After a second and more acute kink, the road straightens. Keep going north for three-quarters of a mile until you come to two farm tracks (both public bridleways) – the first on the right heads east to Low Crag

Farm, then straight afterwards the second on the left goes west to Battle Hill Farm. The only real landmark at this point is a military firing range ahead and to the left (marked on OS maps as "Danger Area") – which has distinctive target mounds and if it's in use red flags will be flying.

Park on western verge of this fairly narrow road (NY 995 167), taking care not to obstruct the Battle Hill track entrance and walk back a short distance to take the bridleway heading E.

If driving to Barnard Castle via A688, the approach is different. After the A67 bridge over the Tees, turn right onto B6277 (signposted Middleton-in-Teesdale). Stay on B6277 for just over two miles until you reach

Lartington, then as it bears right at the village's western end turn left into Lartington Green Lane (signposted Bowes). After a mile there's a T-junction with the Bowes-Cotherstone road where you turn left to drive south for half a mile to park near the Low Crag Farm track.

Public transport: Barnard Castle has good bus links with Durham and Bishop Auckland. Arriva No 75 from Darlington.

Deepdale (east end)

AFTER parking near the White Swan or the picnic site car park north of the town bridge, it's only a few minutes' walk along the B6277 to Deepdale's entrance.

However, to keep away from traffic, it is worth crossing the bridge and taking the footpath that rises to the foot of the castle walls. Continue through the riverside woodlands until

you reach a footbridge. Cross the river and you will emerge virtually opposite the entrance to Deepdale Wood.

Along the river stretch it's worth checking for Grey and Pied Wagtails, which could

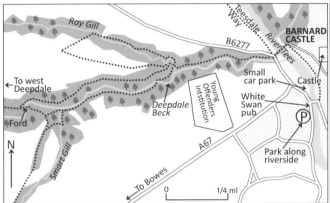

Key points

• Open access throughout but wood's central section is muddy in places.

•Waterproof footwear is essential to cross ford.

• The first mile starting from Barnard Castle is the only section suitable for wheelchairs.

• No facilities in the wood. Shops, cafes, takeaways, public toilet in Barnard Castle centre.

be on rocks jutting from the water, or maybe a Common Sandpiper and Dipper too; if you're lucky a Kingfisher might flash over the surface.

The castle remains atop the rocky cliff provide a splendid backdrop to the Swifts and hirundines darting about overhead from early May.

As you pass through the Deepdale entrance, as the B6277 bends to the left towards Lartington village, you can't fail to notice the extensive grounds and buildings of HM Deerbolt Young Offenders Institution, which extends to the wood's southern edge.

Also expect to see non-birding people out for stroll, as the first half-mile of path is broad, flat and reasonably firm, making it suitable for families with young children, whether on foot or in pushchairs, or babies in prams.

Nevertheless, bird activity is very evident from the start. In 2008, I was delighted to find a singing male Pied Flycatcher as late as May 31. It was just as vocal when I returned three hours later, providing a fitting finale to the visit.

That may not be the case every year but the songs of Blackcaps and Chiffchaffs are almost certain to be sounding, while Willow Warbler melody wafts down from the wood's shrubby fringes. Spotted Flycatchers can be inconspicuous except when performing eye-catching zigzagging aerial pursuits of flying insects.

There used to be Wood Warbler reports regularly from April's final week but over recent years, in keeping with the national decline, finding this species has become harder.

Year-round residents likely to be encountered include Marsh Tits, Nuthatches, Treecreepers and Bullfinches and, in early spring, you may be lucky enough to come across a Lesser Spotted Woodpecker. Deepdale used to be considered one of County Durham's best sites for this elusive rarity and the possibility of coming across it remains to this day.

There should be no problems with Great Spotted Woodpecker; it is prominent throughout much of the woodland. Green

Woodpecker isn't so well distributed; but one recommended spot for sightings is the path along the wood's northern edge, between the Ray Gill 'off-shoot' and the B6277.

Almost a mile into Deepdale the path on the beck's south side narrows and is likely to be muddy, so most likely you'll have it to yourself. Eventually a trail branches to the left, a diversion worth taking; it leads to an open grassy bankside surrounded by large hawthorn bushes from which Garden Warbler song emanates. Willow Warblers and Long-tailed Tits occur here also.

On returning to the woodland floor and continuing westwards, there's a brief section of poor walking conditions, but the path soon improves and emerges into a large clearing – sometimes with a Buzzard soaring overhead – where there's a junction with a path coming

in from Smart Gill to the south-west.

If you just want to cover Deepdale's east end, turn back at this point; alternatively follow the path westwards a little further until it reaches the beck, which is fordable unless running high.

On reaching the other side, turn right on to a path that takes you back along the north side to the Ray Gill junction (or left if you wish to walk right to the west end).

ENTRY from the west is a quite different experience. There is realisation that, for woodland birds, Deepdale represents a last outpost in County Durham's south-west. It points, fingerlike into a virtually tree-less expanse of upland pasture and moorland stretching 15 miles to the Cumbrian side of the Pennines. This enhances the significance of the ravine and its woods.

Deepdale (west end)

The typical sounds on setting off from the Bowes-Cotherstone road are overhead Skylark song interrupted by the cries of Oystercatchers, Lapwings and Curlews.

As I headed along the bridleway coinciding with the start of the track to Low Crag Farm in early June 2008, there was a thrilling moment as a Carrion Crow winging casually over the sheep pastures was given a nasty shock when buzzed playfully by a male Peregrine.

Within 400 yards of the road, as the farm track curves right, the bridleway carries on straight towards The Rigg, a farm more than half-a-mile to the east. This is a little confusing as just 150 yards along it and after crossing a narrow field, you turn right on to a southbound path,

which brings you back on to the Low Crag Farm track – only 300 yards beyond the point where you left it.

It's fairly simple subsequently; the path continues south along the track and through

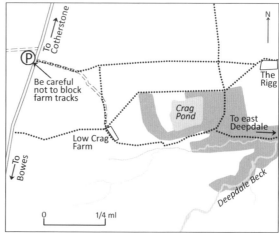

the farmyard – watch out for the slurry oozing from a large manure heap.

From Low Crag an eastbound path takes you down a slope to another farm track. This passes along the south side of Crag (formerly Lartington High) Pond, a man-made fishing lake. It then continues through woods on the lake's east side to connect with Lartington Green Lane, almost a mile to the north. However, as it curves around the lake's south-east corner you turn right onto a path that leads into Deepdale – and continues all the way to Barnard Castle three miles to the east.

The territory, with oak prominent both in the ravine and the more open scattered treescape between it and the lake, looks tailor-made for the likes of Tree Pipit, Redstart, Wood Warbler and Pied Flycatcher. Indeed, on my first visit 30 years ago this quartet was very evident; so too were Spotted Flycatchers and the air throbbed with Lesser Redpoll flight-songs.

These days finding flycatchers is still relatively easy, Redstart song continues to drift furtively from secret tree-top perches and Redpolls, if less numerous, remain very active. As with other former strongholds, there has to be less optimism regarding the numbers of Tree Pipits and Wood Warblers, however.

Though sometimes flushed by day in woodland around the lake, Woodcock is seen more regularly performing evening roding flights during the breeding season.

Watch out too for Tawny Owl in this area, especially in late spring when recently fledged juveniles may be roosting in some not particularly secluded spot.

Also, it's worth scanning in the direction of The Rigg; when I did so in 2008 the most westerly Little Owl I've ever seen in County Durham was on one of the line of telegraph poles leading to the farm.

As for the lake, reedmace-fringed at its west end, its potential is restricted by its modest size and angling, but Wigeon have bred in the past and there are occasional Goosander visits.

For an alternative return to the Bowes-Cotherstone road, take the track running north through the woods east of the lake. After a gate on the wood's northern edge, continue north for about 400 yards until the track crosses the bridleway running east to The Rigg.

Turn left on to the bridleway and keep going west; the path over sheep pastures isn't obvious, so just aim for the gate in each dry stone wall directly ahead. Eventually it brings you on to the Low Crag Farm track, the first stage of the outward walk, and the road.

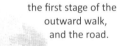

Pied Flycatchers add their song to the spring chorus.

Key points

- Open access all year round.

- Main car parks at picnic sites at NZ 010 517 and NZ 015 532.

- Short walks around picnic areas and shore.

- Wheelchair access in picnic areas only.

- Allow 2 -3 hours to cover area.

- Telescope an asset.

- Nearest toilets in Blanchland.

A MAGNIFICENT winter roost of up to 20,000 Common Gulls is Derwent Reservoir's chief claim to birding fame, but it is capable of producing interesting birds at all times of year and during passage times it has attracted a sprinkling of rarer waders.

Target birds
All year – Dipper (80%), Grey Wagtail (80%), Red Kite (70%), Sparrowhawk (60%), Buzzard (50%). *Spring* – Common Sandpiper (100%), Curlew (100%), Cuckoo (90%), Tree Pipit (80%), Redstart (70%), Common Whitethroat (70%), Yellow Wagtail (50%). *Summer* – Osprey (60%), Little Ringed Plover (50%), Hobby (40%), Common Tern (30%). *Autumn/winter* – Common Gull, Goldeneye, Wigeon, Teal (all 100%), Goosander (80%), Whooper Swan (40%).

Other possible bird species

All year	*Spring/summer*	*Occasional birds*
Greylag Goose	Oystercatcher	Green-winged Teal
Canada Goose	Redshank	Ring-necked Duck
Tufted Duck	Ringed Plover	Scaup
Great Crested Grebe	Lesser Black-backed Gull	Common Scoter
Grey Heron	Swift	Red-throated Diver
Kestrel	Swallow	Bittern
Snipe	House Martin	Buff-breasted Sandpiper
Woodcock	Sand Martin	Pectoral Sandpiper
Tawny Owl	Willow Warbler	Spotted Sandpiper
Stock Dove	Chiffchaff	Curlew Sandpiper
Great Spotted	Pied Wagtail	Quail
Woodpecker		Mediterranean Gull
Goldcrest	*Autumn/winter*	Iceland Gull
Jay	Pink-footed Goose	Glaucous Gull
Rook	Lapwing	
Jackdaw	Black-headed Gull	
Carrion Crow	Redwing	
Reed Bunting	Fieldfare	

Contacts
Northumbrian Water fisherman's lodge (mid-March to end of November) 01207 255 250

Durham Wildlife Trust 01388 488 728

Background information and birding tips

THE RESERVOIR, located at the top of the Derwent Valley with moorland, forestry and grazing fields around it, was opened in 1967 to hold water for use in Gateshead.

There is no full walk/access to the edge of the reservoir as farming land often runs down to the shore but there are several access points, including a country park and picnic spots, so you have plenty of options.

To cover the largest area try the Pow Hill Country Park (NZ 010 517) off the B6306 Blanchland-to-Edmundbyers road on the south side of the reservoir. Here you'll find mixed woodland surrounding car parks and picnic tables which

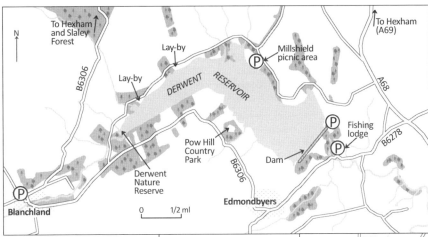

How to get there

(10 miles from Hexham)

The reservoir is best accessed off A68, following the B6306 which winds around the south and west sides of the reservoir. Cover the north side from a minor road which runs back to the A68. From Durham use A691 and A692 to reach A68. From Hexham you can use B6306 or A69 and onto the A68.

attract common birds like Chaffinches, Song and Mistle Thrushes, Blackbirds, Jays, Wood Pigeons and Tawny Owls.

You can walk down to the water's edge knowing that the sun will always be behind you. Feral Canada and Greylag Geese are common but may well bring down passing wild birds such as Pink-footed, Barnacle, European White-fronted and Tundra Bean Geese in winter. You may even spot an occasional Egyptian Goose from an unknown source!

Duck are also more common in winter with flocks of Wigeon grazing the local fields while Teal and Mallard filter mud by the reservoir side. Sea duck such as Scaup and Common Scoters have

dropped in, while Mandarin Ducks may well have come from the breeding site on the North Tyne.

Waders vary according to the season, with breeding Lapwings and Curlews around the fields and Common Sandpipers and Little Ringed Plovers feeding on the edge of the reservoir.

Passing Little Stints, Curlew Sandpipers and Ruff are mainly in the autumn, along with some good rarities

which have dropped in such as Pectoral, Buff-breasted and Spotted Sandpipers.

The water is well-stocked with rainbow trout and they prove an irresistible attraction for Ospreys in summer and some have stayed for a long spell to enjoy the fish.

Anglers will be less excited by the Cormorants when they rise to the surface with a fish. Other fish-eating birds have included Goosanders,

107

Red-breasted Mergansers and a Red-throated Diver.

Clouds of insects encourage large numbers of Swallows, House Martins, Swifts and Sand Martins, while later in the summer Hobbies may come down to the reservoir to feed on these birds.

Other birds of prey species to look out for include Common Buzzard, Sparrowhawk, Goshawk, Red Kite (from the nearby Gateshead release scheme), Peregrine and Merlin.

The Millshield picnic area (NZ 015 532) on the north side off the minor road gives you a great view but you may be looking into the sun if the day you visit is a particularly fine one.

Check the bushes here for warblers, with migrant Chiffchaffs, Willow Warblers, Whitethroats and Garden Warblers all possible. The minor road here has two lay-bys at NY 991 523 and NZ 000 532 you can use to look for feeding Lapwings, Curlews, Redshanks and Golden Plovers, as well as grazing Wigeon in winter along with geese.

The reservoir is famous for its winter gull roost with up to 20,000 Common Gulls using the water, together with smaller numbers of Black-headed, Herring, Great Black-backed and even white-winged gulls.

Mediterranean, Iceland and Glaucous Gulls are all possible, so are well worth looking for in the heaving mass of other gulls.

Derwent Nature Reserve

A small nature reserve at the south-west corner of the reservoir (NY 985 515) provides with a refuge when too many boats are active on the main water. Though there is a bird hide you will need a key to open it. These are obtained from the Durham Wildlife Trust for £10.00. You keep the key for life giving you access at any time.

You can also obtain keys from the Northumbrian Water fishing lodge found before the dam off the B6278 at NZ 032 512. The fishing lodge (Tel: 01207 255 250) is open between mid-March and the end of November. A screen hide has also been erected next to the hide along with a feeding station in front of it.

There is a rookery opposite the hide and the full breeding rituals can be observed as well as the alarm when a raptor approaches the

rookery. Water levels vary, so there is the possibility of wader sightings when there is plenty of mud.

The large gull roost on the reservoir often attracts big numbers of Common Gulls to gather close to the hide. Winter duck include Wigeon, Teal and Mallard with Goosanders and Cormorants throughout the year.

Great Crested Grebes are numerous and well worth watching in the spring as they display, waving their heads and necks before diving under the water.

Other nearby sites
Hamsterley Forest, Slaley Forest, Whittle Dean

THIS PART of the Durham coast is noted for the rich plant life of its cliffs and its special butterfly, the Castle Eden argus, a race of northern brown argus. The cliffs along the three-mile Coastal Path provide superb seawatching and there's good cover for migrants in bushes in its denes and gills.

Target birds

All year – Stonechat (80%), Willow Tit (30%), Tree Sparrow (30%). *Spring/early summer* – Grasshopper Warbler (50%), Lesser Whitethroat (40%), Little Tern (30%). *Late summer* – Little Gull (70%), Roseate Tern (30%). *Autumn* – Sooty Shearwater (50%), Barnacle Goose (30%), Yellow-browed Warbler (20%), Richard's Pipit (10%). *Late autumn/winter* – Snow Bunting (30%), Great Northern Diver (30%), Black-throated Diver (20%), Little Auk (20%), Lapland Bunting (20%).

Other possible bird species

All year
Grey Partridge
Fulmar
Cormorant
Sparrowhawk
Kestrel
Oystercatcher
Ringed Plover
Turnstone
Familiar gulls
Kittiwake
Common woodland and farmland birds
Green Woodpecker
Skylark
Meadow Pipit
Mistle Thrush
Long-tailed Tit
Goldfinch
Linnet
Yellowhammer
Reed Bunting

Spring
Sandwich Tern
Cuckoo
Swift
Hirundines
Redstart
Whinchat
Wheatear

Sedge Warbler
Whitethroat
Garden Warbler
Blackcap
Chiffchaff
Willow Warbler

Summer/early autumn
Great Crested Grebe
Manx Shearwater
Whimbrel
Greenshank
Arctic Skua
Great Skua
Sandwich Tern
Common Tern
Arctic Tern
Guillemot
Razorbill
Puffin

Autumn
Whooper Swan
Pink-footed Goose
Brent Goose
Wigeon
Teal
Common Scoter
Velvet Scoter
Red-breasted Merganser
Red-throated Diver
Great Crested Grebe

Gannet
Knot
Sanderling
Jack Snipe
Snipe
Woodcock
Curlew
Arctic Skua
Great Skua
Long-eared Owl
Short-eared Owl
Redstart
Whinchat
Wheatear
Fieldfare
Redwing
Whitethroat
Garden Warbler
Blackcap
Chiffchaff
Goldcrest

Winter
Red-breasted Merganser
Red-throated Diver
Great Crested Grebe
Knot
Sanderling
Guillemot

Key points

- Parking at: NZ 456 403 (Blackhall); NZ 456 408 (Horden); NZ 439 425 (Warren House Gill); and NZ 439 441 (Easington Colliery).

- Easington Colliery to Blackhall (3 miles) so allow up to four hours for birding.

- Coastal Path suitable for wheelchairs but can be muddy after wet weather.

- Steep cliff steps in places (eg Blackhall side of dene mouth and Blackhills Gill, Horden).

Contacts

Natural England (Denemouth part of NNR), Oakerside Dene Lodge, Stanhope Chase, Peterlee, SR8 1NJ. 0191 586 0004.

Peterlee Tourist Information 0191 586 4450.

How to get there

(Easington is 14 miles east of Durham)

Key roads are: A19 Sunderland-Teesside; A1086 Easington Village-Hartlepool via Horden and Blackhall; B1283 Easington Village-Easington Colliery then turning south to join the A1086 at Horden and B1281, which links the A19 south of Peterlee with A1086 at Blackhall.

There's minor road access to Castle Eden Dene-mouth from A1086 at both Blackhall and Horden. In Blackhall, turn into Eleventh Street at the village north end (if travelling from south it's immediately after a school on the left). Keep straight on over a bridge across the railway, then park in lay-by after allotments.

Horden access is down Cotsford Lane at the south end of the village. It goes downhill past the Comrades Social Club. At a junction near a derelict farm turn under the railway to a narrow lane leading to the car park at the seaward end of Limekiln Gill.

To reach the Coastal Path via Warren House Gill, turn off A1086 onto B1283 (to Easington Colliery) at Horden's north end. Turn right to a civic amenity side and sewage works. Use verge on south side to park without causing obstruction. Follow the

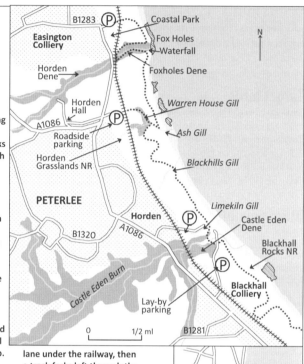

lane under the railway, then a track forks left through the wooded gill to the shore.

For Easington Colliery access, turn from A19 onto A1086 at Easington Village. After half-a-mile go left at the roundabout on the B1432 leading to the village. After half a mile turn right on to B1283 down through Easington Colliery's housing area. At the foot of this hill turn left, then right past a playground into the coastal park.

Public transport: Bus links to all locations with Durham City, Hartlepool, Newcastle and Sunderland.

Background information and birding tips

THIS COASTAL STRIP was used for two iconic British films which says much about how the North-East has changed visually, industrially and socially since the 1960s. The end of cult gangster movie *Get Carter* (1971), starring Michael Caine, was shot at the cliff point where Blackhall Colliery's aerial flight, a conveyor

110

transporting huge buckets filled with debris, dumped waste into the sea for decades.

Most of *Billy Elliot* (2000) was recorded in the village of Easington Colliery but, ironically, the crew had to go elsewhere for pit scenes because the local mine had closed and the area had been landscaped.

The site of the aerial flight has also been transformed. When *BBC Look North* interviewed me in 2000 after I suggested the spot should be named Get Carter Point, the background noise was of terns and Oystercatchers on a foreshore restored by man and nature from the ravages of mining.

I grew up in Horden and this was where I enjoyed my first major 'fall' of migrants. On a misty day in September 1960 Redstarts and Wheatears were everywhere. One of my earliest newspaper articles was headlined 'The day Redstarts invaded Horden Pitheap'.

Memories were re-kindled when thousands of migrants appeared along the coast after torrential rain in early September 2008: Redstarts, Whinchats, Wheatears, Lesser and Common Whitethroats, Garden Warblers and Blackcaps abounded here during that period.

There was also a Greenish Warbler, not recorded previously along this strip. Just three weeks later the strip's first Yellow-browed Warbler was found at the mouth of Castle Eden Dene, demonstrating the potential of the restored area.

Castle Eden Dene mouth is one of several sites between Easington and Blackhall where passage migrants occur. Also promising is Warren House Gill, immediately north of the former Horden Colliery, a smaller, more open gulley with scrub patches.

The even smaller Ash Gill gulley, just south of the former pitheap, hasn't much cover but that makes it easier to find lurking migrants.

Further south is Blackhills Gill, more challenging with steep banks and dense nettle beds flanking its stream. In addition, there are several scrubby clumps, at the back of the beach and on more gently-sloping cliff faces.

The same applies to the Easington area but because its cliffs are steep with limited shore access, birding potential is along their tops and immediately inland. Trees and shrubs planted in the coastal park on the site of the former colliery, are bound to provide increasing cover for migrants.

In late autumn, the small rectangular gulley with hawthorn-covered sides at the park's north-west corner may have migrant thrushes, Goldcrests, Long-tailed Tits, Tree Sparrows and Yellowhammers.

I've seen Willow Tit and even Green Woodpecker in scrub on the railway embankment flanking the park's eastern side. Bushes offer migrant potential and year-

Key points

- Cliff faces not steep along Horden/Blackhall stretches but uneven surface requires care.

- Colliery waste above high tide line should be avoided – you can sink to calf-depth in wet areas.

- No services along Coastal Path. Public toilets in Peterlee town centre near Tourist Information office.

- Pubs, takeaways and shops in local villages but more extensive range at Peterlee.

Though in national decline, it is still possible to find Tree Sparrows in hawthorn bushes at Easington's Coastal Park.

round perches for Stonechats, prominent all along the coastal strip.

While Snow Buntings and, less frequently, Lapland Buntings are possible here during October-March, the chances of finding them are better in local fields.

The mouth of Castle Eden Dene offers the best spring prospects. Blackcaps and Chiffchaffs are the typical warblers of the NNR's woodland but at the seaward end scrub provides scope for Lesser and Common Whitethroats and Garden and Willow Warblers. Listen out for Sedge and Grasshopper Warblers, too.

Whinchat is a regular spring visitor. Cuckoos, Blue-headed Wagtails and Bluethroats are among scarcer spring visitors.

The cliffs at Fox Holes Dene mouth and Get Carter Point are arguably the best for monitoring wildfowl and seabird passage. Frequently such movements are associated with strong and chilling onshore winds and rain, so warm, waterproof clothing is essential.

Even when the sea is placid, 'scoping' can be productive. Great Crested Grebes gather here at the end of the breeding season with 50-plus regularly reported, some remaining in winter.

Common Scoter gatherings of up to 300 often occur in winter with Velvet Scoters sometimes present. Red-throated Divers and Red-breasted Mergansers may be present, joined occasionally by Black-throated and Great Northern Divers and Red-necked Grebes.

Guillemot and Razorbill family groups occur in late summer when they can be involved in feeding frenzies with Manx Shearwaters, Gannets, Cormorants, Little Gulls, Kittiwakes and terns. Inevitably, Arctic Skuas appear to rob terns.

Large numbers of terns and smaller numbers of waders are an indication of this coastline's improved health. Even bigger changes can be anticipated as the recovery continues.

COUNTY DURHAM struck gold when it acquired this truly spectacular river gorge site in the 1974 local government boundary changes. The sometimes physically demanding Brignall Banks walk through the wooded gorge is exhilarating and the birds encountered along the way heighten the thrill, but the shorter circular walk on the southern side is best if time is short.

Target birds *Spring/summer* – Grey Wagtail (90%), Dipper (80%), Nuthatch (80%), Pied Flycatcher (80%), Redstart (70%), Spotted Flycatcher (60%), Goosander (60%), Marsh Tit (50%), Tree Pipit (40%), Wood Warbler (30%).

Other possible bird species

All year		Jay
Mallard	Green Woodpecker	Magpie
Red-legged Partridge	Great Spotted Woodpecker	Jackdaw
Grey Partridge	Skylark	Rook
Pheasant	Hirundines	Carrion Crow
Grey Heron	Pied Wagtail	Starling
Sparrowhawk	Wren	House Sparrow
Buzzard	Dunnock	Tree Sparrow
Kestrel	Robin	Chaffinch
Moorhen	Blackbird	Greenfinch
Oystercatcher	Song Thrush	Goldfinch
Lapwing	Mistle Thrush	Linnet
Curlew	Blackcap	Yellowhammer
Black-headed Gull	Garden Warbler	
Common Gull	Goldcrest	*Spring*
Lesser Black-backed Gull	Long-tailed Tit	Yellow Wagtail
Stock Dove	Blue Tit	Whitethroat
Woodpigeon	Great Tit	Chiffchaff
Collared Dove	Coal Tit	Willow Warbler
Swift	Treecreeper	

Brignall Banks circular walk (NZ 056 114)

SIR WALTER SCOTT, a frequent visitor to the nearby Rokeby estate, included the following phrase: *"O, Brignall banks are wild and fair, And Greta woods are green,"* in his poem *Brignall Banks* and 200 years later this dramatic, winding, wooded ravine continues to have the kind of deep impact on visitors that must have inspired those opening lines.

My visits have generally started in the tiny hamlet of Brignall (only a handful of scattered farmsteads), almost half a mile from the river. Though relatively close to the A66's traffic bustle, it is far enough away to seem pleasantly remote and a good starting point for a circular walk.

Key points
• Open access on rights of way over private land.

• Distance about six miles – leave at least five hours to complete.

• Upstream stretches physically demanding.

• Strong footwear essential.

• Only the Brignall Lane/ Moorhouse Lane sections suitable for wheelchairs.

• Nearest facilities: the Morritt Arms Hotel, Greta Bridge.

• Extensive facilities (shops, cafes, takeaways, public toilet) at Barnard Castle.

Contacts
Tourist Information: Barnard Castle 01833641 001; e-mail: tourism@ teesdale.gov.uk

In springtime it's unusual to hear sounds louder than the cries of Lapwings and Curlews from surrounding agricultural land and Greenfinches and Goldfinches in the treetops.

The lane through the village is barely wide enough for two cars to pass, so the only obvious parking place is the small area of gravel outside the church (NZ 071 123) which can accommodate four or five carefully parked cars. A signpost (Public Footpath to Old Church) points to a gate and the opening stage of the route through the Site of Special Scientific Interest.

The path follows a narrow stream, with Blackcaps, Chiffchaffs and Willow Warblers likely to be singing after mid-April, with possibly Whitethroats performing in the hedge across the small field on the right. Movement in the crops reveals Red-legged Partridges scuttling off.

After this field, a sizeable embankment drops down to a flat riverside area and the remains of St Mary's church. I've seen Tree Pipit song flights performed from the tops of the hawthorn scrub on either side of the boggy-in-places track running down the slope to link with the path that follows the Greta's north bank.

However, before joining it, do a riverbank check. Early rewards could be a Pied Flycatcher or a Nuthatch singing in trees on the opposite side, with a Treecreeper another possibility.

A Goosander or two may be relaxing on this more placid stretch of water, while Grey and Pied Wagtails and Dippers could be occupying protruding rocks. All may be encountered as you head upstream, but this is among the likelier locations. The river birds, it should be stressed, can be hard to find or absent altogether if the river's in full spate.

Three stile crossings of fences along the route ahead present varying degrees of difficulty, two of them particularly for people walking downstream. That's because of the height of the step and the lack of firm points to plonk down your feet below.

The first stile, providing access from the open pasture around the old church site into Tebb Wood to the south, has been improved since the time my wife took a nasty tumble on stepping onto a slippery tree root.

Tebb Wood is mainly a thinned-out mature conifer plantation, so bird potential is limited largely to Coal Tits, Chaffinches and possibly the much scarcer Goldcrests. Beyond a second stile on its far side, there is more than a quarter of a mile of flat grassland. Redstart song or alarm calls may sound from trees by the river or occasional clusters of scrub which may also harbour singing Garden and Willow Warblers, with a Tree Pipit possible too.

Buzzards are among birds that may drift over the valley and Sand Martins and Swallows could well be pursuing insects above. Green Woodpeckers – seen less frequently than Great Spotteds in the ravine ¬ sometimes ventures into this open area. Occasionally a Pied Flycatcher sings from the big ash standing in a line of smaller trees just before that next woodland stretch.

You'll enter the Brignall Banks woodland after the third stile. The going is less than smooth along a short stretch of riverbank that is eroding due to the constant pounding of the river surging round a bend.

Now you are into a spectacular natural dales treescape, with wych elm, ash and oak rising precariously from a bankside verging on the near vertical in places. Bluebells, wood anemones, ramsons and primroses carpet the ground in less steep stretches.

However, after sustained heavy rain, the single file path can become treacherously muddy; at one point floodwater from the

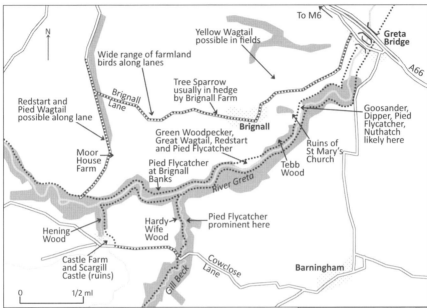

How to get there

(Approx. 15 miles W of Darlington).

For Brignall Banks walk:
From Scotch Corner junction on A1 south of Darlington, head NW along A66 for ten miles. Turn on to minor road signposted to Greta Bridge and Barningham, then immediately right to cross traffic light-controlled narrow bridge over River Greta. Straight after Morritt Arms Hotel turn left on to narrow lane leading to Brignall. Park outside hamlet's church.

For Scargill walk:
Initially as with Brignall Banks but after turning off A66 at Greta Bridge, keep straight on along minor road to Barningham. At T-junction in village turn right to follow narrow lane leading to Gillbeck Bridge and then path to Hening Scar via Castle Farm/ Scargill Castle ruins.

---

fields above is liable to cascade down the bankside and over it. One particular quagmire section demands you stay on your feet to avoid slithering down to riverside rocks 20ft below.

Two trees that have fallen over the path are significant hurdles, though the second blockage has been eased by a passage being chain-sawed through the trunk's upperside, with a big spike hammered in to provide something to grip. Such difficulties, it should be stressed, are confined to three stretches, each of no more than a few hundred yards. In between are broader, flatter areas, where you can concentrate fully on enjoying the ravine's considerable birdlife.

Redstarts and Pied Flycatchers are regularly active from the end of the third week of April, with Spotted Flycatchers later in the spring. Sadly, however, finding a Wood Warbler has become hard, despite much suitable habitat. Marsh Tit, a resident species that has also dwindled nationally, does still occur, along with the more ubiquitous Coal, Blue and Great Tits.

The final hurdle is where a section of path has been washed away by the river surging around the most acute bend along the route. Not long after scrambling around this, there's a semi-open bankside where Garden and Willow Warblers feel more at home amid the bushes and rising saplings while their Blackcap and Chiffchaff cousins sing from adjacent mature woodland.

Long-tailed Tits are more likely to be encountered in this section of the ravine. Then suddenly the path widens and leads you away from the river, steadily upwards to the top of the gorge and into sheep pasture, where it joins a partly-surfaced track. Turn right and soon you're in Moor House farmyard and being 'welcomed' by dogs.

The good news is that the one with aggressive tendencies is securely chained; the others provided no more than a barking escort.

After that it's just a matter of half-a-mile north along Moorhouse Lane, and then you turn east along Brignall Lane for a mile-and-a-half stroll back to your starting point.

If you're in day-listing mode, additions can be made along this final leg through rolling open countryside: Linnets and Yellowhammers in hedgerows; Red-legged and Grey Partridges, Oystercatchers, Lapwings, Curlews and Stock Doves in fields; and in 2008 I was surprised to see a pair of Shelduck by a flooded field depression.

Yellow Wagtail is another possibility and Tree Sparrows seem to be stationed regularly by the entrance to Brignall Farm. There can also be more of the same; I've seen both Redstarts and Pied Flycatchers in Moorhouse Lane's trees.

Scargill-Hening Scar-Hardy Wife Wood circular walk (NZ 058 112)

THIS SHORTER walk on the Greta's southern side is an attractive alternative to the Brignall circular. Inevitably, the bird species will be similar, with Siskin being one of the few possible extras.

The path is mostly along the upper level of the ravine wall and this route offers even more impressive views of the gorge than from the opposite bank. Also, for anyone wishing to visit other Teesdale sites the same day, completing it takes much less time.

The remains of Scargill Castle – actually a fortified house dating from the 13th Century – provide an eye-catching start to a walk well endowed with jaw-dropping sights. However, a No Parking request by the entrance to the

farm on the ruin site, means cars must not be left on this particular stretch of the narrow minor road running west from Barningham village.

Fortunately, parts of Cowclose Lane, between Barningham and Hardy Wife Wood, and Church Lane, west of the wood, have grass verges broad enough to accommodate cars without inconvenience to farm and other traffic. There is even space for one or two cars near Gillbeck Bridge, which carries the road across the stream that flows through the ravine where Hardy Wife Wood is situated.

After parking, head west along Chapel Lane, which is flanked by pastureland, rising to the south to Barningham Moor. Bird species visible over it on a spring day should include Pheasant, Oystercatcher, Lapwing, Curlew, Black-headed Gull, Pied Wagtail and Swallow.

Just past the private driveway to Castle Farm and the Scargill ruin, a signpost points to a stile that leads into the adjacent field. A scarcely-visible public footpath skirts around the farmstead/castle complex's south-west corner, then veers away into a fairly short wooded gulley to join the riverside path at Hening Scar.

After turning right to head downstream, the path rises to continue along a high shoulder of the ravine's south wall. One advantage of this lofty position is that, when there is a clear view through the trees, you are well placed to look down on the likes of Mallard, Goosander, Grey Wagtail and Dipper on the river without disturbing them.

You are also better placed to appreciate the full range of woodland birdsong. Wren, Blackcap, Great Tit and Chaffinch song can usually be heard against the river's noise but, especially when it is running high, quieter vocalists such as Robin, Redstart, Mistle Thrush, Chiffchaff, Goldcrest and Coal Tit can be drowned out by its constant roar.

After a while the path returns to the riverside – generally the gradient is OK but you might want to find a stick to brace yourself at one steep point as there are no adjacent trees to grab if you lose your balance.

After a short spell on the ravine floor you are climbing again, this time to Black Scar to enjoy awesome views along the gorge. Despite the 80ft near-precipice, you can relax thanks to security fencing along the path edge.

This is a superb spot for a Pied Flycatcher encounter. The species' jaunty, see-sawing song can be heard regularly here in late April and May and, scanning around to pin it down is worthwhile. It could be on the very top of one of the ancient trees thrusting skywards from the riverside – and therefore almost at eye-level.

Continuing into the upper reaches of a beechwood, you may well see more Pied Flycatchers and a Redstart too. It's perfect Wood Warbler territory as well but reports are becoming few and far between.

Near this wood's eastern end a left hand track branches off to go down to the River Greta. To return to the road, keep straight on, turning into the Hardy Wife Wood tributary ravine through which Gill Beck flows to the river.

This eventually broadens into a more gently-sided small valley and then you walk alongside the beck, crossing it three times. Take care when stepping on some of the more obvious stones as they can be slippery.

Still there are consolations as in springtime there are more opportunities to see Pied Flycatchers along this stretch of the route leading to the Gillbeck Bridge road crossing – an encore by the site's star bird to round off a most satisfying trek.

Key points

- **Distance inside three miles. With birding stops, allow at least three hours.**

- **A measure of fitness needed to cope with ravine's two more physically-demanding path sections and the stream crossings.**

- **Unsuitable for disabled visitors.**

- **Stout footwear essential.**

Key points
(Hamsterley Forest)

• Car toll payable at machines at eastern entrance to forest drive and at The Grove.

• Car parks off forest drive near Visitor Centre (NZ 094 312), Low Redford (NZ 079 308), Middle Redford (NZ 074 307), The Grove (NZ 067 298) and Blackling Hole (NZ 053 275)

• For security car parks are closed (8pm-8am, summer/5pm-8am, winter). Birders seeking Nightjars need to find safe parking places on the forest drive verge.

• A barrier halts access at Low Redford overnight but The Grove area can be reached from the Windy Bank Road entrance.

DURHAM'S biggest man-made forest and the cluster of fell and woodland locations to the north are rapidly becoming a key raptor-watching area. The spectacle of early spring Goshawk displays are becoming a regular sight and there is the possibility of seeing rare Hen Harriers and Rough-legged Buzzards over adjacent moorland in winter. Siskin and Crossbill flocks provide another reason for late autumn and winter visits.

Target birds *All year* – Common Crossbill (70%), Goshawk (50%), Peregrine (40%), Merlin (30%). *Spring/summer* – Cuckoo (80%), Ring Ouzel , Redstart, Spotted Flycatcher, Pied Flycatcher (all 70%), Tree Pipit (50%), Nightjar (40%), Wood Warbler (30%).

Other possible bird species

All year
Greylag Goose
Mallard
Red Grouse
Grey Heron
Sparrowhawk
Buzzard
Kestrel
Woodcock
Stock Dove
Tawny Owl
Short-eared Owl
Green Woodpecker
Great Spotted Woodpecker
Common woodland birds
Skylark
Grey Wagtail
Pied Wagtail

Dipper
Mistle Thrush
Goldcrest
Long-tailed Tit
Marsh Tit
Coal Tit
Nuthatch
Treecreeper
Jay
Siskin
Linnet
Lesser Redpoll
Bullfinch
Spring/summer
Oystercatcher
Golden Plover
Lapwing
Snipe
Curlew

Redshank
Common Sandpiper
Black-headed Gull
Swift
Swallow
House Martin
Meadow Pipit
Whinchat
Stonechat
Wheatear
Garden Warbler
Blackcap
Chiffchaff
Willow Warbler
Autumn/winter
Fieldfare
Redwing
Brambling

Background information and birding tips

THE FOLLOWING locations all feature upland streams that feed into the main tributary of the River Wear's upper middle section.

Hamsterley's 5,000 acres are spread over the valleys of the Spurlswood, Euden and Ayhope Becks that unite to become the Bedburn Beck at the forest's east end. Pikeston Fell and Hamsterley Common lie respectively to the north and south of the Ayhope.

To the north-east, Harthope Beck passes conifer plantations, then long-established stands of broadleaf trees, before joining Bedburn Beck for the two miles to its confluence with the Wear, upstream of Witton-le-Wear.

1. Hamsterley Forest (NZ 067 298)

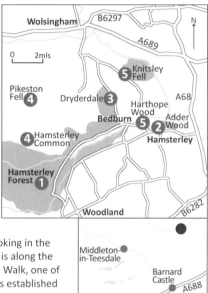

WOOD WARBLER is a species that has become scarcer throughout the whole Hamsterley area, so the forest is something of a last resort. At least ten birds were said to have been singing between the east end toll booth and the visitor centre in early May 2004 and there have been continuing reports from that area during subsequent years.

Pied Flycatchers and Redstarts can be anticipated there also, as well as in the fragments of deciduous woodland around The Grove, the big house in the centre of the forest, and also Oak Bank, a broadleaf oasis amid massed conifers, about three-quarters of a mile further west along the drive.

Meanwhile Tree Pipits crop up in more open forest areas, such as around the fringes of clearings. Such clear-felled zones are likely haunts for a fifth charismatic summer visitor, the Nightjar, a nationally rare breeding species.

Over the decades, the most likely spots have changed following re-planting of these sectors and the harvesting of blocks of mature timber elsewhere.

Having said that, a site well worth visiting in recent years was in the vicinity of Metcalf's House, a ruined former coaching inn (NZ071314) in the Ayhope valley – among the places where I saw Nightjars when I first started looking in the 1970s. The ruin is along the 4.5 mile Orange Walk, one of the official paths established in the forest.

During the past decade I have come across churring Nightjars repeatedly in the extensively cleared areas by the track along the ridge (NZ 04 29) on the south side of the Euden Valley, a mile or so west of The Grove.

However, poor summers since 2006 have brought problems, the dismal weather affecting the moth supply on which these nocturnal aerial hunters depend – and restricting the number of occasions suitable for searching for them. Warm, still nights are ideal – the cold, wet and windy variety a waste of time.

Fortunately early spring weather has been less inclement so a main period for raptor watching has not been similarly hit. Goshawk display is likely during February-April and a session after daybreak can be productive.

Sparrowhawks will be on show over the forest so it's a good chance to sharpen up knowledge of the differences. The forest's layout and the limited field of view along trails between the conifers means it is best to look over the trees from around the fringes of the west end.

Vantage points at Trinity

119

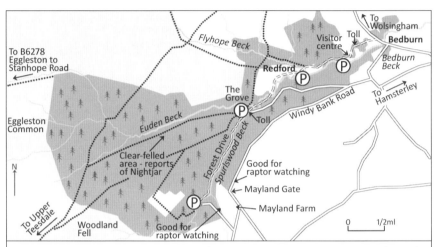

How to get there

(10 miles N of Barnard Castle)

Hamsterley Forest is four miles west of A68, the relevant turn-off being immediately south of the bridge over River Wear.

This turning is 12 miles NW along A68 from J58 on A1(M) by-pass of Darlington. It is also four miles S of roundabout where A690 from Durham City and A1(M)'s J62 links with A68 1.5 miles west of Crook town.

From Hamsterley village, which is two miles along the minor road from the A68, there are three ways into the forest:

• Turn right after Cross Keys pub, then left after 1.5 miles at Bedburn hamlet onto another minor road which, after half-a-mile, brings you to forest drive's eastern end.

• Alternatively, go straight on from village for a mile, turn right on reaching a T-junction and then, after more than half-a-mile, take second right, which descends for almost two miles through conifers to join drive at The Grove in forest's centre.

• For the third option, stay on road along forest's southern edge instead of taking that turning to The Grove. After three miles and just after road swings sharply south from forest, turn right at Mayland Farm, which is on junction. Just under half a mile along this further minor road, turn right on to narrow lane leading to forest drive's western end at Blackling Hole.

Public transport: The Monday to Saturday bus service between Bishop Auckland and Hamsterley village is of little use to forest visitors. The last bus back to the town at 2.59pm means little time can be spent in the forest, with it being a half hour's walk from village.

Rigg (NZ 01 29) and Neighbour Moor (NZ 02 28) on Hamsterley's western edge, offer views eastwards over the forest's four miles. One drawback is the two-to-three mile hike from the nearest parking place on the B6278 Eggleston-to-Stanhope road. Also, if watching on cloudless mornings, you'll be looking directly into sunlight.

Hamsterley's south-western corner is preferred by some raptor watchers – either the Mayland Gate end of Windy Bank Road, along the forest edge, or from the minor road to Blackling Hole at the forest drive's west end. These points provide overviews of most of the forest and there's no walking involved.

Also, because you're looking northwards, the sun isn't in your face.

With luck, bonus birds can be earned during such sessions – and over a wider period of the year than the Goshawk display season. Other birds of prey logged during such watches or in the vicinity have included Honey Buzzard, Red Kite, Hen Harrier, Rough-legged Buzzard, Osprey, Merlin and Peregrine.

A Black Stork that passed over the forest in May, 1989, was only the third for Durham and the first in the 20th Century. A Great Grey Shrike at Trinity Rigg for more than a month provided an extra reason for birders to visit Hamsterley's western extreme during early spring, 2009.

In July that year the forest was among more unlikely Durham inland sites to produce an over-flying Mediterranean Gull report. The same applies to the Quail said to have been calling at Black Hill at its north-west corner.

Winter visits to the forest interior tend to be focused on Crossbills. The population can be hundreds-strong after an irruption but flocks of less than 50 are the norm in more typical years.

Finding a group in such a big conifer complex suggests a needle-in-a-haystack exercise, but it's not so hard except when numbers are very low.

My usual tactic is to wander along trails in The Grove area until I hear the distinctive calls that enable me to home in on them.

The Parrot Crossbill irruption of 1982/83 led to the discovery of two of these rarities, but 1990/91's larger scale arrival saw up to ten stripping seeds from the cone crop of conifers immediately west of The Grove. Hamsterley is definitely a place where this impressive finch can be anticipated during future national influxes.

Unfortunately this cannot be said – certainly not with confidence – about the Hawfinch population. A small group atop a tall deciduous tree near The Grove was often the highlight of past visits but that's no longer so. However, after sightings dried up in the 1980s there were reports towards the end of the next decade, so perhaps another comeback is possible.

Siskins are prominent, especially after autumn invasions by continental birds, Lesser Redpolls feed in alders by the burns and the forest has occasionally produced unusually large Bullfinch counts.

Key points (Hamsterley Forest)

- It can turn chilly after sunset, so take warm clothes. Cover up to minimise midge activity and use insect repellent.

- Five way-marked walking trails range from one to 4.5 miles.

- Also extensive network of tracks, linking with paths over adjacent moorland.

- Tracks mainly firm-surfaced but can be muddy, but is still passable for wheelchairs.

- Visitor Centre at NZ 092 313 (open April-October, 10am-4pm weekdays and 11am-5pm weekends) includes full facilities. Tel: 01388 488 312.

2. Adder Wood/Bedburn Beck (NZ 117 317)

THE MOST easterly of these sites incorporates some of the area's most delightful oak woodland – and if you've built up a thirst by the end of your walk, this can be slaked at Hamsterley village's Cross Keys pub near the start/finishing point.

A public footpath sign in Hamsterley village centre points the way north 500 yards across hedgerow-lined fields to Bedburn Beck valley's southern ridge. From there a path descends steadily down the Adder Wood's western edge to the Wear tributary, passing Snape Gate Farm and then running through a small, dense, relatively birdless conifer

plantation on the way. Finally a footbridge crosses the burn, now the width of a small river.

From the footbridge, the path heads into the grounds of Carrwood Hill House, where it forks. The right turn is on to a wide farm track running east through Spa Wells Bank's attractive deciduous woodland by the burn. After almost half-a-mile there's another bridge, which under normal circumstances, would offer an alternative return as a path on the other side leads to another part of Adder Wood. Unfortunately, signs on either side stress it is private and not for public use. I did sneak across once

Key points (Adder Wood)

• **Ample parking usually available in Hamsterley village centre near the public footpath sign (NZ 118 311) indicating the walk's start.**

• **Distance two to four miles, depending on whether you walk just to Bedburn Beck or continue to the River Wear.**

How to get there

Drive two miles along minor road, branching from A68 immediately south of its River Wear crossing, to Hamsterley village centre. Follow public footpath sign (NZ 118 311) opposite post office and just E of the Cross Keys pub.

Public transport: With Adder Wood just half-a-mile north of village, visiting it is feasible, despite limited Monday to Saturday bus service, from Bishop Auckland.

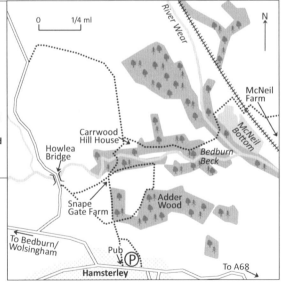

without an ugly Troll emerging to devour me but maybe it was his day off, so I won't advise anyone to repeat such daring.

Soon after this the path veers away from the burn to cross arable farmland. It finishes up, after another half mile, at the River Wear – and as it resumes on the opposite bank, you're tempted to think it might be possible to wade across.

Indeed, it would be brilliant to do so as McNeil Bottoms, flooded former gravel workings, lie on the other side. That's a very productive wetland not much visited by birders due to access problems from the A68 half-a-mile further east. But I certainly wouldn't take the risk unless the water was clearly at an extremely low level. In the spring it tends to be high – and can flow dangerously fast.

However, walking there is made worthwhile by the distinct possibility of Goosander, Common Sandpiper, Kingfisher and Grey Wagtail sightings along this river stretch.

Stay long enough and there may be at least a glimpse of an Osprey – though still mainly a scarce passage visitor to Durham, the occasional bird does linger into the summer in the Wear Valley.

Also, during the relatively short distance between the public and private bridges, singing male Pied Flycatchers were especially prominent when I was there in May, 2008. Two Dipper pairs, one with fledged young, were on show along the Bedburn during the outward and return legs of my trek.

As the private bridge is out of bounds, the only option for a different route back to Hamsterley is to retrace steps to Carrwood Hill footbridge and along the path through the conifers on the other side. Then on reaching the plantation edge, turn left on to a path going east and fringing large open fields north of Adder Wood.

After 600 yards, a path crosses the fields to Adder Wood and continues over an open area, with much gorse scrub, between the woodland's eastern and western sections – leading back to the Bedburn Beck valley's southern ridge and the path to the village.

With oak so prevalent in Adder Wood, it's ideal territory for Redstarts and Pied Flycatchers. Tree Pipits and Wood Warblers are possible, though not with such certainty these days.

Cuckoo, Blackcap, Chiffchaff, Willow Warbler and Spotted Flycatcher are among other summer visitors that can be anticipated, while Green and Great Spotted Woodpeckers, Nuthatches and Jays are among more high profile regular residents.

Key points
(Adder Wood)

- **Allow at least three to four hours.**

- **Ground is too rough for wheelchairs.**

- **Path down Adder Wood's west side to Snape Gate can be muddy in places. Steeper than the alternative path to the east.**

- **Meals at Cross Keys inn at Hamsterley village. Groceries including food and soft drinks available at post office**

- **Nearest public toilets at Hamsterley Forest visitor centre and Low Barns nature reserve visitor centre (three miles east).**

Key points
(Dryderdale)

• Very limited parking on verge near Dryderdale Farm at NZ 093 334. Next nearest convenient spot is 500 yards north along this narrow road from farm at start of track into Dryderdale Plantation (NZ 089 338).

• Shull Bank Wood/Harthope Beck walking distance no more than two to three miles. Allow two to three hours.

• Some parts of Shull Bank Wood boggy and path's start is well churned by cattle. Make sure that rather rickety gate is closed securely.

3. Dryderdale (NZ 09 33)

I WASN'T AWARE of Shull Bank Wood's existence until the Ordnance Survey's Explorer 1:25,000 maps were published. While seeking promising sites on the equivalent sheet in the 1:50,000 Landranger series, I overlooked the unnamed roughly rectangular green area on the east side of the Hamsterley-Bedburn-Wolsingham minor road.

But thanks to Explorer's larger scale I noticed two rights-of-way providing access to both western and eastern ends of the wood. So I checked it out next spring and was so impressed that it has since become one of my late April/early May priority locations.

Surprisingly, it doesn't seem to have hooked other birders for I have yet to come across fellow enthusiasts – or anyone else – during my visits.

I was so used to having the place to myself that I was shocked to arrive one April day in 2007 and find a fleet of liveried 4x4s and a helicopter on adjacent farmland. It was Channel 4's Time Team trying to unravel mysteries surrounding a broad expanse of stones known as The Castles, an Ancient Monument possibly dating from at least the Roman occupation.

One local feature that is firmly on the map is Dryderdale Hall. It was designed by the distinguished Victorian architect Alfred Waterhouse, a few years before his rather more prestigious commission, London's Natural History Museum. The event that really grabbed public attention came a century later, however; it featured as the chief bad guy's residence in the 1971 cult Michael Caine gangster movie, *Get Carter*.

Getting back to the wood, it doesn't look much from the start of the path at the foot of a rather steep road stretch. It's basically a spread of unusually tall birch trees scattered about the southern bank of Dryderdale Beck just before its confluence with Harthope Beck.

With comparatively little shrubbery – just occasional holly bushes and gorse clumps – the habitat looks limited, but conditions certainly seem fine for Tree Pipits and Redstarts. This has become one of my favourite sites for these species each spring.

Regularly I see Woodcock on such visits and breeding Curlews occupy open areas between the trees. Green and Great Spotted Woodpeckers are usually present, while smaller species active in the birch canopies include Long-tailed, Coal, Blue and Great Tits, with Siskins, Lesser Redpolls and Bullfinches likely also.

Very possibly a Buzzard will soar over the trees or adjacent farmland and with the extensive Dryderdale, West Moor and Knitsley Plantations nearby there is also a chance of a Goshawk appearance.

The other significant public footpath runs initially over fields south of Dryderdale Farm. It starts from the road, almost opposite Shull Lodge, the white cottage at the entrance to Dryderdale Hall's long drive. A map is essential as the route over the fields isn't obvious due to it being so little-walked.

Eventually it follows the north bank of alder-fringed Dryderdale Beck's final stage – before the confluence with the Harthope – and goes on to join an equally unmarked path running south from West Shipley Farm. This path then crosses Harthope Beck to continue south towards Hoppyland Farm.

Though this crossing point has only a narrow strip of woodland, it's well worth visiting. A Pied Flycatcher is liable to be singing here just after mid-April and sometimes a Redstart too. Nuthatches and Treecreepers may also be in the trees, while Grey Wagtails and Dippers occur along the beck and very occasionally I've seen a Goosander.

Incidentally, the excellent Harthope

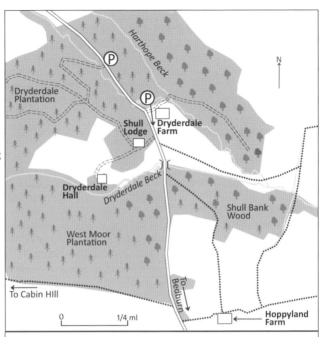

How to get there

From south, take minor road from Hamsterley village to Wolsingham via Bedburn. A mile past Bedburn, there's a long downhill stretch – Shull Bank – with a small bridge over Dryderdale Beck at its foot. Road then rises, passing the white cottage (Shull Lodge) on left and there is limited parking on verge between there and Dryderdale Farm on right.

The other approach is from Weardale four miles to north. At Wolsingham on A689, turn south on to minor road to Bedburn and Hamsterley. This road crosses River Wear bridge and then rises steeply, veering eastwards at top. After another half mile, bear right on coming to a fork and road descends over mainly open farmland towards Dryderdale Plantation on right. Just under half a mile beyond plantation's start, Dryderdale Farm is on left and verge with limited parking is immediately afterwards on right.

Key points (Dryderdale)

• **Waterproof footwear necessary for the Harthope Beck crossing along the other path.**

• **Nearest public toilets at Wolsingham, plus a few shops, takeaways, cafes and pubs.**

Key points
(Hamsterley Common)

• Park on verge at end of St John's Hall cul-de-sac lane and just past Blackburn Lodge (NZ 073 336).

• If starting from Bedburn road, park at West Moor Plantation's south-east corner (NZ 094 324). From Hamsterley Forest, choose Low Redford (NZ 079 308) or The Grove (NZ 067 298) for parking.

• Circular walk from St John's Hall is about six miles (allow five hours). Similar if starting from The Grove or Low Redford. From Bedburn road, it around eight miles (six hours)

• Sections of the moorland tracks likely to be muddy.

Wood begins a short distance downstream from the beck crossing but, frustratingly, there is no public access at this point. Coverage is, however, possible from the other side of the valley – which is why I have dealt with it separately.

One dales' speciality I have never seen at Shull Bank is a Wood Warbler. Indeed, due to the lack of suitable habitat, even Chiffchaffs and Willow Warblers are relatively scarce.

The best place to go for warblers locally is a lay-by 500 yards north along the road from Dryderdale Farm. It overlooks a scrub-covered bankside on the north-east edge of Dryderdale Plantation. Blackcaps, Chiffchaffs and Willow Warblers are usually prominent there and Garden Warblers join them later in the spring.

Actually this isn't so much a lay-by as the start of a rough track for forestry vehicles. Maps don't show a public right of way along this track but there is no sign to indicate the public aren't welcome. It's part of a route system that runs to the plantation's west side and I've ventured along it several times without any objection.

I must admit that, once past that scrub-covered bankside, I've never noted much bird activity among the massed conifers. But on the western side the track links with the public footpath running eastwards from the end of the cul-de-sac minor road to Pikeston Fell's north-east corner – so it offers potential for a more extensive trek.

One sound birding reason for being on that path is that it is a vantage point for looking east over Dryderdale Plantation. As a result there is potential for watching for raptor movement over the conifer expanse.

Equally promising in this respect is Pikeston Fell's Cabin Hill, half-a-mile to the south and reached by the path along West Moor Plantation's southern edge from the Bedburn road.

Moorland birds on show at these two spots include some of County Durham's most easterly and lowest altitude Red Grouse. Though there isn't a place offering all-round views over these plantations on their eastern side, Knitsley Plantation on the hill north-east of Dryderdale Farm can be well observed from the field path starting opposite Shull Lodge.

4. Hamsterley Common/Pikeston Fell (NZ 04 31)

A CIRCULAR walk taking in these locations, particularly during late spring/early summer, usually offers a wider bird range than most other Durham upland treks because it takes in more than just heather moor habitat.

Whether you start from St John's Hall to the north, the Wolsingham-Bedburn minor road to the east or The Grove or Low Redford in Hamsterley Forest to the south-east, there

are woodland or pastureland elements that inevitably boost the variety. Also, the fact it normally seems to be teeming with breeding birds suggests that this most easterly substantial expanse of moorland in the Northern Pennines is less exposed to weather extremes, even though much of it lies above 1,000ft.

Some more sheltered sections of its valleys support a surprising number of woodland

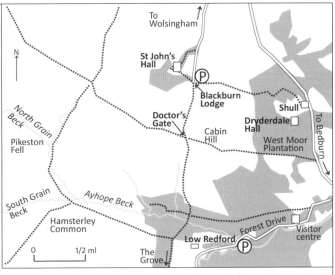

How to get there

From Wolsingham on A689, turn S on to minor road to Bedburn and Hamsterley. Cross the River Wear bridge and when road bends left at the top, turn right onto a narrow lane leading to St John's Hall.

This continues southwards, passing the hall, which stands behind a sheep pasture on right, after 1.5 miles. Lane ends soon afterwards at gated start of path across Pikeston Fell and just beyond Blackburn Lodge, a house on left. Verge just before gate has space for four cars.

Path heads south over fell for 0.5 miles to Doctor's Gate. Beyond there path continues straight on for a mile to Hamsterley Forest's Ayhope Beck section. Also paths cross the route from east rising 1.5 miles from the Bedburn road via West Moor Plantation's southern edge and Cabin Hill. This path continues NW across fell from Doctor's Gate path and I usually head along it.

After more than a mile, paths cross between some

grouse-shooting butts and disused mineworkings. Turn left, heading SW, this path leading into North Grain Beck valley.

On reaching Meeting of the Grains, you can begin second part of an attractive circular route by heading eastwards along Ayhope Beck's southern side. This runs to Potato Hill, Hamsterley Forest, where you turn left to cross beck and continue north back to Doctor's Gate and St John's Hall.

Path south of Ayhope Beck also provides approach to North and South Grain Becks from paths starting from Low Redford and The Grove in forest.

Key points (Hamsterley Common)

- **Descent from fell into North Grain Beck valley and climb from Ayhope Beck are steep. Also two beck crossings along route.**

- **Nearest public toilets at Wolsingham, and at visitor centre at forest's east end.**

- **A few shops, takeaways, cafes and pubs at Wolsingham.**

birds. This is particularly the case with the medieval shield-shaped spur of land – older maps actually name it Ayhope Shield – lying between the North and South Grain Becks as they come together to form the Ayhope Burn.

It figures on all the routes I suggest, and you should find that time spent exploring the lower reaches of the beck valleys, which still have traces of the ancient woodland, is rarely wasted. Indeed, in my experience, this place tends to provide the highlights of an April-July outing.

Expect plenty of noise from Red Grouse and waders, especially Golden Plovers, Lapwings and Curlews, but Snipe and Redshanks too, as you follow the moorland paths as parent birds will express their concern about proximity to nests or young. While heading south from St John's Hall to Doctor's Gate or in the Cabin Hill area, Cuckoos and Wheatears will be on show, while a Merlin may be hunting over the wider fell.

On reaching the tree and shrub cover of the North Grain Beck's final loop around the Shield, the variety of species stretches to include Redstart, Mistle Thrush, Willow Warbler, Spotted Flycatcher and Lesser Redpoll. The more rugged South Grain Beck valley will probably host a Ring Ouzel family. Both Whinchats and Stonechats may be nesting among bracken by the becks and burn.

In sharp contrast, a limited species spectrum is in prospect over the moors at the opposite end of the year. Once, little more than Red Grouse could be expected, but now a Buzzard is always likely and a Peregrine is possible too.

For persistent and patient searchers, there can be rare special rewards: Rough-legged Buzzard has occurred along the South Grain; for me it was the two ringtail Hen Harriers that drifted over the Ayhope valley, landing on rocks on the Common one December afternoon. A regular feature as dusk approaches is the sight of Fieldfare flocks flying in from feeding areas to roost in the nearby forest.

If starting from the north in late spring, don't hurry past St John's Hall to the parking place. That's because its grounds are one of County Durham's most reliable Cuckoo sites; every time I've stopped in recent years, one or two – and three on one occasion – have been perched on the telegraph wires running across the sheep paddock between the lane and the hall.

Also, it's worth strolling along the public footpath that curves through the grounds – ablaze with colourful rhododendron shrubs in late spring – and around the back of the unoccupied hall. Blackcaps, Willow Warblers, Goldcrests, Spotted Flycatchers, Coal Tits, Jays and Lesser Redpolls can be expected.

Obviously forest birds are in prospect along the early stages of the paths starting at The Grove and Low Redford. This applies to some extent to the eastern approach also as the first half mile, from the Wolsingham – Bedburn minor road, is along the southern edge of West Moor Plantation.

I've seen Siskin and Crossbill family parties feeding in the conifers and once, in May, 2005, I was surprised to find a Wood Warbler singing in totally unsuitable habitat at the start of the path.

5. Harthope Wood (NZ 106 325)

IDYLLIC oak-dominated woodland flanking the final half mile of Harthope Beck before it runs into Bedburn Beck is very productive for birds.

Coverage is a little difficult because the only public right of way is restricted to just part of the southern end. However, the open nature of the wood means it's possible to look into it from several points on Howlea Lane along this little valley's eastern edge.

Knowledge of bird song helps, of course; for instance, locating male Pied Flycatchers is relatively easy due to the combination of their distinctive ditties and showy behaviour. Also, it's not unusual for one or two to be singing quite close to the lane.

Sustained alarm calls from Robins and Great Tits may well be an indication of a Tawny Owl roosting in one of the trees.

Green and Great Spotted Woodpeckers, Blackcap, Goldcrest, Spotted Flycatcher, Long-tailed and Coal Tits, Nuthatch, Treecreeper, Jay and Bullfinch may be in this eastern fringe of the wood too. Meanwhile singing Garden

Key points (Harthope Wood)

• Park on verge at NE corner of wood (NZ 107 327) and two points further S along Howlea Lane.

• For Knitsley Fell, park off-road near start of public path (NZ 090 350).

• Section of lane and path around wood's SW corner less than a mile. Allow around two hours.

• Wheelchair access not possible.

• Circular walk around Knitsley Fell/Black Bank Plantation is about four miles (allow three hours). May be muddy in places and some steep sections on slope down to river.

How to get there

From Hamsterley village, take minor road towards Bedburn, but after half-a-mile turn right into Howlea Lane. After less than half-a-mile, lane passes entrance to large caravan site on left and then, after a sharp bend, Howlea Bridge takes it across Bedburn Beck. After a short uphill stretch passing Low Burnlea cottages on right, lane levels out and Harthope Wood is on left. There are just three places where verge is wide enough and sufficiently free of bushes to enable parking

From Wolsingham on A689, turn south onto minor road to Bedburn and Hamsterley, which crosses bridge over River Wear and then rises steeply, veering eastwards at

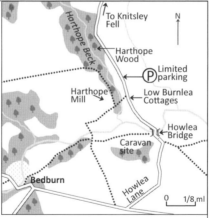

top. After another half mile, turn left into Howlea Lane on reaching a fork in road. This runs for 1.5 miles over Knitsley Fell before descending through open farmland with Harthope Wood on right after another mile. Verge by wood's start provides one of the few off-lane parking places.

and Willow Warblers are likely in the lane's hedgerows.

You can listen for Redstart song but pinpointing these vocalists is harder; as well as being adept at keeping out of sight, they tend to be in the more distant west side of the wood. As I mentioned earlier, the only public access to part of that area is the path crossing its southern end from the lane just below a couple of cottages at Low Burnlea.

This takes you across the beck – watch out for Grey Wagtails and Dippers – to ruined Harthope Mill where you may find another Pied Flycatcher singing.

On reaching the wood's far side, the path divides and the right fork runs for about 300 yards northwards along the edge of the trees before turning west across open farmland. There is a possibility of a Redstart or Tree Pipit along that stretch; once, many years ago, I found a Hawfinch on the wood's western border but the chances of such an encounter now are very slender.

Sadly, the same must be said of Wood Warbler as I haven't heard it in recent years. Fortunately, there is still plenty to enjoy; time spent listening and watching along the edge of this charming location is a worthy addition to a May dales tour.

Knitsley Fell (NZ 09 34), just over a mile north along Howlea Lane from Harthope Wood, is also worthy of attention. Not much

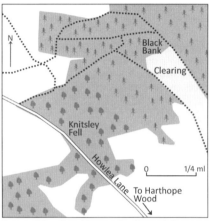

visited by birders in the past, it has gained more recognition since the 1990s, especially with the discovery that this was another site providing Nightjar opportunities.

To reach the site involves considerably less walking than Hamsterley Forest's best place, the favoured viewing site being a clearing near Black Bank Plantation's western side. This can be reached from just a few hundred yards along the public footpath running north-east from the lane at NZ 090 350.

However, be aware that recent wet, chilly summers may have had a detrimental effect on Nightjar numbers.

The plantation – mostly occupying the slope down from the fell to the River Wear – offers a bird range typical of a commercial conifer forest, including Woodcock, Tawny Owl, Goldcrest, Coal Tit, Siskin, Lesser Redpoll and Crossbill. Fell sections that are not forested benefit from hawthorn and willow scrub; the benefit of late autumn/winter checks here were shown with a Great Grey Shrike's appearance in November, 2008.

County Durham's most easterly Red Grouse occur on the fell's open moorland stretches. This area has raptor potential too, a more unusual example being a report of a Marsh Harrier on passage in August, 2001. In summer, feral Greylag Geese family parties can be seen in adjacent sheep pastures.

Key points

• **Public toilets at Wolsingham four miles NW of Harthope Wood stretch of Howlea Lane and at visitor centre at forest's east end.**

130

SAND AND GRAVEL quarrying in the mid-Wear valley brought a new habitat dimension to County Durham, which has no natural lakes. Wildlife was quick to take advantage of flooded workings and Low Barns has long been the flagship reserve of Durham Wildlife Trust (DWT). While Marston Lake is the 120-acre (48ha) site's centrepiece, the habitat range includes woodland, riverbank and more recently created reedbeds and wet grassland.

Target birds
All Year – Dipper (60%), Goosander (40%), Marsh Tit (40%), Kingfisher (30%), Willow Tit (30%). *Spring/summer* – Common Sandpiper (60%), Grey Wagtail (60%), Redstart (30%), Pied Flycatcher (30%), Osprey (10%). *Late autumn/winter* – Siskin (60%), Goosander (40%), Smew (20%), Water Rail (20%), Barn Owl (20%), Bittern (10%), Lesser Spotted Woodpecker (10%), Hawfinch (10%).

Other possible bird species

All year
Mute Swan
Feral geese
Common ducks
Little Grebe
Grey Heron
Sparrowhawk
Kestrel
Familiar gulls
Woodland birds
Stock Dove
Tawny Owl
Green Woodpecker
Great Spotted Woodpecker
Pied Wagtail
Mistle Thrush

Goldcrest
Long-tailed Tit
Coal Tit
Nuthatch
Treecreeper
Jay
Goldfinch
Linnet
Bullfinch
Reed Bunting

Spring/summer
Great Crested Grebe
Oystercatcher
Woodcock
Swift
Hirundines
Sedge Warbler

Reed Warbler
Garden Warbler
Blackcap
Lesser Whitethroat
Whitethroat
Chiffchaff
Willow Warbler
Spotted Flycatcher

Late autumn/winter
Pochard
Goldeneye
Snipe
Fieldfare
Redwing
Lesser Redpoll
Crossbill

Background information and birding tips

LOW BARNS has been a popular birding site since gravel extraction ended in 1964 and an upsurge in management work and new developments since 2000 have boosted future prospects.

Smaller islands and lake fringes have been cleared of scrub that became established over preceding decades, alienating open space-preferring wildfowl and waders that used to occur in the early years. In wooded areas, rotational coppicing is broadening habitat diversity.

This SSSI has been further invigorated by a £500,000 project, completed in 2005 which has

Key points
• Car parking charge for non-members (pay at visitor centre). More parking in small lay-by at reserve entrance.

• Site gate closed in late afternoon (DWT members are given code to open it).

• Paths network totals less than a mile-and-a-half. Allow at least two hours.

• **All paths wheelchair-accessible, as are the hides, but not visitor centre's first-floor viewing gallery.**

• **Visitor centre (open 10am-4pm daily, except over Christmas-New Year) has toilets (disabled access), and shop with food.**

Contacts
DWT Head Office
0191 584 3112; www.durhamwt.co.uk

Low Barns
01388 488 728

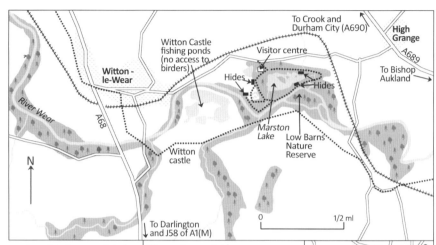

produced eight acres (3ha) of phragmites reedbed, one section on an old sewage farm site that has been added to the reserve. Now, as well as reeds, there is open water and an artificial Sand Martin nesting bank, overlooked by a large hide.

The rest of the reeds are in a marshy pool with a boardwalk created over an area cleared of alien conifers between Marston Lake and the path down the reserve's former western edge. Another new hide looks across wet pastureland on the other side of that path.

It is encouraging that Reed Warblers were noted at Low Barns in August 2006, just over a year after the project's completion and numbers have continued to increase.

Bittern was always going to

How to get there

(Five miles NW of Bishop Auckland)

Reserve is half-way along two-mile minor road between A68 (turn-off at Witton-le-Wear, 12 miles NW of J58 on A1(M) Darlington by-pass) and the A689 Bishop Auckland - Crook road (junction near High Grange three miles north-west of Bishop Auckland). Brown signs with duck logo along approach from A68.

Public transport: **Arriva 88 bus**

service (Bishop Auckland – Barnard Castle) stops at Witton-le-Wear (15 minutes walk to reserve) but only two-hourly, Mon-Sat, with last bus back to Bishop Auckland at 3pm.

be a harder target to attract but birds have been seen flying over the new beds. The total phragmites area may be too small for future breeding by these secretive herons but at least they could help Low Barns to become a more regular wintering site.

The reserve is a favourite place for catching up with summer visitors, including scarcer species such as

Redstart and Pied Flycatcher – perhaps making use of its extensive nest box accommodation or en route to breeding sites higher up the dale. It's also a reliable place for encounters with thinly-distributed wetland specialists like Kingfisher and, particularly in late autumn and winter, Water Rail.

Similarly, there's still a reasonable chance of coming

across woodland residents that in recent times have become much harder to see elsewhere, such as Marsh and Willow Tits.

There is, it should be stressed, no pattern of rarity occurrences. Records of Little Bittern, Night Heron and Cattle Egret (only the 12th for Britain) during 1976-79 gave an impression of a pace being set but it didn't continue. However, appearances by Ring-necked Duck, Wryneck and Red-rumped Swallow since 2000 emphasises a continuing ability to surprise.

Osprey is the most consistent of the scarce visitors on the site list, with sightings involving both passage and summering birds. More can perhaps be anticipated of Little Egret, Red Kite, Marsh Harrier and Hobby in future in view of the improvement in their national and regional status.

I recommend starting your visit at the feeding station beside the car park. Most birds on show can be seen while walking around the reserve, but you're unlikely to enjoy such close-up views of Nuthatch or Great Spotted Woodpecker. Sometimes Marsh Tit and Brambling come to the feeders and there have even been exceptional occasions when a comparatively rare Hawfinch has joined the feast.

It's also worth climbing the outside steel stairs to the visitor centre's first-floor gallery looking over Marston Lake's west end. While the windows aren't really suitable for telescope use, it's useful for checking through hirundines over the water in spring and diving ducks – which very occasionally include a Smew – in winter.

To the left of the path from the visitor centre to the North Hide, the Alder Wood occupies a swampy hollow where the River Wear flowed until changing course dramatically during 1771's historic November flood. The elevated path is ideal for looking into the tree canopies – a particular target during leafless winter months being Lesser Spotted Woodpecker. While this small, elusive species isn't recorded annually, it's worth spending some time seeking it among the branches and listening for its calls in early spring.

Green and Great Spotted Woodpeckers are seen regularly and, with alders predominating, this is a likely place for Siskin and Lesser Redpoll feeding flocks in winter. Marsh Tit, Nuthatch and Treecreeper are possible all year.

The North Hide overlooks a reedmace bed that hosts the occasional long-staying Bittern; it's a regular Water Rail location too. After this, the path descends gently along the rest of Marston's north side. Willow Tit may occur in adjacent saplings and shrubs and a passage or wintering Green Sandpiper can be the reward for checking mud opposite the screen hide near the lake's east end.

Subsequently the path loops westwards along the riverbank to the South Hide, a further vantage point for viewing Marston's west end waterfowl (which in April 2002 included no less than three Ring-necked Ducks, two males and a female). Often Kingfisher is seen from here, either in flight or on a branch over the water.

Another possible Kingfisher spot is a little to the west where the river forks to flow around a fairly substantial island. Scan along the south fork's bank and there's a chance of catching sight of one perched and watching for prey.

Upstream from this point are the best local prospects of Dipper and, during spring and summer, Common Sandpiper and Grey Wagtail. The slower moving water above the weir across the river near the reserve's south-west corner may offer Goosander and Grey Heron, which are also Marston Lake regulars.

A TOTAL OF 94 young Red Kites released in the valley during 2004-06 was one of the later programmes to reintroduce the species to England, Scotland and Northern Ireland. Now, with a breeding population established, these elegant raptors can be seen widely, further enhancing the already impressive birding potential of this well-wooded area which also has a significant wetland site.

Target birds *All year* – **Red Kite (70%), Siskin (60%), Buzzard (50%), Marsh Tit (50%), Willow Tit (50%), Water Rail (40%), Kingfisher (40%), Common Crossbill (30%)**. *Spring/ summer* – **Grasshopper Warbler (50%), Reed Warbler (50%), Little Egret (30%), Garganey (30%), Redstart (30%), Tree Pipit (30%)**. *Late autumn/winter* – **Mediterranean Gull (30%), Iceland Gull (20%), Glaucous Gull (20%)**.

Other possible bird species

All year
Common waterfowl
Shoveler
Pochard
Goosander
Grey Partridge
Cormorant
Grey Heron
Sparrowhawk
Kestrel
Lapwing
Curlew
Snipe
Woodcock
Familiar gulls
Common woodland/farmland birds
Stock Dove
Little Owl
Tawny Owl
Green Woodpecker
Great Spotted Woodpecker
Jay
Goldcrest
Coal Tit
Long-tailed Tit

Nuthatch
Treecreeper
Dipper
Mistle Thrush
Grey Wagtail
Pied Wagtail
Goldfinch
Linnet
Lesser Redpoll
Bullfinch
Yellowhammer
Reed Bunting

Spring to early autumn passage
Little Ringed Plover
Ruff
Black-tailed Godwit
Greenshank
Common Sandpiper
Lesser Black-backed Gull
Common Tern
Cuckoo
Swift
Hirundines
Chiffchaff
Willow Warbler
Blackcap

Garden Warbler
Lesser Whitethroat
Whitethroat
Sedge Warbler
Spotted Flycatcher
Whinchat
Wheatear
Pied Flycatcher
Tree Sparrow

Autumn/winter
Whooper Swan
Pink-footed Goose
Barnacle Goose
Shelduck
Wigeon
Gadwall
Golden Plover
Jack Snipe
Green Sandpiper
Barn Owl
Fieldfare
Redwing
Brambling

Background information and birding tips

THE DERWENT WALK brings countryside close to the heart of the Tyneside conurbation. This 11 miles of converted former railway, stretching to the Pennine fringes, is a popular haunt of ramblers, long-distance runners, horse riders and especially cyclists.

It also offers much to birdwatchers. The most northerly stretch of the route passes through the 435 acre (174ha) Derwent Walk

Key

1   Chopwell Wood
2   Far Pasture Nature Reserve
3   Shibdon Pond Reserve
4   Thornley Woodlands Centre

Country Park which includes areas of mature oak woodland. Extending from Swalwell to Rowlands Gill, it is owned and managed by Gateshead Council and has direct links with, or is close to, several sites of birding interest. From west to east they include:

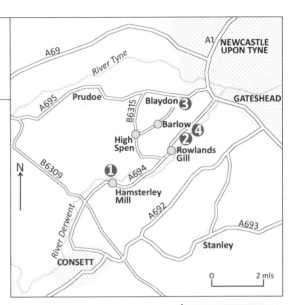

1. Chopwell Wood (NZ 139 589)

WHILE THE North-East has bigger and, more bird-rich conifer concentrations, these 900 acres (360ha) managed by the Forestry Commission have one advantage. They're much nearer the region's biggest population centre, a significant factor on short winter days.

Only very occasionally does Chopwell figure in notable national bird reports. The most recent example was during Britain's major influx of Parrot Crossbills during autumn 1990. The wood attracted one of the irruption's biggest flocks – at least 27 – which lingered for five weeks from mid-November.

Nowadays Common Crossbill is one of the species most sought by visiting birders. Numbers vary, depending on the state of the conifer cone seed food supply, but a search of trails radiating from the central road is usually rewarded, even if just with a brief view of a small fly-over party.

Though pines dominate the plantations, larch occurs in places and there are stands of alder and birch. These may well hold a flock of Siskins, with Goldfinches possibly present as well.

You may encounter Lesser Redpolls and Bullfinches along the trails too and in past times Hawfinch would have been another possibility. The latter may still occur in the valley but the odds in favour of coming across it are low.

Key points (Chopwell Wood)

• Main car parks at NZ 137 586 and NZ 132 580. Smaller parking spaces further along road.

• Alternatively, park off A694 at Lintzford, a mile SW of Rowlands Gill, and take public footpath (NZ 149 572) entering wood's SE corner after 0.3 mile. This path is unsuitable for wheelchairs.

135

Key points
(Chopwell Wood)

• **Always open – and free. Trails mostly firm-surfaced and suitable for wheelchairs but some stretches can be muddy.**

• **Some uphill sections at southern end and not suitable for wheelchairs**

• **It's unlikely you'll walk more than 3-4 miles. Allow 2-3 hours.**

• **Nearest toilets: Thornley Woodlands Centre (see centre account).**

Woodcock, Tawny Owl, Green and Great Spotted Woodpeckers, Goldcrest, Coal Tit, Treecreeper and Jay are among Chopwell's other resident bird species. Grey Wagtail, Dipper and, in summer, Common Sandpiper can be found along the stretch of the Derwent skirting the wood's southern edge.

In springtime there's a chance of Redstart in the remains of an old oakwood by the river and possibly Tree Pipit along clearing fringes but both are more likely higher up the valley.

Sparrowhawk is the raptor most frequently seen along the trails. Red Kite and Buzzard fly overhead regularly but sightings are liable to be brief due to the restricted field of view

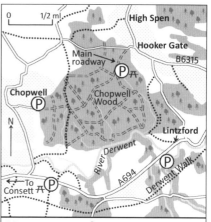

How to get there

(10 miles from Newcastle town centre)

From the A694 at Rowlands Gill turn on to B6315. Head W for two miles to Hookergate where there's a double bend followed by a signposted left turn into Chopwell Wood.

Public transport: Buses between Rowlands Gill and High Spen stop at Hookergate (where wood's central road begins). Also Newcastle-Consett Red Kite buses stop at Lintzford near wood's southern access.

while walking between tall conifer stands. In 2010, an Osprey was reported in April and there was an account of a Hobby pursuing hirundines on the wood's eastern side in mid-June.

2. Far Pasture Nature Reserve (NZ 173 593)

FINDING THIS POPULAR Gateshead Council-managed reserve can be a headache for first-time visitors because the A694 turn-off to the very minor road leading to the secluded site isn't particularly obvious.

However, once you've located the junction (first-on-the-left if driving from Thornley Woodland Centre) the rest is fairly simple. The lane descends to the valley floor, via an

old railway bridge over the Derwent Walk, and ends at a sewage works. However, first there's a large, grassy field on the left and to the right the reserve's small car park.

Nearby a spacious hide – opened in 2000 by Bill Oddie – provides all-round views of a six acre (2.4ha) pool and its islands. The pool has a woodland background, there is extensive scrub on the banks and reedmace, phragmites and rushes rise from the shallows. Its wildfowl range isn't extensive and numbers are low, but there are occasional Shoveler and Garganey reports and a Green-winged Teal lingered in February 2006.

Waders tend to be limited to a few Snipe and the odd winter-visiting Jack Snipe and Green Sandpiper. However, watchers prepared for a long sit can be rewarded with Water Rail and Kingfisher and sometimes an otter swims into view.

Woodland species that may be seen or heard include Woodcock, Tawny Owl, Green Woodpecker, Goldcrest, Willow Tit, Jay and Bullfinch. Sedge Warbler is prominent in reeds and waterside bushes during spring/summer when Grasshopper Warbler is usually present also. Now and again a Reed Warbler is reported,

raising hopes of breeding.

More unusual passage birds include Red-rumped Swallow (April), Marsh Warbler (June) and Common Rosefinch (June and September). A Firecrest discovered in the hedge by the sewage works in February 2010, remained through March. Another was ther in early 2012.

Spring and autumn migration can also lead to Osprey sightings, with several records over the past two decades and a Montagu's Harrier passed over one May. Far Pasture is a noted dragonfly site, raising the possibility of a hunting Hobby in late summer.

The raptor seen most frequently through the year is, of course, Red Kite; the lane leading to the reserve is an ideal spot for witnessing pre-roost assemblies over the Gibside Estate woodlands across the river.

Key points (Far Pasture)

- Car parking (NZ 172 592) at foot of minor road branching from A694 at Lockhaugh.

- Hide can be visited at any time with key from Thornley Woodlands Centre (see centre account for details). Fully wheelchair accessible.

- Enjoy an hour or two in the hide – though you may have to wait longer for Water Rail or Kingfisher sightings

- Nearest toilets: Thornley Woodlands Centre (see centre account).

- A few shops/pubs at Rowlands Gill.

How to get there

(9 miles from Newcastle town centre)

Turn-off to Far Pasture from A694 is first on left (signposted Derwent Walk Country Park and Lockhaugh Farm) south of Thornley Woodlands Centre (distance: 0.75 mile). After bridge over Derwent Walk, turn right at T-junction (signposted Far Pasture). Car park is less than a 0.25 mile further, on right.

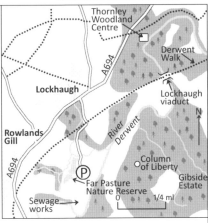

Public transport: Red Kite Buses to Consett from Eldon Square, Newcastle, stop near turn-off to Far Pasture.

Key points
(Shibdon Pond)

• Park at Blaydon Swimming Pool off B6317 immediately SW of reserve (NZ 192 627).

• View pool at any time – reserve paths always open. Some stretches may be muddy. Hide keys available at Thornley Woodlands Centre (see centre account).

• Allow at least 2-3 hours to walk trails (they add up to two miles) and watch from hide.

• Bikes, wheelchairs and mobility scooters can be hired at Swalwell Centre (for use in country park and along Derwent Walk)

• Local wildlife info on Gateshead Birders' website - www. gatesheadbirders. co.uk

3. Shibdon Pond Nature Reserve (NZ 195 628)

IRONICALLY, the valley's most productive birding site is where prospects might appear nil – beside the otherwise development-flanked A1 Gateshead Western Bypass. Industrial estates occupy the space between the dual carriageway and the River Tyne, across which is the western end of Newcastle's sprawl. Nearby is the crowd-pulling MetroCentre out-of-town shopping mall.

Shibdon Pond reserve, a Site of Special Scientific Interest, consists of a ten-acre (4ha) pool and 25 acres (10ha) of adjoining land, including scrub and marsh, with a nature trail. It is on the site of a former colliery and the pool, created by mining subsidence, is fed by spring water rising from old underground workings.

With an outflow channel to the Tyne, water levels can be controlled, which enables the continued provision of habitat for passage waders.

The reserve – managed by Durham Wildlife Trust on behalf of Gateshead Borough Council – was in good form during the 2010 summer. Up to five Little Egrets – still unusual on Tyneside – were on show in late July/early August but during the next month the main focus was on a much scarcer Spotted Crake, Shibdon's first since 1991.

Other species recorded included Garganey, Water Rail, Spotted Redshank, Greenshank, Green Sandpiper, Mediterranean Gull and Kingfisher.

Sand Martin and Chiffchaff can be expected in March, with possibly a three-figure presence of the former plus a few Swallows by early April. The reserve provides a stop-over for summer visitors, such as Cuckoo, Tree Pipit, Spotted Flycatcher and Redstart, perhaps making for higher up the valley.

Autumn is better for waders but Little Ringed Plover and Common Sandpiper may appear in spring. A fly-over Osprey is always possible and there can be late spring surprises along the nature trail, with May/June records of Wryneck, Marsh Warbler, Icterine Warbler and Golden Oriole.

Up to nine warbler species may hold territory if Grasshopper Warbler and Lesser Whitethroat join the more regular range in the woods, scrub and marsh. The habitat is well suited to Sedge Warblers and there is a sufficient phragmites spread to support a few Reed Warbler pairs.

Floating platforms have helped a Common Tern colony to become established; they arrive usually in May, a month when Black Terns may linger briefly en route to Baltic regions. A Black

How to get there

(6 miles from Gateshead centre)

Turn off A1 Gateshead Western Bypass less than 0.5 mile beyond MetroCentre into Swalwell, then right at roundabout and right soon afterwards on to B6317 to Blaydon. After passing rugby ground go straight on at A694 crossroads roundabout, continuing for 0.5 mile. After pond appears on right - park at Blaydon Swimming Pool

If driving from north on A1, turn off onto first slip road beyond bridge over River Tyne (0.75 mile). Go right at roundabout on to A694 and after this passes under A1 turn right at crossroads roundabout on to B6317 to Blaydon, then same as above.

Public transport: Regular bus services to Blaydon from Newcastle and Gateshead.

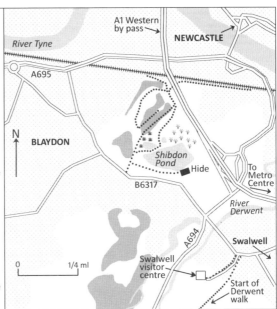

Tern, typically a juvenile, may stay longer during return passage in August. At this time more wader variety can be anticipated, with Ruff, Black-tailed Godwit and Greenshank the more regular.

Warm weather can spark dragonfly activity over the marsh – which, in turn, can arouse the interest of a passing migrant Hobby. Out-of-the-ordinary autumn migrants have included Bee-eater and Barred Warbler (August), Bluethroat and Red-backed Shrike (September) and Pallas's Warbler (October).

Autumn/winter has always been Shibdon's prime period for wildfowl and it remains well stocked with Teal, with up to 370 counted in recent years, but the numbers of some species are much lower than in the past.

Shoveler maxima have been only half the 30-50 logged regularly during the 1980s-90s but diving duck declines have been even more acute, possibly due to the silting-up of the pool. Fewer than ten Pochard and between 20 and 40 Tufted Ducks compare with as many as 400-plus of each in the 1980s.

Garganeys, scarce spring/ autumn passage visitors, have nested on the reserve, as have Shoveler and Pochard, which are also nationally rare breeding species. Small numbers of Shelduck, Wigeon, Gadwall, Goldeneye and Goosander occur at various times. Green-winged

Key points
(Shibdon Pond)

• **Nearest toilets at Swalwell Visitor Centre (open 10am - 5pm daily and spring/summer Bank Holidays). Turn off B6317 at Blaydon rugby ground (0.75 mile SE of reserve), following Derwent Walk Country Park signs (NZ 197 620). Tel 0191 414 2106.**

Teal has been the only comparative rarity since the 1990s.

Autumn brings the prospect of fly-over goose skeins – Barnacles following the Tyne westwards to the Solway Firth (late September/early October) and Pinkfoots heading south. Whooper Swans pass over too and sometimes a party spends a few days on the reserve.

Winter gull gatherings are always worth checking as Mediterranean and Iceland Gulls appear with some regularity and, to a lesser extent, Glaucous too. Yellow-legged Gull is another possibility, though there've been few accepted records in recent years.

An outstanding past rarity was the Laughing Gull on Tyneside during 1984-1987; it was discovered initially at Shibdon and made several return visits. Notable too was the Ring-billed Gull seen intermittently one mid-1990s autumn/winter.

Peregrines hunt occasionally in autumn/winter and there has been the odd report of a Goshawk doing likewise. Over those months Water Rail and Kingfisher, which occur all year, tend to be well reported.

Up to 200 Redshanks may roost and Snipe are on show too, but not as many as in the past. Other waders present include Jack Snipe and Green Sandpiper and there's a chance of Woodcock sightings around the nature trail. Goldfinch, Siskin and Lesser Redpoll feeding flocks are likely and Waxwing parties may appear during an irruption year. Long-eared Owls sometimes roost in the scrub.

4. Thornley Woodlands Centre (NZ 178 604)

Key points (Thornley)

• Park at centre (NZ 178 604) off A694 between Winlaton Mill and Rowlands Gill.

• Centre (open 12 noon - 2pm weekdays, 12noon - 5pm weekends/Bank Holidays) offers booklets and leaflets about area and local wildlife news. Also toilets.

THORNLEY makes an ideal starting point for first-time visitors to the valley. The visitor centre provides information about wildlife and footpaths in the area and, for £5, you can obtain a key for access to hides at the various Gateshead reserves. Also, it's in one of the area's most bird-rich woodlands.

The centre is on the left of the A694, off a long uphill stretch, half a mile south of Winlaton Mill. From it, paths lead to the Derwent Walk, into the Paddock Hill woodland and into Thornley Wood Country Park across the A694.

The country park's top winter attraction is an excellent wild bird feeding station overlooked by one of the hides for which keys are needed. Species regularly seen there include Stock Dove, Great Spotted Woodpecker, Long-tailed, Marsh and Coal Tits, Nuthatch, Treecreeper, Jay, Brambling, Siskin, Bullfinch and Yellowhammer.

During the breeding season these species may be encountered along the extensive paths network – along with a wide range of summer visitors, though not as many as in former times. Up to the early 1990s, Tree Pipit, Redstart, Wood Warbler and Pied Flycatcher song could be heard regularly but now this quartet is seen normally seen only as passage visitors heading for locations higher up the valley.

Spotted Flycatcher still occurs but is scarcer than in former times.

This isn't a location with a rare bird history but there was a memorable occasion when a Lesser Spotted Woodpecker foraged obligingly in trees near the visitor centre – inadvertently co-operative behaviour much appreciated by birders.

One of the North-East's scarcest woodland residents, the LSW continues to be hard to locate but Lower Derwent Valley woodlands are among the likelier places for a lucky encounter.

Red Kites nest relatively close to the visitor centre and are often seen over the woods. Paths from the centre linking with the Derwent Walk provide views across the valley to the Gibside Estate woods, a main kite roost site during autumn/winter. Spectacular pre-dusk aerial gatherings of 40-plus have been seen in early 2012.

Key points
(Thornley)

• **Paths network always open. Several miles of trails in woods on both sides of A694 and your visit could easily run to 3-4 hours.**

• Some stretches may be muddy and there are steep flights of steps in places.

• Wheelchair users can reach the visitor centre and flat paths from Winlanton Mill car park.

• Key to enter six Gateshead reserve hides (including Thornley Wood's) can be bought (£5) at centre.

• A few shops/pubs at nearby Rowlands Gill and Winlaton Mill.

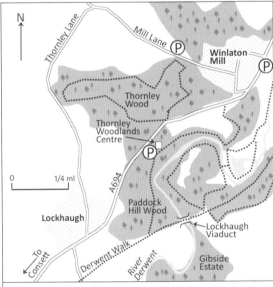

How to get there
(Eight miles from Newcastle centre)

Centre (signposted) is by A694 midway between Rowlands Gill and Winlaton Mill and three miles south of A694/B6317 roundabout near Blaydon.

Public transport: Red Kite buses from Newcastle's Eldon Square to Consett stop there. Also centre has direct link (walkers only) with Derwent Walk

Key points

• **Off-road parking space for two or three cars on narrow minor road between Healeyfield Lane and Muggleswick: in the Coalgate Gorge (NZ 061 488); above it (NZ 056 486); and above the Derwent Gorge at NZ 054 487.**

• **Derwent Gorge and Muggleswick Woods NNR closed to public – view from minor road and public footpaths.**

• **Footpath (0.75 miles) along the Coalgate Burn's southern rim reaches Goldhill Lane, another minor road between Healeyside Lane and Muggleswick. It is boggy in places.**

ALL SECTIONS of the Derwent Valley offer something to birders but this stretch below the Derwent Reservoir dam has particular plus points. The river – more of a large burn at this point – twists and turns through a landscape that hasn't changed much over the centuries. It rushes through a narrow ravine, with remnants of ancient woodland clinging to the steep side before joining the Coalgate Burn. These two neighbouring gorges have long been a top County Durham location for the classic range of Dales summer visitors.

Target birds
All year – Buzzard (70%), Lesser Redpoll (70%). *Spring/summer* – Cuckoo (60%), Redstart (60%), Tree Pipit (50%), Spotted Flycatcher (50%), Pied Flycatcher (50%), Wood Warbler (30%), Marsh Tit (30%).

Other possible bird species

All year
(*indicates species just on nearby moorlands)*
Mallard
*Red Grouse
Red-legged Partridge
Grey Partridge
Grey Heron
Kestrel
Black-headed Gull
Common Gull
Stock Dove
Common farmland/woodland birds
Tawny Owl
Kingfisher
Green Woodpecker
Great Spotted Woodpecker
Grey Wagtail

Pied Wagtail
Dipper
Song Thrush
Mistle Thrush
Goldcrest
Long-tailed Tit
Coal Tit
Nuthatch
Treecreeper
Jay
Greenfinch
Goldfinch
Siskin
Linnet
Bullfinch
Yellowhammer
Reed Bunting.

Spring/summer
Goosander
Oystercatcher

*Golden Plover
Lapwing
*Snipe
Woodcock
Curlew
*Redshank
Common Sandpiper
Swift
Sand Martin
Swallow
House Martin
Skylark
Meadow Pipit
*Wheatear
Blackcap
Garden Warbler
Whitethroat
Chiffchaff
Willow Warbler

Background information and birding tips

THOUGH three small reservoirs and moorland to the south-west provide limited wildfowl and raptor potential during autumn and winter months and this site's species list includes many year-round residents, a birding trip outside spring and early summer is likely to be disappointing.

The altitude and exposed position means that anyone visiting the woods around the Coalgate/Derwent confluence too early in spring is likely to be frustrated. In the first half of April, they resemble the county's

142

How to get there

(Approx four miles W of Consett)

The gorges are two miles west of the A68, which runs north-west from J58 on the A1(M) by-pass of Darlington into Scotland. There are three routes to the gorges from the A68.

In Castleside, cross the A68 onto a minor road (signposted Stanhope) which is initially Church Street (church on right) and then, beyond the village, becomes Healeyfield Lane. Soon after Healeyfield Farm on left comes the right turn (signposted Muggleswick and Edmundbyers) to the gorges. If walking to gorges from there, park on verge by wooden seat at junction.

If travelling north on A68, turn left at the Rowley crossroads onto lane signposted to Stanhope, Muggleswick and Healeyfield (a mile south of Castleside). This lane joins Healeyfield Lane west of Castleside. The rest of the route is as above. From Durham City turn left off A691 at Lanchester onto B6296 heading south-west. After three miles as the road bends left, turn onto the middle of three lanes branching right. This is Longedge Lane running north-west for 3.5 miles to the

A68 Rowley crossroads.

If driving south on A68, turn right at Carterway Heads (eight miles S of the A69 junction in Tyne valley) onto B6278 to Stanhope. After 0.75 miles, turn left into a lane to Muggleswick. Half a mile south take left fork and continue for a further half mile past a right hand turn. As the lane bends right after a further 250 yards, the small parking space above the Derwent Gorge is on the left.

Public transport: Buses run to Castleside from Consett, which has service links with Newcastle,

Durham City and Sunderland. From there it is 0.75 miles walk along Church Street/Healeyside Lane to the gorges turning. The gorges are just a mile north-west of the Coast-to-Coast cycle route.

lower woods much further east in late February.

However, unless we're experiencing a prolonged cold spell, they start to come alive generally during the final days of April. To be on the safe side I rarely go there

until the first week of May; even then many trees are likely to be still in the early stages of unfurling their leaves.

This can benefit birders as by then the target species such as Tree Pipit, Redstart,

Wood Warbler and Pied Flycatcher are all likely to be singing and therefore much easier to locate. Finding them once the leaf canopies become fully established during the second half of May is much harder, so it's

143

Key points

• Footpath running south from Coalgate Burn footbridge to Healeyside Lane (just over a mile) worth exploring.

• Allow at least three hours for a visit – longer if you plan comprehensive coverage of this area's lanes and footpaths.

• Gradients as the Healeyfield Lane to Muggleswick road negotiates the Coalgate Burn gorge are among the North-East's steepest, with tortuous hairpin bends.

• The Moorcock Inn (NZ050467) off Healeyfield Lane and between Smiddyshaw Reservoir and the Honey Hill Water Treatment Works offers the immediate area's only facilities.

necessary to use this narrow window of opportunity to be sure of maximum satisfaction. It is also vital to make the most of the restricted access to the woodland because much of it is officially out-of-bounds.

The first information displayed about the Derwent Gorge and Muggleswick Woods National Nature Reserve link on the Natural England website is that the 71 hectare (almost 180 acres) NNR is "currently closed to the public." This, it explains, is because either: the site is unsafe; or Natural England's tenure doesn't allow public access; or the site is so fragile that any form of access would damage the wildlife interest.

This sound positively discouraging but, actually, much can be enjoyed from the area's minor roads and public footpaths network. Indeed, during 2001's Foot and Mouth Disease crisis all local footpaths had been closed but I still managed Pied Flycatcher and Wood Warbler encounters along the road from Healeyfield Lane (branching west from the A68 at Castleside) to Muggleswick hamlet.

Only just wide enough for vehicles to pass, this road dips down, via a series of hairpin bends, to cross the Coalgate Burn, then rises equally sharply up its north bank and runs for several hundred yards along the ravine's top. Subsequently it skirts along the Derwent Gorge's southern

end before veering away north-westwards.

With nowhere to park until the Coalgate Burn gorge bottom, it's worth leaving the car at the Healeyfield Lane/Muggleswick road junction and descend on foot if you have the time and inclination for a long walk. Flanking the lane are oakwoods, which may hold Wood Warbler and Pied Flycatcher.

Where it bends into the valley of the Horsleyhope Burn (which joins the Coalgate at the bottom) there's a view across birch scrub over which Tree Pipits perform song flights. From the gorge bottom the road zigzags up to the top where you may hear Redstart in trees and shrubs bordering the sheep pasture to the right of the lane and Pied Flycatcher singing in oaks clinging to the precipitous ravine bank on its left side.

After the road bends north-westwards from that ravine, the Derwent Gorge's woodland begins on the right. In the past I've seen both Wood Warbler and Pied Flycatcher in these trees but not in recent years. Both still occur in the gorge, but deeper into the NNR where, as explained earlier, there's no public access.

At the road's next bend use a small off-road parking area. Walk through a gate onto an old forestry track into a riverbank conifer plantation below the broad-leafed woodland of the gorge's western slope. After just a few paces you'll see the Natural England notice board diverting the public to steps down to a footbridge over the river into Northumberland on the opposite bank.

Actually there is value in lingering a while on the footbridge – possible glimpses of Goosander, Common Sandpiper, Kingfisher, Grey Wagtail and Dipper along the river. Across it, after passing through the grounds of an isolated cottage, the public path becomes a driveable unsurfaced track through woodland occupying a peninsula left by the river looping acutely northwards.

Redstarts, Blackcaps, Garden and Willow Warblers are among species to be anticipated here but soon the track leads into open farmland. At this point I usually backtrack to the minor road above the gorge where a stile leads to another birding option. This is a public footpath dropping to a footbridge over the Coalgate Burn before it flows through its gorge. Subsequently the path rises through birch scrub filled with Willow Warbler song, before levelling-out along the southern rim of the burn's valley.

To the south is a mature birchwood where Tree Pipit and Redstart song can be heard. Sometimes a Tree Pipit launches into its song flight from tall conifers further along the path; the rhythmic calls of Lesser Redpolls on the wing are likely here also.

A Cuckoo's voice may carry from pastures west of the mature birchwood or from moorland to the north-west. Buzzard soars regularly over this area and, with Red Kite successfully re-established not too far away in the Lower Derwent valley, this graceful raptor could glide into view too.

Stock Dove, Green and Great Spotted Woodpeckers, Marsh Tit, Nuthatch, Treecreeper, Jay and Bullfinch occur in these outstanding woodlands. Also, moors to the west are at their liveliest at this time of year; Red Grouse, upland-breeding waders, Cuckoo, Skylark, Meadow Pipit and Wheatear can be anticipated from public footpaths crossing them.

Key points

• **Further afield is the Punch Bowl, at Edmundbyers, two miles west of Muggleswick. More pubs and also a few shops at Castleside on A68.**

• **Nearest public toilets: Derwent Reservoir's east end (two miles N of Muggleswick); Allensford Country Park (where A68 crosses River Derwent north of Castleside). More at Carrick's Haugh picnic site at reservoir's west end (six miles west of Muggleswick) and Blanchland village (two miles further west).**

THE SEVEN MILES of coastline between the mouths of the Rivers Tyne and Wear offer exceptional birding opportunities. Several sites are noted for migrants, including outstanding rarities, that appear, especially during autumn. Also, there is first-rate seawatching potential, foreshore habitat that supports a wide range of overwintering waders and spectacular cliffs that house thousands of nesting seabirds in summer.

Target birds

Spring/early summer – Firecrest (30%), Red-backed Shrike (30%), Icterine Warbler (20%), Marsh Warbler (10%).

Late summer/autumn – Roseate Tern (80%), Sooty Shearwater (70%), Curlew Sandpiper, Mediterranean Gull, Black Redstart, Yellow-browed Warbler (all 60%), Pomarine Skua, Barred Warbler, Firecrest (all 40%), Red-necked Grebe, Balearic Shearwater, Wryneck, Richard's Pipit, Greenish Warbler, Pallas's Warbler, Red-backed Shrike (all 30%), European Storm-petrel, Long-tailed Skua, Sabine's Gull (all 20%), Cory's Shearwater (10%).

Late autumn/winter – Mediterranean Gull (60%), Snow Bunting (50%), Iceland Gull, Glaucous Gull, Little Auk, Lapland Bunting (all 40%), Great Northern Diver (30%), Water Pipit (30%), Black-throated Diver (20%), Slavonian Grebe (10%).

Other possible bird species

All year
Mute Swan
Mallard
Tufted Duck
Eider
Common Scoter
Grey Partridge
Red-throated Diver
Fulmar
Gannet
Cormorant
Shag
Grey Heron
Sparrowhawk
Kestrel
Moorhen
Coot
Familiar gulls
Common farmland/woodland/garden birds
Oystercatcher
Ringed Plover
Guillemot
Little Owl
Tawny Owl

Great Spotted Woodpecker
Skylark
Meadow Pipit
Rock Pipit
Pied Wagtail
Stonechat
Mistle Thrush
Tree Sparrow
Goldfinch
Linnet
Yellowhammer
Reed Bunting

Spring/early summer
Manx Shearwater
Lapwing
Sanderling
Dunlin
Whimbrel
Redshank
Turnstone
Arctic Skua
Great Skua
Little Tern
Sandwich Tern

Common Tern
Arctic Tern
Guillemot
Razorbill
Puffin
Swift
Sand Martin
Swallow
House Martin
Tree Pipit
Yellow Wagtail
White Wagtail
Whinchat
Wheatear
Ring Ouzel
Grasshopper Warbler
Blackcap
Lesser Whitethroat
Whitethroat
Chiffchaff
Willow Warbler
Spotted Flycatcher
Pied Flycatcher

Late summer/mid-autumn
Brent Goose
Barnacle Goose (on passage usually Sept 25 – Oct 10)
Shelduck
Common wildfowl
Scaup
Long-tailed Duck
Velvet Scoter
Goldeneye
Red-breasted Merganser
Goosander
Manx Shearwater
Merlin
Peregrine
Golden Plover
Grey Plover
Lapwing
Knot
Sanderling
Dunlin
Snipe
Woodcock

Black-tailed Godwit	Tree Pipit	Pintail	Redshank
Bar-tailed Godwit	Grey Wagtail	Shoveler	Turnstone
Whimbrel	Redstart	Scaup	Arctic and Great Skua
Curlew	Whinchat	Long-tailed Duck	Little Gull
Greenshank	Wheatear	Velvet Scoter	Razorbill
Redshank	Fieldfare	Goldeneye	Long-eared Owl
Common Sandpiper	Redwing	Red-breasted Merganser	Short-eared Owl
Turnstone	Migrant warblers	Goosander	Kingfisher
Arctic Skua	Spotted Flycatcher	Great Crested Grebe	Grey Wagtail
Great Skua	Pied Flycatcher	Merlin	Waxwing
Little Gull	Long-tailed Tit	Peregrine	Fieldfare
Black Tern	Coal Tit	Water Rail	Redwing
Sandwich Tern	Brambling	Golden and Grey Plovers	Blackcap
Common Tern	Siskin	Lapwing	Chiffchaff
Arctic Tern	Lesser Redpoll	Knot	Long-tailed Tit
Razorbill	*Late autumn/winter*	Sanderling	Coal Tit
Puffin	Whooper Swan	Purple Sandpiper	Brambling
Cuckoo	Pink-footed Goose	Dunlin	Siskin
Long-eared Owl	Brent Goose	Jack Snipe	Lesser Redpoll
Short-eared Owl	Shelduck	Snipe	
Sand Martin	Wigeon	Woodcock	
Swallow	Gadwall	Bar-tailed Godwit	
House Martin	Teal	Curlew	

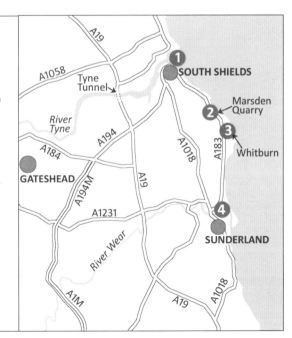

How to get there

Reach all sites by A183 Sunderland-to-South Shields coast road.

Approach from A1(M): leave at J65, heading for South Shields on A194(M)/A194, then turn right on to A1300; follow Coast signs until reaching A183; turn left for Trow Quarry (one mile) and sea front parks (two miles).

From A19, turn on to A194 south of Tyne Tunnel after which as above.

Public transport: **E1 bus service (Sunderland - South Shields) stops along A183 by leas and parks.**

Metro rail service runs direct to South Shields from Newcastle .

From Sunderland, change at Pelaw Metro station for South Shields).

147

Key points
(South Shields)

• Free parking on A183 (nearest point to Trow Quarry at NZ 384 662). For seafront parks, use Beach Road and Bents Park Road (NZ 37 67).

• Up to three miles walking in quarry/leas area. Parks/pier coverage could total two miles. Allow 2–3hrs for each.

Background information and birding tips

EACH SECTION of the Tyne-Wear coast has made significant contributions to its near-300 bird species list, one of the region's biggest. From north to south, they are:

1. South Shields (NZ 384 662)

BRITAIN'S first Eastern Crowned Warbler might have seemed destined for Fair Isle but instead provided jackpot-time for many birders at Trow Quarry at the northern end of the South Shields Coastal Leas.

What had been a municipal rubbish dump was landscaped into a public leisure area during the 1960s. Its maturing trees and shrubs soon started to prove attractive to migrants – with the October 2009 warbler sensation providing the ultimate endorsement.

More recent planting of bushes on a nearby mound and a new hedge across the more southerly leas now ensure Black Redstarts and Yellow-browed Warblers occur in the Trow area most years.

Other scarce species recorded include Wryneck, Firecrest, Red-breasted Flycatcher, Red-backed Shrike, Common Rosefinch and Icterine, Subalpine, Barred,

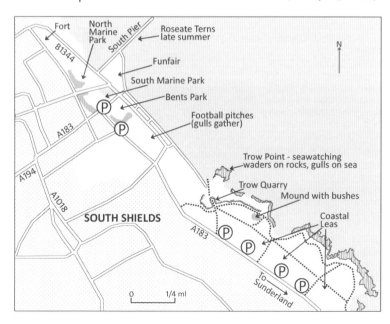

Greenish, Pallas's and Radde's Warblers.

Stretching for more than a mile, the grassland of the leas is among the North-East's more promising places for coming across Shorelarks and Richard's Pipit in autumn. Small numbers of Lapland Buntings may be present from September to the following spring, with Snow Buntings a further possibility along the clifftop between Frenchman's and Marsden Bays.

The area doesn't hold Short-eared Owls as in the past but you might expect a newly-arrived bird in autumn.

It's unusual if autumn passes without a Yellow-browed Warbler in the South Shields seafront Bents and North Marine Parks; the species has been found even in the young sycamores by the pay-and-display car park at the base of the South Pier.

Firecrest, Red-breasted Flycatcher and Greenish and Pallas's Warblers are among other scarce migrants that have made park appearances.

South Marine Park's lake is worth checking in winter. It has been visited by Ring-necked Duck, Scaup, Black-throated Diver and Little Auk and is among the Tyneside sites where Mediterranean, Iceland and Glaucous Gulls might be seen.

The Tyne's mouth has a distinguished rare gull history, peaking in the 1970's Ross's and Ivory Gull Christmas double - and there is still a chance of something unusual in flocks now. Football pitches beside Bents Park, the sea off Trow Point and the shore by the South Pier are the main assembly points.

In recent late summers, Roseate Terns have been prominent by the pier, with up to 29 adults and juveniles on the beach, on rocks at the pier's base or on the ledge along its outer wall. Late autumn/winter storms may lead to sea duck, diver, grebe or Grey Phalarope harbour appearances.

Key points
(South Shields)

• **Quarry/leas grassland and coastal path firm and generally wheelchair-accessible (except in very wet weather).**

• **Seafront park paths all hard-surfaced. Soft sand in dunes.**

• **Public toilets at several seafront points (disabled access at those by A183 at Pier Parade (NZ 373 676) and in South Marine Park. May be closed during late autumn/ winter.**

• **Coin-op autoloo (disabled access by RADAR key) at amusement park.**

2. Marsden Quarry (NZ 393 646)

A CLUSTER of birding sites on the extreme south-eastern fringe of South Shields has been performing magnificently in spring and especially autumn since the 1960s

The 48-acre (19ha) Marsden Old Quarry nature reserve extends west from Lizard Lane, with sycamores and elder-dominated scrub at its more sheltered western end. More bushes, bramble tangles and nettle beds cover one-time spoil heaps on its northern side. Nearby is Quarry Lane, a tree and scrub-flanked path

to Cleadon Park housing estate half-a-mile to the south-west.

Trees and bushes at Marsden Hall above the quarry's eastern end and at the Lizard Lane edge of Whitburn golf course are important birding areas too.

Comprehensive coverage brings rewards. The most recent were a Blyth's Reed Warbler (second for Durham) in a willow-herb patch between the A183 and Whitburn golf course's north-east section in 2010 and a Booted/

Key points
(Marsden Quarry)

• Limited parking near quarry's Lizard Lane entrance (NZ 398 646) and in Valley Lane (NZ 393 646) near NW corner.

• Coverage of all sites totals 2-3 miles. Allow 3-4hrs.

• Unsurfaced Quarry Lane and trail sections in and above quarry may be muddy. Not suitable for wheelchairs but clifftop Coastal Path is OK in fine weather

• Public toilets (closed in winter but disabled access all year) by A183 at Marsden Grotto.

• Toilets (disabled access) also at Souter Lighthouse (open 11am-5pm, weekends and Mon-Thurs, mid-March to end of October).

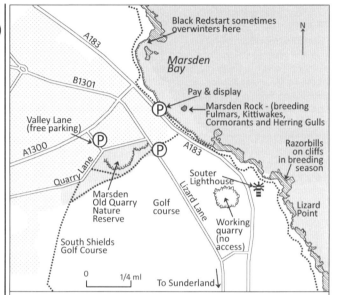

How to get there

(Six miles from Sunderland town centre)

Approach from A1(M) and A19 as for South Shields until reaching Marsden Inn roundabout on A1300. Turn right there into Lizard Lane and quarry entrance is on right after quarter-of-a-mile (just beyond houses). Alternatively, turn right from A1300 a quarter-of-a-mile before Marsden Inn into Valley Lane to park near quarry's NW corner.

Public transport: Lizard Lane is on routes of E2 and E6 bus services (Sunderland – South Shields) which stop at Whitburn golf course.

Sykes's Warbler (probably Booted but BBRC ruled much rarer Sykes's couldn't be eliminated) in Quarry Lane in 2009.

A 1999-2004 purple patch involved Durham's first Isabelline Shrike (quarry's north-west corner), the initial sighting of the county's third Pallid Swift (much-watched later over the South Shields Coastal Leas), its first Red-flanked Bluetail (south-west corner) and third Red-eyed Vireo (Quarry Lane).

Migrants occur everywhere but some species are associated with certain places. Invariably, Wryneck appears in the quarry's small bay immediately inside the Lizard Lane entrance, while Black Redstarts and Ring Ouzels tend to be along the west end's higher cliffs.

South-west corner sycamores are ideal for Pallas's and Yellow-browed Warblers (as are trees at Marsden Hall, along Quarry Lane and at the golf course's Lizard

Lane end). Richard Pipit and Ortolan and Rustic Buntings have lingered on grassland between the golf courses and Quarry Lane. Late spring Marsh and Icterine Warblers have sung in bushes at the quarry's north-west corner.

South Tyneside's most scenic spot is Marsden Bay, where breeding seabirds are spread along the bay's more southerly mainland cliffs, on 90ft (27m) high Marsden Rock and three smaller stacks. It remains spectacular, though its Kittiwakes (3,000 pairs), Cormorants (100 pairs) and Herring Gulls (50 pairs) used to be more numerous and there have been ups and downs for its Fulmars (200 pairs) too.

Razorbills (30 pairs), the most recent colonists, have maintained slow progress since young were first reared in the late 1980s.

Bay activity is lowest in winter but Fulmars are usually back by January, Razorbills by February and there are diver, grebe and sea duck possibilities offshore. Often a Mediterranean Gull is by the car park north of the Grotto pub, a Peregrine may be hunting feral pigeons along the cliffs and sometimes a Black Redstart lingers around caves at the bay's north end.

A few dozen Shags roost on narrow ledges on Marsden Rock's sheer south-eastern face. Numerous Cormorants once roosted on the top in winter but not in recent years – maybe a consequence of the landmark's famous arch collapsing in February, 1996.

3. Whitburn NZ 410 635)

V ERSATILITY gives Whitburn the birding edge over the rest of this coastline. Migrant passerines are widespread and this is a premier UK seawatching point. Also, an impressive range of raptors has been recorded over the years and the foreshore sustains thousands of waders.

The National Trust-maintained Coastal Park, created during 1989-90's £1m-plus clean-up of former colliery dereliction, is a consistent performer. Since 2000 it has scored with Durham's second Red-flanked Bluetail and Isabelline Shrike and the county's first Melodious Warbler.

At the village's southern end, the Church Lane/Cornthwaite Park area has produced two county firsts – a Blyth's Reed Warbler (2007) and a Pallas's Grasshopper Warbler (2010) – with past glories including Pallid Swift, European Bee-eater and Arctic Warbler.

Yellow-browed Warblers are likely at both sites each autumn, with Firecrest, Red-breasted Flycatcher and Icterine, Barred, Greenish and Pallas's Warblers possible too.

Other migrant-friendly Whitburn sites include the cemetery north of the small shopping centre and Jackie's Beach (small bay with

Key points
(Whitburn)

• Park at Coastal Park (NZ 410 635) or, when closed to traffic, at White Rocks Grove (NZ 409 633).

• For observatory, park in Marsden Avenue (NZ 409 631).

•Allow at least 2hrs to check for migrants in scrub areas in nature reserve.

• Whitburn Steel overlooked by Sea Lane pay/display car park (NZ 408 613) but parking free across A183 in Cornthwaite Park (NZ 407 615) – also handy for Church Lane area.

• Cornthwaite Park/Church Lane's best spots are park's NW corner, trees along its W edge and tall trees beside lane, including churchyard.

How to get there

(Two miles from Sunderland town centre)

All sites off A183 which can be joined at Sunderland from A1(M) by leaving at J64 to join A195 into Washington.

Turn left (third junction) on to A182, then leave it (second junction) to join A1231 to Sunderland. This leads on to B1289, then follow Coast signs to seafront and head north on A183 to Whitburn (two miles).

From A19, turn on to A1231 at North Hylton Bridge over River Wear (after which as above).

Public transport: E1, E2 and E6 bus services (Sunderland – South Shields) all stop at Whitburn Cricket Ground (close to Cornthwaite Park and Whitburn Steel), E1 and E2 at Whitburn Lodge (south end of Coastal Park) and E1 at Arthur Street (near CP main entrance).

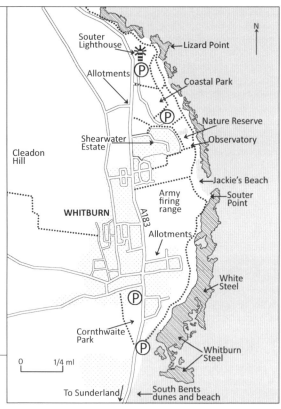

Key points
(Whitburn)

• **Coastal Path firm and wheelchair accessible, as are hard-surface paths in Cornthwaite Park/ Church Lane area. Each less than a mile (allow 1-2hrs).**

• **Steel's wader/ tern gatherings best viewed from clifftop on rising tide but beware crumbly cliff edge!**

scrub patches south of the Coastal Park).

Actually migrants may drop into any Whitburn garden with a tree and bushes; two addresses on the western edge were the locations for Durham's second Hume's Leaf Warbler and fourth Booted Warbler.

Raptors often pass over farmland or Cleadon Hill to the west at passage times – Marsh Harriers and Ospreys quite regularly, with Honey Buzzard, Red Kite, Hobby and Hen and Montagu's Harriers also logged since the 1990s.

Whitburn's seawatching observatory at the Coastal Park's south-eastern corner is well used during July-November, the peak time for seabird and wildfowl passage. Rarities since 2000 include White-billed Diver, Fea's/Zino's Petrel and Gull-billed and Caspian Terns.

More frequently-seen

species sometimes pass in huge numbers; site record day counts over the same decade include 11,000 Little Auks and 1,271 Sooty Shearwaters.

Observatory keys can be bought from the National Trust at Souter Lighthouse but usually the hide's door is open when in use. If locked during a seawatch, just knock and someone will open the door.

In fine weather, seawatching is possible from wooden benches along the Coastal Park's cliffs.

Whitburn's shorebirds include nationally important Golden Plover numbers (5,000 in January 2009). They mass on White Steel at low tide, many switching to the army firing range or local farmland over high water.

Carefully checking through flocks can be rewarding; both American and Pacific Golden Plovers have been found in the past.

Up to 540 Redshanks have been spread around Whitburn Steel and the South Bents shore in recent winters, with Oystercatcher, Ringed Plover, Sanderling, Dunlin, Curlew and Turnstone numbers peaking in the 100-250 range.

One or two Curlew Sandpipers, Whimbrels and Greenshanks may linger in late summer.

Roseate Terns (up to 12 adults and juveniles recently) are another August/September attraction; they mingle with Sandwich and Common Terns on both Whitburn and White Steels.

Several Mediterranean Gulls are in the area between July and the following spring. Iceland and Glaucous Gulls occur less often and a Bonaparte's Gull was around during the 2010 autumn.

A few Snow Buntings may be in the South Bents dunes/beach area in winter. A sighting of Water Pipit is possible too, as birds forage about washed-up seaweed piles there or below the cliffs further north.

Key points (Whitburn)

- **Observatory keys available by post (£13 incl p&p) from The Warden National Trust, Souter Lighthouse, Coast Road, Whitburn, Sunderland, SR6 7NH.**

- **Also available (for £12) at lighthouse shop (open 11am-5pm, weekends and Mon-Thurs, mid-March - end October).**

- **Coin-op autoloo (RADAR key access for disabled) in Cornthwaite Park. Also toilets at Souter Lighthouse when open (see above).**

Birders at Whitburn Observatory have recorded some remarkable seabird sightings – Little Auks are regular in autumn, sometimes in large numbers.

Key points (Sunderland)

- Free parking by Mere Knolls Cemetery's Dykelands Road entrance (NZ 403 602). Also at nearby seafront supermarket (NZ 404 604).

- Free parking along A183 above North Dock (NZ 407 586), in lower promenade car park by harbour (NZ 409 585) and in roads around Roker Park (NZ 405 590).

- About two miles walking at both Mere Knolls/ Cut Throat Dene and North Dock/harbour areas. Just a few hundred yards in Roker Park's lake/ravine area. Checking all three could take at least 4hrs.

4. Sunderland (Harbour, Roker Park and Seaburn)

SECRET VISITS by mega-rarities have become a speciality of the coastline's most built-up section. Britain's seventh Siberian Rubythroat spent three days on a back lawn in the Roker district in October 2006. Depending on BBRC deliberations, the Brown-headed Cowbird photographed in a garden at neighbouring Seaburn in May 2010 could be declared the country's sixth.

Both times the news broke only after the bird had disappeared. In contrast, many birders enjoyed Durham's first-ever Red-eyed Vireo at Seaburn in October 1990. It was in sycamores at Mere Knolls Cemetery's seaward end, one of its better migrant spots.

Another is the group of trees at the Hole-in-the-Wall, as the north-west corner of this older eastern section is known (due to a boundary wall breach). The gap provides access to a scrub-fringed path, also with a history of unusual migrants, between Monkwearmouth School's grounds and Cut Throat Dene (a shallow gulley with stream).

Britain's latest-ever Arctic Warbler (November 17, 1984) is on the cemetery/dene bird list, along with Dusky and Radde's Warblers, Woodchat Shrike, Golden Oriole, Common Rosefinch and Ortolan Bunting. This is one of the Tyne-Wear coast's likelier places for finding Pallas's and Yellow-browed Warblers; other species recorded include Wryneck, Icterine and Barred Warblers, Firecrest and Red-breasted Flycatcher.

Mere Knolls was Sunderland's only regular migrant site north of the Wear until the 1990s' facelift of the formerly derelict rivermouth.

Trees and shrubs planted on the steep slope between the North Dock and the A183's Harbour View stretch have since produced Pallas's and Yellow-browed Warbler records.

Barred Warblers have repeatedly occupied elder trees by the walkway to the Italian restaurant topping the dockside Marine Activities Centre. Two Alpine Swifts delighted birders here in October 2006, after appearing initially over nearby Roker Park.

This 15-acre (6ha) park is well endowed with trees and shrubs, with the most promising section being the ravine linking Roker's lower promenade with the bandstand area.

This includes a small gulley with a stream and, to the south, the park's lake. In winter, the gulley stream may have a Water Rail and sometimes a Kingfisher is seen catching lake tiddlers.

Sea duck, divers and grebes occur periodically in the outer

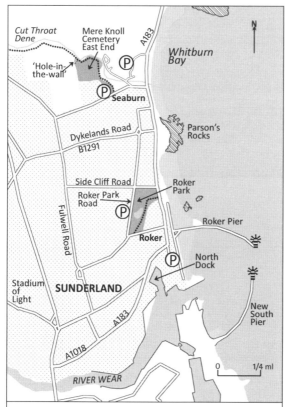

Key points
(Sunderland)

• Mere Knolls coverage mostly over grass. Cut Throat Dene path may be muddy. Paved or tarmac surfaces elsewhere good for wheelchairs.

• Cut Throat Dene path and some parts of cemetery unsuitable for wheelchairs.

• Public toilets on seafront and in Roker Park but some are closed in winter and no disabled access. Seaburn seafront Morrison's supermarket has toilets with disabled access.

• Pubs, restaurants, takeaways and supermarket on Seaburn seafront. Pubs and corner shops near North Dock.

How to get there

Sites by A183 along Sunderland's Roker and Seaburn seafront (see Whitburn for routes from A1(M) and A19).

Public transport: E1, E2 and E6 bus services stop at one or more sites (E1 at or near all three, E2 at Seaburn and E6 in Dykelands Road near Mere Knolls entrance).

harbour. Iceland or Glaucous Gulls may be in New South Pier gull roosts but always several hundred yards from the nearest public access point (the old North Pier where the river meets the outer harbour).

Curlew Sandpiper is sometimes among waders feeding north of Roker Pier during early autumn. This was also one of several places visited by 2010 autumn's wandering Bonaparte's Gull.

155

Key points (Bowlees)

- Park (free) at Bowlees picnic site (NY 908 283). Toilets open all year.

- Limited parking also in B6277 lay-by (NY 905 281) close to path across field to Wynch Bridge.

- Durham Wildlife Trust visitor centre open daily (10.30am-5pm), Easter to end September. Tel: 01833 622 292.

- About two miles to High Force. Watch out for uneven surfaces on Pennine Way's large stones. One short steep stretch.

Contacts

Tourist Information: Barnard Castle, 01833 696 356

Middleton-in-Teesdale, 01833 641 001

YOU WON'T FIND the name Uppermost Teesdale on any map but I'm using it to delineate the picturesque area lying at the highest point of the dale above Barnard Castle where you will find the famous High Force waterfall, a reliable Black Grouse lekking site, riverside broadleaf woodland and other highly productive birding habitats.

Target birds *All year* – Black Grouse (70%), Peregrine (40%), Raven (40%), Merlin (20%). *Spring/summer* – Dipper (80%), Grey Wagtail (80%), Ring Ouzel (50%), Spotted Flycatcher (50%), Redstart (40%), Tree Pipit (30%), Twite (10%). *Winter* – Snow Bunting (10%).

Other possible bird species

All year
Common wildfowl
Teal
Goosander
Red Grouse
Grey Partridge
Grey Heron
Sparrowhawk
Buzzard
Kestrel
Woodcock
Woodland/farmland birds
Stock Dove
Tawny Owl
Great Spotted Woodpecker
Goldcrest
Coal Tit

Long-tailed Tit
Mistle Thrush
Siskin
Lesser Redpoll

Spring/summer
Oystercatcher
Ringed Plover
Golden Plover
Lapwing
Dunlin
Snipe
Curlew
Common Sandpiper
Redshank
Lesser Black-backed Gull
Cuckoo
Swift

Skylark
Hirundines
Chiffchaff
Willow Warbler
Blackcap
Garden Warbler
Wheatear
Pied Wagtail
Meadow Pipit
Greenfinch
Goldfinch
Linnet

Winter
Fieldfare
Redwing
Brambling

Background information and birding tips

ALL THE VALLEY of Durham's longest river above Barnard Castle is classed as Upper Teesdale and as I've covered several locations such as Baldersdale/Lunedale, Blackton

Beck and Deepdale elsewhere in the book, I've used the superlative Uppermost for these three remaining sites.

These locations include productive stretches of the Tees itself, the dale's highest riverside broadleaf woodlands, fells rising to more than 2,000ft, and parts of one of England's biggest national nature reserves (NNRs). Also featured are some very well-walked sections of the 267-mile Pennine Way; it's not just coincidence that they happen to pass the dale's most outstanding scenery. The sites are:

1. Bowlees (NY 90 28) to High Force (NY 88 28)

YOU CAN anticipate a wider range of bird species along this two-mile walk than anywhere else at the higher end of the dale, especially during May/early June.

Park at Bowless picnic site and stroll to the Wynch Bridge over the Tees and you will surely hear Blackcap, Chiffchaff and Willow Warbler songs from woodland surrounding the site and the path leading to the Durham Wildlife Trust visitor centre.

Swallows and House Martins are busy around the hamlet's few cottages and farmstead by the B6277, while Redstarts and Spotted Flycatchers can be found in riverside beech and oak trees before you cross the footbridge.

Over the suspension bridge, you're on the Pennine Way, which follows the river closely for much of the rest of this walk. Immediately upstream is Low Force, the smallest of the dale's waterfall trio, but very picturesque nonetheless.

The outing's first Dipper may be visible, either along the rock-walled gorge below the falls or along the fast flow towards them.

More will be further upstream, along with other stalwarts of rushing dales waterways: Oystercatchers, Common Sandpipers and Grey and Pied Wagtails.

A few hundred yards above the falls, the Tees is split by a substantial rock expanse clothed in birch and willow. In summer, the lower water level means the narrower channel on the Pennine Way side dries up, so it's possible to cross to this island.

The remaining water flow is usually gentle, so if you're lucky, you may find a flotilla of Goosander ducklings competing for the best seats on the back of their red-headed mother if she swims to a more secluded spot.

The island is also a good vantage point for viewing the canopies of mature broadleaf and conifer trees on the opposite side of the river. A variety of woodland species, including Spotted Flycatcher, are likely to be here.

Sometimes Siskins are in the conifers. It's also worth checking around the edges of the birchwood clearing in the island's

Key points (Bowlees)

- **Tight squeeze stile between path from B6277 and Wynch Bridge. Unsuitable for wheelchairs.**

- **Shops, cafes, fish and chips, pubs at Middleton-in-Teesdale (three miles SE from Bowlees along B6277). High Force Hotel (accommodation and meals), 01833 622 222 (1.5 mile NW).**

157

centre; occasionally I've found a Tree Pipit there.

Over flat, damp pastureland extending up to Holwick Fell to the south, a Snipe may be delivering its *'chippa'* song from a drystone wall. Lapwings, Curlews and Redshanks express outrage noisily whenever a Carrion Crow appears.

Where the path veers away from the river it presents the walk's only distinctly uphill section. At the top of this short, sharp rise, you enter the near 18,500 acre (7,387 ha) Moor House-Upper Teesdale NNR, which covers the 20 miles of river from its source on the saddle between Cross Fell and Little Dun

Fell in Cumbria. Also, you stride into a new habitat, a long-established expanse of juniper which supports a wide range of woodland birds. You may have encountered Lesser Redpolls earlier along the trail but here they may be particularly prominent.

At the far end of the junipers, a short diversion enables a splendid view of the Tees plunging 70ft down a black whin sill precipice. High Force is not England's highest waterfall but it's arguably the most impressive.

At this point I usually return to Bowlees on the same track as any alternative route usually produces few birds.

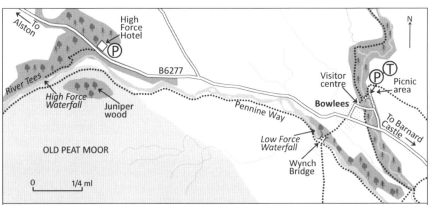

How to get there

(Approx 15 miles NW of Barnard Castle)

Bowlees is three miles NW along B6277 from Middleton-in-Teesdale.

Look for signposted turn-off to picnic site on right just before Bowlees hamlet. Middleton is 12 miles north along B6277 from junction with A66 (12 miles west of A1's Scotch Corner or 37 miles east of J40 on M6 at Penrith).

Middleton can also be reached via A688 from J61 on A1(M) and A689 from J60 (links with A688 at West Auckland). Head for Staindrop on A688, then turn right to reach well signposted Middleton via B6279, B6278 and B6282.

Public transport: Bus services 95/96 run to Middleton from Barnard Castle (Mon-Sat only from April 2011) and services 75/76 from Darlington.

Services higher up dale, including Bowlees, have been restricted to Wednesdays (market day at Barnard Castle) since April, 2011. Check tourist information for latest information.

2. Langdon Beck (NY 85 32)

AS DAYBREAK spreads light across the exposed fells, the early spring soundscape becomes progressively more complex and intense as breeding birds are sparked into a fresh round of display and territorial defence.

What makes Langdon Beck different are vocal eruptions that are rare nationally, especially south of the Scottish border. From the valley floor come bubbling, pigeon-like 'roo-oo-roo' cries and angry hissing. As wisps of mist clear, it comes as no surprise to see they are produced by male Black Grouse.

All the purple prose written about this lekking ritual seems entirely appropriate as the Blackcock strut their stuff. Medieval jousting knights may be a cliché, but it's the metaphor invariably in mind as these avian contestants square-up to each other, wings bowed, lyre tails spread and white undertail coverts flared. Witnessing it is ever-enthralling – the sleep lost to ensure being there at dawn is a happy sacrifice.

Lekking is such an important feature of the Black Grouse breeding cycle that generally it isn't wise to publicise site locations. However, the Langdon Beck lek is already well known and can be viewed without disturbance from a public road.

Blackcock gather on grassland at the foot of the slope below the road, far enough away to be not disturbed by watching birders – provided they remain inside cars. Please don't be tempted to step outside to set up a telescope and tripod – or to try to creep closer.

Please stick to this rule because the Black Grouse is on the conservation concern Red-List, its vulnerability underlined by the project running since 1996 to encourage a North Pennines recovery.

Surveys showed the number of males between the Yorkshire Dales and the Scottish border increased from 773 in 1998 to 1,200 in 2007. Sadly they slumped to 400 by spring 2010 following poor breeding seasons in 2007 and 2008 caused by wet weather and the prolonged, severe 2009/10 winter.

Despite the ups and downs, numbers of males at Langdon Beck recorded in the DBC's annual *Birds in Durham* since 1990 have been consistently around 20-30, with 30-plus in both 2008 and 2009. However, that trend's maintenance won't have been helped by more prolonged severe weather during the 2010/11 winter.

The Game and Wildlife Conservation Trust-led recovery project cannot influence the weather, of course, but at least there's hope the effects can be lessened by improved feeding habitat and other conservation

Key points (Langdon Beck)

• View lek from car at approx NY 850 323 on minor road to St John's Chapel, Weardale from B6277 at Langdon Beck hamlet.

• Stay in car – stepping outside will scare birds away.

• Verge for parking is barely half a car's width but road isn't much used at daybreak.

• No views of lek from off-road parking area by bridge at foot of hill.

• Nearest toilets at pay car park by High Force Hotel, three miles SE along B6277.

Contacts

Langdon Beck Hotel (accommodation/ meals), 01833 622 267

Langdon Beck youth hostel, 0845 371 9027

159

How to get there

(Approx 10 miles NW from Middleton-in-Teesdale)

Langdon Beck (an hotel, a youth hostel and a very few widely-spread farmsteads) lies ten miles NW along B6277 from Middleton-in-Teesdale (see Bowlees for routes to Middleton) and 14 miles SE of Alston, Cumbria.

To view lek, turn off B6277 (0.5 mile NW of hotel) on to minor road to St John's Chapel, Weardale. After 0.25 mile, road bears left to descend into Langdon Beck valley; just after cattle grid pull on to verge and view down slope to valley floor where Blackcock gather.

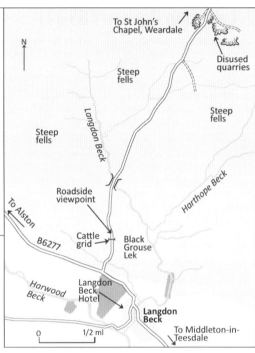

measures that are being promoted.

Late March/early April is a good time to enjoy the spectacle. Getting there for sunrise doesn't require such an early start then. Of course, you may be satisfied with just seeing Black Grouse doing nothing in particular in which case, there's a reasonable chance of at least a few at the site at any time of day during the protracted season. For instance, after walking elsewhere in the dale in June, 2010, I stopped briefly in early evening before returning home and saw six males half-heartedly involved in display.

However, when the daybreak show ends, most disperse widely. Some males may be seen later – often with Pheasants – in fields by the B6277 stretch between the Langdon Beck Hotel and the turn-off to St John's Chapel. Usually they are some distance back from the B6277 in which case closer views may be possible from the minor road, between the junction and the cattle grid.

What you tend not to see during lekking are females. The much less conspicuous Greyhens are extremely shy and watch the proceedings out of sight in surrounding longer vegetation. Actually they're very adept at escaping attention most of the time; regularly *Birds in Durham* features Black Grouse reports from around 30 widespread moorland sites but only a small minority refer to females. That's why populations are assessed on the basis of counts of males.

While Black Grouse are invariably centre stage, expect a full range of other moorland species and there's always a possibility of a surprise; it's one of several Teesdale locations where Rough-legged Buzzard has been reported in winter.

Also, after the minor road crosses the beck, its next two miles rise to Harthope Head, more than 2,000ft. Disused quarries there are worth checking for Wheatear and Ring Ouzel early in spring and there has been the occasional winter Snow Bunting report.

3. Widdybank Fell (NY 82 29)

A FULL CIRCUIT of Widdybank Fell is a great experience, passing through the dale's most awesome scenery, but it does amount to almost eight miles of footslogging.

Also, while around two-thirds of the route is relatively easy, much of the rest is physically challenging and should be tackled only by the well-equipped and fully fit. Fortunately there are more modest alternative options for those daunted by such prospects.

As the route includes the road from Langdon Beck to Cow Green Reservoir, you can walk much shorter distances to two key points – the Widdybank Farm area and over the western side of the fell to Cauldron Snout waterfall – from different parking places.

The full circuit begins with the 1.25 mile track to the farm, now the base for the Natural England (NE) team involved with the NNR. This track presents no particular physical demands as it winds across Widdybank Pasture, which throbs with life in springtime, particularly waders such as Oystercatcher, Lapwing, Snipe, Curlew and Redshank.

A few Black Grouse may be on the pasture – or you could see some flying to higher ground on the fell. Twite, which used to occur regularly near the farm, continue to be a possibility.

After passing through the farmyard, you'll join the Pennine Way along the Tees bank. Watch out for Wheatears and Ring Ouzels along the broad, flattish riverside area known as Holmwath.

Across the river, expect bird activity in the juniper scrub rising up the boulder-strewn slope to the base of rugged Cronkley Scar. A careful check along this craggy spread could reveal a perched Peregrine. If not, there's a good chance you'll see one in flight before long. A Raven appearance is also possible here.

The Pennine Way stretch – extending almost two miles – is the walk's hard section. Beyond Holmwath, the riverside rises steeply to Falcon Clints, the lengthy crag line at Widdybank Fell's southern end.

Repeatedly the path crosses boulder fields with uneven surfaces and in between are boggy areas with boardwalks which become slippery after wet weather.

Finally there is Cauldron Snout, a series of cataracts during which the Tees descends 200ft at a very steep gradient. Reaching the top is quite a scramble – almost a rock-climbing exercise in places.

To avoid becoming the subject of a Mountain Rescue operation, you need to be super alert, taking care where to place your feet as well as looking out for a

Key points (Widdybank Fell)

• For full circuit, park on side of Cow Green Reservoir road at start of track to Widdybank Farm (NY 847 309).

• If just visiting Cow Green-Cauldron Snout section, use car park at reservoir (NY 811 309).

• Full circuit almost eight miles. Progress slow between Holmwath and Cauldron Snout. Allow five hours and take adequate clothing and refreshments.

• Distance between Cow Green car park and Cauldron Snout 1.9 miles. Allow at least two hours. Wheelchair accessible.

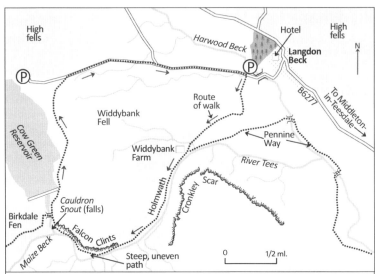

How to get there

(Approx 18 miles NW from Barnard Castle)

At Langdon Beck, turn from B6277 on to minor road to Cow Green Reservoir (junction near Langdon Beck Hotel). This crosses Harwood Beck, a Tees tributary, after 0.25 mile and start of track to Widdybank Farm (gateway with Natural England notice board) is on left after another 250 yards. If just visiting Cow Green-Cauldron Snout, continue two miles to car park overlooking reservoir.

Public transport: Only bus service from Barnard Castle beyond Middleton is on Wednesdays (check tourist information). This goes to Langdon Beck but will take you all the way to Cow Green on request.

Peregrine wheeling about high overhead, the occasional Goosander flying along the river or the Grey Wagtail and Dipper on stones jutting from the rushing water. It's very satisfying to eventually stand at the Snout summit – the view seems even more stupendous after all the effort.

The other reward is an easy 1.9 miles along Widdybank Fell's western edge. To the left Cow Green Reservoir stretches two miles towards the mighty Cumbrian fells, marking the Tees birthplace. You'll have seen many Red Grouse by now; along this well-maintained hard-surfaced trail you'll see more, with Golden Plovers very much on show as well.

If you're there during May, you may see Dotterels taking a break from their northward migration. Merlins and Peregrines may be hunting over this area and sometimes there are more unusual raptors; an Osprey, possibly summering, was at Cauldron Snout in late May 2009 and a Rough-legged Buzzard was reported at nearby Birkdale Farm (along the Pennine Way after it veers into Cumbria from the waterfall) in March 2011.

This location has a history, also, of November and January Snow Bunting appearances, including a flock of 30 once, but mostly during 1974-76, suggesting lack of coverage in more recent winters. Shorelark was recorded in the mid-1970s too.

One reason for the good standard of path over the fell is to encourage visitors to stay on it rather than trample adjacent delicate sugar limestone grassland with its rare flowers such as Teesdale violet and spring gentian.

This alpine flora, a relic of post-glacial times, led to fierce opposition to the reservoir constructed during 1967-71 with the loss of a tenth of the habitat.

While the developers won, there were concessions to the challengers, including the declaration of the NNR to conserve what remains of this remarkable environment.

Certainly, the reservoir hasn't been much use to birds through being 1,500ft above sea level, very exposed and often frozen in winter. Wildfowl tend to be limited to a few

Teal, Mallards and Goosanders, augmented by the occasional Whooper Swan party and the odd Wigeon, Pochard, Tufted Duck and Goldeneye.

Oystercatchers and Common Sandpipers occur along the shore during the breeding season; Ringed Plovers and Dunlin may be present too. Rare waterfowl appearances are very isolated – nothing since a Spoonbill's brief visit in April, 1977.

The circuit's final stage is the easiest – the Cow Green to Langdon Beck minor road, downhill all the way to the parking place at the starting point.

You're unlikely to come across any fresh birds but the panoramic view down the dale is ever magnificent.

Key points

• Two-mile Holmwath-Cauldron Snout stretch is heavy going and the climb alongside waterfall steep. Stout walking boots essential.

• Nearest toilets at pay car park by High Force Hotel, three miles SE along B6277 from Langdon Beck.

A summer walk at Widdybank Fell may produce a sighting of a singing Ring Ouzel, as well as Wheatears.

163

Key points

• Access free to WWT members. For non-members, prices vary (see website for latest fees) – children under four free.

• Visitor centre has toilets (with disabled access and parent-and-baby room), café and shop. CCTV shows heronry activity in breeding season. Play-areas for under-fives and older children.

• Perimeter circuit, including Hawthorn and Spring Gill Wood sections, covers more than a mile; allow at least three hours.

Contacts

WWT Washington Wetland Centre
0191 416 5454
Email:
info.washington
@wwt.org.uk

THE WETLAND CENTRE resulted from an unsuccessful 1970s campaign to safeguard under-threat Barmston Ponds, which was then an outstanding wader site. Twenty years after one pond was drained, the sole survivor was declared a nature reserve, though by then its glory days were very much in the past and it is the Wetland Centre that has the greater birding significance now.

Target birds
Spring/summer – Avocet (100%, if still nesting), Little Ringed Plover (60%), Reed Warbler (50%), Garganey (30%), Little Egret (10%). *Autumn/winter* – Bullfinch (80%), Willow Tit (60%), Water Rail (40%), Kingfisher (40%), Mediterranean Gull (30%), Waxwing in irruption years (20%).

Other possible bird species

All year
Common waterfowl
Shelduck
Gadwall
Teal
Shoveler
Cormorant
Grey Heron
Sparrowhawk
Kestrel
Lapwing
Redshank
Familiar gulls
Common woodland/farmland birds
Tawny Owl
Great Spotted Woodpecker
Pied Wagtail
Mistle Thrush
Goldcrest
Long-tailed Tit
Coal Tit
Treecreeper
Jay
Greenfinch
Goldfinch
Linnet
Yellowhammer
Reed Bunting

Spring/summer/early autumn
Little Grebe
Great Crested Grebe
Oystercatcher
Ruff
Snipe
Black-tailed Godwit
Whimbrel
Curlew
Greenshank
Green Sandpiper
Common Sandpiper
Little Gull
Lesser Black-backed Gull
Black Tern
Common Tern
Swift
Skylark
Sand Martin
Swallow
House Martin
Meadow Pipit
Wheatear
Grasshopper Warbler
Sedge Warbler
Lesser Whitethroat
Whitethroat
Garden Warbler
Blackcap
Chiffchaff
Willow Warbler
Spotted Flycatcher

Late autumn/winter
Pink-footed Goose (passage skeins flying over)
Wigeon
Pochard
Goldeneye
Snipe
Curlew
Grey Wagtail
Fieldfare
Redwing
Blackcap
Chiffchaff
Brambling
Siskin
Lesser Redpoll

How to get there

(Five miles W of Sunderland city centre)

The Wetland Centre and Barmston are off the same junction of the A1231, the main road between Washington and Sunderland city centre and which links the A1(M) at J65 with the A19 Sunderland by-pass. Brown duck logo signs point the way to the centre from the A19 and from A1(M)'s J65 (and also from J64 from which the A195 and A182 lead to the A1231).

The centre is reached from the south exit from the roundabout of the relevant A1231 junction (the first west from A19, the sixth east from A1(M)'s J65 and the fourth from the A182/A1231 junction)). For Barmston Pond, take roundabout's north exit which leads into Nissan Way then, after 300 yards, turn left into unsigned cul-de-sac to park. A path leads to pool viewing screens.

Public transport: Several bus services (eg Lime 8 service between Sunderland and Stanley) from local cities/towns stop at Waterview Park, the government building near Wetland Centre, but not all operate on Sundays. One that is seven-day is Go Northern's 50/50A Durham City - South Shields service. Check Traveline 0870 608 2608 for more details.

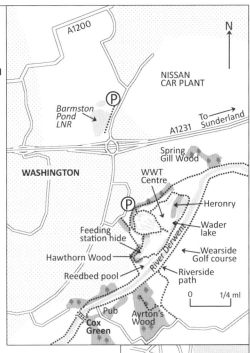

Background information and birding tips

IN COMMON with the rest of the Wildfowl and Wetlands Trust network, the centre combines a display of captive world-wide waterfowl with a refuge for wild birds. The collection area radiates from the visitor centre, while the wilder birds will be found on the outermost area beside the River Wear and also the centre's northern flank.

From the outset local birders doubted that man-made pools carved out of a sloping cornfield could repeat the phenomenal run of waders logged at Barmston Ponds during 1967-77. Up to a point they were right, for the 110-acre (45ha) centre has matched that performance only very occasionally over its four decades. However,

it has enriched the City of Sunderland's wildlife scene in other ways.

Ironically one wader – Avocet – that was never recorded at Barmston has become a centre speciality. In view of past passage records, it always seemed likely that Teesmouth – if

165

Key points

- **Four hides overlook Wader Lake and there's another at Hawthorn Wood feeding station.**

- **Five electric buggies available free of charge (not in wet weather) to disabled at Centre. Early booking recommended.**

- **Most paths are hard-surfaced but riverside track to accessible Wader Lake hides isn't. Normally OK for wheelchairs, but may be muddy.**

- **Return walk from Wader Lake is uphill and includes slightly steep stretch.**

anywhere – might become this spectacular marshbird's first nesting location in the region. By the time two pairs did rear young there in 2008, however, Washington was celebrating its third successive season as the species' most northerly nesting site in Britain.

The centre's Wader Lake still held that status in 2010, though hopes of expansion beyond a single nesting pair hadn't been fulfilled up to then. A third adult was present for almost a fortnight in spring 2008 and a second pair appeared in 2009 but left after a month, without attempting to breed.

Usually the pair arrives in March and they and their fledged young, fitted with colour rings, depart during July. Ringing has produced some knowledge of subsequent movements; it led to the two 2010 youngsters being spotted among a flock of 45 Avocets at Cley, North Norfolk, 160 miles (260km) to the south-east in late July.

Oystercatcher, Little Ringed Plover, Lapwing, Redshank and Common Sandpiper are also on the centre's breeding species list. The ability to adjust Wader Lake water levels has benefited both nesting and passage shorebirds. Ruff, Black-tailed Godwit, Greenshank and Green and Wood Sandpipers are among the more regular callers, particularly during July-September. More unusual visitors recorded since

2000 include Temminck's Stint and Lesser Yellowlegs.

With up to 50 pairs, the shingle island's Common Tern colony is full of bustle during the breeding season – as is the North-East's biggest heronry in the trees and shrubs behind the lake. It has held up to 45 nests and with Little Egret occurring increasingly in the region, there's hope this coloniser might choose to raise families there too eventually. Significantly, the first Durham record of the species away from Teesmouth was on Wader Lake in May 1995.

Springtime is particularly lively, with wooded areas and scrub belts reverberating with the vocal output of resident and summer-visiting songbirds, while Swifts, Swallows and martins are active overhead. Checking through the latter paid off in April 2002 with the discovery of a Red-rumped Swallow, only the third for Durham. With the Wader Lake's Lesser Yellowlegs just a few weeks later, that was one year when the centre certainly did rekindle some of that old Barmston magic.

There are other reasons for being alert for spring and autumn aerial activity. Marsh Harrier and Osprey on passage have been seen with some regularity and Honey Buzzard and Hobby are further possibilities.

Icelandic Whooper Swan parties and Pink-footed Geese skeins migrating south to East Anglia for the winter are liable to pass over and sometimes Svalbard-breeding Barnacle Geese follow the Wear valley on their equivalent journey westwards to the Solway Firth.

A top winter attraction is the Hawthorn Wood feeding station in the centre's southern corner. It attracts a broad species spectrum, including Great Spotted Woodpecker, Willow Tit, Nuthatch, Jay, Brambling, Bullfinch and Reed Bunting. Sometimes overwintering Blackcap and Chiffchaff show up there too.

While in this part of the centre it's also worth checking treetops across the river for Hawfinch which used to be recorded there. A comeback isn't out of the question, with other woods in the Wear valley's Washington to Chester-le-Street stretch continuing to produce sightings.

Between Hawthorn Wood and the river is another example of how Wearside has gained from the centre's development. Previously Reed Warbler occurred in the area only as a scarce passage migrant on the coast but by the late 1970s a male sang in the phragmites bed established in the most upstream of the riverside pools and since then the species has been a regular centre summer visitor.

The reedbed is also ideal Water Rail territory; this ace skulker is reported mainly during autumn and winter but there are occasional breeding season sightings.

Wader Lake's outstanding late autumn/winter events are Curlew roosts; the assembly has grown steadily, with almost 800 in October 2010 a new record high. This is also a time for peak Redshank gatherings, with up to 170 in recent years.

Wildfowl are particularly prominent there in winter and the Wear should be checked (through the chain link perimeter fence) in case it holds something interesting. A few Goldeneye occur regularly on this river stretch and there have been infrequent appearances by Long-tailed Duck, Smew, Red-necked and Slavonian Grebes and Grey Phalarope during cold weather.

As with other seasons, winter birding potential is not confined to the riverside refuge area. For instance, near the visitor centre Siskin and Lesser Redpoll flocks may be feeding in alders. The centre's viewing gallery overlooks a stream visited by Grey Wagtail; sometimes a Kingfisher zips past the huge window also. In irruption years there's a possibility of Waxwings being attracted by the berries of guelder rose around the grounds.

Barmston Pond (NZ 327 571)

THIS IS THE surviving relic of a pair of mining subsidence pools that came to the attention of birders during the 1960s – and very quickly became famous as a top North-East site for rare waders.

A Grey Phalarope in August 1974 was the 34th shorebird species recorded there in just eight years. Illustrious predecessors included Collared Pratincole, Kentish Plover, Broad-billed Sandpiper, Lesser Yellowlegs and Wilson's Phalarope, with Spoonbill

and White-winged Black Tern among other notable visitors. Not bad for two partially flooded fields on either side of a farm lane crossing a disused railway that once carried coal from local pits to ships at Sunderland.

Forty years on, the once rural landscape has changed dramatically. That former mineral line became Nissan Way leading to Europe's most productive automobile plant (opened in 1986). The field which held the easterly pool until drainage in 1975 is now the entrance

Key points

- **Parking place (NZ 328 573) on former farm lane (now a cul-de-dac) off Nissan Way.**

- **Always open. Two viewing screens (subject to vandalism), the furthest just 300 yards from parking place.**

- **Path to screens can be muddy but probably not enough to trouble wheelchair users.**

- **Nearest public toilets at Galleries shopping centre, Washington (off A1231 two miles to west).**

to the industrial complex's test track.

To the west, the pool that remains is next to a vast parking lot for newly-built cars, with a fire brigade training centre across the road. Unfortunately, Barmston Pond – a Local Nature Reserve since 1993 – is now a shadow of its former self.

In the early years it used to dry up partially in summer but gradually it became a more permanent water body, lacking shallow feeding areas for waders. Also, an end to cattle-grazing in the field meant its fringes were no longer churned, enabling thick vegetation to grow where previously there had been shorebird-attracting mud.

However, including it in a tour of local birding sites can still be fruitful. With the viewing screens just a short walk from the parking place, checking it doesn't take much time and there can be more than just a spattering of routine waterfowl. Black-necked Grebe, Little Egret and Water Rail have occurred since the end of the 1990s and there is still a chance of Little Gull or Black Tern at passage times. Mixed winter

gull gatherings may include a Mediterranean and there have been reports of Yellow-legged and Iceland too.

It is sad that adjacent farmland which used to support breeding Lapwing, Snipe, Redshank and Yellow Wagtail has disappeared since the mid-1980s. On the plus side, however, extensive tree and shrub planting in the pool's vicinity has improved prospects for woodland and hedgerow birds.

This can be a promising site for songbird migrants both in spring and autumn; in October 2008 it produced Durham's most inland Yellow-browed Warbler record. Sometimes Waxwing parties are seen in winter.

Meanwhile Barmston shouldn't be written off totally as a haunt for passage waders. They certainly responded well during the series of Augusts up to 2006 when Nissan pumped out water to produce the required muddy fringes and shallow feeding zones. If effective water level management measures could be carried out in future, the reserve's fabulous past could be revived.

NORTHUMBERLAND SITES

The Farne Islands enjoy a worldwide reputation for the
richness of its breeding seabird populations.

Key points

- Site open from dawn to dusk. No admission charge.

- Morralee Wood stroll is under two miles. Combined walk is four miles. Allow at least three hours for both.

- Wheelchair users should manage part of path along river's west bank from car park. First 300 yards of path to Raven Crag too steep for easy access.

- Pay and display car park with disabled-friendly toilets at walk's start.

Contacts

National Trust Hexham office 01434 344 218

ALLEN BANKS has, arguably, the best spring birding potential of the North-East's dales, with outstanding scenery, a 70-plus bird species list and an array of other significant wildlife credentials, including red squirrels. Though other dales sites have their own special features, a tremendously high standard is set along the course of this river's final northward flow to join the South Tyne.

Target birds

Late April/early May – Pied Flycatcher (90%), Wood Warbler (80%), Redstart (70%), Spotted Flycatcher (60%), Tree Pipit (40%). *Winter* – Hawfinch (20%).

Other possible bird species

All year	Goldcrest	Grey Wagtail
Goosander	Jay	Pied Wagtail
Grey Heron	Goldfinch	Garden Warbler
Buzzard	Common farmland	Blackcap
Green Woodpecker	species	Chiffchaff
Great Spotted		Willow Warbler
Woodpecker	*Spring/summer*	
Dipper	Common Sandpiper	*Winter*
Long-tailed Tit	Swift	Fieldfare
Coal Tit	Sand Martin	Redwing
Nuthatch	House Martin	Siskin
Treecreeper	Swallow	Lesser Redpoll

Background information and birding tips

NORTHUMBERLAND'S largest expanse of ancient woodland, dating from at least medieval times, is textbook territory for Wood Warblers. Sadly, as part of this species' national slump, recently reported numbers of singing males are only small fractions of the 48 counted there in 1967. However, Allen Banks remains a comparative regional stronghold.

What hasn't changed is the magnificence of woodland, with a strong presence of sessile oak, ash and wych elm, along with beech introduced from the late 1700s. It can be well appreciated from the network of paths, created during the mid-19th Century, when the woods were part of the estate of adjacent Ridley Hall.

Eventually Ridley Hall became the home of Francis Bowes-Lyon, whose elder brother, the 14th Earl of Strathmore, was the maternal grandfather of Elizabeth II. Six years before his death, aged almost 92, Francis gave Allen Banks to the National Trust in 1942, since when it has become a popular visitor attraction.

The starting point for walkers is the hall's former kitchen garden, now a pay-and-display car park with picnic tables and a toilet block. The hall, not in the NT's

How to get there

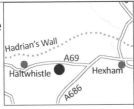

(Approx 32 miles W of Newcastle)

Allen Banks is just south of A69, with turn-off between Haydon Bridge and Bardon Mill, 25 miles east of Carlisle. A minor road crosses River South Tyne, then goes under Newcastle-Carlisle railway, immediately after which a left turn leads to signposted car park entrance on right.

Public transport: The 685 Newcastle-Carlisle bus service's nearest stop is just half a mile away. Nearest Newcastle – Carlisle railway stop is Bardon Mill, 1.5 miles away. The site lies 2.5 miles from National Cycle Network route 72, which follows Hadrian's Wall.

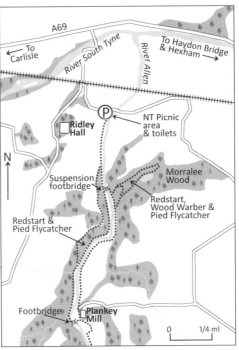

portfolio, isn't open to the public.

Three colour-coded walks totalling more than six miles are on offer and my advice to birders seeking the quickest results is to opt for the purple one, which in early May I found particularly productive.

It runs around Morralee Wood above the river's east bank. You access it via a swaying footbridge half a mile down the west bank from the car park.

Even before stepping onto the bridge you may hear Wood Warbler and Pied Flycatcher song resounding from the beeches on the opposite bank. As the path climbs sharply then loops through mixed deciduous and coniferous woodland expect to hear the songs of Redstarts, Blackcaps, Chiffchaffs, Willow Warblers, Goldcrests, Coal Tits, Nuthatches and Treecreepers.

The two other walks can be combined if you are feeling energetic. Orange begins just beyond the car park, with a path branching off to the right. This runs along the crest

of the Allen's west bank with, to the left, predominantly beech woodland occupying the severe slope down to the riverside path. On the right is initially Ridley Hall parkland, then a conifer plantation and finally farmland.

While Allen Banks looks ideal for the supreme spring-visiting Dales songbirds quartet – Tree Pipit, Redstart, Wood Warbler and Pied Flycatcher – finding them in the NT's 190 acres can be difficult. The best strategy is to listen for their distinctive songs, but they become much less vocal as the season advances.

Even if some are still singing after mid-May, locating them is hampered by the burgeoning leaf canopy. Morning visits, the earlier the better, in late April or early May, are likely to produce the most satisfying results.

171

Key points

- **Dogs under close control are welcome.**

- **Once Brewed Visitor Centre (three miles NW) has toilets, shop and Tourist Information, 01434 344 396.**

- **More facilities at Haydon Bridge, three miles E along A69. Extensive shopping centre seven miles further east at Hexham.**

A few hundred yards beyond Raven Crag, the highest point of this walk, with a splendid view up the Allen gorge, the path descends, by means of steps to the river. There, the Orange route returns to the car park, but if you're game for more, turn right and you're on the Black route that carries on upstream and out of NT woodland into Briarwood Banks, an SSSI owned by the Northumberland Wildlife Trust.

The path passes through a flatter, more open wooded area, emphasised in springtime by Willow Warbler song from bushes fringing one particular clearing.

Spotted Flycatchers may be hawking insects along the riverside, sometimes from rocks protruding from the Allen. This more sheltered river stretch tends to have Goosanders, Grey and Pied Wagtails and Dippers on show more often than the lower stretches.

A rigid bridge provides a crossing to Plankey Mill and the walk's return leg along the Allen's east bank. On fine weekends the riverside here may be packed with picnicking families but, beyond the farm, you're back in tranquility, between riverside alders and sheep pastureland.

Garden Warblers may be singing in bushes at the southern end of this large open area. Watch out, also, for Buzzards soaring.

Where the river bends around Raven Crag, it slows down into a calm pool where people are often splashing, so bird potential is limited, but after sunset Daubenton's bats, one of eight species recorded locally, feed there. This is one of the Allen valley's scarcer mammals that can at least be seen.

Unless exceptionally lucky, otter encounters tend to be no more than footprints in riverside mud. The valley is also England's most northerly site for the rare and endangered dormouse.

After this bend, the path climbs above the river to pass below rock outcrops, which rule out scrambling higher to locate any Pied Flycatchers that may be singing in trees at the top.

Access to Morralee Wood does becomes possible 500 yards along the path, where it links with the track rising from the footbridge half a mile upstream from the NT car park and the walk's end.

While spring is the period of most birdwatching visits to Allen Banks, there is also potential during the winter months when Fieldfares, Redwings, Bramblings, Siskins and Lesser Redpolls are likely to be present. Also, locating and checking through feeding flocks of tits and associated species becomes simpler with the deciduous woodland in a leafless state.

DURING THIS WALK in the heart of the Cheviot Hills, virtually all you see in every direction is rolling grassy uplands, which may not sound too promising bird-wise and, to be honest, it isn't. However, this route includes other habitats, such as the course of the River Alwin and the southern end of Kidland Forest. Along the way you can build up a respectable bird list and the views over the hills are splendid.

Target birds *Spring/summer* – Whinchat (90%), Stonechat (80%), Common Crossbill (80%), Tree Pipit (60%), Ring Ouzel (50%), Spotted Flycatcher (50%).

Other possible bird species

Spring/ early summer	Cuckoo	Wheatear
Goosander	Swift	Mistle Thrush
Grey Heron	Skylark	Blackcap
Buzzard	Sand Martin	Willow Warbler
Kestrel	Swallow	Coal Tit
Oystercatcher	House Martin	Goldfinch
Curlew	Meadow Pipit	Siskin
Common Sandpiper	Grey Wagtail	Reed Bunting
Common woodland and farmland birds	Pied Wagtail	
	Dipper	

Background information and birding tips

THE TERRAIN over much of this circular walk is a bit like America's Wild West prairies, a notion strengthened by thoughts that 200 years ago Scottish Borders-reared cattle were driven to Tyneside markets along a trail dating from Roman times.

Clennell Street, as it is now known, is tramped mainly by ramblers these days and it figures in the start and most of the return leg of this circular walk.

My first advice is: don't hurry away from Alwinton because its broadleaf trees and house gardens are something of an oasis in the sea of grassland and dense commercial conifer plantations that occupy the seven miles between the village and the Scottish border, You will log most of the walk's possible common woodland and hedgerow species around the village.

Indeed, several will have been seen and heard in the car park trees while tying your bootlaces. Also look south over the fields towards the River Coquet and you could add Grey Heron, Oystercatcher, Swift and Sand Martin to the tally and maybe even a Goosander flying up or down river.

Inevitably, this is not an area with a reputation for rarities but the immature Red-footed Falcon that spent a couple of days in the vicinity of the village in May,

Key points

- National Park pay and display car park with toilets at Alwinton (NT 919 064)

- Open access but avoid in wet or very windy weather

- Distance about eight miles. Allow at least five hours.

- Wheelchair users can use track following River Alwin to Kidland Forest. Access (NT 922 061) is from the road 0.25 miles south of Alwinton.

- Refreshments at Rose & Thistle pub, Alwinton (01669 650 226).

Contacts

Clennell Hall (hotel/camping and caravan site 01669 650 377)

Rothbury Tourist Information, 01669 620 887

1980, shows its potential.

While strolling along the village street, there's an element of literary history to consider as well. With cattle drovers featuring in his 1817 novel, *Rob Roy*, Sir Walter Scott did some of his research here, staying at The Rose and Thistle pub, very much the village's social hub then as it is now.

Soon after the pub, cross the village green and a footbridge over the Hosedon Burn to bring you onto Clennell Street, which takes you northwards past a small rookery in tall conifers.

After a few hundred yards, turn right from the lane via a ladder stile to follow a barely visible path across two large fields. This leads to a footbridge across the River Alwin, which is flowing south to join the Coquet. By the bridge is another rookery in a line of Scots pines and to the north-east, Clennell Hall, a country hotel with a popular camp site.

Across the bridge, turn left onto the unsurfaced track beside the Alwin and this takes you to Kidland Forest, two miles to the north. Oystercatchers, Common Sandpipers, Grey and Pied Wagtails and Dippers can all be anticipated on the way.

The hillsides lack trees and scrub so much of the time you're conscious only of the songs of Meadow Pipits and, higher up, Skylarks. However, after the first river bridge,

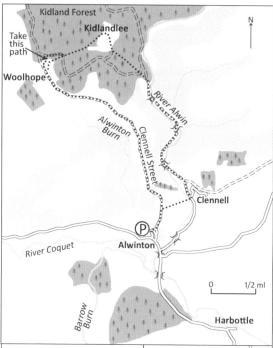

How to get there

(24 miles W of Alnwick)

From Newcastle, drive north on A1 for 17 miles, then take A697 Coldstream road. After eight miles, there's a long, straight downhill stretch as road crosses Coquet valley.

At the bottom, turn left on to B6344 and head W to Rothbury (seven miles) and on for a further four miles to the tiny hamlet of Flotterton.

Here the B6344 swings south-west but, by the hamlet's few buildings, you turn right (though it seems more like straight on) onto minor road heading NW higher up the

dale. Passing the small villages of Sharperton and Harbottle, after seven miles, you reach Alwinton.

Drive past the Rose and Thistle pub and the National Park's car park is on the right at village's west end.

Public transport: Not a practical option in this remote region.

short metallic warbles emanating from the lower slopes draw attention to the presence of Whinchats. They're fairly easy to locate in May and early June, but tend to become elusive later in the season.

The same applies to Stonechats, which also occur along the lower slopes. Wheatears should be on show too; one regular place is around the Rookland Sike/Alwin confluence, near the second bridge. There's an outside chance of Ring Ouzel, perhaps on Clennell Hill's higher rugged western slopes south of that confluence.

Overhead Buzzards and Kestrels could well be soaring on thermals, along with Jackdaws, Rooks, Carrion Crows – and just possibly a Raven, a species that's increasing in the Cheviots.

Listen for Blackcap and Willow Warbler song at Kidland's entrance. Take the path that forks left there for an uphill slog along a narrow corridor between tightly-ranked evergreens. The habitat is meagre and you'll be lucky to find many birds.

Eventually, however, the path flattens and after a mile you're in the clearing around Kidlandlee, 1,250ft above sea level. A massive shooting lodge that dominated this isolated spot for more than half a century was demolished by explosives in 1956, so a farm and two holiday cottages are the only signs of habitation now.

The path passes to the east and north of these before angling south-west to bring you back on to Clennell Street at Wholehope. Birdwise, I have found this to be the most interesting part of the walk's forest section.

South-west of Kidlandlee the scene is changing. Much of this corner of the forest had already been clear-felled before my 2008 visits and this has since been extended.

Significantly, I noted more bird activity from the path across this clearing than elsewhere in the forest in early June when Siskins were particularly prominent. I came across a Crossbill party and on the west side a Tree Pipit was launching into its song flight from a clump of broadleaf trees.

How to rejoin Clennell Street at Wholehope isn't blindingly obvious. When that clearing path reaches an unsurfaced road near the forest edge, don't – as maps indicate – go straight on into a gulley strewn with tree-felling debris. Instead turn right onto the road which subsequently bends left to a dry stone wall with a rickety gate.

Through the gate, cross a rush-filled field, guided by a waymarker just visible in the middle. After a small gulley, you're in a sheep pasture with a shelter-type structure ahead and then you turn left on to the well-defined trail back to Alwinton.

The trail runs close to Kidland's south-west corner. Being sheltered on a day chilled by a brisk NE wind, this edge of the forest was comparatively bristling with birds – including Siskins, a Crossbill family group and a Spotted Flycatcher – during my late May visit.

Working a huge expanse of commercial timber is never easy but sheltered plantation edges and clearings do seem to be the best bets.

As the trail swings away from the forest it forks; while both options lead to Alwinton, the right hand one is preferable. The final three miles is mainly gentle downhill, the ground firm and mostly grassy. Birds tend to be limited to Skylarks, Meadow Pipits and the occasional Buzzard but the impressive Cheviot panorama helps to compensate.

PROXIMITY to Druridge Bay and Newbiggin-by-the-Sea means these sites 15 miles north of Newcastle can sometimes be overlooked in the minds of birders heading for the mid-Northumberland coastal area. However, they add up to a substantial amount of habitat that supports many birds and each has shown a capacity to attract unusual species. Visiting them can be rewarding.

Target birds

All year – Tree Sparrow (40%), Bullfinch (40%), Willow Tit (30%), Water Rail (20%). *Late autumn to early spring* – Whooper Swan (40%), Glaucous Gull (30%), Iceland Gull (20%). *Summer and spring/autumn passage* – Little Ringed Plover (40%), Black-tailed Godwit (40%), Little Gull (40%), Garganey (30%), Green Sandpiper (30%), Wood Sandpiper (30%), Spotted Redshank (30%), Black-necked Grebe (10%), Little Egret (10%), Spoonbill (10%), Temminck's Stint (10%).

Other possible bird species

All year

Common waterfowl
Wigeon
Gadwall
Teal
Shoveler
Pochard
Grey Partridge
Little Grebe
Grey Heron
Kestrel
Lapwing
Familiar gulls

Common farmland/ woodland birds
Little Owl
Kingfisher
Goldcrest
Coal Tit
Skylark
Long-tailed Tit
Pied Wagtail
Meadow Pipit
Greenfinch
Goldfinch
Linnet

Lesser Redpoll
Bullfinch
Yellowhammer
Reed Bunting

Summer and spring/ autumn passage

Great Crested Grebe
Oystercatcher
Little Stint
Dunlin
Ruff
Common Sandpiper

Spotted Redshank
Greenshank
Little Gull
Black Tern
Common Tern
Swift
Hirundines
Chiffchaff
Willow Warbler
Blackcap
Garden Warbler
Lesser Whitethroat
Whitethroat
Grasshopper Warbler
Sedge Warbler
Whinchat
Wheatear
Yellow Wagtail

Late autumn to early spring

Pink-footed Goose
Shelduck
Pintail
Goldeneye
Merlin
Peregrine
Golden Plover
Snipe
Curlew
Barn Owl
Short-eared Owl
Fieldfare
Redwing
Grey Wagtail

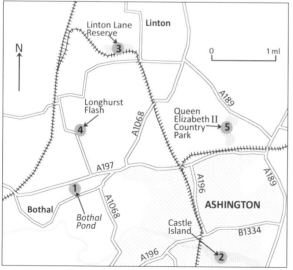

Background information and birding tips

THESE SITES are on the fringes of Ashington, once known as 'the largest coal mining village in the world' when it was a major hub of Northumberland's former deep mining industry.

Four are the results of past mining activity and one of these is at the time of writing having its surroundings re-shaped by a new opencast project.

The five, in alphabetical order, are:

1. Bothal Pond (NZ 24 87)

WHAT MAY SOUND like a modest patch of water is actually a substantial small lake. Its status is further enhanced by the impressive range of wetland birds it has attracted over the years.

Though on private land with no access, this mining subsidence pool sits conveniently between two roads. Its northern tip can be viewed from the verge of the A197 Ashington-to-Morpeth road. Meanwhile the broader, shallower-edged southern end is close to the lane from the A1068 to Bothal village.

There is usually a hedge stretch low enough to be overlooked by birders of average height, but it can pose problems for shorter people or the wheelchair-bound.

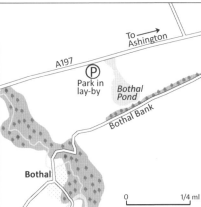

Key points
(Bothal Pond)

• To view from A197 embankment, park in lay-by (NZ 241 875) near pool's north end and walk back.

• From minor road between A1068 and Bothal village, park at NZ 245 872 to view pool from behind hedge.

• Public toilets with disabled facilities in Ashington town centre and also Woodhorn Mining Museum (see Queen Elizabeth II Country Park).

• Shops, cafes, takeaways and pubs in town centre. Also, 24-hour Asda hypermarket two miles E along A197 from Bothal.

How to get there
(One mile W of Ashington)

Reached via A189 Newcastle – Ashington road (linked to A1 by A19 Tyne Tunnel road). Switch to A197 at roundabout junction NE of Ashington, the head W for three miles (five roundabouts as it skirts town's N edge). When N end of pool appears on left, don't park there but in lay-by 150 yards further along road. To view pool's S end, continue W along A197 for almost a mile, then turn left on to minor road leading to Bothal village (one mile). After steep uphill stretch and passing buildings on both sides, pool is on left.

Public transport: No 35 Ashington to Morpeth bus service stops on A197 by junction with minor road to Bothal village (NZ 229 871), almost a mile W of pool's N end.

177

Key points
(Castle Island)

• **Park carefully in Nursery Park Road near start of path to riverside (NZ 282 861).**

• **Hard-surfaced path to riverside descends steeply at first. Unsuitable for wheelchairs due to barrier to keep out motorbikes.**

• **Path reaches riverside opposite island's west end, but you need to walk almost 0.25 mile along riverside path (also hard-surfaced) to view eastern end.**

• **Allow up to two hours if birding.**

It has a history of surprises, such as the Glossy Ibis in May 1989, which was Northumberland's fourth and the first since 1908. Just two decades passed before the next ibis record – and Bothal was among several of the county's wetlands visited by that first-winter bird in September 2009 before it settled for more than three weeks at Druridge Pools.

Northumberland's first Lesser Scaup was recorded at the pond in May 1999 and the pair that toured the area in May 2009 called there too. The county's second-ever Caspian Tern did likewise during a July 2007 wandering session.

Great White Egrets dropped in during July 1999 and June 2003. American Wigeon, Green-winged Teal, Ring-necked Duck and Marsh Harrier have been among other notable visitors.

Not all unusual callers linger briefly; a Long-billed Dowitcher was on show for 18 days in April 2004. Avocet, Temminck's Stint and Pectoral Sandpiper stand out among scarce-visiting waders recorded.

A broad range of more regular species has been logged, with above-average numbers sometimes. After easterly winds and heavy rain in August 2004, the shorebird presence included up to 13 Greenshanks, seven Wood Sandpipers and 21 Common Sandpipers.

A few hundred Wigeon and Teal tend to be Bothal's most numerous winter ducks. In recent years up to 25 Gadwall have been noted in springtime but generally Shovelers haven't reached double figures in any season. Pochard numbers tend to be less than 20 while Tufted Ducks don't exceed 50 – in contrast to the 1980s when there were three-figure peak counts. A few Goldeneyes may be present in winter.

Garganey and Black-necked Grebes can be anticipated at passage times and there are past isolated records of Common Scoter in October and Red-crested Pochard in November. Whooper Swans are a winter possibility, either on the pool or, more likely, on farmland by the A1068 to the east. Occasionally a few Bewick's Swans have been in the fields too.

2. Castle Island (NZ 28 85)

THE 280 ACRE (112ha) Wansbeck Riverside Park stretches more than two miles between the A1068 and A189 bridges, but the main focus of interest for birders is in the easterly section and in the centre of the broadest part of the waterway.

Castle Island, a Local Nature Reserve since 2003, is the remains of saltmarsh habitat

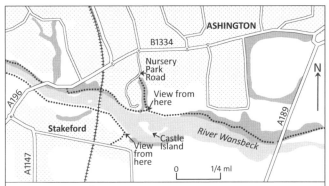

• **Alternative entry points (both banks) from A196 bridge (car park on N side at NZ 274 859). This is 0.7 mile upstream of island but easier access to riverside for wheelchairs.**

• **Fairly short but steepish path to southern riverbank near island from West Sleekburn village. Path starts at NZ 278 855 (reached from second turning on left after railway level crossing).**

• **Toilets with disabled facilities: (see Bothal and QEII Country Park). Also toilet block (no disabled facilities) at eastern end of West Sleekburn, near Foresters Arms.**

How to get there

(Southern edge of Ashington)

After A189 bridge over River Wansbeck, turn left at roundabout onto B1334. At third roundabout (The Elephant pub on right), turn left into Nursery Park Road.

Path descending to Castle Island riverside stretch begins as road bears right into private housing estate.

To view island from Wansbeck's south side, continue along B1334 and, after next roundabout, take the A196 which crosses river to Stakeford. Turn left there onto A1147 at roundabout, then left again, after a short distance, onto minor road signposted to Cambois (turning as A1147 bends right). After a railway level crossing you are in West Sleekburn where path descends to riverside.

isolated from the daily tidal flow after the construction of a barrage across the Wansbeck just upstream of the A189 and 0.5 mile from the sea. Slightly off the beaten track and therefore perhaps not visited as frequently as other local sites, checking it can prove worthwhile, as indicated by its performance over the years.

It is one of several Northumberland locations that have benefited from the increased UK occurrence of Spoonbills during recent years. Up to three were there in late May/early June 2007 and two in June 2011.

The island's credentials were polished further by two Great White Egrets in May 2011.

Wader activity is mainly between July-September. Species that have occurred on autumn passage include Little and Temminck's Stints, Curlew Sandpiper, Ruff, Black-tailed Godwit, Green Sandpiper, Spotted Redshank, Greenshank and Wood Sandpiper. There have been spring Little Ringed Plover appearances and that is the season when the site's sole rare wader, a Terek Sandpiper, occurred in May 1990 after overwintering in the nearby Blyth estuary.

Key points
(Linton Lane)

• Small parking area (NZ 256 907) on right just before short stretch of Linton Lane comes to mineral line crossing (open only to walkers).

• Firm paths (each 0.25 mile) to hides from lane on N side of crossing.

• Paths and hides are wheelchair-accessible.

• Plough Inn, Ellington, 1.5 miles due NE does meals. See QEII Country Park for more facilities.

A few Little Gulls, invariably first-summer birds, turn up between May and July and Black Tern is a further passage possibility. Iceland Gull is recorded occasionally during winter months.

Over recent years, Goldeneye has been among the more prominent wildfowl species, with November/December counts in the 15-30 range.

As well as occurring in winter, Red-breasted Merganser has been recorded in springtime and Goosander in summer. There

have also been isolated Scaup appearances.

The rest of Wansbeck Riverside Park (given LNR status in 2007) includes both woodland and grassland. There are paths along the north bank of the park's stretch of the Wansbeck and the central part of the south bank. Kingfisher sightings are possible along the river and you can expect to encounter typical woodland birds such as Great Spotted Woodpecker, Nuthatch and Treecreeper.

3. Linton Lane Reserve (NZ 25 90)

THIS RESTORED, former opencast coal mining site covers 120 acres (48ha) and

includes two pools with small islands. The larger one, on the west side, is fringed by reedmace

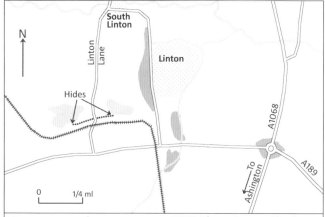

How to get there

(Three miles NNW of Ashington)

Turning to lane leading to reserve is one mile along minor road W from roundabout at Junction of A189 and

A1068. It's not signposted but is first on right less than 0.5 mile past a railway level crossing.

At end of short lane, pull into small parking area on right.

and other marsh vegetation, with nearby grassland and woodland.

The smaller pool is in a more open situation, but the Northumberland Wildlife Trust hopes its surroundings will become marshland, grading into alder/willow carr, species-rich grassland, woodland and scrub. You can reach the hides overlooking the pools from the north side of the gated mineral line crossing at the end of Linton Lane.

Early highlights for this improving site included Great White Egret in May 2003 (later seen mostly at Longhirst Flash), a Green-winged Teal in December 2004 and February 2005, a Red-necked Phalarope in September 2005 and a Spotted Crake on two 2006 summer dates.

A Ring-necked Duck in May 2007 was followed a week later by two Lesser Scaup, a male and female – the first English record of more than a single bird since this species' 1987 British debut (there had already been Scottish records of up to three).

Large white-winged gulls brought further focus on the site. After a slump in Northumberland reports over preceding years, Glaucous Gulls made a distinct comeback from 2007.

One was a first-year bird that flew to Linton repeatedly between foraging sessions at New Moor landfill site, less than a mile to the south-east, during early spring. More was seen of the species at Linton during subsequent winters, as well as reports of occasional Iceland Gulls, also.

The reserve is on the edge of one of Northumberland's main zones for wintering Whooper Swans. It's not unusual for a herd to be in nearby fields or to fly on to the west pool to roost.

With a four-figure presence of Pink-footed Geese regularly in the wider Druridge Bay area, up to 1,500 have been seen in fields near Linton in recent years. Taiga Bean Goose, White-fronted Goose and Barnacle Goose have made isolated appearances also.

Generally, duck numbers are modest, though up to 300 Wigeon and 100-plus Teal have been logged. Also, monthly counts of Gadwall, which has bred on the reserve, have occasionally been higher than elsewhere in the county.

Tufted Duck is the most numerous diving duck, but usually numbers don't exceed 40, despite increased on-site breeding. In 2010, there was a redhead Smew in late January and a Garganey in early September.

While not ideal for shorebirds, Linton has produced the odd Black-tailed Godwit and Green Sandpiper report. As for marsh vegetation skulkers, Water Rail has been recorded regularly over recent winters.

At passage times, there's a possibility of fly-over Marsh Harriers, Ospreys and Hobbies, while winter offers Merlin and Peregrine prospects. As for owls, Barn, Little and Short-eared have been reported occasionally in recent years.

The path to the west hide passes through woodland and scrub where Blackcaps, Garden Warblers, Chiffchaffs and Willow Warblers are among spring songbirds. Grasshopper and Sedge Warblers are more likely to be heard during the east hide walk, while Whitethroats sound off in the lane's hedgerows.

Resident passerines include Willow Tits, Treecreepers, Tree Sparrows and Bullfinches.

Key points
(Longhurst Flash)

- Park at small unsurfaced lay-by (NZ 244 888) on 90-degree bend in Longhirst Lane.

- Flash only viewable from cut-down section of high mound along E side of lane (viewpoint reached by short path from parking space).

- Viewpoint not wheelchair accessible in summer 2011 due to churned-up surface of approach path.

- Take care when parking at or leaving lay-by (tight bend restricts view of approaching traffic).

- Public toilets (see Bothal Pond and QEII Country Park)

4. Longhirst Flash (NZ 2488)

SPECTACULAR marshbirds have taken a liking to this subsidence pool over the years so it will be interesting to see whether that pattern continues, considering its surroundings are subject to major change at the time of publication.

The flash and an adjacent small conifer plantation used to be in a large area of open arable farmland. However, that was before the new Potland Burn Surface Mine began work – by spring 2011 it stretched almost to the southern edge of the water.

Over six years more than 2m tonnes of coal and 500,000 tonnes of fireclay are due to be scooped from more than 600 acres (242ha) on both sides of Longhirst Lane, which runs north from the A197 Ashington-Morpeth road.

Fortunately the flash remains visible despite the construction of a high mound which blocks views of the mining east from the lane. At the nearest point to the pool (crucially beside the narrow lane's only parking space), a watchpoint has been created on the mound.

When I called there in May 2011 it looked very much 'business as usual', with the usual waterfowl selection, two Little Ringed Plovers patrolling its shore and a Black-tailed Godwit wading in the shallows.

UK Coal pledges to not only preserve the flash and other local wetland and woodland sites, but also to generally improve the environment of the whole affected area after the coal and clay extraction.

Promises include the creation

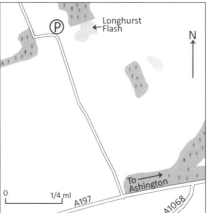

How to get there
(Two miles NW of Ashington)

Head W on A197 and turn right onto minor road about 0.5 mile past junction with A1068. Flash is on right, 0.8 mile along this straight stretch of lane – but opposite a 90 degree bend in road. Small lay-by with limited parking space actually on bend. NB: turning to Linton Lane Reserve is two miles further along minor road from flash.

of wildlife-friendly meadows, marshland and wetlands on 170 acres (69ha) of the eastern side of the mine area, plus almost 90 acres (34.55ha) of new woodland and hedgerow and nearly nine miles of new footpaths and bridleways.

Whether the flash continues to attract off-beat species remains to be seen, of course. The most recent example of its pulling power was the Glossy Ibis that paid a short visit during September 2009 while touring local wetlands.

Great White Egret has been recorded twice since the late 1990s, the second one spending most of its fortnight stay at the flash.

Meanwhile Little Egrets have been recorded almost annually from 2005. Spoonbills have been reported several times in late spring too, usually singles, but during a May 2002 influx, five or six were present for a while. Two Common Cranes in the area in late March 2008 paid occasional visits. There have been August Marsh Harrier and Osprey sightings also.

The wader list includes nothing more remarkable than Little Ringed Plover, Ruff, Black-tailed Godwit, Spotted Redshank, Greenshank and Green and Wood Sandpipers.

Gulls drifting across from the New Moor landfill site a mile to the north-east have included the occasional Iceland and Glaucous.

Ducks may be limited to small numbers of Shelduck, Wigeon, Teal, Mallard and Tufted, along with a few Gadwall and Shoveler and the odd Pintail. Garganey is possible at passage times, especially spring.

5. Queen Elizabeth II Country Park (NZ 28 88)

THE MOST regally-named of the area's wildlife sites was landscaped out of a ghastly industrial eyesore – the biggest colliery spoil heap in Europe.

However, the near-150 acre (59ha) Local Nature Reserve, comprising woodland, scrub, grassland and a 40 acre (15.7ha) lake, was designed for multi-recreational use. A popular spot for fishing, canoeing and wind-surfing, it is perhaps not too surprising that the lake's birding track record is less impressive than those of the other sites.

The lake's most productive time of year tends to be winter and early spring, as indicated by December-to-March records of Smew, Black-throated Diver, Red-necked, Slavonian and Black-necked Grebes and Iceland and Glaucous Gulls.

There have also been occasional outstanding visitors to adjacent

Key points (Queen Elizabeth II CP)

• Car parks at N end of lake (NZ 286 893) and at Woodhorn Museum (NZ 289 884).

• Path (flat, firm, easy) around lake totals about 1.5 mile. Circuit takes about an hour depending on birding stops.

• Mining museum facilities include café and toilets with disabled access. Open Wed-Sun, also Bank Holiday Mondays and Mon-Tues during school holidays (10am-5pm, April-October, 10am-4pm (November-March). Tel: 01670 528 080.

• Premier Inn, including Brewer's Fayre restaurant, overlooking N end of lake

farmland, such as the two Common Cranes that also showed up at Longhirst Flash during March 2008. Up to 50 Whooper Swans were in the fields in early 2010 and four Greenland White-fronted Geese were there in January 2011.

Spring passage can lead to Little Gull and Black Tern stop-overs and there are occasional Marsh Harrier sightings. Great Crested Grebes bred successfully in 2008.

A standard range of woodland residents and summer visitors can be anticipated in the park.

Waxwings may appear during irruption years and, in February 2011 a Lesser Redpoll flock included a Mealy Redpoll.

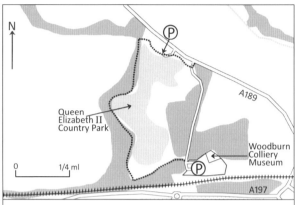

Queen Elizabeth II Country Park

Woodburn Colliery Museum

A189

A197

0   1/4 ml

How to get there

(Above Ashington's NE corner)

Driving N on A189 from Newcastle – Ashington road, keep straight on at roundabout junction with A197. You are now briefly on A197 which immediately passes under a railway bridge and then come to a mini-roundabout where you turn left on to resumed

A189. Sign-posted turn-off to Woodhorn Mining Museum (from which direct access to country park's S end) soon after mini-roundabout. Car park at lake's N end just over 0.5 mile further along A189.

Public transport: Park's southern end and museum are 15 minutes' walk from town centre bus station (regular services from Newcastle).

Winter waterfowl gatherings usually include Pochards and Goldeneyes. Sometimes Goosanders are present too and there has been the occasional Scaup and Red-breasted Merganser visit.

The lake's north end can be viewed from the car park off the A189. Next to the car park is a Premier Inn with a Brewer's Fayre restaurant. If the object of your visit happens to be at the south end, it is best to approach from the neighbouring Woodhorn Mining Museum's car park (see museum opening times and other details in Key Points).

Originally managed by Wansbeck District Council, the park and museum have been Northumberland County Council's responsibility since 2009 when the district authority was abolished under local government reorganisation.

THIS IS ONE of several Northumberland coastal stretches that lives up fully to all the tourism hype with its magical blend of pristine beaches that are never crowded, elegant sand dunes and rugged, dark whin sill outcrops. From the birding standpoint, there's a wetland nature reserve, trees and shrubs that hold migrant passerines and a miniature estuary as two burns combine in a saltmarsh before flowing into the sea. Visits at any time of year can be rewarding.

Target birds *All year* – Water Rail (40%). *Late spring/summer* – Little Tern (80%), Roseate Tern especially in late July/August (50%) Garganey (20%). *Autumn* – Sooty Shearwater (40%), Yellow-browed Warbler (40%), Pomarine Skua (30%), Firecrest (30%), Pallas's Warbler (10%). *Late autumn/winter* – Twite (70%), Snow Bunting (50%), Long-tailed Duck (40%), Little Auk (30%), Lapland Bunting (30%), Slavonian Grebe (20%), Grey Phalarope (10%).

Other possible bird species

All year

Mute Swan	Goldfinch	Willow Warbler
Greylag Goose	Linnet	Blackcap
Shelduck	Yellowhammer	Whitethroat
Mallard	Reed Bunting	Chiffchaff
Tufted Duck		Spotted Flycatcher.
Eider	***Spring/early summer***	
Grey Partridge	Manx Shearwater	***Late summer/early***
Little Grebe	Ruff	***autumn***
Gannet	Whimbrel	Whooper Swan
Cormorant	Greenshank	Pink-footed Goose
Shag	Common Sandpiper	Barnacle Goose
Grey Heron	Turnstone	Brent Goose
Sparrowhawk	Arctic and Great Skuas	Wigeon
Kestrel	Little Gull	Teal
Moorhen	Sandwich Tern	Common Scoter
Coot	Common Tern	Velvet Scoter
Oystercatcher	Arctic Tern	Red-breasted Merganser
Ringed Plover	Guillemot	Red-throated Diver
Lapwing	Razorbill	Fulmar
Familiar gulls	Puffin	Manx Shearwater
Common farmland/	Swift	Gannet
woodland birds	Sand Martin	Arctic Skua
Collared Dove	Swallow	Great Skua
Skylark	House Martin	Terns and auks
Meadow Pipit	Yellow Wagtail	Golden Plover
Rock Pipit	White Wagtail	Knot
Pied Wagtail	Redstart	Curlew
Stonechat	Whinchat	Turnstone
Greenfinch	Wheatear	Little Stint
	Grasshopper Warbler	Spotted Redshank
	Sedge Warbler	Greenshank

Key points (Beadnell Bay)

- Pay-and-display car park at Newton Links (NU 235 260). Arrive early to get a space in summer.

- Pay-and-display car park at Beadnell village is bigger but if exploring both bays, Newton Links is best option.

- Nearest public toilets at Low Newton beside Coastal Path behind the Ship Inn. (NU241 245).
- Long Nanny is a mile NW of Newton Links car park. Allow at least three hours.

- Main links path firm but can be muddy in places. Soft sand in dunes and along shore.

Green Sandpiper	Spotted Flycatcher	Shoveler	Purple Sandpiper
Wood Sandpiper	Pied Flycatcher	Pochard	Dunlin
Woodcock	Short-eared Owl	Scaup	Snipe
Redstart	Fieldfare	Long-tailed Duck	Woodcock
Whinchat	Redwing	Common and Velvet	Bar-tailed Godwit
Wheatear	Brambling	Scoter	Curlew
Reed Warbler	Siskin	Goldeneye	Redshank
Blackcap		Red-breasted Merganser	Turnstone
Garden Warbler	***Late autumn/winter***	Red-throated Diver	Short-eared Owl
Lesser Whitethroat	Pink-footed Goose	Merlin	Kingfisher
Whitethroat	Brent Goose	Peregrine	Fieldfare
Chiffchaff	Wigeon	Golden Plover	Redwing
Willow Warbler	Gadwall	Grey Plover	
Goldcrest	Teal	Sanderling	
	Pintail		

Background information and birding tips

THESE TWO BAYS make up just five of the 39 miles of the Northumberland coastal Area of Outstanding Natural Beauty, but incorporate some of its finest sections. In addition, each bay offers different birding delights and Newton Point, the headland separating them, is also excellent for seawatching.

The most productive sites are within easy walking distance of car parks reached by minor roads from the B1339 Scenic Coastal Route; one of them is ideal for wheelchair users. The main sites are:

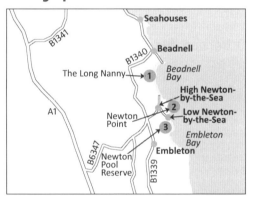

1. The Long Nanny (NU 235 260)

THE LINKS backing Beadnell Bay's magnificent crescent of sand are broken at only one point – by a tidal creek that adds a saltwater element to the low-lying farmland behind the dune system.

The first of two streams that run into it is called Brunton Burn after the hamlet where its short meanderings begin to the south-west; the second flows from West Fleetham to the north-west, but Long Nanny is its well-established name.

That has a rather charming ring to it, which

is perhaps why it has been given also to the area around the channel leading to the sea after the pair's confluence, despite Brunton Burn being arguably the more substantial water.

Newton Links ,lying to the south, have Site of Special Scientific Interest (SSSI) status because they are one of the Northumberland coast's best examples of calcareous sand dunes supporting species-rich vegetation. However, the citation gives due regard also to the saltmarsh associated with the Long

Nanny inlet and the important tern colony nearby.

The latter is watched over by National Trust wardens from a hut standing prominently in the dunes. They need to be constantly alert to minimise the many pressures which can affect the colony – from natural predators and visitors' dogs running loose, to sustained downpours and exceptionally high tides.

The picture emerging from breeding results over recent years emphasises the problems. For instance, in 2009, 31 Little Tern pairs fledging 22 young may not sound too encouraging, but it was better than in the 2004 summer when 32 pairs fledged just 14 of the 53 young hatched from 68 eggs laid.

Disaster struck in 2007 when 88 eggs laid by 40 pairs were destroyed by high tides and bad weather during June, though re-laying led to 17 young fledged eventually. When it comes to caring for Little Terns, an ability to be grateful for small mercies is essential.

At least the Little Tern colony has remained generally in the 30 – 40 pairs range over this period. The Long Nanny's Arctic Tern colony, on the other hand, has declined markedly. In the space of five years it more than halved but at least the 700 pairs in 2009 reared 175 young (one for every four pairs) whereas 1,473 pairs in 2004 raised just 110.

Sand-eel availability was greater during the 2007 summer and that ought to have boosted productivity, but the colony was not immune from the severe weather and high tide combination that hit the Little Terns. The eggs and young of many of the 1,200 pairs were lost.

By early August the only evidence of such struggles is likely to be the wardens' hut standing prominently in the dunes, no longer occupied but with a notice pinned to the door giving details of the breeding outcome. Some terns may still be on show offshore, but the majority will have dispersed along the coast.

Occasionally there are appearances by Roseate Terns moving on from their main UK colony on Coquet Island; up to 61, including eight juveniles, reported at the burnmouth in the first half of August 2008 was rather more than usual, however. Roseate visits can occur earlier in the summer, too.

The Long Nanny colony has attracted vagrant terns on isolated occasions but all well in the past. This is particularly so in the case of the Gull-billed Tern seen hawking over the salt marshes on June 30, 1973.

More recently, the Lesser Crested Tern that visited the nearby Farne Islands each summer during 1984-97 called here in May 1992 and July 1995. It was among several Northumberland sites graced by

Key points
(Beadnell Bay)

• In tern breeding season, colony is cordoned off and shore walkers must divert through dunes via the Coastal Path to the west. Always follow wardens' instructions.

• Only local facilities are The Joiner's Arms at High Newton and The Ship Inn at Low Newton.

• To the north, there are pubs and a few shops at Beadnell and more extensive facilities – cafes, takeaways, shops and pubs - at Seahouses (Also Tourist Information there, 01665 –720 884).

187

a second-summer White-winged Black Tern in late June, 1996.

Also, June has been a particularly productive month for appearances by non-seabird species since the mid-1990s. The list includes Little Egret, White Stork, Spoonbill, Osprey, Quail, Common Crane, Terek Sandpiper, Lesser Grey Shrike and Rose-coloured Starling.

Ringed Plover is the site's other locally significant breeding species and shares the difficulties faced by the terns. The nine pairs in 2009 reared just three young, though there was better productivity in 2007 – with the efforts of 12 pairs leading to 16 fledging, despite the bad weather and high tides. Outside the breeding season, gatherings occur here; counts in recent years include up to 125 in the first quarter of the year and 68 in the final.

Also the saltmarsh by the Brunton Burn, just before it joins the Long Nanny, provides a roost for Curlew; counts have reached 300-plus. A Golden Plover flock may be in the fields between Links House and the Long Nanny.

While passage waders, including the occasional rarity such as the aforementioned Terek Sandpiper, call in spring and autumn, Beadnell Bay is not noted particularly for migrant passerines, probaby because the dunes are not well-endowed with bushes. There are isolated scrub clumps, especially between

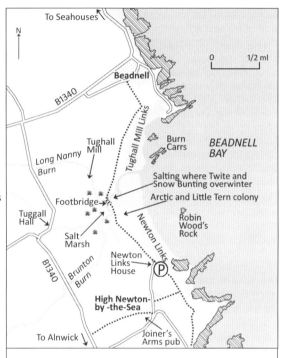

How to get there

(10 miles NE of Alnwick)

Take B road links from the Newcastle-Berwick stretch of the A1. From south, turn off A1 at Denwick (north end of the Alnwick bypass, 36 miles north of Newcastle) onto B1340 which leads to Seahouses (13 miles).

After nine miles (immediately after it joins with the B1339 from Embleton), turn right to High and Low Newton-by-the-Sea. At High Newton (three-quarters of a mile), turn left after The Joiner's Arms pub into a narrow lane ending at Newton Links car park.

From the north, leave A1 at Belford, 14 miles south of Berwick, for B1341/B1340 to Beadnell village (11 miles), but if Newton Links is your intended starting point stay on B1340 as it heads inland for a mile. It then turns southwards for about three miles to reach turn-off to High and Low Newton (first on the left).

Public transport: Two-hourly 501 Newcastle-Berwick bus service stops at Beadnell but it operates only from April to October. Check with tourist information office for latest information.

the Long Nanny and Beadnell village, and at least some potential is indicated by early autumn reports of Icterine Warbler and Red-backed Shrike since year 2000.

This is a period when encounters with passage raptors may occur; there have been early September reports of Marsh Harrier and Hobby in recent years. As for seabirds, Mediterranean Gull can show up at the burnmouth at this time and there has been the occasional report of Long-tailed Skua, Sabine's Gull and, more frequently, Glaucous Gull.

October-March can be eventful, also. During the 2007-08 winter, for instance, a Short-toed Lark was a popular attraction for almost six weeks. Usually feeding on saltings extending into the dune system immediately west of the tern wardens' hut, this was only the third mainland record of the species in Northumberland.

Its sojourn provided some short-term consolation for Shore Lark having become an increasingly scarce winter visitor to the county in recent years. The last substantial presence up to the time of writing was at the Long Nanny when 12 appeared in early November 2003, five remaining until March 2004 and four were still there in April.

Twite have proved to be a more reliable winter speciality on the saltings, though their numbers appear to be dwindling. Up to 120 were reported in the final quarter of 2003, but around 80 was the peak over the next two winters, then no more than 64 during 2006-08.

Snow Bunting numbers have tended to be inconsistent too; around 40 were reported during the 2003-04 and 2007-08 winters but there were significantly fewer in between. Lapland Bunting has become scarcer too, with usually no more than two or three. However, early spring return passage led to five in March, 2004, and 13 in March, 2006.

It's unclear whether a Ring Ouzel at the Links House Farm manure heap for a month from early February 2009 had overwintered or was a very early spring migrant.

With finch and bunting flocks in the dunes, one can anticipate coming across a Merlin seeking prey during the winter months. Equally, with many Golden Plovers and Curlews in the area, plus wildfowl, Peregrine sorties can be anticipated. Short-eared Owl – and occasionally the much rarer Hen Harrier – can be seen hunting over these fields.

Meanwhile Kingfishers put in appearances now and again so it's certainly worth spending some time checking along the waterway. One suitable point is the footbridge carrying the coastal path over the burn at the point where it starts flowing across the beach. Further useful lookouts are provided by the tops of taller sand dunes.

2. Newton Point (NU 239 347)

NORTHUMBERLAND'S coast is well endowed with headlands and on days of onshore winds, particularly between July and November, most tend to deliver results.

Newton Point, it must be admitted, is not among the top locations due to the promontory being quite low (the highest point of its outer part is just over 32ft above sea level) and its seaward tip is very exposed in severe weather.

However, if you are in the area already and changing weather makes seawatching a productive possibility, the Point could well add extra satisfaction to your visit. When the Farne Islands wardens set a new national record with 28,803 Little Auks passing during

Key points
(Newton Point)

• **Pay-and-display car park above Low Newton village (NU 239 247).**

• **Protect road verge by the 'Tin Church' by obeying no parking signs.**

• **Public toilets at Low Newton beside Coastal Path behind the Ship Inn. (NU241 245).**

• **Newton Point is 0.75 of a mile NE of Low Newton. Follow Coastal Path from village (the path passes within half-a-mile of the headland). Football Hole is immediately north of the headland.**

• **Main links path firm but can be muddy in places.**

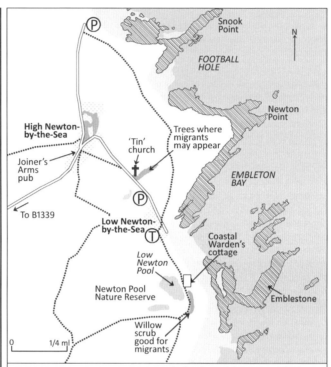

How to get there

Follow instructions for Long Nanny, but on reaching High Newton, stay on minor road from B1340 for another half-mile until the pay-and-display car park on the right above Low Newton. The path leading to Newton Point is at the foot of the slope down to the village.

a continuous sea-watch on November 11, 2007, Newton Point, ten miles down the coast, was in the thick of the action with a total of 1,936 passing in just one hour.

Similarly, there have been Sooty Shearwater and Pomarine Skua sightings at the Point on the same days that movement has been evident elsewhere. Long-tailed Skua occurrences are more irregular, but on any day (mainly late summer/ autumn and more rarely in late spring/early summer) when the species is reported passing other Northumberland headlands in a north-east wind, it is possible off Newton too.

The same applies, of course, to the full range of seabirds and wildfowl involved in regular autumn movements. Newton

Point has the benefit of a small bay, Football Hole, barely half-a-mile across, immediately to the north. This is always worth checking for late autumn/winter regulars such as Eider and Red-throated Diver, plus occasional Long-tailed Duck, Velvet Scoter and Mediterranean Gull. Grey Phalarope is among other notable visitors over the years.

In addition, the headlands on either side of Football Hole provide useful vantage points for scanning the considerably bigger Beadnell Bay to the north and Embleton Bay to the south for sea-duck, divers and grebes.

Searching for grounded songbird migrants during spring or autumn falls can be concentrated mainly on two small bushes at Football Hole. Bluethroat, Red-backed Shrike, Subalpine Warbler, Barred and Yellow-browed Warblers are among scarcer species reported from there.

At Newton Point itself, the place to check is a small former military compound, now used by the National Trust as offices and a workshop. Even at its starkest it provided shelter for grounded migrants, but the Trust has boosted its potential by planting shrubs for cover. Species that have taken advantage include Wryneck, Black Redstart, Redstart, Ring Ouzel and Pied Flycatcher.

As the headland's outer section is grassland, Wheatears can be prominent at passage times. Also, it can be well covered in Scandinavian thrushes if flocks crossing the North Sea make landfall at the Point.

A short distance north along the road from the Low Newton pay-and-display car park is St Mary's Church, known as the 'Tin Church' because it was built with corrugated steel sheeting bought by the local community in kit form in the late 1800s.

Here is the first substantial cover migrants encounter on moving inland from the Point. There's a line of trees and shrubs behind the church and a roadside conifer belt. Across the road from the church is a scrub-fringed track to Quarry House; it's private but the nearer bushes can be viewed from the road. This area has accommodated Waxwing, Barred, Pallas's and Yellow-browed Warblers, Firecrest and Great Grey Shrike in autumn.

Mature trees in the walled garden by the Links House turn-off in High Newton village have held Pallas's and Yellow-browed Warblers and they look a good bet for Red-breasted Flycatcher.

Key points (Newton Point)

• Wear warm clothing if seawatching in onshore winds in autumn and winter.

• Wheelchair access possible on path behind dunes from Beadnell Harbour car park.

3. Newton Pool Reserve (NU 239 347)

CREST THE BROW of the rise beyond the 'Tin Church' on a hot summer's day and you might well question the wisdom of going further because Low Newton's small natural haven is likely to be bustling with watersport activity and the adjacent beach crammed with families.

Even the village green, surrounded on three sides by early 19th Century cottages, is liable to be heaving as real ale enthusiasts flock to the Ship Inn to sample the products of its own brewery. But it is worth persisting: at the foot of the hill you'll see a Coastal Path signpost pointing to a path which, after

Key points
(Newton Pool)

- Car parking/ toilets – same as Newton Point.

- Pool is less than 0.5 miles south of village. Allow two hours, depending on how much is on show.

- Boardwalk gives all-year access, including wheelchairs, to pool/hides.

- To check Emblestone from the soft sand dunes, cross to shore north of warden's cottage. The dunes are steep so can be physically challenging.

- Facilities: same as Long Nanny.

How to get there
As with Newton Point except that at foot of slope below car park, continue south following signpost pointing to path running behind village.

passing a garden where migrants may take shelter, takes you around the back of the cottages and between the rear of the pub and the public toilet block. Very soon they are heading south on a boardwalk over soft sand behind the dune system.

The National Trust is responsible for this coastal stretch, and after passing the local warden's cottage, the path comes to their Newton Pool reserve. Two hides (one suitable for wheelchair access) look out over the pool which during the breeding season offers a routine wetland waterfowl range, including a small Black-headed Gull colony.

Well fringed with reeds and rushes, it is one of the county's better sites for Water Rail sightings, particularly in winter, when Bearded Tit has shown up very occasionally. Kingfisher can sometimes be seen from the hide in winter.

Passage times are inevitably going to be the most productive periods to visit the pool. It does not have an outstanding wader history but September 1983 was clearly exceptional, with Wilson's and Grey Phalaropes and Pectoral Sandpiper recorded in the space of a few days.

The 1980s were arguably its best decade for Spotted Crake, a very rare visitor to the county, which had extended stays during

October, 1984, and August, 1989.

Since then Pectoral Sandpiper has turned up locally on several occasions, the most recent on a flash in a field just north of the pool in the 2007 autumn. Grey Phalarope is also a likely prospect– with its proximity to the coast and the regularity of phalarope sightings over the sea during strong onshore winds, there has to be a chance of an occasional bird seeking refuge.

Birders tend to focus their autumn attention on the willow scrub occupying the boggy area between the boardwalk and the dunes, from the warden's cottage to the hides.

Yellow-browed Warbler is recorded here virtually annually and the spot has had a share of the Barred, Greenish and Pallas's Warblers, Firecrests, Red-breasted Flycatchers and Red-backed Shrikes logged along the Northumberland coast over the years. A Cetti's Warbler was recorded in 2011.

Don't expect to find much there in August but it's certainly worth climbing to the top of the adjacent dunes at low tide to scan the extensive Emblestone whin sill outcrop that snakes out to sea.

The particular attraction at this time may well be roosting Roseate Tern families that have moved north from the Coquet Island colony.

SINCE THE END of gravel extraction, Caistron has become a trout fishery and its promising status as Northumberland's leading inland water for birds in the 1990s has faded somewhat. Nevertheless, birding visits can still be rewarding and with new gravel workings having already created a fresh lake downstream, there are some grounds for optimism.

Target birds *All year* – Buzzard (90%), Kingfisher (50%). *Spring/summer* – Little Ringed Plover (70%), Reed Warbler (60%), Redstart (50%), Spotted Flycatcher (50%), Osprey (30%). *Winter* – Goldeneye (100%), Goosander (60%), Whooper Swan (50%), Green Sandpiper (50%), Short-eared Owl (50%), Water Rail (40%), Smew (30%), Hen Harrier (30%).

Other possible bird species

All year		*Autumn/winter*
Mute Swan	Mistle Thrush	Common Sandpiper
Greylag Goose	Long-tailed Tit	Cuckoo
Canada Goose	Coal Tit	Swift
Shelduck	Goldfinch	Sand Martin
Gadwall	Common farm/	Swallow
Mallard	woodland birds	House Martin
Tufted Duck	Linnet	Sedge Warbler
Cormorant	Lesser Redpoll	Blackcap
Grey Heron	Bullfinch	Garden Warbler
Sparrowhawk	Yellowhammer	Willow Warbler
Kestrel	Reed Bunting	*Autumn/winter*
Moorhen	*Spring/summer*	Wigeon
Coot	Shoveler	Teal
Lapwing	Ruddy Duck	Pochard
Familiar gulls	Oystercatcher	Golden Plover
Skylark	Ringed Plover	Curlew
Meadow Pipit	Curlew	Redwing
Grey Wagtail	Redshank	Fieldfare
Pied Wagtail	Greenshank	Brambling

Background information and birding tips

MORE SPECIES were recorded at this site than at any other inland location during the 1996-99 fieldwork for the *Atlas of Wintering Birds in Northumbria*. A check through its 180-plus species list showed high productivity in other seasons during the final quarter of the 20th Century too.

Unfortunately, fly fishing now takes place over 40 of Caistron's 50 acres and an eight acre worm fishing lake is also on offer. With prospects of hooking rainbow, blue or wild brown trout of up to 15lbs, it has become popular with anglers. Cheap boat hire means there are liable to be more of them on the water, than wildfowl, during busy periods. While

Key points

• Park on minor road verge 200 yards SW of Bickerton (NT 993 002).

• Open access at all times.

• Two miles each way. With birding stops this could take at least four hours.

• Unsuitable for wheelchairs due to stile access to path by lake.

• Shops, pubs, takeaway food, toilets at Rothbury (by B6342 bridge over Coquet).

Contacts
Tourist Information, 01669 620 887.

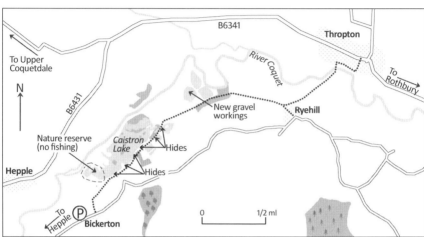

How to get there

(Approx 20 miles NW of Morpeth)

From A1 at Morpeth, take A697 Coldstream road, turning left after eight miles and at the foot of a long straight downhill stretch on to B6344 to Rothbury (six miles). Turn left there on to B6342, cross Coquet bridge and turn right onto minor road. Follow signs to Little Tosson and Bickerton; after Little Tosson farmstead, the lake appears in the valley to your right.

Continue to Bickerton, parking on the verge on the right as the road rises just beyond the hamlet.

Walk back to take the public footpath to the lake from the steel gate at the east end of the hamlet.

Public transport: Bus service 516 (doesn't operate Sundays and public holidays) runs from Newcastle (via Morpeth) to Rothbury and on to Thropton from where there's a two-mile walk via Ryehill to Caistron Lake.

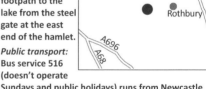

during busy periods. While this activity peaks during summer months, rainbow trout fishing is available all year, depending on winter weather.

This explains why this SSSI location in a scenic setting has slid down the birding rankings. It was once Northumberland's only far inland water to hold more than 1,000 wildfowl regularly. While there are still liable to be hundreds of birds present, a substantial number will be Canada Geese. When they fly off into surrounding fields, the lake can look disappointingly birdless.

The decaying hides emphasise the dramatic change; on their walls are mouth-watering lists of species recorded in the past glory days and photographs of the junketing when the Ryton Gravel Company received an award for conservation work in 1980.

So what's it doing in a *Best Birdwatching Sites* edition? The answer is simply that Caistron and its surroundings continue to offer a great deal to birders and the nearby New Workings, with an extensive lake and islands, could mean exciting times to come.

It's possible that fewer

unusual species have been recorded recently because birders have been shunning the place since the angling take-over: certainly no-one else has been viewing the birds whenever I've been there in recent years. The fact interesting reports keep trickling through suggests that improved coverage could increase the flow.

Since the end of 2004, reports of Red-necked Grebe, Whooper Swans (up to 100), Smew, Goshawk, Osprey, Peregrine, Green Sandpiper, Water Pipit and Common Redpoll indicate its continuing potential.

Early spring has produced three-figure counts of Oystercatchers and Curlew, 1,000-plus Lapwings and later passage waders such as Temminck's Stints. In winter there are still likely be in excess of 100 Wigeon and 30 Goldeneyes and the strong presence of Greylag and Canada Geese can draw scarcer species such as Bean, White-fronted and Barnacle. Untypical wildfowl species recorded in recent winters include Common Scoter and Mandarin.

Smaller pools north-east of the lake remain promising for Water Rail and Kingfisher, while Sedge and Reed Warbler song can still be heard coming from their reed beds in spring/summer.

A Great Reed Warbler sang at Caistron during June, 1990, showing the potential of this habitat, which should not be affected by intensive angling. In its heyday, the reserve was credited with 75 breeding species; a significant number of these would have been in this part of the site.

One benefit of birders staying away is that car parking is not a problem. Access to the public footpath running along the lake's south-east facing side can be either from Bickerton or Ryehill.

As conflict with farm traffic looks likely at the latter location, I usually pull onto the grass verge as the narrow minor road starts to go uphill just south-west of Bickerton. However, there is room only for one or two cars and the next possible space is much further along the lane.

There can be bird activity around this parking place. Fieldfares and Redwings are liable to be in the fields during winter months and as sunset approaches there can be a procession of Buzzards heading to roost in the conifer plantations to the south-west. In spring, I've heard Redstart song from here, while Blackcaps can sound from the gardens of Bickerton's few houses and a Grey Wagtail may be on the stream.

A roadside steel gate provides access to the path that crosses two sheep fields to reach the lakeside right of way. However, it's a wise tactic to view the lake's south-west section before climbing over the stile, because unless very careful, your sudden appearance may well cause jumpier wildfowl to depart.

Though the trout fishery operator has declared the south-west end a nature reserve where angling is barred, the public footpath hasn't been screened off, so the birds are being disturbed constantly. Further north, there is a mound alongside the path, together with hides, dating from when the whole site was managed as a nature reserve. However, their value is minimal as they overlook the fishing areas.

At the north end of the lake the path meets a farm-type track to which left or right access is not permitted. Instead you cross it and enter a field, turning immediately right and making for its north-east corner. This leads to the New Workings (keep well away from gravel haulage vehicles!) which in their raw state look perfect territory for Little Ringed Plovers. What comes next is awaited with interest.

WINTER WILDFOWL SPECTACLES, superb seawatching, rarities appearing among a wide range of passage waders, equally off-beat delights among falls of songbird migrants … just some of the reasons why this is one of the North-East's most rewarding birding areas. With four nature reserves and a country park spread around the bay's six miles and a nationally-important seabird breeding site offshore, the potential is considerable.

Target birds
Spring/summer – Marsh Harrier (60%), Roseate Tern (40%), Spoonbill (30%), Avocet (30%), Temminck's Stint (30%). *Late summer/autumn* – Sooty Shearwater (60%), Pomarine Skua (30%), Yellow-browed Warbler (30%). *Late autumn/winter* – Whooper Swan (70%), Pink-footed Goose (70%), Twite, (70%), Water Rail (50%), Barn Owl (50%), Lapland Bunting (50%), Red-necked Grebe (30%), Bittern (30%), Slavonian Grebe (20%), Little Auk (20%).

Other possible bird species

All year
Common waterfowl
Shelduck
Wigeon
Gadwall
Teal
Shoveler
Eider
Grey Partridge
Gannet
Cormorant
Shag
Grey Heron
Great Crested Grebe
Sparrowhawk
Kestrel
Oystercatcher
Ringed Plover
Lapwing
Redshank
Familiar gulls
Farmland/woodland birds
Skylark

Contacts
Tourist Information Centre (open Apr-Oct), 01665 712 313.

Northumberland Wildlife Trust – 0191 284 6884.

Stonechat
Tree Sparrow
Pied Wagtail
Rock Pipit
Greenfinch
Goldfinch
Linnet
Lesser Redpoll
Bullfinch
Yellowhammer
Reed Bunting.

Summer and spring/ autumn passage
Barnacle Goose
Brent Goose
Garganey
Fulmar
Manx Shearwater
Little Egret
Little Ringed Plover
Knot
Sanderling
Little Stint
Curlew Sandpiper
Dunlin
Ruff
Snipe
Woodcock
Black-tailed Godwit
Whimbrel
Curlew
Common Sandpiper
Green Sandpiper

Spotted Redshank
Greenshank
Wood Sandpiper
Arctic Skua
Great Skua
Kittiwake
Little Gull
Mediterranean Gull
Black Tern
Sandwich Tern
Common Tern
Arctic Tern
Guillemot
Razorbill
Puffin
Cuckoo
Swift
Goldcrest
hirundines
Chiffchaff
Willow Warbler
Blackcap
Garden Warbler
Lesser Whitethroat
Whitethroat
Grasshopper Warbler
Sedge Warbler
Reed Warbler
Ring Ouzel
Fieldfare
Redwing
Spotted Flycatcher
Redstart

Whinchat
Wheatear
Pied Flycatcher
Yellow Wagtail
Brambling
Siskin.

Late autumn/winter
Brent Goose
Pintail
Pochard
Scaup
Long-tailed Duck
Common Scoter
Velvet Scoter
Goldeneye
Red-breasted Merganser
Red-throated Diver
Merlin
Peregrine
Golden Plover
Sanderling
Snipe
Bar-tailed Godwit
Curlew
Iceland Gull
Glaucous Gull
Short-eared Owl
Waxwing
Black Redstart
Water Pipit
Crossbill
Snow Bunting

How to get there

(Southernmost site – Ellington – is approx five miles NE of Ashington).

All sites are reached by minor roads from A1068 - which links to A19 Tyne Tunnel road and Newcastle's A1 Western Bypass via A197 (joining A1 beyond Morpeth) and the A189 to Ashington and Newcastle. A1068's northern end joins A1 at Alnwick. See Bothal site for (Pp xx) more details, mileages etc.

Public transport: Newcastle – Alnwick hourly 518 bus service stops at Amble at bay's north end (also at Hadston by access road to Druridge Bay CP).

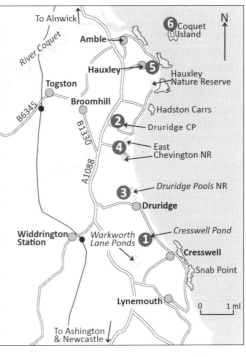

Background information and birding tips

DRURIDGE BAY is where – if approaching from the south – Northumberland's coast starts to live up to the tourist hype. However, if not for a strong opposition campaign in the 1980s and a later government policy change, a nuclear power station might now be its dominant central feature.

During the 20th Century's last three decades, this splendid coastal crescent was scarred by opencast coal mining, but ultimately the environment benefited, with extensive wetland habitat being created in the wake of these huge operations.

The main attractions, (in alphabetical order), are:

1. Cresswell Pond (NZ 284 946)

THIS EXTREMELY productive wetland preceded the bay's opencast era, but the former deep mining industry influenced its creation, causing already low-lying land behind the dunes to sink and flood. Eventually, with the sea so close, this lagoon became brackish due to occasional briny incursions via its outlet channel.

The result was habitat for a wide species range. Farmland shelving gently into its western and northern ends and the sand/mud bar in the south-east corner ensure ideal conditions for waders. Equally there is scope for both surface-feeding and diving waterfowl. A reedbed on the eastern side caters for more secretive species and provides a buffer against disturbance from the adjacent, often quite busy minor road.

The 50 acre (20ha) reserve – owned by Alcan Farms Ltd but NWT-managed – is visited

Key points
(Cresswell Pond)

• **Free parking: for hide in rough and sometimes muddy lay-by (NZ 284 946) at start of track to Blakemoor Farm; for lake's north end mud-free surfaced car park (NZ 284 946) from which also access to beach through dunes.**

• **From lay-by, walk up track to farm then turn right on to path to hide at pond's S end. Distance: about 0.25 mile.**

• **Hide wheelchair-accessible but gate at start of path from farm may pose difficulties.**

• **Toilets at Cresswell village (across road from ice cream shop).**

• **Meals at Plough Inn, Ellington.**

regularly by rarities. Lesser Scaup, Glossy Ibis and Semipalmated and Baird's Sandpipers are among more recent examples. They extended an already impressive list that, since the early 1960s, included Blue-winged Teal, Great White Egret, Purple Heron, Long-billed Dowitcher, Wilson's Phalarope, White-rumped, Buff-breasted, Terek and Marsh Sandpipers, Bonaparte's and Ross's Gulls and Gull-billed, Whiskered and Lesser Crested Terns.

Meanwhile nationally rare breeding species such as Bittern, Little Egret, Spoonbill, Marsh Harrier and Osprey are seen more often than in the past. In the case of Bittern, the reserve produced records annually during 2008-12, with sometimes two and very occasionally three reported. With the hide close to the reedbed's southern end, close-up views of this masterful skulker are possible.

Cresswell was always one of the likelier locations for Avocet breeding due to the pool's saline condition and hopes were fulfilled in the 2011 summer following the appearance of eight in early April. As a result the reserve took over from WWT Washington on Wearside as England's most northerly nesting site.

The pool's wader list also includes Temminck's Stint, Pectoral Sandpiper, Greater Yellowlegs and Red-necked and Grey Phalaropes and it continues to be a reliable place for connecting with more regular passage species. Bad weather can produce unusual numbers (up to 79 Ruff after August 2004's sustained rainfall and 128 Black-tailed Godwits following an April 2005 deluge).

Among the delights of remaining in Cresswell's hide until dusk in winter is the sight and sound of Whooper Swans flying in to roost from fields further inland. With thousands of Pink-footed Geese now regularly wintering, there is the further spectacle as they head for their overnight quarters. Nightfall's approach also boosts the chances of Water Rail appearances along the reedbed fringe.

If birds gathered at the lake or on neighbouring fields erupt suddenly into the sky, it may signal the presence of a hunting Merlin or Peregrine. A winter afternoon can be rounded off by the sight of a Barn Owl hunting over the marshy area with a small pool, between the lake's south-east corner and the track to Blakemoor Farm at dusk.

More than a dozen duck species are recorded annually, with Wigeon (winter peaks usually 300 to 500) and Teal (up to 300) standing out numerically. Checking carefully through such gatherings has led to the discovery of the occasional American Wigeon or Green-winged Teal.

Garganey is a spring/autumn passage visitor and Smew an irregular winter visitor. Sea ducks, particularly Red-breasted Mergansers, may be on show with Scaup, Long-tailed Duck and Common Scoter much less frequent.

The roomy hide provides the best general view of the lake but not the shallow-mud-fringed extension into the field beyond the bridleway along the reserve's northern edge. Often well stocked with feeding waders, this is best viewed from the bridleway or, to avoid possibly disturbing the flock, the roadside across from the car park used mainly by beach visitors.

Adjacent sites can lay on occasional passerine thrills. Outstanding examples are the male Pine Bunting (the 22nd for Britain) that fed at Blakemoor Farm sheep troughs in early 1992 and Northumberland's third Isabelline Shrike in the dunes in October, 2006.

Autumn migrants recorded in bushes by the path between the farm and the hide include Wryneck, plus Icterine, Greenish and Yellow-browed Warblers.

Just 0.5 mile north of Cresswell Pond is Hemscott Hill Farm from where a public footpath leads to Bell's Pond, a small water often overlooked during birding whistle-stop dashes around the bay. Spoonbill, Common Crane and Lesser Yellowlegs are among rarer species recorded there since the 1990s.

Usually a Twite flock – typically 20-70 but

Map labels:
Hemscott Farm
Bell's Pond
Cresswell Pond
Hide
Warkworth Lane Ponds
Warkworth Lane
A1068
Closed lay-by possible Whooper Swans
Ellington
To Ashington & Newcastle
Dunes area - Twite, Snow and Lapland Bunting
Park here for hide
Cresswell
T (opposite ice cream shop)
Caravan site
Snab Point (sea watching)
N
0   1/2 ml

How to get there

(Approx five miles NNE of Ashington)

All Druridge Bay sites are E of A1068 Ashington-Alnwick road. The A189 N from Newcastle (connecting with A19 between Tyne Tunnel and A1) joins A1068 two miles N of Ashington. For Cresswell Pond, turn right at roundabout a mile N along A1068 into Ellington village. After passing Plough Inn, turn left on to minor road to Cresswell village (two miles). At T-junction at Cresswell, turn left and, after a mile, reserve is on left. Hide at lake's S end reached from Blakemoor Farm (park in lay-by at farm track entrance). To view mud at lake's N end, cross road from dunes car park.

Public transport: Bus service 340 operates between Cresswell village and Ashington from where services X31, 32 and 33 run to Newcastle (Haymarket bus station). Reserve is half a mile N along minor road from Cresswell village.

there can be up to 200 – is at Hemscott Hill Links between November and March, either near the small burn running into the sea, or in the vicinity of feeding cattle. A few Snow Buntings may be there also and possibly a Lapland Bunting or two. Shore Lark is more irregular; three during the 2006/07 winter were the most recent occurrence at the time of writing.

Warkworth Lane Ponds, a mile south-west of Cresswell Pond, is another site often missed out by birders touring the bay, mainly because these four subsidence pools are somewhat off-the-beaten-track and offer a narrower species range than the seaside reserves.

Rarity appearances at the ponds are much more infrequent, but they were visited by the Pied-billed Grebe that was in the area during 1992-94. More recently, a Great White Egret was there in April 2010 and Black-necked Grebe, Marsh Harrier, Little Gull and Black Tern are seen occasionally at passage times. Winter brings the prospect of Whooper

Swans and Pink-footed Geese feeding on nearby farmland, with Short-eared Owl a further possibility.

The pools, 0.5 mile from the nearest public road, can be reached by public footpaths. The bridleway between Ellington village and the A1068 via Highthorn Farm passes the main pool. This track is intersected by the bridleway and path between Cresswell Pond and the A1068. You can drive closer to the pools via the tarmac-surfaced access to Ellington Caravan Park but this is narrow and parking is limited.

2. Druridge Bay Country Park (NZ 271 998)

Key points (Druridge Bay CP)

• Free parking places near lake's west end (NU 259 001). Pay-and-display parking near visitor centre and beach (NZ 271 998).

• If you wish to visit Hadston Carrs (noted for seawatching/ migrants) just North of CP, there's free parking (NU 008 278) at end of minor road leading to this spot from A1068 (see Access details).

THOUGH earmarked for general public leisure and non-motorised water sports, the Country Park created from the land restored after open-cast mining, has earned a place on the Northumberland birding map.

Indeed, the county species list was extended in mid-August 2010 with the identification of a Sykes's Warbler (only ten previous British records) in scrub in the Park's dune system. The site was half-a-mile north of the park's visitor centre, near Hadston Carrs, which is also one of the bay's main seawatching points.

Half the park's 200 acres (80ha) resulting from open-casting is occupied by Ladyburn Lake, its narrower, shallower west end a designated nature reserve. The rest is the domain of sailing craft, canoes and wind surfboards, but

only during April-September. From October to March it's strictly for birds and, particularly during the earliest times, they have taken full advantage.

Ladyburn gained a reputation as the region's number one Smew location before the park's official launch in 1989. Up to 12 were recorded in the early months of 1985-87. Also there were unusually high October-December assemblies (up to 56) of Red-breasted Mergansers during 1987-89.

Other comparatively large counts included 270 Pochard, 115 Tufted Ducks and 61 Goldeneye, all during October-December 1988. Up to 18 Scaup and a few Long-tailed Ducks occurred too over this period.

However, Smew visits are irregular nowadays (with two in 2010 and 2011 and three in 2012). Meanwhile counts of

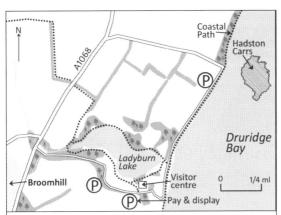

• Country Park open daily, 9am – dusk. Closed to vehicles at night.

• Walk around lake takes an hour. Allow longer if diverting on to linked paths through surrounding woodland.

• Lakeside paths are accessible to wheelchairs.

• You might also want to spend some time sea-watching.

• Country Park visitor centre, tel. 01670 760 968, includes wheelchair-accessible café and toilets (open 9am-5pm).

How to get there

(Approx nine miles NNE of Ashington)

Turning to Country Park is a mile further north along A1068 from junction with B1330 to Red Row and is prominently signposted. Opposite junction to Hadston village, it takes you on to an unclassified road that runs for 0.75 mile to visitor centre and pay-and-display car parks between Eastern end of Ladyburn Lake and bay dunes.

If limiting your visit to Hadston Carrs, an alternative is to continue north along A1068 past Country Park turn-off for almost a mile, taking first right (unsigned). This minor road (0.75 mile) links with coast path at Hadston Carrs (free parking space there).

Public transport: Newcastle-Amble-Alnwick 518 bus service stops at Broomhill and Hadston, just ten minutes' walk from CP.

common wildfowl have declined also, with no more than 37 Pochards, 77 Tufted Ducks, 20 Goldeneyes and 17 Red-breasted Mergansers in recent years. One reason for this is the creation of East Chevington reserve immediately south of the park. Its pools offers significantly more choice to wildfowl than in the 1980s.

While the lake isn't suitable for waders, Greenshank and Common and Green Sandpiper are seen occasionally. The general lack of muddy fringes wasn't, of course, a problem for the Red-necked Phalarope that took shelter for two days after being blown in during stormy weather in August 1986. There are Grey Phalarope sightings from time to time at Hadston Carrs; an outstanding four spent two days on the sea there in late September, 2007.

The park's bird list includes around 50 breeding species,

mostly in woodland – both coniferous and mixed – and scrub established during the post-open cast landscaping operation. Summer visitors include Grasshopper, Sedge, Garden and Willow Warblers and Crossbills occur some winters.

In between, scrub cover in the park's

dunes is as likely a place to find migrants as anywhere around the bay's curve. Chibburn Mouth (see East Chevington for more details) at the southern end of the park's three miles of dunes has a notable migrant track record too.

Key points
(Druridge Pools)

• **Free parking off unclassified road by start (NZ 275 966 and NZ 276 962) of paths to reserve hides. This road runs N behind dunes from 90-degree bend as minor road from Cresswell turns inland to join A1068.**

• **The two northerly hides are just 5mins walk from roadway, the screen looking W across marsh's S end even closer. Coverage within an hour is possible if your schedule is tight.**

3. Druridge Pools (NZ 275 966)

IT REMAINS possible – at the time of writing – that Druridge Pools could gain the dubious distinction of being one of the last places to provide a confirmed record of a species that may have become globally extinct.

After four years of research and deliberation, both the BOU records committee and BB rarities committee decided that a wader present in early May 1998 had been correctly identified as Britain's first Slender-billed Curlew.

However, wider birding opinion remained divided, resulting in a review that was still in process in 2012. In the meantime this "critically endangered" species may have ceased to exist. There has been no confirmed sighting since a report of three juveniles on passage in Oman in the Middle East in August 1999.

Previously, Druridge Pools' most landmark event was the Pied-billed Grebe – only the 14th for Britain – present over three periods between late 1992 and spring 1994. Also notable was the Black-winged Stilt which visited

the reserve in late summer 1993; it was thought to be the same individual that, soon afterwards, appeared at RSPB Titchwell, Norfolk. There it became famous, remaining for almost 12 years. Known as Sammy, it was hailed eventually as the most watched bird in history.

Great White Egret, Pacific Golden Plover, White-rumped and Broad-billed Sandpipers and Red-throated Pipit provided further1980s -'90s highlights. The flow continued into the new century, the most outstanding recent visitor being the first-winter Glossy Ibis that was mostly at this reserve during its month-long autumn 2009 sojourn in the bay area.

Also, there have been Spotted Crake, Avocet, Temminck's Stint, Pectoral Sandpiper, Lesser Yellowlegs and White-winged Black Tern appearances since year 2000.

Following the trend of the other bay reserves, Little Egret, Spoonbill (four together during May-June 2011) and Marsh Harrier sightings have become

How to get there

(Approx seven miles NNE of Ashington)

Turn off A1068 at roundabout by Widdrington Arms (three miles north of Ellington). This brings you on to a narrow, coast-bound minor road with a series of 90-degree bends. At the last of these, as road bends south (directly ahead is a stand of weather-beaten conifers), turn left on to unclassified road behind dunes leading to paths to reserve hides/screen.

If moving on to this reserve from Cresswell Pond, simply drive north for a mile then, at 90-degree bend, go straight ahead on to unclassified road.

Druridge Bay

Oddie Hide

Little Hide

Budge screen

Druridge Pools Reserve

Park along track

High Chibburn

To Widdrington & A1068

Druridge

To Cresswell (pond and village)

0　　1/4 ml

---

more frequent in recent years and it's a further location for a Bittern encounter.

The wide range of waterfowl recorded include Garganey regularly on passage and Black-necked Grebe occasionally. This sites has a history of winter Smew appearances; after early 2010's severe weather, four were present during February.

The 60-acre (24ha) NWT reserve straddles the public footpath between the access roadway to the dunes and Widdrington village on the A1068 about 1.5 miles inland. North of the path, hidden behind a mound, is a large deep pool, a left-over from opencast mining operations up to the 1970s. This is much favoured by diving ducks and grebes.

On the south side, also shielded by a mound, are extensive wet fields with three Trust-created small shallow pools, particularly popular with wading birds.

The large and spacious Oddie Hide overlooks the main pool while a smaller hide across the public footpath provides views of the wet fields and particularly the most northerly of the small pools. These are about 300 yards along the path; a screen hide on the east side of the fields and closest to the other pools is even closer to the roadway. Sadly, the hides suffer occasional vandalism from a tiny minority of the thousands of fun-seekers who flock to nearby beaches each year.

The paths to the hides and screen pass through a long strip of planted saplings and shrubs bordering the reserve's eastern edge, which are likely to hold grounded migrants. September/October can be particularly productive, with Wryneck, Radde's Warbler, Firecrest and Little Bunting among scarcer species recorded since year 2000. Firecrest has turned up

Key points
(Druridge Pools)

• Paths to hides/screen may be boggy, posing difficulties for wheelchair-users. Also, only large hide is wheelchair accessible (steps up to other hide and screen).

• Nearest toilets at Cresswell village to S (two miles) and CP visitor centre disabled access to N (five miles).

• Meals at Widdrington Inn (junction of A1068 and minor road to Druridge Pools) Also, café at CP visitor centre.

in springtime too and in 2008 there was a singing Marsh Warbler.

Migrants also take refuge in isolated bushes in the Druridge Links dunes; species logged over the years include Pallas's and Yellow-browed Warblers, Red-backed and Great Grey Shrikes and Rustic Bunting.

Stonechats are regular breeders in this area and survived the harsh winters of 2009-10 and 2010-11.

Key points (East Chevington)

- Free parking for a few cars near most-used hide (south end of North Pool) on unclassified road verge at NZ 268 987) or, if no space available, at end of lane behind dunes (NZ 272 985).

- Short distance to steel hide overlooking North Pool. Firm path starts across road from parking space.

- Wheelchair users can reach southern hide.

- Reserve's South Pool, on other side of lane, can be viewed from hedge gap by parking space.

4. East Chevington (NZ 368 987)

EACH OF THE BAY'S main wetlands offers something different. In the case of East Chevington, the most recent and biggest of the NWT reserves, it is reedbeds – and the birds associated with them – that are the special feature.

Considering the East Chevington phragmites expanse was planted as recently as 1999, we didn't have to wait long for some positive results. After likely breeding by Marsh Harriers in 2007, nesting was confirmed in 2009 when a pair successfully raised four young. Further breeding followed in 2011 and 2012. Due to the raptor eradication policy of Victorian gamekeepers nationwide, the species hadn't bred in Northumberland since the early 1880s. During the next 60 years there wasn't even a definite passage report.

Hopes that Bittern might eventually follow suit have yet to be fulfilled but optimism continues; the species appeared annually during 2004-12, with reports in every month except May. Bearded Tit, however, remains an irregular visitor; at least four were noted from November 2004 and a pair was seen in March 2005 but, after a single female in April 2006, none has been recorded up to the time of writing.

Clearly the Squacco Heron, Northumberland's third-ever, that stayed for seven weeks in autumn 2004, felt very much at home. The reserve was also among Druridge wetlands visited by autumn 2009's Glossy Ibis. Spoonbills appear regularly – including six in May 2002 when a Purple Heron, the county's fourth, spent three days there too. Little Egret has occurred annually since 2007 and Great White Egret, first noted in June, 1998, appeared in both 2010 and 2011.

The reedbeds provide much potential for Water Rails; there have been summer as well as winter sightings. Meanwhile ringing operations indicate how well summer-visiting songbirds have taken to the new habitat; 28 adult and 25 juvenile Reed Warblers were mist-netted in August 2007 and 164 Sedge Warblers in August 2009.

East Chevington's two pools,

each almost half-a mile long, lie north and south of an unclassified narrow lane between the A1068 Red Row by-pass and the bay's dunes. They are the legacy of the huge operation that scooped 3.5m tones of coal from 650 acres (260ha) of farmland during 1982-93.

Two years of repairing the devastated landscape included creating a 460 acre (184ha) nature reserve, which was passed to the NWT in 2003. The following years weren't without problems as arson attacks destroyed traditional wooden hides. Their green-painted steel replacements survive but can be very cold in winter and hot in summer.

Many birders prefer to mount their telescopes outside the hides in good weather, without disturbing waders, gulls and terns on the nearest mudbank.

Rare shorebirds were prominent in East Chevington's rapid acquisition of regional hotspot status. It was among bay sites visited by Northumberland's second-ever Long-billed Dowitcher in autumn 1998. Since then Pacific Golden Plover, Lesser Yellowlegs and White-rumped, Broad-billed, Buff-breasted and Terek Sandpipers have provided further wader highlights.

In addition, Avocet, Temminck's Stint (including a county record party of six in May 2004) and Pectoral Sandpiper have been recorded several times. Also notable were appearances by Red-necked Phalarope (spring) and Grey Phalarope (late autumn). During the relevant seasons, the reserve also hosts a broad selection of more regular passage waders, sometimes in exceptional numbers (eg 110 Black-tailed Godwits and 80 Whimbrel in July 2006).

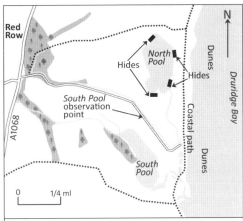

How to get there

(Approx eight miles NNE of Ashington)

Turning for East Chevington from A1068 is two miles north of Widdrington Inn roundabout (or five miles north of Ellington roundabout). Stay on A1068 when B1330 forks left to Red Row and Broomhill but be prepared for a sudden unsigned right turn to reserve after another 0.3 mile. This is opposite the next left into Red Row, which is well signed. Turn right and travel for 0.75 mile along narrow lane with passing places until reserve's North Pool appears on left and there's an obvious off-road parking place on right.

Public transport: Newcastle-Amble-Alnwick 518 bus service stops at Red Row, a mile W of reserve.

The reserve has also figured in Northumberland's more recent rare gull records, with a Ross's (June 1999) and a Bonaparte's (September 2006). North Pool gull gatherings have included Mediterranean, Yellow-legged, Iceland and Glaucous. A few Little Gulls can be expected during April-September, with larger groups in the 20-50 range occasionally.

Roseate and Little Terns are present sometimes among North Pool assemblies of Sandwich, Common and Arctic Terns in summertime. Black Tern sightings involve

Key points
(East Chevington)

• Allow at least an hour to check through North Pool birds from southern end hide. Spend time looking over South Pool from hedge gap; for something more unusual.

• Allow at least two more hours if you wish to visit all four of North Pool's hides (those on east side and north end reached from coastal path).

• If you wish to visit North Pool's two most northerly hides, an alternative option is to use Druridge Bay CP pay-and-display car park (NZ 271 998) which is closer to them.

• Nearest toilets and café at CP visitor centre.

mainly one or two birds, often juveniles, in August or September. Meanwhile, in line with its loss of national rarity status, there has been almost a mini-spurt of White-winged Black Terns (five records during 2003-11).

Autumn wildfowl activity can be intense as Iceland-breeding Pink-footed Geese migrate south to East Anglia and Svalbard-nesting Barnacle Geese (late September/early October) head west to the Solway Firth.

As many as 1,300 Barnacles have been known to land on the North Pool after crossing from Norway. Most Barnacles move on quickly but a small number may stay into the winter – a practice adopted increasingly by Pinkfeet (up to 3,500 visitors now winter in the area). Four Snow Geese accompanied Pinkfeet that arrived in September 2011.

The reserve is among roosting sites for locally overwintering Whooper Swans. Generally, the range and numbers of ducks is similar to those at the other main local wetlands, including the occasional Green-winged Teal.

Garganey appear fairly regularly, especially in spring. Unusually large gatherings of some species can occur in exceptional circumstances – for example 185 Goldeneyes (two or three times more than typical peaks) as coastal passage birds

sought shelter from bad weather.

Smew isn't recorded annually, but some years there can be more than the typical one or two (eg six in January 1997 and, after severe weather, five in February 2010). Sea ducks that can occur include Scaup, Long-tailed Duck, Common Scoter and Red-breasted Merganser.

As for other waterbirds, all three scarce grebes have been logged, Black-necked mainly at passage times, with Red-necked and Slavonian during winter (when they are also possible offshore).

As well as being the region's most reliable site for connecting with Marsh Harrier, East Chevington has other raptor potential. Osprey is a spring and autumn passage visitor, while Merlin and Peregrine are more likely during autumn/winter when there's also a chance of Hen Harrier.

Unusual visitors include an immature Montagu's Harrier that passed through in mid-June 2006. Short-eared Owl reports tend to be mainly between November and April (one to four birds in recent years). Barn Owl may also be hunting near the pools.

Bushes in the dunes and small reed-fringed pools at the Chibburn's mouth are worth checking for migrants in the appropriate seasons. Past rewards include Wryneck,

Bluethroat, Red-backed and Great Grey Shrikes and Greenish, Hume's, Subalpine and Marsh Warblers.

Occasional Lapland Buntings and up to 40

Twite and 20 Snow Buntings may be around the Chibburn Mouth in winter. Shore Lark has occurred much less regularly.

5. Hauxley (NU 283 024)

THIS IS THE most visitor-friendly of the bay's NWT reserves. Varied habitat has accumulated an outstanding bird species list and there is plenty of free car parking from which well-maintained paths lead to the hides.

It used to have a visitor centre with a great view of much of the reserve, a small exhibition area and space for the occasional telescope and binoculars sales weekend.

It benefited local residents too, providing a meeting place for community groups but unfortunately, the goodwill hasn't always been returned by all who set foot on it.

A mystery arsonist struck during 2010 and at the time of writing, the £120,000 centre, which opened in 2001, remains a blackened, burned-out shell. The Trust plans to replace it eventually.

Meanwhile a converted former toilet block by the car park acts as a temporary reception centre. A notice advises that until the new centre opens the nearest public toilets are at Amble to the north or at the country park visitor centre to the south (both about three miles by road).

The 80 acre (32ha) reserve occupies part of the 1970s Radcliffe open-cast mining site – which wiped the village

of Radcliffe from the map, with the 700 population moved to a new housing estate at Amble. Landscaping after the coal-scooping operation ended included the creation of a lake and this part of the site was bought by the NWT in 1983. The Trust has since developed it into one of the bay's most popular wildlife locations.

Now, 30 years later, we see a substantial stretch of water, 'divided' into more compact areas by islands and peninsulas, with reedbeds and other waterside vegetation

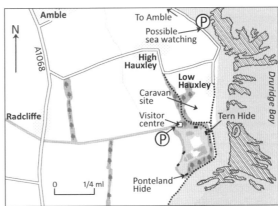

How to get there

(Approx 11 miles NNE of Ashington)

Turn off A1068 to reach Hauxley Reserve two miles north of CP turn-off and a mile south of Amble. Site is indicated by a prominent brown reserve sign. A minor road then brings you to

High Hauxley. At eastern end of village road bends 90 degrees to right, then soon afterwards bears left at a similar angle. At this second bend, turn right on to track leading to reserve and a caravan site (both well signposted). When track forks, go right to reach reserve car park.

Key points
(Hauxley)

- Car park (free) at NU 283 024.

- Reserve (free access) open at all times.

- Small, temporary visitor centre by car park open 10am-5pm in summer and 10am-3pm in winter. These times likely to apply also when new centre opens (scheduled for autumn, 2012).

- Hides accessed from paths (totalling about 0.5 mile). Paths firm and hides wheelchair accessible.

- Allow at least two to three hours if you plan to visit all the hides.

- Until new toilets built as part of visitor centre, nearest facilities at Amble and at CP visitor centre.

Contacts
Reserve
01665 711 578

providing cover. With firmly established tree and scrub belts around its fringes as well, the reserve accommodates a large percentage of the 60-plus bird species that breed in the Hauxley area.

Some aspects of the lake are less than ideal. In particular, its north and east banks rise quite steeply from the water with minimal scope for waders. However, there are more suitable conditions for shorebirds around the edges of the islands – which, by adjusting water levels, can be improved further at migration times.

Tern Hide on the seaward side is so-named because Sandwich, Common, Roseate and Arctic Terns nesting on Coquet Island, gather on the muddy shore it overlooks. Britain's second-ever Lesser Crested Tern which summered on the Farne Islands from 1984 to 1997 visited Hauxley during four of those years.

A Bridled Tern (tenth for Britain) seen on Coquet Island on several July-August dates in 1988 did likewise and then presumably the same individual showed up almost exactly a year later. The reserve was among sites visited by the White-winged Black Tern that opted to spend most of the 2003 summer in the area. Black Tern occurs regularly while on spring and autumn passage and the same goes for Little Gull.

As with the bay's other reserves, Hauxley caters for a wide shorebird range, including species that use it as a high tide roost

after feeding on the foreshore. The Wader Hide on the lake's west side is just one point where they might be seen around the reserve. The Ponteland Hide (reached via the Coastal Path) overlooks specially-created wader scrapes at the southern end. Some rare visitors – eg the Baird's Sandpiper in June 2003 have been seen from the Tern Hide.

More recent rarities include a Terek Sandpiper in May 2011 – just over 25 year after Northumberland's first was recorded on the reserve in June 1986 and Northumberland's first Greater Yellowlegs in late 2011. Hauxley has also been visited twice by White-rumped Sandpiper (in 1984 and 1998 – remarkably both on July 14) and by Lesser Yellowlegs (May 2003 and 2008).

Further rare/scarce waders logged include Avocet, Temminck's Stint, Pectoral, Buff-breasted and Marsh Sandpipers and Red-necked and Grey Phalarope. Of more regular passage species, notable records include 69 Black-tailed Godwits in April 2005.

Other wetland species are well represented also. The wildfowl spectrum includes Garganey on passage, Smew in winter and the occasional Scaup, Long-tailed Duck and Red-breasted Merganser at various times. Both American Wigeon and Green-winged Teal have been recorded since 2005.

Little Egret, Spoonbill and Marsh

Harrier sightings have increased during recent years. There was a Great White Egret appearance in June 1998 and a flyover bird was reported in August 2011.

Trees and shrubs around the reserve's fringes provide cover for songbird migrants. An example of the potential was the Western Bonelli's Warbler (only the fourth for Northumberland) in bushes near the Tern Hide in August 2006. A late migrant Marsh Warbler sang for a couple of days in early July 2011 and Firecrest is among other notable spring visitors.

Autumn delights have included Icterine, Barred, Greenish and Yellow-browed Warblers and Red- backed Shrike.

6. Seawatching/Coquet Island (NE 65 0DW)

SEAWATCHING can be rewarding throughout the year on this stretch of the Northumberland coast. While headlands at either end of the bay are the best locations for observing storm-related movements, any tall dune around its six-mile curve can provide a useful vantage point.

The dunes, indeed, are ideal on a calm winter day when birds are very visible on a flat sea, drifting closer on a rising tide. It would be unusual if there weren't at least several Red-throated Divers in view, sometimes a lot more (eg 50-plus in October 2009). There's a chance a much scarcer Black-throated or Great Northern Diver could be out there too.

In the case of grebes, Red-necked or Slavonian Grebes are possible as well as the expected Great Cresteds. Checking through a Common Scoter raft could reveal a few Velvets; very occasionally Surf Scoter has been recorded. Long-tailed Ducks and Red-breasted Mergansers are further possibilities.

Watching from the dunes is also enjoyable, in summer when Gannets, terns and auks are likely to be feeding or passing offshore, or in early autumn when seabird and wildfowl passage is accelerating in still comparatively balmy weather. However, some of the North-East's most exhilarating seawatching is conducted in the teeth of stiff north-easterly winds, with rain or hail squalls, so warm, waterproof clothing is vital.

In the worst conditions it's better to watch from the shelter of a car in suitable parking places around the bay. One is just north of Low Hauxley at NU 286 033, off the seafront road leading to Amble. Two miles to the south, another is at NU 279 009, just south of Hadston Carrs (see

How to get there

(Amble approx 12 miles NNE of Ashington, Snab Point, S of Cresswell village is six miles to NE).

A1068 Ashington-Alnwick road passes through Amble. Turn-off to reach harbour.

Public transport: Newcastle – Alnwick hourly 518 bus service stops at Amble.

Key points
(Coquet Island)

• **Parking and toilets next to Tourist Information Centre (open April-October, tel 01665 712 313) in Queen Street, Amble.**

• **No access to Coquet Island, but hour-long boat trips around island run April-Sept. Birding groups can charter boats for longer outings.**

Details: Dave Gray, Puffin Cruises, 21 Broomhill Street, Amble, Morpeth, NE65 0AN, 01665 711 975.

Key points
(Coquet Island)

- Time spent seawatching depends on events. On a calm day you may not wish to stay for more than an hour. A stiff onshore breeze in autumn could mean a continuous seabird and wildfowl passage and you'll want to stay much longer.

- Warm clothing, a waterproof outer layer and hot drinks are essential for seawatching in bad weather.

- If watching from dunes, take care to avoid sand grain damage to sensitive optical equipment. Soft sand makes the dunes inaccessible to wheelchair-users (car park option advisable).

- Wheelchair-users cannot be lifted aboard boats for cruises around island.

Druridge Country Park for access details).

At the opposite end of the bay, there's the car park at Snab Point (NZ 301 928), 0.5 mile south of Cresswell village along the coast road to Lynemouth. As well as being productive for seawatching, this site has had its moments as far as landbird vagrants go too. A Siberian Stonechat was near the car park in September 2001 and Northumberland's third Desert Wheatear spent ten days at this promontory in November 1999.

One advantage of Druridge's reserves being close to the sea is that pager-equipped birders visiting them can switch quickly to looking out from nearby headlands or dunes on receiving alerts that something 'hot' is heading their way.

For example, a northbound White-billed Diver in October 2008 and a Great Shearwater in August 2005 were seen off Hauxley following sightings off Newbiggin ten miles to the south.

Two Gull-billed Terns passed Snab Point in May 2006

after first being reported off Hartlepool, Cleveland, 50 miles away.

Britain's rarest breeding seabird is the Roseate Tern, with just around 100 pairs – mostly nesting on tiny Coquet Island, immediately north of the bay and a mile offshore. Thanks to the efforts of RSPB wardens the colony has grown steadily from 34 pairs since year 2000 to an average 80-90 pairs in recent years.

Nests of Common, Arctic and Sandwich Terns, Eider and Black-headed Gulls cover much of the rest of the surface, while Puffins – up to 19,374 pairs in recent years – raise their young underground.

Such is the concentration of nesting birds that landing is out of the question but boats operating from Amble harbour cruise around the island from April to September. A CCTV link enabling the seabirds to be viewed on a screen at Amble ended during the 2011 summer and there is uncertainty over whether it will be resumed in future.

210

BRITAIN'S only east coast archipelago is one of the region's prime birding locations. During the summer months the accent is strongly on nesting seabirds, with Puffins and Guillemots present in their tens of thousands. Falls of migrants in spring and autumn can be on a par with some of the country's hottest spots for passage. The excitement of the boat trip, stunning scenery, close-up views of grey seals and a history spanning 14 centuries are further reasons why a visit to these islands is a landmark event. This really is an extra special place.

Target birds
Summer – Manx Shearwater (60%), Arctic Skua (60%), Roseate Tern (40%). *Spring passage* – Bluethroat (40%), Red-backed Shrike (40%). *Autumn passage* – Wryneck (40%), Greenish Warbler (40%), Ortolan Bunting (40%).

Breeding birds (usual abundance)

Fulmar (200-300 pairs)	Herring Gull (700-800 pairs)
Cormorant (100-150 pairs)	Great Black-backed Gull (12 pairs)
Shag (900-1,000 pairs)	Sandwich Tern (500-600 pairs)
Eider (600-700 nests)	Common Tern (100 pairs)
Red-breasted Merganser (1 nest - bred in 2007 for first time)	Arctic Tern (1,800 pairs)
	Guillemot (48,000 individuals)
Oystercatcher (40 pairs)	Razorbill (400 pairs)
Ringed Plover (8 pairs)	Puffin (36,500 pairs)
Kittiwake (3,000-4,000 pairs)	Rock Pipit (24 pairs)
Black-headed Gull (400-500 pairs)	Pied Wagtail (6 pairs)
Lesser Black-backed Gull (500-600 pairs)	Wren (1 pair – first-ever breeding record for islands)

Other possible bird species

Spring/autumn

Swallow	Reed Warbler	Spotted Flycatcher
Robin	Lesser Whitethroat	Pied Flycatcher
Redstart	Whitethroat	Brambling
Whinchat	Garden Warbler	Chaffinch
Wheatear	Blackcap	Brambling
Ring Ouzel	Chiffchaff	Siskin
Grasshopper Warbler	Willow Warbler	
	Goldcrest	

Background information and birding tips

MOVEMENT of the Earth's tectonic plates laid the foundations for North-East England's tourist industry – in operation 295 millions years later.

Stunning scenic attractions such as the Great Whin Sill were formed by intrusions of magma from far underground. Run-off from the Pennine Fells pouring over one such exposure gave us Upper Teesdale's High Force Waterfall, while two to five miles off the Northumberland coast, the eastern extremity of this hard, basaltic formation is among

Key points

• Large pay-and-display car park with toilet block opposite Seahouses harbour entrance.

• Shops, pubs, cafes and takeaways at Seahouses.

• Visitor access only to Inner Farne and Staple Island. Boat trip that includes an hour on Inner Farne or Staple lasts approximately 2.5 hours. The National Trust levies a landing fee for non-members.

• All-day boat trips (May-July) last about 5.5 hours (two hours on Inner Farne and Staple).

• Half-mile circular boardwalk on 16-acre Inner Farne can be slippery in wet weather).

• Watch your step for straying seabird chicks.

How to get there

(Seahouses lies 15 miles NE of Alnwick)

All boat trips leave from Seahouses, which is reached by B roads leading from A1.

From the south, turn off A1 at Denwick (north end of the Alnwick bypass) onto B1340 which leads to Seahouses (13 miles). From the north, leave A1 at Belford, about 14 miles south of Berwick-upon-Tweed, and take B1340 to Bamburgh (six miles) where it becomes the B1340 to Seahouses (three miles).

The nearest A1 turn-off to Seahouses (both directions) is at NU 139 274, about five miles south of Belford (two miles south of Purdy Services) but the six-mile drive along a winding minor road is no quicker than the other routes.

Public transport: By bus: The following buses from Berwick and Alnwick are routed via Seahouses. The 501, 505 bus service is operated by Arriva (0844 800 44 11). The 401, 525 service is operated by Travelsure (01665 720 955).

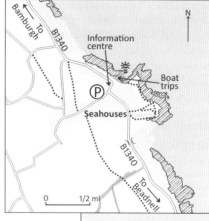

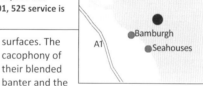

England's most outstanding nature reserves.

The Farnes' scatter of 15 dolerite masses that always remain above the waves (another 13 appear only when the tide drops) teem with seabirds each summer. Puffins and Guillemots are far ahead of the rest numerically, with Kittiwakes, Arctic and Sandwich Terns, Shags and Eiders only in the lower thousands.

There's also a small but slowly increasing Razorbill population, while Fulmars, Cormorants and Common Terns are stable. Several hundred pairs of Herring, Lesser Black-backed and Black-headed Gulls plus a few Great Black-backs make up the rest of the cast.

Staple Island, one of only two major breeding sites where visitors are permitted to go ashore, is a highlight whether viewed from land or sea. Guillemots crowd the tops of The Pinnacles, three rock columns on its south-east side.

Kittiwake nests are plastered to precarious ledges, while the home life of Shags and Razorbills is played out on broader rugged surfaces. The cacophony of their blended banter and the colony's distinctive aroma ratchet up the deep sense of atmosphere.

A half-mile boardwalk on Inner Farne, the largest of the islands, is a memorable experience too, though this is not exactly a relaxing stroll. While constantly looking down to avoid trampling on straying chicks, there's an expectation of imminent dive-bombing from above by nearby nesting Arctic Terns.

In contrast, female Eiders mimic plastic decoys as they sit tight on eggs close to passing feet. Equally Puffins, with fish dangling from multi-coloured bills, couldn't be less interested in human presence as they stand by their nest burrows.

Puffins seem to be everywhere but there are concerns that this may not always be so. That's because a 2008 survey found that in just five years the population had fallen from 56,674 to 36,500 pairs, a serious setback that ended an upward trend spanning more than 30 years.

The loss of 40,000-plus birds is in spite of plenty of sand-eels, their main summer food, and substantial numbers of young reared annually. The only conclusion is that there has been much increased mortality in their oceanic winter range due to food shortages. The colony has now reverted to almost its early 1990s level of 34,000 pairs. Now the question is: will this downturn continue?

The 3,800-strong grey seal colony, one of England's biggest, is a further aspect of the multi-layered appeal of the Farnes. Yet another is the rich history of the islands; the small 14th Century chapel on Inner Farne commemorates St Cuthbert, who lived there as a hermit until his death in AD 687.

All-day boat trips between May and July take around 5.5 hours and are particularly suitable for groups of birders and photographers. As well as landings on both Inner Farne and Staple Island, they include a cruise around all the islands to view nesting seabirds on cliff faces and grey seal colonies at various vantage points.

Birders can expect to see Gannets from the Bass Rock colony passing during boat cruises. Skimming over the waves could be Manx Shearwaters on fishing trips from even more distant colonies – and later in the summer maybe the occasional Sooty on its 'winter break' from the southern oceans (as many as 2,005 in a day have been counted in mid-September).

Any Arctic Skuas hanging around the islands will be trying to rob terns returning from fishing trips.

Of more unusual species, one possibility is Roseate Tern, Britain's rarest regularly nesting seabird. Though the species hasn't nested on the Farnes since 2006, there's a well established colony elsewhere on the Northumberland coast, and birds continue to appear periodically. They may not stand out too well among thousands of nesting Sandwich and Arctic Terns, but this wasn't a problem with the eye-catching summer plumage White-winged Black Tern recorded off Brownsman in June 2004.

An outstanding list of much rarer summer visitors suggests the Farnes are capable of attracting seabirds from all over the world. Most remarkable of all was the Aleutian Tern, at Inner Farne, in May, 1979, a first European record of a species that nests on coasts and islands of Alaska and easternmost Siberia.

In June, 1966, there was a Sooty Tern from equatorial waters, and then, from Arctic regions came a Brünnich's Guillemot in July, 1978. The latter was the most southerly ever recorded off eastern Britain and one of only two recorded alive anywhere around the country's coasts during 1958-85.

After earlier visits to Norfolk and Teesmouth, only the second Lesser Crested Tern for Britain, a female, was recorded in August 1984. Clearly it wasn't a problem that the North-East has a less balmy climate than the Mediterranean, the location of the species' nearest colonies, for it returned each summer during 1985-97.

Pairing with male Sandwich Terns, it was incubating in 1985 and next summer it

Key points

• Wear a hat as protection from dive-bombing by Arctic Terns defending their nests.

• Information centre and toilets, including provision for the disabled, on Inner Farne.

• Wheelchair users should seek guidance from boat owners about access.

was seen for the first time with a chick. It succeeded again in 1989, 1990, 1992, 1996 and 1997. The final chick was colour-ringed and seen at La Paracou, near Sables d'Olonne, Vendée, France, on September 23.

The importance of the islands as a stop-over site for migrant landbirds doesn't always receive the recognition it deserves – which is odd considering that such species account for much of its near-300 species list.

Notable August-October statistics include the fact that, at the time of writing, it's the only British location outside Scotland's Northern Isles to have been graced by Red-flanked Bluetail, Pallas's Grasshopper Warbler and Lanceolated Warbler.

Of Northumberland's 11 Yellow-breasted Buntings, ten were on the Farnes. Each of only three Booted Warblers on the county list were found on the islands.

The April-June track record isn't bad either. Britain's seventh Calandra Lark in 1999 placed the Farnes in an elite club with Fair Isle, Scilly, St Kilda, Dorset's Portland Bill and Norfolk's Scolt Head. White-throated Sparrow in 2007 was a first American songbird for the Farnes, joining three New World sandpipers

Contacts

Tourist Information 01665 720 884

Billy Shiel Farne Island Ferries
01665 720 316 (booking office)
01665 721 297 (further details about trips)
e-mail: skipper@farne-islands.com
www.farne-islands.com

Golden Gate 01665 721 210 / 721 819;
e-mail: bookings@farneislandsboattrips.co.uk
www.farneislandsboattrips.co.uk/bookings.html

Hanvey's Boat Trips 01665 720 388 / 720 718
www.farneislands.co.uk/farne.html

Sovereign 01665 721 554 / 720 760
e-mail: theoldeschoolhouse@hotmail.co.uk
http://theoldeschoolhouse.com/page003.html

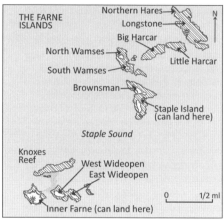

(Semipalmated, White-rumped and Buff-breasted) already on the list.

Spring 2008 saw the accent on variety; a fine run included a Honey Buzzard, two Marsh Harriers, two Ospreys, five Bluethroats, ten-plus Black Redstarts, three Marsh Warblers, two Icterine Warblers, a Subalpine Warbler, a Yellow-browed Warbler, seven Red-backed Shrikes, three Common Rosefinches and a Lapland Bunting.

As many such migrants drop onto accessible Inner Farne and in weather that shouldn't prevent boats from leaving Seahouses, it's surprising more birders don't venture out at passage times.

Bird clubs planning excursions to the islands tend to opt for dates between mid-June and late July when the seabird breeding season is at an advanced stage. The possibility of unusual passerine migrants in addition to seabirds is a compelling reason for considering visits in the mid-May to early June period.

A speculative visit in August or September, by which time a lot of the seabirds will have departed, is more of a gamble, inevitably. However, if boats are running on a day of light easterly winds and mist, it can be rewarding.

WHILE Hadrian's Wall attracts tourists from around the globe, the special attraction for birdwatchers is a few hundred yards of water a mile south of the near-1,900-year-old, coast-to-coast relic of Roman occupation. The World Heritage Site pulls its biggest crowds in summer, but the lough's most consistent birding potential is in winter, though it offers something of interest in every season.

Target birds

Winter – Greenland White-fronted Goose (80%), Pink-footed Goose (70%), Buzzard (70%), Merlin (50%), Peregrine (50%), Raven (50%), Smew (40%), Hen Harrier (30%), Goshawk (20%). *Spring passage* – Little Ringed Plover (60%), Black-tailed Godwit (60%), Osprey (40%). *Autumn passage* – Ruff (60%), Spotted Redshank (60%), Greenshank (60%), Spotted Redshank (50%), Green Sandpiper (50%), Wood Sandpiper (50%), Barnacle Goose in late September/early October (40%).

Other possible bird species

All year		
Mute Swan	Familiar gulls	Swallow
Greylag Goose	Stock Dove	House Martin
Canada Goose	Little Owl	Meadow Pipit
Shelduck	Pied Wagtail	Yellow Wagtail
Teal	Mistle Thrush	Wheatear
Mallard	Goldfinch	Willow Warbler
Tufted Duck	Reed Bunting	Linnet
Cormorant		
Common farmland birds	*Spring to autumn*	*Winter*
Grey Heron	Gadwall	Whooper Swan
Sparrowhawk	Garganey	Wigeon
Buzzard	Ruddy Duck	Pintail
Kestrel	Oystercatcher	Shoveler
Moorhen	Ringed Plover	Pochard
Coot	Common Sandpiper	Scaup
Golden Plover	Cuckoo	Goldeneye
Lapwing	Short-eared Owl	Goosander
Snipe	Swift	Fieldfare
Curlew	Skylark	Redwing
	Sand Martin	Brambling

Background information and birding tips

GRINDON LOUGH has been the only regular location for seeing Greenland White-fronted Geese in Northumberland since the early 1990s, but because it is located in the centre of England (admittedly at its narrowest point), it's a drive of an hour or more for most North-East birdwatchers, whose activities tend to be coastal strip-oriented.

Indeed, it is the only annual

Key points

• Park on verge on The Stanegate road overlooking lough – obvious used places (NY 806 676) at east end of lough.

• Other verge strips are half-a-car width; avoid partially blocking this narrow road (used by farm and forestry traffic).

• A larger lay-by available above west end of lough and beside conifer plantation (NY 804 674)

• The walk between these two points is half a mile each way.

• Road too narrow for safe use of wheelchairs.

Contacts

Tourist Information
01434 344 396

215

How to get there

(Approx seven miles NW of Hexham).

Take A69 from Newcastle to Haydon Bridge. Ignore bypass and drive into village, (speed camera partially hidden just before South Tyne bridge). Just after bridge turn right (signposted Roman Wall) onto minor road. After three miles, Hadrian Lodge (angling hotel) is on left and soon after that there's a crossroads (woods with a few houses on north side). Turn left onto minor road (The Stanegate) and drive W for a 1.5 miles until Grindon Lough appears on right.

The crossroads isn't obvious so if you come to a T junction, with The Old Repeater Station B&B on right, you've gone two miles too far north.

From Carlisle, leave M6 motorway at J43 to drive east on A69. After 16 miles and a long stretch crossing Denton Fell's moors, turn left (just after speed camera) on to B6318 at Greenhead. After nine miles Housesteads Roman Fort is on left (roadside car park) but keep going for two miles until reaching The Old Repeater Station B&B at minor road junction on right.

Turn right there and drive south for two miles until, immediately after woods on both sides, there's a crossroads. Turn right on to The Stanegate for final 1.5 miles to Grindon Lough.

Public transport: Regular bus services run between Carlisle and Newcastle and Hadrian's

Wall Bus (appropriately numbered AD122, the wall's earliest date) operates all year. Details from Tourist Information centres.

Hadrian's Wall Country Bus service operates for much of year. Nearest stop on B6318 at Housesteads Fort, about a mile away.

English site for the *flavirostris* race that overwinters in western Scotland and Ireland, but numbers remain consistent with this sub-species' status as a scarce visitor to the North-East.

Generally, reports since 1999 have been in the range of six to nine birds, so 13, including four juveniles, during the 2007/08 winter raised hopes of an upward trend. The disappointing news was that only a single bird appeared during the winter of 2011-12.

Bear in mind that while the Whitefronts roost at the lough during their mid-October to April sojourns, they feed at a number of preferred sites a few miles away. Awaiting their return as dusk approaches provides opportunities to appreciate the wider assets of this site.

Small parties of Ravens have been reported in recent winters and with patience and persistence, it's possible to see more birds of prey than just Sparrowhawks and Kestrels. Common Buzzard, following its post-1980s national population expansion, is most likely, but there's a reasonable chance of Peregrine too, with Merlin another possibility.

Hen Harriers have been seen hunting over fields around the lough on several occasions but even more so over nearby Muckle Moss to the south of The Stanegate. However, as with other North-East upland locations, the population is well below potential due to illegal persecution. To see this species will mean being prepared to visit repeatedly and to invest many hours of watching and waiting.

The same applies to Goshawk, past sightings of which have been spread thinly over a greater part of the year. For instance, one was watched hunting Teal on the lough at dusk in early September, 2004. Early autumn and spring is when a visit might coincide with an Osprey appearance; there have been records in both seasons.

Due to its steadily growing national population, Marsh Harrier is another outside prospect at passage times, an example being two birds reported hunting around the lough on different dates in May, 2005.

Waters in elevated locations tend not to attract large numbers of waterfowl, but Grindon Lough,

leased to the Northumberland Wildlife Trust (NWT) since 1972, is very much an exception. Being a mesotrophic lake, it contains a narrow range of nutrients at medium concentration levels and therefore supports high plant and animal diversity.

When it comes to birds, Grindon is unrivalled in the North's hills, outshining even its larger and deeper mesotrophic near neighbours, Broomlee, Crag and Greenlee Loughs.

The most prominent wildfowl are Greylag Geese, including winter-visitors from Iceland as well as feral birds, and feral Canada Geese. In late September or early October their presence may attract skeins of Barnacle Geese to stop off when migrating from their nesting grounds in Svalbard to their Solway Firth winter territory.

Equally, Icelandic Pink-footed Geese may be tempted to break their journey as they fly south to Norfolk. Sometimes small numbers of both linger through the winter.

Regular overwintering by very small numbers of Greenland Whitefronts has filled the gap left by the once-regular Bean Geese of the *fabalis* race, now a scarce winter visitor to Britain.

Isolated Bean Goose appearances can still occur, such as the out-of-season bird of late May, 2007. However, like the Lesser White-fronted Goose of early September 2003 and the

Key points

• **Once Brewed Visitor Centre, with toilets, shop, café, internet access, tourist information (01434 344 396) and picnic tables is three miles to west on B6318.**

• **Similar facilities at nearer Housestead Fort information centre, tel 01434 344363, email: customers@ english-heritage. org.uk**

• **More facilities at Haydon Bridge four miles (by road) and Hexham (seven miles away).**

lone Snow Geese of June 2002, October 2005 and late February/early March, 2007, it belongs perhaps in the 'birds of dubious origin' category.

Whooper Swans are less common thanks to the stronger attraction of major winter refuges established at the Ouse Washes in East Anglia and Martin Mere, Lancashire. However, Grindon continues to hold an impressive duck variety during winter months; of surface-feeders, there are liable to be a few Shelduck, Pintail and Shoveler, as well as Wigeon, Teal and Mallard, with Gadwall possible during the spring/summer period and Garganey occasionally on passage.

A Green-winged Teal's lengthy stay in 2002 underlined the need for thorough checks of hundreds of the Eurasian counterpart of this comparative rarity from North America.

The Northumberland Wildlife Trust website declares the lough's water is 'too shallow for diving ducks' but clearly the birds disagree as Tufted Ducks can be seen throughout the year and are joined in autumn and winter by Pochard and Goldeneye and Scaup occasionally.

Goosander may also occur and two drake Smew were on show in both early 2004 and 2005 and one at the start of 2006. A drake Red-crested Pochard was an attraction during the 2001/02 winter. Little and Great Crested Grebes and Cormorant are further diving birds on the site list – plus Black-necked Grebe recorded during the 2007 winter.

Waders tend to take centre stage during the periods between winter seasons. At least 25 species have been recorded since 2000, spread across every month from March to October inclusive.

Among the more regular passage birds are Black-tailed Godwits in April (usually less than ten but a flock of 30 in 2008) and Ruff, Spotted Redshank, Greenshank and Green Sandpiper in August.

Little Ringed Plover has been recorded in both spring and late summer. There are September and October records of Little Stint but the only fairly recent Curlew Sandpiper was a late spring mover on June 01, 2002.

More unusual species since the start of the new millennium include Temminck's Stint (May 2005) and single Pectoral Sandpipers (July, 2002 and April, 2008).

August, 2008, produced a rarity, with an adult winter plumage Wilson's Phalarope present for at least five days over the mid-month period. Many birdwatchers travelled to see it – possibly the most Grindon has had within a week, but with around 200 yards between the bird and the roadside watchpoint, it was only possible to obtain 'record shots'. Others equipped only with binoculars realised that, at a site like this, a telescope is essential.

The area's wider regular possibilities include – despite the seemingly inappropriate exposed, marginal upland habitat – Little Owl, which was confirmed to have nested locally for the first time in 1978. So don't be surprised to see one perched on a dry stone wall, farm building or similar structure further west along The Stanegate.

Also, it's worth checking the conifer plantation by The Stanegate to the south of the lough's west end, as Lesser Redpoll can be very evident there during spring and summer months. Crossbill parties are possible, though far from certain, at any time of year.

To the east, in some winters there's a Brambling flock in woods at Grindon Hill where The Stanegate is crossed by the minor road from Haydon Bridge to the B6318.

THIS VALLEY at the northern end of the National Park is one of half-a-dozen Northumberland sites in the 'absolutely unmissable' category because of their high landscape value and wildlife riches. The open woodland of the valley floor is well endowed with classic dales birds and the massive hills on either side provide a spectacular backdrop.

Target birds
All year – Buzzard (90%), Common Crossbill (50%), Peregrine (30%). *Spring/summer* – Tree Pipit (80%), Whinchat (70%), Redstart, Ring Ouzel, Spotted Flycatcher (all 60%), Pied Flycatcher (40%), Wood Warbler (20%), Dotterel (5%). *Winter* – Rough-legged Buzzard (10%).

Other possible bird species

All year		*Spring/summer*
Mallard	Skylark	Reed Bunting
Red Grouse	Meadow Pipit	*Spring/summer*
Grey Partridge	Grey Wagtail	Golden Plover
Grey Heron	Pied Wagtail	Common Sandpiper
Sparrowhawk	Dipper	Swift
Kestrel	Song Thrush	Hirundines
Snipe	Mistle Thrush	Wheatear
Woodcock	Goldcrest	Whitethroat
Black-headed Gull	Long-tailed Tit	Blackcap
Stock Dove	Coal Tit	Garden Warbler
Barn Owl	Treecreeper	Chiffchaff
Tawny Owl	Jay	Willow Warbler
Green Woodpecker	Siskin	
Great Spotted	Linnet	*Late autumn/winter*
Woodpecker	Lesser Redpoll	Redwing
Common farmland/	Crossbill	Fieldfare
woodland birds	Bullfinch	Brambling
	Yellowhammer	

Background information and birding tips

DOMINATING the scene at Harthope is The Cheviot, the county's highest point at 2,681ft (815m); there's one circular route that enables you to visit this summit and enjoy the best of the valley's woodland in one session.

Inevitably, Harthope's woodland thins higher up the valley, petering out, with just a few scattered, stunted rowans above Harthope Linn waterfall. Amazingly, once spring is in full swing, each of those isolated saplings may hold a singing Willow Warbler

Lower down as you stroll along the burn every tree or shrub can seem alive with family parties of not only Willow Warblers, but also Siskins, Lesser Redpolls and more beside.

Most birders must travel some distance to enjoy this off-the-beaten-track spot near the

Key points
• Park off-road before Carey Burn Bridge (NT 975 250).

• Full circular walk (9 miles) takes six hours. Allow four hours to tackle Langleeford to Harthope Linn and back (four miles).

• Langleeford to The Cheviot mostly uphill, the final stage especially steep. Descent to Harthope Linn involves ill-defined path over frequently boggy slope.

Contacts
Wooler Tourist Information (open daily Easter to end October, 10am-4.30pm)
01668 282 123

Northumberland National Park 01434 605 555; www.northumberland nationalpark.org.uk

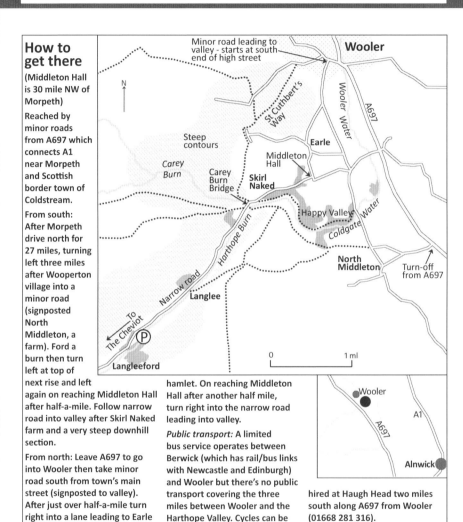

How to get there

(Middleton Hall is 30 mile NW of Morpeth)

Reached by minor roads from A697 which connects A1 near Morpeth and Scottish border town of Coldstream.

From south: After Morpeth drive north for 27 miles, turning left three miles after Wooperton village into a minor road (signposted North Middleton, a farm). Ford a burn then turn left at top of next rise and left again on reaching Middleton Hall after half-a-mile. Follow narrow road into valley after Skirl Naked farm and a very steep downhill section.

From north: Leave A697 to go into Wooler then take minor road south from town's main street (signposted to valley). After just over half-a-mile turn right into a lane leading to Earle

Map labels: Minor road leading to valley - starts at south end of high street; Wooler; Steep contours; Carey Burn; Carey Burn Bridge; Skirl Naked; St Cuthbert's Way; Wooler Water; A697; Earle; Middleton Hall; Happy Valley; Coldgate Water; North Middleton; Turn-off from A697; Harthope Burn; Narrow road; Langlee; To The Cheviot; P; Langleeford; 0 1 ml

hamlet. On reaching Middleton Hall after another half mile, turn right into the narrow road leading into valley.

Public transport: A limited bus service operates between Berwick (which has rail/bus links with Newcastle and Edinburgh) and Wooler but there's no public transport covering the three miles between Wooler and the Harthope Valley. Cycles can be hired at Haugh Head two miles south along A697 from Wooler (01668 281 316).

Inset map labels: Wooler; A1; A697; Alnwick

Scottish Border, but it's well worth the effort. Tree Pipits remain prominent as they launch into their showy song flights from trees by the track above Langleeford but the area's Redstart population is more elusive and harder to see.

Harthope's cul-de-sac road is linked to two equally narrow lanes, one branching from the A697 some 27 miles north-west of its A1 junction at Morpeth, the other running south from area's only small town, Wooler. They meet at Middleton Hall and from there you must drive along a valley road barely wide enough for two cars to pass.

On the way you pass a farm called Skirl Naked, but any thoughts of nude bagpipe-playing prompted by that tag will disappear rapidly as you suddenly descend precipitously to reach the valley's start by the Carey Burn Bridge.

The waterway with that name is joined by Harthope Burn to form Coldgate Water – which then flows eastwards through Happy Valley. It's worth stopping here as you can be reasonably sure of seeing Common Sandpiper, Grey and Pied Wagtails and Dipper. Also, a footbridge over the Hartburn leads to a small oakwood which looks promising for the likes of Wood Warbler and Pied Flycatcher.

You can drive just two miles into the Harthope Valley because only local farm traffic is permitted beyond the point where the Hawsen Burn links up with the Harthope, just downstream of Langleeford. Park on the broad, flattish grassy strip between the road and the Harthope and explore further on foot along a selection of trails radiating from here into the adjacent hills.

For birders with no desire for such lengthy treks, the best option is the unsurfaced track running a further 1.5 miles up the valley to Langleeford Hope near the woodland's upper limit. This is where Tree Pipits can be prominent in late April and May, while Cuckoos, Redstarts and Spotted Flycatchers can also be seen.

Goshawks have been reported in recent springs and an Osprey lingered in May, 2006. Buzzards, Peregrines, Woodcock, Stock Doves, Green and Great Spotted Woodpeckers, Long-tailed Tits, Siskins, Lesser Redpolls and Bullfinches are among other species in prospect during the course of the full year.

However, if you're feeling more energetic, are fit enough, and suitably equipped, there's the option of a circular walk taking in both that valley woodland stretch and The Cheviot summit.

It adds up to around nine miles and involves climbing more than 1,800ft, with the final stage to the summit particularly steep, but it can pay dividends.

Migrating Dotterels sometimes take a break on the Cheviot plateau during May and there was also excitement when a Golden Eagle appeared over the summit on May 27, 2007.

Key points

- **Unsurfaced track between Langleeford Hope and Langleeford muddy in places.**

- **The Cheviot route best avoided in bad weather.**

- **Public toilets in Wooler town centre and at picnic site off minor road between Middleton Hall and North Middleton.**

- **Shops, takeaways and pubs at Wooler.**

More likely species of the walk's upland section will include Golden Plovers, Lapwings, Curlews, Skylarks and Meadow Pipits.

As you're tramping over mainly grassland, even Red Grouse can't be guaranteed, apart from maybe hearing an occasional call from one of the nearer heather moors. However, the hike itself is exhilarating and you can't fail to be impressed by the views from the summit.

In sharp contrast to the walk so far, the second half is downhill all the way. Initially you head further south-west along an extension from the Pennine Way which otherwise runs west of The Cheviot summit while following the Scottish Border. But you

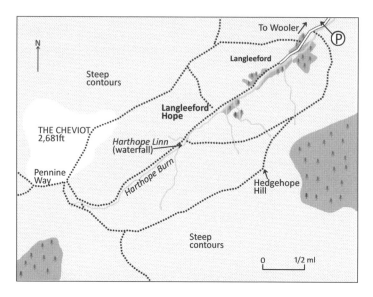

leave it on reaching Cairn Hill at the plateau's southern end to loop back into the Harthope Valley.

Initially the going is heavy – with no marked path, you're basically following the burn as it trickles down Cairn Hill's boggy south-eastern flank. This continues for much of the 1.5 miles to Harthope Linn; subsequently both path and burn are more clearly defined.

Half-a-mile beyond the waterfall is Langleeford Hope, the valley's first sign of human habitation. Just before it, there are sheep pens where, early in the spring, a Ring Ouzel is sometimes found.

Later on, a pair of Whinchats may be in the vicinity; by July there could be a whole family group of them clicking about the tops of bracken fronds.

Also worth checking is the group of conifers at Langleeford Hope as I've known them to

hold a party of Crossbills, along with Siskins and Lesser Redpolls.

It's a good idea to start this walk as early as possible so there is plenty of time left to enjoy the final leg back to the parking place. The woodland bird variety along this stretch is top notch, so it should not be hurried.

As I stated earlier, there are other trails that can offer something to birders. For instance, Wheatears and Ring Ouzels appear along the Hawsen Burn path from Langleeford in early spring (a Black Redstart reported near the Hawsen/Harthope confluence coincided with a light influx on the north Northumberland coast in April 2008).

Ten Ring Ouzels were seen along the Carey Burn in early April, 2006, and a Great Grey Shrike haunted the Langleeford – Threestoneburn path in spring 2008. Rough-legged Buzzard is one dream – sadly rarely fulfilled – of winter visiting birders.

HARWOOD'S range of coniferous woodland species is similar to Kielder's, but its considerably smaller size makes finding them less of a needle-in-haystack exercise... and it is only an hour's drive from Newcastle-upon-Tyne. It is possible to tramp the forest's many miles of trails for hours without seeing anyone else..... and there is moorland to the west also worth visiting.

Target birds *All year* – Common Crossbill (80%), Goshawk (40%), *Merlin (30%) *Peregrine (30%), *Raven (30%). *Spring/ summer* – *Cuckoo, *Redstart, *Ring Ouzel, Spotted Flycatcher (all 60%), Tree Pipit (40%), Nightjar (20%). *Late autumn/early spring* – Great Grey Shrike (20%).
* indicates species more likely to be seen over moorland and along the Grasslees Burn valley to the west of the forest.

Other possible bird species

All year		
*Mallard	Stonechat	*Redshank
*Red Grouse	Mistle Thrush	*Common Sandpiper
*Red-legged Partridge	Goldcrest	Meadow Pipit
Pheasant	Long-tailed Tit	Grey Wagtail
Sparrowhawk	Coal Tit	Pied Wagtail
Buzzard	Jay	*Sand Martin
Kestrel	Siskin	Swallow
Woodcock	Linnet and Lesser	*House Martin
Common woodland birds	Redpoll	Meadow Pipit
Tawny Owl	*Spring/summer*	Whinchat
Green Woodpecker	*Oystercatcher	*Wheatear
Great Spotted	*Golden Plover	Grasshopper Warbler
Woodpecker	*Lapwing	Whitethroat
*Skylark	*Snipe	Willow Warbler
	*Curlew	

Background information and birding tips

THOUGH DWARFED by Kielder Forest and with much less habitat diversity, this near 9,000 acre (3,548ha) spread of mainly Sitka spruce created in the 1950s, has plenty of benefits for birders.

Most birding action happens in Harwood's southern half, as it is the only section with direct road access. Even then, the three clearings which have produced recent Great Grey Shrike records are two to five miles away from parking areas, so if you can bring a mountain bike you'll have a distinct advantage over the footsloggers.

Of course there is birding potential while tramping to those far-off clearings: in the Fallowlees Burn/Redpath Farm area; at Tutehill Moss, to the north-west; and by Chartners, an isolated house even further north.

Key points
• Cars barred in forest (except for rallies).

• No parking in private Harwood village.

• Forest open to walkers and mountain bikers except when car rallies are held. Some sections may close during timber felling operations.

• No facilities in the forest; few signposts and no marked trails, so bring a map.

• Public toilets at Elsdon village on the B6341 may re-open if funding can be found.

• Alternative toilets ten miles away at Rothbury.

Contacts
Tourist Information (National Park Centre) 01669 620 887

How to get there

(30 miles NW of Newcastle)

Harwood occupies 60 square miles of former grazing land and moors between the B6342 and B6341, south of Rothbury.

From Newcastle: From A1 western bypass, take A696 past Newcastle Airport, to Belsay hamlet (14 miles). After another six miles, turn right onto B6342 (signposted Wallington, Cambo and Rothbury, a narrow road with some very sharp bends.

Beyond Cambo (three miles), the B6342 is almost straight for more than two miles, but where it eventually bends tightly right (at Harwood Gate), turn left onto a minor road leading towards Elsdon village. After a mile, turn right into an even more minor road, signposted Harwood but don't drive into this tiny residence for forestry staff. Instead, turn left after a quarter of a mile onto a westbound unsurfaced track. There is ample parking on this track's verge. Don't drive beyond the end of the conifers on the right. From now on you must rely on your feet or pedalpower.

From Scotland: From A68, turn left 13 miles south of the border onto A696, then left again after another three miles and just past Otterburn village on to the B6341 to Rothbury.

At Elsdon village after three miles, turn right onto a minor road and go left when it forks just outside the village. After a mile, it straightens out to head east along Harwood Forest's southern edge.

The turning leading to the parking place south-west of Harwood village is 2.5 miles beyond Winter's Gibbet.

Public transport: Reaching the forest by public transport is difficult. The nearest regular bus service involves travelling from Newcastle to Morpeth where you change to Service 516 to Rothbury, where mountain bikes can be hired at Rothbury (Black Sheep Bikes, tel: 01669 631 121) to enter the forest's northern end via the Simonside Hills.

Map labels

N

To Rothbury & A697

Grasslees

Grasslees Burn

Billsmoor Park

B6341

Tosson Hill

SIMONSIDE HILLS

Sandy Crags

Boddle Moss

Darden Burn

Miller's Moss

Darden Lough

Dough Crag

Chartners

St Oswald's Way

Elsdon

To A696

Tutehill Moss

Redpath

Fallowlees Burn

Winter's Gibbet

Harwood village (private)

To Rothbury

To A696

B6342

0   1/2 ml

Rothbury

A697

A696

A68

224

During winters when Crossbill numbers are high, it's possible to catch sight of several fly-over groups or come across a feeding party or a group drinking from a water-filled rut in an unsurfaced forest road.

The major nationwide Crossbill influx during the early 1990s added a couple of rarities to Harwood's bird list: an adult male Two-barred Crossbill between December 24, 1990 and March 16, 1991, with two female Parrot Crossbills recorded on the 17th.

The Lesser Spotted Woodpecker reported a mile north of Harwood village in March, 2003, was even more remarkable because Northumberland is at the extreme northern end of the British range.

Carrying a telescope and tripod can be hard work but they come in handy when searching for a Great Grey Shrike in the particularly extensive Fallowlees Burn/Redpath Farm clearing. The most recent was in early March, 2012 , continuing a run of annual records.

The clearings look just right for Hen Harrier but reports are few and far between in recent times. Short-eared Owls hunting over the clearings are now becoming rarer too.

On the plus side, the forest has become a reliable site for Goshawk, with annual sightings over the last decade – occasionally up to four birds. These were spread across every season, but mainly during February-April and October-December.

Great Spotted Woodpecker, Stonechat, Fieldfare, Redwing, Siskin and Lesser Redpoll are among other species I've seen during clearing watches. One November day a familiar flight call drew my attention to a lone Waxwing over the Fallowlees Burn site. These open areas, where scrub is becoming established can be productive in spring and summer too, with potential for Tree Pipits, Whinchats, Grasshopper Warblers, Whitethroats, Willow Warblers and Spotted Flycatchers. A late evening visit during the breeding season is bound to lead to sightings of roding Woodcocks. Nightjars can sometimes be heard.

While limited motorised access is confined to Harwood's southern edge, footpaths lead into it from the west and east; walkers and mountain bikers enter also from the Simonside Hills to the north.

One path worth exploring that doesn't actually reach the forest is to Darden Lough, a former Teal breeding site, 300 yards from its western fringe. This trail starts from a lay-by on the B6341 four miles north of Elsdon. After a footbridge over the Grasslees Burn, it rises for two miles – sometimes fairly steeply – to the peaty lough more than 1,000ft above sea level, and then loops back to the road around the western side of boggy Miller's Moss.

This elliptical route has much to offer. Buzzards may be soaring and there's a chance of Merlins, Peregrines and Ravens over the moors. Black Grouse is another possibility, (I saw two females on Miller's Moss in February, 2006 but none have been reported since). Red Grouse, on the other hand, occurs widely.

Skylark and Meadow Pipit song, the Cuckoo's voice and wader calls sound over the fells in the breeding season. Occasional sandstone crags are likely spots for finding early-arriving Wheatears and Ring Ouzels. Later in the season, areas of bracken become Whinchat family nurseries and alders and birch along Grasslees Burn harbour Redstarts.

The area's most unusual raptors since the 1990s have all been just outside Harwood. An immature Golden Eagle overflew the B6341 north of Elsdon in March 2004. Just over a year later a first-winter White-tailed Eagle soared above Simonside, while in March 2009, a Rough-legged Buzzard reportedly flew north-west near a gruesome tourist attraction, Winter's Gibbet.

Key points

- Many miles of wheelchair-friendly paths, including Lakeside Way around reservoir's 27 mile shoreline.

- Forest Drive (£3 toll) 12 miles from Kielder Castle to Byrness on A68 (open only from Easter to Christmas).

- Visitor centres at Kielder Castle (Open daily April - October/weekends only November-December 18); Leaplish (February – October); Tower Knowe, 01434 240 398 (June-September).

- Food and drink: Duke's Pantry (tea-room) at Kielder Castle and Angler's Arms nearby; Boat Inn Restaurant and Bar, Leaplish; and Waterside Café, Tower Knowe.

- Toilets at Kielder Castle, Leaplish Waterside Park and Tower Knowe.

ROLLING OUT the superlatives is most appropriate when focusing on the upper North Tyne valley. Its centrepiece is northern Europe's biggest man-made lake (by volume), nestling within the Forestry Commission's largest tree expanse. Admittedly, some speciality birds can be seen closer to the North-East's main built-up areas, but for the overall experience of a most spectacular location, the extra miles are worthwhile.

Target birds

All year – Siskin (80%), Mandarin Duck (70%), Common Crossbill (70%), Lesser Redpoll (60%), Raven (40%). *Winter/early spring* – Goshawk (50%). *Spring/summer* – Osprey (80%), Goosander (60%), Spotted Flycatcher, Redstart, Grasshopper Warbler (all 50%), Pied Flycatcher (40%), Tree Pipit (30%), Wood Warbler (20%).

Other possible bird species

All year			
Common waterfowl	Great Spotted Woodpecker	Oystercatcher	Ring Ouzel
Tufted Duck	Jay	Golden Plover	Whinchat
Red Grouse	Goldcrest	Lapwing	Wheatear
Grey Partridge	Coal Tit	Dunlin	Grey Wagtail
Cormorant	Skylark	Snipe	Pied Wagtail
Grey Heron	Long-tailed Tit	Curlew	
Sparrowhawk	Nuthatch	Common Sandpiper	*Autumn/winter*
Common Buzzard	Treecreeper	Redshank	Whooper Swan
Kestrel	Dipper	Black-headed Gull	Pink-footed Goose
Merlin	Mistle Thrush	Common Gull	Wigeon
Peregrine	Stonechat	Cuckoo	Teal
Woodcock	Meadow Pipit	Short-eared Owl	Pochard
Common woodland/	Goldfinch	Swift	Goldeneye
farmland birds	Bullfinch	Hirundines	Waxwing
Tawny Owl	Reed Bunting	Chiffchaff	Fieldfare
Long-eared Owl		Willow Warbler	Redwing
Green Woodpecker	*Spring/summer*	Blackcap	Brambling
	Little Grebe	Garden Warbler	
	Great Crested Grebe	Whitethroat	
		Sedge Warbler	

Background information and birding tips

THIS SITE covers a vast area, containing, according to Campaign to Protect Rural England, the location of the nation's most tranquil spot (kept secret for obvious reasons). That's as well as Britain's cleanest air and the least light pollution.

Ospreys nesting successfully from 2009 reinforced Kielder's status as a leading North-East bird of prey-watching location. Already the 155,000 acre (62,000ha) conifer expanse was the region's main centre for Goshawks.

The Osprey success had long

been anticipated. The male of the pair that reared three young in both 2009 and 2010 was thought to have summered annually from 2006. In 2008 an abandoned nest was blown down, during a gale. Subsequently Forestry Commission (FC) rangers erected a nesting platform in a more secure conifer – an effort duly rewarded after the pair returned the following spring and two pairs have bred in 2011 and 2012.

News of Northumberland's first-ever recorded nesting by Ospreys aroused much public interest, despite the closest suitable location for a public viewpoint being Mounces car park off the C200 road north of Leaplish Waterside Park. This was two miles from the nest and on the opposite side of the reservoir. Even through powerful telescopes the birds at the nest were just distant specks – and rather blurred if you were there on a warm day with a heat haze.

The official viewpoint was switched to Leaplish from spring 2011, although Mounces remains available to birders using their own telescopes. The security of the Ospreys is paramount, of course, but continued successful breeding should lead to an increased future presence in Northumberland.

That will boost the chances of seeing these handsome raptors around the 27 miles of reservoir shoreline. Meanwhile, intimate views of nest activity are at least possible through CCTV feedback to a screen at Kielder Castle.

While Ospreys star from late May to late July (the period the public viewpoint operates) Goshawks are centre stage during February to April when males perform their skydancing displays above breeding territories.

Since this species' late 1960s British breeding comeback following 19th Century extirpation, the Border Forests have become a nationally significant stronghold, with about 15 pairs rearing young successfully in 2010. Conifer expanses around Kielder village, on Deadwater Fell's slopes to the north and around Kielder Burn to the north-east are among areas producing regular reports.

Due to increased interest in the spectacular displays, FC ranger-led walks are usually staged over the first weekend of March (see Key Points for details). However, most Goshawk-seekers visit independently and are not disappointed, despite the lack of a dedicated bird of prey-focused site since the former Bakethin Raptor Viewpoint closed some years ago.

Basically, it's worth observing from anywhere with a good overview of the forest's north-western area, especially if you can see clearly to Deadwater Fell, the 1,867ft (571m) highpoint at the dale's head.

One promising place, with commanding views in every direction, is the top of Cat Cairn (NY 613 928), a rock outcrop beside Skyspace, one of several artworks in the park. Reached by waymarked paths from Kielder Castle or from the locked gate at the Skyscape car park off the C200, it's a 1.5 mile trek – unless you have a key (see Access Details) to open the gate and drive to it.

Meanwhile views over substantial forest

Key points

- Forestry Commission Goshawk Walks in first weekend of March. Early booking essential (01434 220 242). Also check News page on www.forestry.gov.uk

- Special ferry trips to watch for fishing Ospreys. Details from visitor centres.

- A pay-and-display ticket entitles access to all Forest Park car parks.

tracts are possible from the Forest Drive, some within a much shorter walking distance of the castle.

Further south, on the reservoir's eastern side, is a site near another artwork, Silvas Capitalis (NY 657 905), a giant head comprising 3,000 specially shaped larchwood pieces. Along Lakeside Way, the 27-mile footpath around the entire shoreline, it's a likely point to watch for an Osprey fishing, but is three miles from the nearest car park.

Nearer the dam end, and involving much less walking, the Otterstone Viewpoint (NY 675 873) on the Bull Crag Peninsula off the C200 is another spot where you might catch up with Osprey.

Sparrowhawks used to be Kielder's commonest day-flying raptor but they are now comparatively scarce. Today Common Buzzards are by far the most numerous; in 2011 at least 46 pairs nested.

The reason for the Sparrowhawk decline – just 12 pairs fledged young in the Border forests in 2011 – is not absolutely certain. However, as it has coincided with the Buzzard increase, it may be due to some form of pressure from the greater presence of the larger raptors.

Kestrel numbers have dwindled also – a result of the Goshawk upsurge. A study of the latter's diet at Kielder during 1973-96 (*Ibis: Vol 145;* pp 472-483) showed that six raptor species made up 4.5 per cent of 5,445 Goshawk breeding season prey items recorded. Pigeons and crows made up two-thirds of the total, but more Kestrels were killed than the total of the other five raptors. This suggested an obvious reason for the falcon's decline from 30 pairs to 10 by 2011. During the same period Goshawk numbers rose from one to 20 pairs.

Peregrines (11 nests in the area in 2011) may well be seen over the park and there's a chance too of Merlin which breeds on nearby moorland. Marsh Harrier and Hobby sightings prospects have grown following their increased North-East occurrence in recent years.

Hen and Montagu's Harriers (both nested locally during the late 1950s-mid 1960s) may pass over on migration, while past reported rare visitors include spring passage Honey Buzzard and Black Kite. Golden Eagles appear occasionally in Northumberland's uplands and they continue to be the ultimate hope of Deadwater ridgeline-scanners.

Raptors may provide a particular incentive to tackle the long drive up the North Tyne valley, much of it along slow, country roads, but depending on the season there is potentially a much wider range of bird delights to make the journey worthwhile.

Inevitably, there is great expectation of Crossbills among Kielder-bound birders. A visit to such a vast conifer concentration without seeing them is almost beyond contemplation, but numbers fluctuate according to food availability.

Sightings were easy during the 1990-91 winter when an estimated 30,000-plus Crossbills were present due to a bumper supply of conifer seeds coinciding with a major influx of birds from across the North Sea. In years when the opposite extreme applies, they are much more thinly distributed.

Fortunately, their loud, distinctive 'chip-chip-chip' calls make finding a party less of a needle-in-a-haystack exercise even in years of low numbers. Spend some time in areas that regularly hold flocks – such as Bakethin, the Bull Crag Peninsula, Lewis Burn and Plashetts – and you could well come across a group.

Siskins, which can be found in birch and alder woodland as well as conifers, occur widely throughout the forest. As with

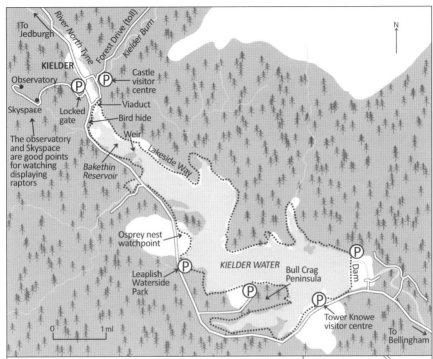

How to get there

(Approx 40 miles NW of Newcastle)

Leave A69 at Hexham (18 miles W of Newcastle) onto A6079. After five miles turn left onto B6318 – but just for 0.25 mile. At roundabout after bridge over North Tyne at Chollerford, switch to B6320 to Bellingham (12 miles) where you turn left on to C200 road to Kielder Water. C200 reaches reservoir after 12 miles, runs along its W side to Kielder village (nine miles). If driving S on A68 from Scotland, turn right five miles after Rochester on to the B6320 to Bellingham (nine miles).

Access to Skyspace artwork (for raptor watching from Cat Cairn viewpoint): Key to open locked gate to drive to Skyspace available to disabled (for £10 returnable deposit) from Kielder Castle Visitor Centre, Leaplish Waterside Park or Calvert Trust Kielder. Non-disabled motorists interested in driving to Skyspace should inquire at Kielder Castle.

Public transport: Snaith's Service 880 from Hexham bus station (direct link with Arriva 685 Newcastle-Carlisle service) to Kielder Castle on Tuesdays, Fridays and Saturdays (more details 01830 520 698). Arriva Service 714 runs from Gateshead and Newcastle to Kielder Castle on Sundays and Bank Holiday Mondays from late May until mid-October (timetable on www.arrivabus.co.uk).

Contacts

Kielder Castle: 01434 250 209
Leaplish visitor centre: 01434 251 000

Tower Knowe visitor centre: 01434 240 398
The Calvert Trust Kielder (outdoor activities and care for disabled) 01434 250 232

229

Crossbill, winter numbers can be particularly high after a large-scale arrival of overseas birds during the autumn.

Close-up views can be obtained at the Kielder Castle feeding station (where red squirrels tend to be the ultimate show-stealers). Lesser Redpolls are more thinly spread and mainly summer visitors, though post-breeding flocks linger into the autumn and some overwinter.

Since the 1980s, the FC has developed an extensive mosaic of blocks of trees of different ages to maximise bird diversity. Another feature of this policy is the maintenance of broadleaf woodland corridors along the forest's water courses, which is why Kielder Castle, Lewis Burn and the Sidwood/Comb area around the Tarset Burn, are particularly productive.

Tree Pipits, Blackcaps, Garden Warblers, Chiffchaffs and Willow Warblers make for such locations on returning in spring, with the declining Wood Warblers a further possibility. Aided by FC-erected nest boxes, these areas also provide vital habitat for Redstarts and Pied and Spotted Flycatchers.

Meanwhile Grasshopper Warbler 'reeling' may be heard in newly-planted forest clearings, habitat also favoured by Whinchats. Sometimes forest clearings harbour an overwintering Great Grey Shrike.

Another key birding site is Bakethin Reservoir, purposely developed as a nature conservation area. It is separated from the main lake by a weir so its water level remains constant.

From Bakethin's car parks a path along a former railway extends through the east bank's broadleaf woods after crossing the North Tyne via a 19th Century viaduct, a fine vantage point. Another path through west side conifers – a red squirrel haunt – leads to a hide overlooking three man-made islands, one fitted with an artificial otter holt.

Bakethin's potential is underlined by a bird list that includes scarcer species such as Long-tailed Duck, Smew and Red-necked and Slavonian Grebes. Even Bittern has been recorded. Occasionally there are sightings of Whooper Swans and Pink-footed and Barnacle Geese on passage.

Small numbers of Goldeneyes overwinter; boxes have been fixed to trees in the hope some will stay to nest. Meanwhile Goosander has bred in the North Tyne valley since the 1950s and Bakethin is among places where a brood can be anticipated.

Both Kielder Water and Bakethin are visited by non-native Mandarin Ducks, present in the North Tyne valley since the mid-1990s. However, they are seen most regularly on the river in the vicinity of Ridley Stokoe, a picnic site off the C200 about 2.5 miles downstream of the reservoir dam.

In February 2006, there was an exceptional count of 63, a Northumberland record high, along the Smalesmouth-Ridley Stokoe stretch (numbers have since been much lower). Breeding occurs, with 27 broods reported in the wider Border Forests area in 2009.

For birders keen to tackle more challenging treks, paths lead out of the forest or from higher points along the Forest Drive to moorlands. This is the domain of Red Grouse and upland waders – Golden Plover, Lapwing, Dunlin, Snipe and Curlew – while Wheatears and the increasingly scarce Ring Ouzels may be in more rugged places.

Ravens, likely to be seen during raptor-watching sessions from lower altitudes, range over these open expanses with double figures reported sometimes in winter.

INTERNATIONALLY IMPORTANT as the only British wintering site for the Svalbard/Spitzbergen race of pale-bellied Brent Goose, the reserve can boast an impressive bird list in excess of 320 species. So while the castle, ruined Priory, 12th Century church and picture postcard village attract almost a million visitors annually, it is also a magnet for birders, particularly when migrants are on the move.

Target birds
Spring – Gannet (100%), Little Tern (70%), Black Redstart (60%), Ring Ouzel (60%). *Summer* – Manx Shearwater, Arctic Skua, Guillemot, Razorbill (all 80%), Puffin (60%). *Autumn passage* – Fieldfare (90%), Redwing (90%), Yellow-browed Warbler (40%). *Winter* – Pale-bellied Brent Goose, Wigeon, Bar-tailed Godwit, Grey Plover (all 100%), Peregrine, Slavonian Grebe, Red-throated Diver (all 70%), Red-necked Grebe (40%).

Other possible bird species

Spring/autumn (regular migrants)	Lesser Redpoll	Blackbird
Pink-footed Goose	Snow Bunting	Song Thrush
Barnacle Goose	Lapland Bunting	Sedge Warbler
Little Gull		Blue Tit
Black Tern	*Breeding birds*	Chaffinch
Roseate Tern	Eider	Greenfinch
Blackbird	Mallard	Goldfinch
Ring Ouzel	Fulmar	Linnet
Song Thrush	Oystercatcher	Starling
Wheatear	Ringed Plover	Carrion Crow
Whinchat	Lapwing	Jackdaw
Robin	Common Tern	House Sparrow
Black Redstart	Arctic Tern	Reed Bunting
Redstart	Barn Owl	
Willow Warbler	Woodpigeon	*Occasional species*
Chiffchaff	Collared Dove	Marsh Harrier
Garden Warbler	Swallow	Hen Harrier
Whitethroat	House Martin	Long-tailed Skua
Lesser Whitethroat	Robin	Pomarine Skua
Pied Flycatcher	Dunnock	Balearic Shearwater
Spotted Flycatcher	Wren	Firecrest
Chaffinch	Skylark	Pallas's Warbler
Siskin	Meadow Pipit	Hume's Leaf Warbler
Brambling	Rock Pipit	Red-breasted Flycatcher
	Stonechat	
	Pied Wagtail	

Background information and birding tips

THE MAINLAND section of the National Nature Reserve stretches a distance of seven miles along the Northumberland coast and is connected to Holy Island by a causeway that is swiftly covered

Key points
• Free parking available at Budle Bay, Lowmoor Point, Beal shore and Snook.

• Pay and display car park at Chare Ends. Disabled parking at Green Lane park in the village.

• Toilets at Green Lane car park and in Crossgates, village centre.

• Wheelchair access to hides at Lowmoor Point and Rocket Field. Access available at Lough but paths from village can be very muddy.

• Two pubs, two hotels, six B&Bs, three cafes/coffee shops on island and many cottages for rent.

Contacts
Lindisfarne.org.uk details safe crossing times and available accommodation.

Island heritage centre 01289-389 004 or 389 015 (www.lindisfarne-centre.org)

by high tides, so leave enough time for a safe crossing.

The reserve, established in 1964 and managed by Natural England, forms part of the Northumberland Coast Area of Outstanding Natural Beauty. Covering 8,534 acres from Budle Bay northwards to Cheswick Black Rocks, it comprises extensive rich inter-tidal mud, sand and silt between the island and mainland. A further 1,800 acres of botanically important sand dunes are included in the Lindisfarne SSSI.

While internationally important for the wintering Brent Geese from Svalbard/Spitzbergen, Lindisfarne also holds internationally important populations of Pink-footed Geese, Wigeon, Bar-tailed Godwits and Grey Plovers.

It is nationally important for Red-necked and Slavonian Grebes, Shelduck, Golden Plovers, Knot and Dunlin. Ringed Plover and Sanderling are nationally important as passage species.

Massed waders and wildfowl present a magnificent spectacle during the winter. On cold and sunny days the mudflats resound to the harsh grunting calls of Brent Geese, wader calls and the explosive whistles of drake Wigeon gathered in feeding areas or on the water.

The best time to see all areas is two or three hours each side of high tide when birds are close to shore. Equally spectacular can be the mass panic created by the regular presence of four or five hunting Peregrines. It is an unusual winter outing when a Peregrine fails to appear. Sparrowhawks, Merlins and Kestrels are also regular and, occasionally, a Hen Harrier.

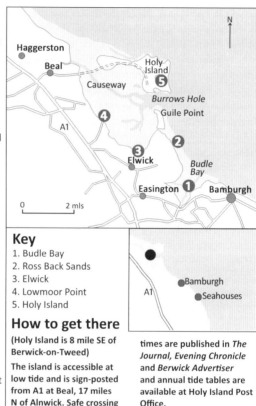

Key
1. Budle Bay
2. Ross Back Sands
3. Elwick
4. Lowmoor Point
5. Holy Island

How to get there
(Holy Island is 8 mile SE of Berwick-on-Tweed)

The island is accessible at low tide and is sign-posted from A1 at Beal, 17 miles N of Alnwick. Safe crossing times are published in *The Journal, Evening Chronicle* and *Berwick Advertiser* and annual tide tables are available at Holy Island Post Office.

The pale-bellied Brent Geese are among the world's rarest geese. They first arrive from Arctic breeding grounds by late August and most are present by October, remaining until March. Normally around 3,000 are present, about half the total Svalbard race, with the rest wintering in Denmark.

The big attraction for them is eel grass or *Zostera* which grows in huge swathes on the mud. It is also the favourite food of Wigeon. By mid-winter, as *Zostera* runs out, the geese are forced to feed on grass and other plants and congregate on island and mainland fields.

232

Most Wigeon leave altogether at that stage.

Pinkfeet, with up to 6,000 normally present, use the reserve mainly to roost and feed inland during the day. Barnacle Geese pass through in autumn in large numbers en route to the Solway, although from 2009 small numbers have wintered around Budle Bay. Up to 20,000 Wigeon are usually present in autumn and early winter. The reserve is also the region's main spot for Pintail, with up to 600 sometimes accompanying the Wigeon.

The winter population of Bar-tailed Godwits is around 3,000, though 9,600 were present in February 1986. They feed on the tide line in huge excitable parties, particularly along the Pilgrims Way, the line of poles which marks the safe route across the flats. The poles often act as handy perches for ever-watchful Peregrines.

Counts in recent winters have also shown around 2,000 Grey Plovers, 1,000 Shelduck, 6,000 Golden Plovers and 4,000-6,000 Knot. The commonest wader is Dunlin, though numbers have crashed from a peak of 31,000 in 1978 to 6,000-7,000.

The reserve is so large that for birdwatching it is best divided into sections:-

1. Budle Bay (NU 153 348)

LARGE NUMBERS of duck, waders and gulls can be viewed easily from the parking area (NU 153 348) along the main B1342 Bamburgh-Waren Mill road. Though not signposted, the parking area is on the south side of the bay alongside the main road.

The road is elevated, and the roadside parking provides ideal watching conditions for birders in wheelchairs.

A telescope is advisable for all areas of the reserve as birds can be distant at low tide.

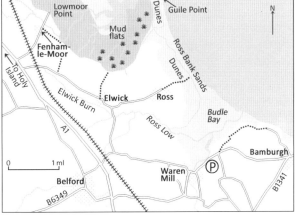

2. Ross Back Sands (NU 133 370)

ACCESS is from Ross village (NU 133 370), three miles further north along the same route. The village is signposted at a junction with a red telephone box.

Park in the village and walk east down the lane towards the sea and then cross the half-mile track across farmland and dunes to the beach. This route is not suitable for wheelchairs. The walk is worthwhile as it is excellent for all four local tern species in summer.

In winter there's the chance to see Red-necked and Slavonian Grebes, Red-throated Diver (occasional Great Northern and Black-throated), Long-tailed Ducks, Common Scoters and often Velvet Scoters.

3. Elwick (NU 116 369)

HALF A MILE north of the Ross turn-off is Elwick (NU 116 369) where a bridleway runs to the southern shore of the main flats, always a good area for geese, duck and wader species, all in large numbers. The bridleway is rough and often muddy so the route is unsuitable for wheelchairs.

4. Lowmoor Point (NU 099 399)

THE EASIEST viewing by far is from the double-decker hide (NU 099 399) reached via Fenham-le-Moor, which comprises a farm and a few cottages and is signposted from the A1.

Follow the road down to the shore where the hide is situated on the left. As the tide floods in, most birds fly north into the bay at Fenham Mill for a few extra minutes of feeding. The flats can also be scanned from the road to the island.

The southern part of the reserve, including Budle Bay, is a sanctuary area while part of the central section is a shooting zone between September 1 and February 20. Up to 200 shooting permits are issued annually with Wigeon, Mallard, Teal and grey geese being the main quarry species. The annual total 'bag' is around 700 birds.

The flats can also be viewed from Holy Island itself, with the Heugh (the high ridge overlooking the harbour) often giving the closest views of grebes, divers, hundreds of Eiders and noisy parties of Brent Geese on the sandbars.

The best time period from the Heugh is low tide when birds are concentrated in the channels and on exposed bars. The old coastguard tower on the Heugh provides welcome shelter for winter watching.

5. Holy Island (NU 105 438)

THE HISTORIC ISLAND, cradle of Christianity in the north, remains a place of pilgrimage so can be crowded with tourists from spring to late autumn, but the bulk of them tend to keep close to the village and castle.

The island has a reputation for producing good birds, something best judged from its mouth-watering list of rarities. Of the 400 species so far recorded in Northumberland, 34 have made their first, and in some cases only ,appearances here.

A good migration day, with winds from the east or north and clear weather over Scandinavia to prompt mass departures of northern species, can be truly spectacular.

Spring can be rewarding but autumn is the best period, making the island an essential destination for many birders, if only for a long day out. If you want to stay longer, booking accommodation well in advance is wise.

There are a couple of rough lay-bys on the left side of the road as you drive on to the island which give an opportunity to stop and scan the flats.

Birds can turn up anywhere but some areas are more important. The scattered bushes and trees on The Snook (NU 105 438), the promontory that points towards the mainland, holds migrants during 'falls', so arriving birders often makes it their first stop.

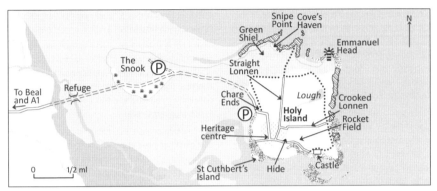

Free parking is available along the rough track on the left side of the road.

Ground conditions on the Snook, where there are often large areas of floodwater, make it unsuitable for wheelchairs.

In recent seasons this area has produced Wryneck, Great Grey Shrike, Red-backed Shrike, Shore Lark, Yellow-browed Warbler, Pallas's Warbler, Icterine Warbler, Radde's Warbler, Western Bonelli's Warbler and Firecrest. In May 2008 it held a Great Snipe, the first Northumberland record since 1976.

The Snook is equally important as a botanical hotspot with a superb array of orchids and other plants. It has the distinction of its own unique orchid, the recently recognised Lindisfarne helleborine *Epipactis sancta*.

The island is large so it is best after visiting the Snook to drive the further mile towards the village and use the pay and display car park on the left just as you enter the village.

While the Snook can be good, the prime spots for migrants are around the village. As most of these hotspots are gardens, discretion and common courtesy are needed, though locals are used to birders and are tolerant. The gardens at Chare Ends, the main road into the village, can hold large numbers of small migrants, which have included Pallas's, Yellow-browed and Hume's Leaf warblers, Red-breasted Flycatcher and Firecrest.

You'll find the churchyard and famed vicarage garden are similarly excellent for both common migrants and rarities. Again, courtesy is essential. Don't, for example, use gravestones as rests for telescopes or as picnic tables (incredibly, it has happened).

These sites have attracted Arctic and Subalpine Warblers, Red-breasted Flycatcher, Nightjar, Little Bunting and even a stray Kingfisher. In November 2008 the garden was shared by a Red-flanked Bluetail and an equally showy Pallas's Warbler. Yellow-browed Warblers are annual on the island in autumn with up to eight in a day being nothing unusual.

The island's two lonnens (tracks through the main farmland) can hold many migrants. The Straight Lonnen runs north from St Coomb's Farm and the Crooked Lonnen eastwards to the sea. Two other areas always worth checking are the isolated bushes along the track at Chare Ends (NU 125 425) and willows at Greenshiel excavations (NU 128 444), the site of an 8th Century Anglo-Saxon settlement, half a mile on towards the North Shore.

The track is reached through the gate (with Natural England information board) just as you turn left off the causeway road towards the village. To reach Greenshiel, continue along this track for half a mile and then bear left through a gap in the dunes and follow the rough path towards the North Shore.

On a good autumn migration day the island can be alive with northern thrushes and common migrants including Robins, Goldcrests, Chaffinches, Bramblings, Siskins and occasional Short-eared and Long-eared Owls. Such mass movements also bring sought-after rarities.

It is not unusual to count 5,000 or 6,000 Fieldfares, Redwings, Blackbirds and Song Thrushes in the first couple of hours after dawn. When conditions are fine most pass straight overhead to the south-west but during rain or strong winds many take cover on the island.

The biggest single arrival involved Redwings one morning in October 1991 when villagers awoke to find the streets and gardens carpeted with birds grounded by a dense wall of fog. An estimated 20,000 Redwings were present, most flying off soon after dawn when the fog lifted. The same morning an estimated 15,000 were on the Farne Islands.

The Rocket Field pools (NU 133 420) are seasonal and can be viewed from the new information centre hide located alongside the road to the castle, 150 yards east of Ship Inn in Marygate, the village's main street.

The area floods in late summer and has attracted waders including Pectoral Sandpiper, Ruff, Green, Wood and Curlew Sandpipers, Temminck's and Little Stints and Grey Phalarope.

In September 1998 it produced Northumberland's second Baird's Sandpiper. In winter large numbers of Teal are present and it is the county's most regular site for Black-tailed Godwits.

The Lough (NU 138 428) a mile north-east of the information centre is reached by walking along the Crooked Lonnen towards the sea and then turning north. It has common breeding species and, occasionally, a Black-necked Grebe.

A Black-headed Gull colony was wiped out by otter predation in 2004 and has not re-established. The water has also attracted Spotted Crake, Bittern and Grey Phalarope.

Emmanuel Head (NU 140 437) is marked by a 200-year-old white navigation pyramid and provides good seawatching with on-shore winds. The Head is quarter of a mile on from the Lough and the pyramid is visible from afar.

From March-November many Gannets are offshore, as are all three auk species from the Farne Islands. Manx and Sooty Shearwaters and Arctic and Great Skuas are regular. Long-tailed and Pomarine Skuas and Balearic Shearwater are recorded in most late summers/autumns but in much smaller numbers.

Other regular passage species in small numbers include Black and Roseate Terns and Little Gull. During autumn and winter occasional influxes of Little Auks can provide an incredible spectacle as they speed past against a background of mountainous waves. During a two-day period in November 2007 many thousands passed north, hundreds skimming low over the island having to clear field walls and dunes.

North of Emmanuel Head, the ridge of sand dunes and rocky promontory of Coves Haven (NU 128 438) provides a breeding site for Fulmars. A few pairs also nest around the castle.

During winter the island is a very reliable site

for Lapland Buntings, with groups feeding in stubble around Chare Ends and in bare areas around the old limestone quarry (NU 128 438). This area is reached by going through the gate at the north end of the Straight Lonnen and continuing for 300 yards through the gap in the dunes. Again, it is rough underfoot, so unsuitable for wheelchairs.

The birding richness of the area can be judged by its many rarities. In spring/summer they have included: White-billed Diver, Night Heron, White Stork, Honey Buzzard, Red Kite, Black Kite, Montagu's Harrier, Red-footed Falcon, Common Crane, Broad-billed Sandpiper, Black-winged Stilt, Stone Curlew, Dotterel, Hoopoe, Golden Oriole, Red-rumped Swallow, Black-headed Wagtail, Red-flanked Bluetail, Eastern Black Redstart, Red-throated Pipit, Nightingale, Marsh Warbler and Ortolan Bunting.

Pine Grosbeak in the Crooked

Loaning in May 1975 and Trumpeter Finch at Castle Point in August 1987 are the sole records of these species in Northumberland.

Autumn/winter rarities include: Ross's Goose, Snow Goose, King Eider, Black Scoter, Surf Scoter, American Wigeon, Blue-winged Teal, Cory's Shearwater, Great Shearwater, Rough-legged Buzzard, Corncrake, Spotted Crake, American Golden Plover, Lesser Yellowlegs, Wilson's Phalarope, Roller, Bee-eater, Olive-backed Pipit, Richard's Pipit, Citrine Wagtail, Short-toed Lark, Desert Wheatear, Woodlark, Greenish Warbler, Roller, Red-eyed Vireo, Serin and Rustic Buntings.

A Black-throated Thrush in Chare Ends in January 1979 and a Chimney Swift over the village square in November 2005 are the only Northumberland records.

Though seabirds and wildfowl dominate the birding scene within the reserve, passerine migrants such as Redstarts are recorded annually.

Richard Allen

OCCUPYING a distinct North Sea headland, Newbiggin is well-placed both for seabird and wildfowl coastal passage and migrant arrivals. The full extent has become clear only since the late 1980s thanks to a great effort by a small team of dedicated birders. This area has repeatedly shown that it ranks among the region's top-performing migration sites, with some rarities more typical of national hotspots.

Target birds *All year* – Mediterranean Gull (80%). *Spring/early summer* – Garganey

(30%), Icterine Warbler (20%). *Late summer/mid-autumn (Jul-Oct)* – Roseate Tern (70%), Sooty Shearwater, (50%), Wryneck (40%), Black Redstart (40%), Barred Warbler (40%), Yellow-browed Warbler (40%), Pomarine Skua (30%), Sabine's Gull (30%), Pallas's Warbler (30%), Red-backed Shrike (30%), Balearic Shearwater (20%), Red-necked Grebe (20%), Long-tailed Skua (20%), Greenish Warbler (20%), Red-breasted Flycatcher (20%). *Late autumn/winter (Nov-Mar)* – Great Northern Diver (30%), Little Auk (30%), Black-throated Diver (20%).

Other possible bird species

All year	Reed Bunting	Spotted Flycatcher	Regular Terns
Common waterfowl		Redstart	Black Tern
Pochard	*Spring/autumn passage*	Whinchat	Razorbill
Eider	* = most likely July to Nov; # = mainly March	Wheatear	Puffin
Common Scoter	to June	Pied Flycatcher	
Grey Partridge	Little Ringed Plover	Yellow Wagtail	*Winter*
Red-throated Diver	*Golden Plover	#White Wagtail	Brent Goose
Fulmar	*Grey Plover	Brambling	Shelduck
Gannet	Knot	Siskin	Wigeon
Shag	Sanderling	Lapland Bunting	Gadwall
Grey Heron	*Curlew Sandpiper	Snow Bunting	Teal
Sparrowhawk	Dunlin		Shoveler
Kestrel	Ruff	*Seabird/wildfowl passage (July – Nov)*	Scaup
Oystercatcher	*Woodcock	Whooper Swan	Long-tailed Duck
Ringed Plover	Black-tailed Godwit	Pink-footed Goose	Velvet Scoter
Lapwing	Bar-tailed Godwit	Barnacle Goose	Goldeneye
Snipe	Whimbrel	Brent Goose	Red-breasted Merganser
Curlew	Common Sandpiper	Shelduck	Golden Plover
Redshank	Green Sandpiper	Wigeon	Grey Plover
Familiar gulls	*Spotted Redshank	Gadwall	Knot
Guillemot	Greenshank	Teal	Sanderling
Common farmland/	Wood Sandpiper	Pintail	Purple Sandpiper
woodland birds	Turnstone	Shoveler	Dunlin
Stock Dove	Cuckoo	Scaup	Jack Snipe
Coal Tit	*Long-eared Owl	Long-tailed Duck	Bar-tailed Godwit
Skylark	*Short-eared Owl	Velvet Scoter	Turnstone
Mistle Thrush	Swift	Goldeneye	Iceland Gull
Stonechat	Goldcrest	Red-breasted Merganser	Glaucous Gull
Pied Wagtail	Hirundines	Goosander	Barn Owl
Rock Pipit	Migrant warblers	Manx Shearwater	Fieldfare
Goldfinch	Ring Ouzel	Arctic Skua	Redwing
Linnet	*Fieldfare	Great Skua	Lapland Bunting
Yellowhammer	*Redwing	Little Gull	Snow Bunting

Background information and birding tips

NEWBIGGIN is anything but a one-stop shop. The birding potential is spread along almost two miles of coastline and reaches half a mile inland. So making the most of it on a really eventful day can involve driving from place to place and a fair amount of walking.

The most productive locations are:

1. Newbiggin Point (NZ 320 880) to Beacon Point (NZ 317 894)

ICONIC St Bartholomew's Church, dating from the 13th Century and the town's most seaward building, overlooks the exposed promontory where watchers, suitably clad to cope with weather extremes, gather to monitor seabird and wildfowl movements.

Thousands of Little Auks passing Newbiggin Point on November dates in 2001, 2004 and 2007 are just one indication of the scale of activity witnessed there in fairly recent times. Sooty Shearwaters and Pomarine and Long-tailed Skuas have also been prominent.

Also, it's one of the region's more regular watchpoints for sightings of Cory's, Great, and Balearic Shearwaters, European and Leach's Storm-petrels and Grey Phalaropes. Rarities logged include White-billed Diver and Zino's/Fea's Petrel.

Sabine's Gull is another seabird that can make an autumn seawatch memorable as it's not unknown for Newbiggin observers to log one or two more than elsewhere (six passed one day during September, 2007). Extended, comparatively close-up, views have been possible on occasions when these Arctic-nesting beauties have lingered off the Point.

A much rarer small gull in no hurry to depart from Newbiggin was the Bonaparte's Gull that was in the bay for more than seven weeks during autumn, 2006. It was seen regularly on the shore near the headland car park, a section of beach that has also become the region's main gathering point for Mediterranean Gulls. Numbers have grown sharply during recent years – with 28 reported between July and October, 2010.

However, this part of Newbiggin isn't just about seabirds. November, 2005's Pallid Swift ranged about over the High Street-St Bartholomew's area.

Though the churchyard offers virtually no cover, it can be productive during falls of migrants. October 2004's Pied Wheatear spent time there; Wryneck and especially Black Redstart are among more typical passage visitors that have cropped up among the gravestones.

Dotterel and Grey-headed Wagtail were found near the church during the significant fall

Key points
(Newbiggin Pt)

• **Free seafront car park (NZ 317 881) south of bus turning circle by St Bartholomew's driveway – 200 yards from seawatch point.**

• **Walk from car park to Beacon Point about a mile, plus extra 0.5 mile to check dunes and shore to NW.**

• **Path may be muddy in places. Allow an hour each way.**

• **Main seawatching season July-November plus passage in late spring/early summer too. Little Auks movements possible through winter.**

Key points
(Newbiggin Pt)

• Seawatch point exposed totally during NE gales. Waterproof and warm clothing essential.

• Public toilets by golf club entrance. Also coin-op superloo outside Black Pearl pub about 0.25 mile along promenade from car park.

• Wheelchair access possible to watch point.

of early September 2008 and a Yellow-browed Warbler later in the month.

Walking to Beacon Point, a mile north of St Bartholomew's, can be worthwhile, especially at passage times. The trail there follows the eastern edge of the town's golf course – reached by a path starting from High Street's east end, then passing between the golf clubhouse and caravan site.

Expect Eiders on the sea and typical wader species – Oystercatcher, Ringed and Golden Plover, Sanderling, Dunlin, Curlew, Redshank and Turnstone – around the point's rocky foreshore, numbers growing from late summer and a strong presence through autumn and winter. Curlew Sandpiper, Whimbrel, Common Sandpiper and Greenshank are possible during July-September.

Such gatherings presumably contributed to isolated Beacon Point autumn appearances by King Eider and American Golden Plover. Meanwhile the adjacent golf course has accommodated Dotterel, Pacific Golden Plover and Buff-breasted Sandpiper.

With Britain's main Roseate Tern colony at Coquet Island ten miles to the north, there's a possibility of summer sightings at Newbiggin. Following dispersal from the colony, family parties may use Beacon Point as an early stop-over, though not usually as many as in late August 2009 when up to 40, including ten juveniles, were counted.

A September 2010 report of Marsh Warbler in dead scrub north of the golf clubhouse indicates the value of checking the limited available cover. Wheatears may be prominent along the path in both spring and autumn.

The 2004 Pied Wheatear frequented its southern end during part of its visit and a Desert Wheatear found on the semi-derelict beach near Lynemouth power station in November 2008 also spent some of its four-day stay around Beacon Point, as did another in December 2011/January 2012.

Shore Larks, Twite and Lapland and Snow Buntings have occurred at the Point or in nearby dunes during autumn/winter.

2. The Mound/Settling Ponds Embankment

DOMINATING Newbiggin's north-western skyline are Lynemouth power station and the eight chimneys of Alcan aluminium smelter which, sadly for the local economy, has now closed. They are not a pretty sight but have figured in some of the town's rare bird triumphs.

The power station's settling ponds stretch more than half a mile to the edge of the town. At their south-east corner is a large, tree-covered mound, presumably a landscaping measure to eliminate the industrial backdrop from the view of local residents.

Those trees provide the first substantial cover for migrants drifted onto the headland by easterly winds on murky autumn days. As a result the mound has become one of the region's more reliable sites for finding the kind of birds that make September-November

How to get there

(Approx 15 miles NE of Newcastle)

From A189 Newcastle-to-Ashington road (linked to A1 by A19 Tyne Tunnel road turn onto B1334 North Seaton roundabout (to E of Ashington) to head NE to Newbiggin. After 1.5 miles, B1334 terminates at end of High Street by seafront, with free parking nearby.

From N via A1068 Alnwick-Amble-Ashington road, turn onto A189 a mile south of Ellington (two miles N of Ashington). After 1.5 miles, you come to a T-junction with a mini-roundabout. Go left on to A197 which leads to Newbiggin, joining B1334 in town centre where you turn left to reach seafront car park.

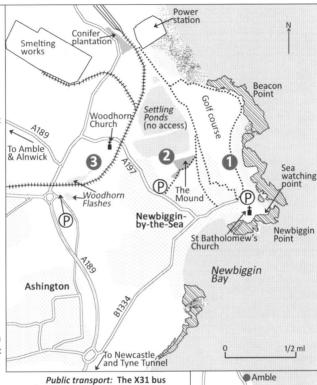

The A197 passes Woodhorn Church and access road to The Mound if you wish to check these sites first.

Public transport: The X31 bus service from Newcastle (also more local services) run to Headland.

The Mound/Settling Ponds Embankment

Mound can be reached from Oakwood Avenue off A197 (turn-off at war memorial about 0.25 mile N of A197 junction with B1334) in town centre). Alternatively from East Lea housing estate (reach via Woodlea, the first turning on left S along A197 from war memorial).

Woodhorn Church and Flash

Woodhorn Church stands by A197 in fairly open country, 0.5 mile beyond mini-roundabout (junction of A189 and A197) or, if approaching from Newbiggin, a mile NW of town centre junction of A197 and B1334.

such a special time of year. Yellow-browed Warbler is an almost routine mound delight, especially when above-average numbers reach Britain's east coast.

An early highlight, in November, 1989, was registered correctly at the time as a Yellow-browed "showing the characteristics of the race *P. i. humei.*" It was another seven years before BOURC declared what had previously been regarded as the south-central Asian

Key points
(The Mound/ Settling Ponds Embankment)

• Park in Oakwood Avenue (NZ 308 884) off Woodhorn Road at War Memorial or at East Lea housing estate (NZ 312 886). Take care not to inconvenience local residents.

• Path by settling ponds embankment is about a mile to NW.

• Allow plenty of time to check scrub between embankment and golf course during big falls of migrants.

• Path too muddy for wheelchairs. and there's a boggy area to SW of golf course.

form to be a separate species, Hume's Warbler. A review of past records placed the Newbiggin bird as only the sixth for Britain and the second for Northumberland.

The mound is also a likely spot for a Pallas's Warbler encounter, though this species' visits are less regular (records in just three of the 2003-11 autumns). Radde's and Dusky Warblers, Firecrest, Red-breasted Flycatcher, Golden Oriole, Arctic Redpoll and Rustic Bunting have also provided thrills over the years – particularly in autumn.

A Honey Buzzard landed briefly on a tree during this species' significant mid-September 2008 movement.

A notable spring surprise was a Greenish Warbler in May 2009 (nationally the species occurs

mainly during August-October and this was a spring first for Northumberland).

Around the corner from the mound is the start of the path beside the embankment along the eastern flank of the settling ponds. There is much potential, with scrub providing cover for migrants on both the embankment (fenced off but viewable from the path) and between the path and the golf course.

After a heavy fall of migrants involving commoner species such as Redstart, Blackcap, Garden Warbler, Chiffchaff, Willow Warbler, Goldcrest and Pied Flycatcher, there can be something to check out in every bush.

Comprehensive coverage of this extensive area will often pay dividends. One vivid example was the Pallas's Grasshopper Warbler on the embankment on September 29, 2001 – only the fourth British mainland record of this Siberian vagrant (most of the 42 before 2010 were on Shetland, especially Fair Isle).

That was exceptional but, in most years, spring, autumn or both will lay on something interesting here. Such delights have included Hoopoe, Wryneck, Bluethroat, Black Redstart, Icterine, Subalpine, Barred, Greenish and Yellow-browed Warblers, Firecrest and Red-backed and Great Grey Shrikes.

Heavy rain can lead to floodwater forming in the south-west corner of the golf course. This can lead to passage wader appearances if it occurs in spring or autumn. There was an example in mid-August 2004 when such a temporary wetland attracted 12 Ruff, four Spotted Redshanks and a Wood Sandpiper.

3. Woodhorn Church (NZ 302 888) and Flash (NZ 297 884)

THE TREES AND BUSHES closest to the sea are where migrants might be expected to shelter in adverse weather but some of the Newbiggin area's most remarkable

discoveries have been almost a mile inland.

Woodhorn Church, dating from the 11th Century and a Grade 1 listed building, was a heritage museum and then a base for local artists after its original role ended in 1973. As far as birders are concerned, its most important features are the churchyard trees and a sheltered hedge at the back, which have earned a reputation for attracting rare birds of national as well as regional significance.

Realisation that this was a special place was kindled by the Olive-backed Pipit, the fourth for Northumberland, in the churchyard and adjacent paddock in October, 1990. An even more distinguished discovery was Britain's second-ever Black-faced Bunting in the hedge during October 1999.

A further county first – an Iberian Chiffchaff, the ninth for Britain, that sang in the churchyard trees in April 2004 – showed the site could deliver in springtime too. Northumberland's third Western Bonelli's Warbler in October 2002 and seventh Blyth's Reed Warbler in September 2007 were further highlights for the hedge.

Early May 2008 produced Golden Oriole and Red-backed Shrike sightings. The site has also had a share of Newbiggin's autumn Yellow-browed and Pallas's Warbler reports over the years.

Commoner species such as Redstart, Blackcap, Garden Warbler, Chiffchaff, Willow Warbler and Pied Flycatcher are liable to be prominent in the trees after big influxes.

South of the church the land dips with an embankment carrying a mineral railway curving across it. On either side of this embankment are flashes, mining subsidence pools which have further enhanced the birding credentials of Newbiggin's western outskirts.

Britain's second Hooded Merganser (March 2002) and Northumberland's first Franklin's Gull (April 2005) stand out especially, but a supporting cast which has included Green-winged Teal, Garganey, Slavonian and Black-necked Grebes and Red-necked Phalarope, further emphasise the advantages of checking these pools regularly.

Routine passage waders recorded include Little Stint, Ruff, Black-tailed Godwit, Greenshank and Green and Wood Sandpipers. Fly-over Honey Buzzard and Marsh Harrier have been logged and nearby farmland can be productive too – as indicated by records of Pacific Golden Plover, Short-toed Lark, Richard's Pipit and Lapland Bunting.

A few Greenland White-fronted Geese lingered in nearby fields during the early months of 2010 and 2011.

Even a small conifer plantation, by the power station's access road half a mile north of the church, has scored. A Hume's Warbler, Northumberland's seventh, famously overwintered there during January – April, 2002.

Key points (Woodhorn Church)

- Parking at Woodhorn Church (NZ 302 888).

- For flash south of railway embankment, park on shoulder of roundabout immediately by railway bridge over A189 at NZ 295 883 (junction with A197 to Ashington).

- Flash on north side of railway embankment can be viewed from side of A189 just N of railway bridge. Flash on south side can be approached along a path running from A197/ A189 junction roundabout to W edge of Newbiggin.

243

Key points

- Access beyond sentry box banned when firing range in use.

- First gateway watchpoint just beyond army sentry box (0.4 mile north of Mayfair House).

- Second watchpoint where Blackpool Drain branches east from bridleway.

- Dont drive along lane across carr east of Mayfair House – potholes! OK for walking except when flooded.

- Lane partly wheelchair-accessible.

- Nearest public toilets at Ponteland (two miles west). Extensive facilities at Kingston Park shopping centre off A1/A696 junction.

Contacts

Tourist Information: 0191 277 8000.

THIS PRODUCTIVE bird of prey site lies mostly within the Newcastle city boundary and two miles from a Metro rail service terminal. As well as raptors, there's always a wide range of woodland and farmland birds on show and excessively wet weather at passage times can lay on wader thrills too. The fact it includes one of Europe's most threatened habitats – a raised mire – emphasises that this is a very special place.

Target birds *All year* – Willow Tit (50%), Water Rail (30%), Barn Owl (30%), Red Kite (20%). *Spring to early autumn* – Grasshopper Warbler (60%), Kingfisher (30%), Garganey (20%), Marsh Harrier (20%). *Late autumn to early spring* – Short-eared Owl (40%), Merlin (30%), Peregrine (30%), Hen Harrier (20%).

Other possible bird species

All year		
Common waterfowl	Meadow Pipit	Grey Wagtail
Grey Partridge	Pied Wagtail	White Wagtail
Grey Heron	Mistle Thrush	Redstart
Sparrowhawk	Long-tailed Tit	Whinchat
Buzzard	Treecreeper	Wheatear
Kestrel	Jay	Ring Ouzel
Lapwing	Linnet	Sedge Warbler
Snipe	Bullfinch	Garden Warbler
Woodcock	Yellowhammer	Lesser Whitethroat
Curlew	Reed Bunting	Summer warblers
Redshank		
Familiar gulls	*Spring to early autumn*	*Late autumn to spring*
Common woodland/	Oystercatcher	Wigeon
farmland birds	Ruff	Golden Plover
Stock Dove	Black-tailed Godwit	Waxwing
Little Owl	Whimbrel	Fieldfare
Tawny Owl	Greenshank	Redwing
Long-eared Owl	Green Sandpiper	Chiffchaff
Green Woodpecker	Common Sandpiper	Goldcrest
Great Spotted	Cuckoo	Tree Sparrow
Woodpecker	Swift	Brambling
	Skylark	Siskin
	Hirundines	Lesser Redpoll

Background information and birding tips

A RADIO-TAGGED White-tailed Eagle from eastern Scotland's reintroduction programme that wandered south in spring 2010 became the 14th bird of prey species, not including owls, recorded at Prestwick Carr since the end of the 1990s.

A similarly tagged Scottish-bred Marsh Harrier called in during 2004's autumn passage. After leaving the Tay estuary where it was reared, the juvenile made its initial English appearance in Cumbria. However, before continuing south to overwinter in West Africa, it diverted east to linger around Newcastle's fringes, one location being this former fen just inside the city boundary. Since then Marsh Harrier occurrences between March and May and August to October have become almost routine.

The location is noted also for Hen Harriers, particularly between October and January, with one or two, sometimes more, reported regularly. There are occasional fly-through Osprey sightings and Honey Buzzard is possible at passage times too.

Spring and autumn sightings of Goshawk and April and June Hobby occurrences in recent years illustrate further potential. Merlins and Peregrines are mainly seen during autumn/ winter – a period marked also by two Rough-legged Buzzard records since the 1990s. Maybe more will be seen of Red Kite in future, following its re-introduction in nearby Gateshead's Derwent Valley.

Seeing unusual raptors depends on being in the right places at appropriate times – plus luck. With some in view for just minutes as they drift over on a very few dates and not necessarily every year, that applies even to birders covering the site regularly. Casual visitors are fortunate to see more than the standard Sparrowhawk, Buzzard and Kestrel ... but it can happen.

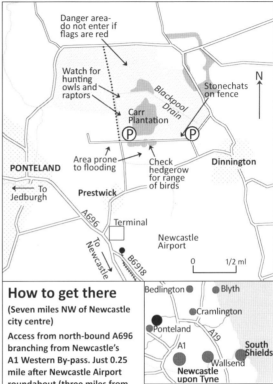

How to get there

(Seven miles NW of Newcastle city centre)

Access from north-bound A696 branching from Newcastle's A1 Western By-pass. Just 0.25 mile after Newcastle Airport roundabout (three miles from A1 junction), turn right at next roundabout onto minor road to Prestwick hamlet (0.5 mile). From north-west, this turning is first on left after Ponteland (shortly after Badger pub on left).

At Prestwick, watch for unsigned left turn (so inconspicuous you might miss it) just after last house. Go along narrow lane to Mayfair

House crossroads (0.75 mile). Turn right, parking almost immediately on left verge (NZ 186 736). Also 0.5 mile to west near Prestwick Mill Farm (NZ 180 736). At east end of lane across carr (NZ 200 737).

Public transport: Bus service 45 runs between Newcastle Haymarket and Dinnington (carr's east end a 0.75 mile walk from village).

Owls are well represented too, with Barn, Little, Tawny and Long-eared nesting. Barn Owls can be seen hunting over wet grasslands and fields before dusk and Short-eareds, quite a local speciality, throughout the day from August to April. Numbers vary, with up to six during September-December 2009, and 14 in the winter of 2011-12.

A total of 127 acres (51ha) of Prestwick Carr have SSSI status because it's a rare example of lowland raised mire – a mound of peat lying above the local water table and fed only by rain. This used to maintain the former extensive wetland but it dried out after an 1850s drainage project lowered the water table. Now work is in progress to retain water through improved ditch management and sluice-use.

Public access is restricted to dead straight lanes and a bridleway criss-crossing the carr. From the Prestwick to Dinnington road, a narrow lane runs northwards for half-a-mile and then, after crossing its west-east counterpart by Mayfair House, becomes an unsurfaced bridleway to the Berwick Hill minor road nearly 1.5 miles away.

The other lane runs eastwards from Ponteland golf course and Prestwick Mill farm for 1.5 miles almost to Dinnington. Major deterioration has occurred to the mile-long stretch beyond the Mayfair House crossroads and you'll risk damaging your car if you attempt to drive it.

One complication for birdwatchers is the MoD firing range between Prestwick Mill Farm and Berwick Hill. Red flags indicate when it is being used and most of the carr's northern section cannot be entered.

Much of the bridleway is in this 'danger area', including two gateways enabling birders to look east across farmland towards Carr Plantation (hedgerows block the view along most of the bridleway).

However, the lane across the carr is always open – except when flooded. Its eastern end lies between extensive wet grassland, which can be viewed from gateway breaks in the substantial flanking hedgerows which bristle with birds in every season.

At the lane's western end, horse paddocks on the north side can hold many waders if flooded at passage times. After a September 2008 deluge left much of the carr under water, Little Stint, Pectoral and Curlew Sandpipers, Ruff and Greenshank were among waders on show.

A Common Crane and 86 Black-tailed Godwits followed similar flooding in mid-April 2005. The obvious message is: check Prestwick Carr after heavy rain during peak passage periods.

With just a few small permanent pools – one south of the central lane (0.75 mile east of Mayfair House), another west of the bridleway – wildfowl possibilities are mostly unexceptional, though Garganey can occur on passage.

As for other wetland species, Water Rails lurk in marshy spots, and ditches, where a Kingfisher may also flash into view. Quail is an occasional spring/early summer visitor to the grassland but, inevitably, is heard rather than seen. The same applies, but on a regular basis, to Grasshopper Warblers. In contrast, Whinchats and Stonechats can be on show along fences.

Whitethroats and Willow Warblers are prominent in hedgerows in spring and summer. Sedge Warblers, Garden Warblers and Lesser Whitethroats are likely to be encountered also.

Listen for Redstart song, with breeding confirmed in recent summers. Willow Tit is a resident, though mainly seen most in autumn/winter in mixed tit flocks active in the hedgerows.

Fieldfares and Redwings can be expected then too, along with small parties of Siskins and Lesser Redpolls. Hawthorns still with berries may attract Waxwings during irruption years.

THIS ACTIVELY-MANAGED forest dating from the 1930s is now a leisure location for all seasons, but for birders it is especially interesting in the summer when roding Woodcocks are joined by purring Nightjars and moorland and farmland birds are found around its edge.

Target birds
All year – Common Crossbill (100%), Red Grouse (100%), Goldcrest (90%), Sparrowhawk (70%), Buzzard (70%), Woodcock (40%), Goshawk (20%), Green Woodpecker (20%), Long-eared Owl (20%), Black Grouse (10%). *Spring/summer* – Spotted Flycatcher (90%), Whinchat (80%), Cuckoo (70%), Tree Pipit (70%), Wheatear (50%), Redstart (50%), Nightjar (50%), Wood Warbler (30%), Merlin (20%), Golden Plover (10%). *Autumn/ winter* – Fieldfare (80%), Redwing (80%), Brambling (40%), Hen Harrier (30%), Great Grey Shrike (30%), Red Kite (30%).

Other possible bird species

All year	Lesser Redpoll	Meadow Pipit	Black Kite
Tawny Owl	Chaffinch	Willow Warbler	Marsh Harrier
Robin	Greenfinch	Chiffchaff	Golden Eagle
Blackbird	Bullfinch	Whitethroat	Rough-legged
Song Thrush		Blackcap	Buzzard
Mistle Thrush	*Spring/summer*	Garden Warbler	Osprey
Long-tailed Tit	Kestrel	Linnet	Hobby
Blue Tit	Lapwing		Whimbrel
Great Tit	Curlew	*Occasional Birds*	Barn Owl
Coal Tit	Great Spotted	Pink-footed Goose	Short-eared Owl
Siskin	Woodpecker	White Stork	
	Swallow	Honey Buzzard	

Background information and birding tips

SLALEY FOREST was once part of a Red Grouse moor managed for its heather only. Forestry Commission planting started in the mid 1930s with a mixture of Scots pine, larch, Norway spruce and Sitka spruce with enough light reaching the ground to allow heather to continue growing. The subsequent clear felling allowed heather seed to regenerate and create a bird-friendly habitat.

Regular tree cover management is carried out in the centre of the forest around the Ladycross area, where you'll also find a stone quarry. The 290-million-year-old sedimentary layers are worked by hand, not explosives, so for the past 300 years the quarry has been a magnet for wildlife.

More than 140 species of birds have been seen, along with ten species of dragonfly and 14 species of butterfly, but because this is a working quarry it is only open to the public at certain times of the day.

The forest itself is noted for a summer population of Nightjars that love the clear fell

Key points

• Forest tracks open at all times.

• Quarry open 8.30am – 12.30pm (Mondays to Saturdays).

• Park along B6306 at NY 978 551 and NY 954 552 at Ladycross.

• Keep to forestry tracks.

• Wheelchair access on rough forestry tracks will depend on a strong pusher.

• Use car as a hide on some tracks.

• Allow up to 4 hours to find birds – 30 to 40 species likely.

Contacts
Forestry Commission Rangers
01388 488 312

Ladycross Quarry
01434 673 302
www.ladycrossstone.
co.uk/index.php/
nature

management. As trees grow up the birds move to where the cover is less intrusive. This evening show can be observed from the forest's many tracks, but remember that the peak time for display it is also the peak time for midges!

Woodcocks are common but it is best to find a clear fell area so you'll have a longer period to observe the birds flying over, rather than simply crossing a forest ride.

This would apply for Crossbills as well. Conifer seed is vital for this bird, so good years for Crossbills coincide with heavy cone crops. Red squirrels also love feeding on the cones, with larch ideal in winter when no needles are found on the trees.

The southern edge of the forest backs onto the Blanchland Red Grouse moor. Here you can observe many species not always found in the forest. Stonechats and Whinchats are more likely here, as well as Curlews and Lapwings. Golden Plovers may be heard calling away from the trees.

Birds of prey are limited due to persecution but Merlins still exist and Hen Harriers are more likely in winter passing through the area. Meadow Pipits and Skylarks are common prey for the Merlins but Wheatears and even Ring Ouzels may fall prey over this moor.

Migrating birds on passage have included birds of prey such

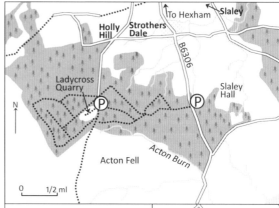

How to get there

(Quarry is 7 miles S of Hexham)

From Hexham take B 6306 southwards for seven miles to the car park at NY 978 551. It takes 20 minutes to walk from here to Ladycross Quarry.

From A68, head NW from Castleside (near Consett) and take B6278 signposted to Edmundbyers before turning onto B6306 northwards through the village of Blanchland.

Alternatively you can drive to the hamlet of Strothers Dale (NY 974 568) and follow the signs for Ladycross, turning left up a narrow road into the forest. A Forestry Commission sign is found in the car park (NY 954 552) opposite the gate to the quarry.

From this point you can walk/ drive/bike across the moor and search for moorland birds. There is presently a clear-fell in front of you and a track runs across the moor (NY 953 546). This area is where the Great Grey Shrike has been found in winter.

as Marsh Harrier, Hobby, Rough-legged Buzzard and even Golden Eagle seen from the quarry. White Storks, Whimbrels and Pink-footed Geese are classic spring/autumn passage birds.

The owls of the forest are always hard to see, but ground-nesting Long-eared Owls are not what most people would be looking for! Both Tawny and Long-eared Owls normally use the nest of other birds such as Carrion Crow or Magpie, but a lack of suitable holes means Barn Owls need nestboxes to be provided.

THIS GALAXY of sites is an attractive alternative to more distant wetlands for Newcastle birders keen to get their fill of wildfowl, waders, raptors and more unusual species. Three are long-established mining subsidence pools and two are flashes established fairly recently. The sixth site, Holywell Dene, isn't a wetland as such, being a long, wooded ravine, but flowing through it is Seaton Burn, which does attract certain wetland species.

Target birds *All year* – Tree Sparrow (50%), Water Rail (30%), Willow Tit (30%). *Spring to early autumn* – Reed Warbler (60%), Garganey (50%), #Black-necked Grebe, (50%), Marsh Harrier (30%), Little Egret (20%), Osprey (20%), Hobby (20%), Temminck's Stint (20%), Pectoral Sandpiper (20%).

Late autumn/winter – Whooper Swan (60%), Short-eared Owl (60%), Mediterranean Gull (50%), Peregrine (30%), Iceland Gull (30%), Bean Goose (20%), White-fronted Goose (20%), Smew (20%), Merlin (20%), Long-eared Owl (20%).

= Most likely to be seen in August/September

Other possible bird species

All year
Familiar waterfowl/gulls
Shelduck
Gadwall
Pochard
Tufted Duck
Grey Partridge
Little Grebe
Cormorant
Grey Heron
Sparrowhawk
Buzzard
Kestrel
Lapwing
Stock Dove
Barn Owl
Little Owl
Tawny Owl
Kingfisher
Green Woodpecker
Great Spotted Woodpecker
Common farmland/
woodland birds
Skylark
Meadow Pipit
Pied Wagtail
Dipper
Mistle Thrush

Long-tailed Tit
Coal Tit
Nuthatch
Treecreeper
Jay
Greenfinch
Goldfinch
Linnet
Bullfinch
Yellowhammer
Reed Bunting

Spring to early autumn
* = Most likely to be seen in spring/early summer
Great Crested Grebe
Oystercatcher
Little Ringed Plover
Curlew Sandpiper
Ruff
Black-tailed Godwit
Spotted Redshank
Redshank
Greenshank
Green Sandpiper
Wood Sandpiper
Common Sandpiper
Lesser Black-backed Gull
Black Tern

Common Tern
Swift
Hirundines
Whinchat
Yellow Wagtail
*White Wagtail
Wheatear
*Grasshopper Warbler
*Sedge Warbler
*Lesser Whitethroat
*Whitethroat
*Garden Warbler
*Blackcap
Chiffchaff
Willow Warbler
Lesser Redpoll

Late autumn/winter
Pink-footed Goose
Wigeon
Teal
Goldeneye
Snipe
Jack Snipe
Curlew
Fieldfare
Redwing
Brambling
Siskin

Background information and birding tips

WITHIN EASY REACH of the Newcastle/North Tyneside conurbation, these six sites offer a wide variety of birding experiences east and north of the A19 stretch between its junctions with the A1 (north of Newcastle) and the A1058 (two miles north of the Tyne Tunnel).

Key:
1. Holywell Pond
2. Holywell Dene
3. Beehive Flash
4. Backworth Pond
5. Arcot Pond
6. West Hartford Flash

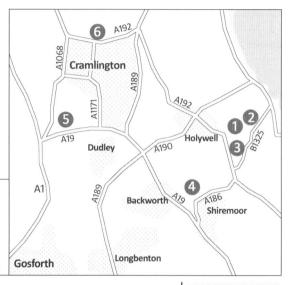

1. Holywell Pond (NZ 320 753)

BRITAIN'S second Ross's Gull at Holywell Pond on April 30, 1960, wasn't cause for celebration because an adult male was found "freshly dead from shot", as the *British Birds* rarities report put it.

Eventually a live one was seen on the reserve – in late May 1997 when a summer-plumage adult visited on two dates while lingering for a month on the Northumberland coast. By then more than 70 had been recorded in Britain and the county's total had risen to eight, so it perhaps wasn't so sensational.

Particularly outstanding during the 37 years between the appearances by those diminutive Arctic wanderers were Collared Pratincole (only the eighth British record for the 20th Century) in

July 1966 and two Great White Egrets in May 1989 and July 1992 (the 1980s national total was less than 50).

Also notable were two White-winged Black Terns (a juvenile in August, 1969 and a second-summer in June 1996) and an immature Night Heron (August 1977, and again in the year's final quarter).

Several wildfowl rarities to occur over these decades include Ferruginous Duck and, from across the Atlantic, American Wigeon, Green–winged Teal, Blue-winged Teal and Ring-necked Duck.

Other notables just outside this period were May 1959's Alpine Swift, February 1960's Great Snipe

Key points
(Holywell Pond)

• **Park in vicinity of Holywell Dene Road (NZ 319 746) but don't inconvenience residents parking in East Grange, the cul-de-dac at end of this road.**

• **Off-road parking in Hartley Lane (B1325) at start of path to pond via Holywell Dene (NZ 333 747) is on a sharp bend.**

and August 1998's Black Stork.

In the 21st Century another White-winged Black Tern in August 2002, and more Green-winged Teal and Ring-necked Duck appearances provided some echoes of the glory days, but in other ways Holywell has maintained or even stepped up its former momentum. For instance it has continued to attract passage Black-necked Grebes in August or September (when the number of Little Grebes present can top 30).

Red-necked and Slavonian Grebes are much rarer visitors; the most recent records up to the time of writing were, respectively, in December, 2005, and November, 2007. As well as hosting the occasional Bittern and Spoonbill, it has shared in the county's steadily increasing number of Little Egret sightings.

Marsh Harrier stands out among scarce raptors recorded at or near the site, a Northumberland Wildlife Trust reserve since 1970 and also an SSSI. During 2004-08 there were reports in every month from April to September, but especially during April- June.

In 2005 there was a particular concentration, but several of these appearances were brief, involving fly-overs, so though prospects of seeing this species at Holywell have improved, it's still a matter of being on the spot at the right time.

With the spread of Britain's Osprey population, the situation is similar as far as these spring and autumn passage raptors are concerned. As Hobby sightings increase in the North, the chance of seeing this falcon at Holywell is growing too.

Honey Buzzard becomes a possibility in the light of the nationally-significant September movements of displaced Continental birds in 2000 and 2008. During the latter passage, three were seen in a day in this area.

The generally flat, open landscape means a lot of sky can be viewed, providing much scope for sharper-eyed birders to catch sight of fly-over raptors.

Hen Harrier sightings are possible at passage times and in winter, either at the reserve or hunting over open farmland between Seaton Delaval, Whitley Bay and the coast.

Over the past decade there have been several reports, one in the 2004-05 winter, when the star local raptor attraction was a juvenile Rough-legged Buzzard that spent two months roaming over much of this area. Even more unexpected was a different Rough-legged that overflew the pond on the unusually late date of May 1, 2005.

Merlins and Peregrines can be anticipated, particularly during winter months when Short-eared Owl may be hunting over the farmland. Barn Owls have been recorded during recent breeding seasons.

Key points
(Holywell Pond)

• **Public screen hide is almost half a mile along path starting at East Grange or just over a mile from Hartley Lane parking area. Allow minimum of two hours.**

• **Allow up to four hours if covering surrounding farmland paths network.**

• **Paths around fields can be muddy in wet weather.**

• **Reach public screen hide (always open) overlooking SE corner of pond by path around field from East Grange cul-de-sac.**

• **The hide has a wheelchair ramp but the path from the parking area is often wet and overgrown making access difficult.**

Key points
(Holywell Pond)

• **Wildlife Trust permits required for entry to limited reserve sections that are accessible.**

• **At pond's SW corner there's a locked hide (keys available from Trust) and a screen overlooking a bird feeding station,**

• **Good public toilets (NZ 305 755) in Seaton Delaval centre, just E of roundabout at A192/A190 crossroads.**

• **More toilets at St Mary's Island car park on coast seven miles by road to east (NZ 350 752).**

• **Pubs and a few shops in local villages. More extensive facilities at Cramlington and Whitley Bay.**

Wildfowl variety and numbers have changed over time. Overwintering Whooper Swan numbers approached and occasionally exceeded 200 during the 1970s and early '80s. Now, although parties sometimes have brief stays, usually sightings involve flocks passing over en route to or from East Anglia's Ouse Washes.

A few hundred feral Greylag Geese are around in winter and they can attract wild Pink-footed Geese (eg 420 in December, 2007). Scarcer Tundra Bean and White-fronted Geese (both Eurasian and Greenland) may turn up too. The geese gather, generally, in the fields to the west of the pond. Large skeins of migrating Pink-footed and Barnacle Geese may overfly the area at passage times.

Once Holywell was a winter haunt for 100-150 Wigeon but now there may be no more than a handful. Similarly, Teal counts are well below the 1,000-plus peaks of 1959 and 1966. However, it is still a reliable site for spring or autumn passage Garganey.

Small numbers of Gadwall and Shoveler are seen regularly and now and again Pintail occurs, as does the introduced Mandarin Duck.

As for diving ducks, the pond is a Pochard breeding site and often figures in the county's largest

monthly counts of this species (usually 20-40).

Normally no more than 20-30 Tufted Ducks are present but there were up to 57 in late 2007/ early 2008. A few Goldeneyes overwinter and a Goosander group may be present also. Red-crested Pochards, Scaup, Long-tailed Ducks, Common Scoters and Smew are occasional visitors.

Passage waders during 2004-08 included Little Ringed Plover, Ruff, Black-tailed Godwit, Whimbrel, Spotted Redshank, Greenshank and Green and Wood Sandpipers.

There's a chance of Little Gulls and Black Terns at such times, while recent years have produced reports of Mediterranean Gulls (mainly August-December) and Iceland Gulls (January-March).

Water Rails and Kingfishers are seen and Reed Warbler song has become a regular breeding season sound. The calls of one or more Quail were heard in May, June and August, 2005 but Holywell's reedbed has attracted Bearded Tit only once (a lone bird in December, 1977).

Willow Tits and Tree Sparrows (a flock of 40 in late 2005) are among more notable residents. An Icterine Warbler singing by the bridleway running east from the village's Holywell Dene Road in May, 2008, underlined the wider area's potential.

How to get there

(Seven miles from Tyne Tunnel)

Turn off A19 four miles north of Tyne Tunnel onto A186 leading to Earsdon village (two miles). Turn left at Earsdon roundabout onto A192 leading to Holywell, then take first right into Holywell Dene Road.

This leads to East Grange cul-de-sac (path to pond starts from cut between houses in this small cul-de-sac). If approaching via the longer path from Hartley Lane (B1325), turn right into this road off A192 a short distance north of Earsdon roundabout.

Public transport: Bus links with Newcastle and Whitley Bay/Tynemouth and the pond is just two miles north of the Shiremoor and Monkseaton stations on the Tyne-Wear Metro rail service.

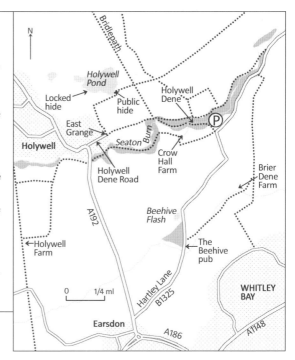

Key points
(Holywell Dene)

• Space for a few cars off-road (NZ 333 747) in Hartley Lane (B1325) – on sharp bend so take care – two miles north of turn-off from A192. Take short public footpath across field to link with path along dene top.

2. Holywell Dene (NZ 330 747)

THIS NARROW tree-filled ravine, extending from the south-east edge of Holywell village to Hartley and Seaton Sluice on the A193 coast road and well-equipped with public footpaths, has offered much more than standard woodland species over the years.

The Dene is well served with paths from the point where it is crossed by the A192 just south of Holywell village to its seaward end four miles to the NE. The main area of woodland lies in the 1.5 mile stretch east from the

waggonway crossing near Crow Hall Farm, with paths both along upper edges and beside Seaton Burn. Allow at least two hours to cover the area thoroughly.

Close to the sea and in an otherwise mainly open landscape, it attracts grounded migrants seeking cover. A striking historical example was the Tengmalm's Owl of December, 1911.

Rather more recently, the late 1980s proved particularly productive, BBRC-accepted records including Rustic Bunting (April 1986), Subalpine Warbler

253

Key points
(Holywell Dene)

• Allow at least two hours to cover all paths.

• Paths may be muddy in places. Steep flights of steps between upper and lower paths. Footbridges over Seaton Burn make site unsuitable for wheelchairs.

• Nearest public toilets at St Mary's Island car park on coast (three miles by road) to east, NZ 350 752.

• Beehive pub in Hartley Lane (just over a mile south of off-road parking space) serves meals. Also pubs and a few shops in local villages, with more extensive facilities at Cramlington and Whitley Bay.

(May 1987) and Pallas's Warbler (October 1988). No less than three Night Herons (two adults and a second-summer) roosted in the dene's trees for at least ten days in May, 1997.

Scrub habitat at the east end accommodated a Barred Warbler along with Garden Warblers, Chiffchaffs and Spotted and Pied Flycatchers in September, 2002. Yellow-browed Warbler was recorded in October, 2005.

The dene is among several Northumberland sites where Red Kites have put in appearances since the Lower Derwent valley

re-introduction project.

Meanwhile the Seaton Burn, flowing through the ravine has broadened its species range, with occasional records of Common Sandpiper and, in winter, Water Rail and Green Sandpiper. Kingfishers, Grey Wagtails and Dippers have been noted in all seasons.

Woodland species occurring throughout the year include Stock Dove, Tawny Owl, Great Spotted Woodpecker, Long-tailed Tit (up to 40 reported in February, 2008), Nuthatch, Treecreeper and Bullfinch.

How to get there
(Six miles from Tyne Tunnel)

Turn off A19 four miles N of Tyne Tunnel on to A186 leading to Earsdon village (two miles). Turn left at Earsdon roundabout on to A192 and then, after a short distance, right into Hartley Lane (B1325). Off-road

parking space at start of path to dene is on a sharp bend two miles N of this junction and a mile N of Beehive pub.

Public transport: Tyne-Wear Metro rail service to Whitley Bay and then bus to Hartley village near east end of Dene's main woodland.

3. Beehive Flash (NZ 327 737)

THE B1325 between Earsdon and Hartley is narrow, with several sharp bends, so it's quite possible for drivers correctly focused on the road to pass this wetland without noticing it. Though just a few yards from passing traffic, it is small and only visible through a couple of gaps in the hedge along a stretch where parking prospects are virtually nil.

Beehive Flash's history is relatively short. There is no mention of it in the 2004 edition

of *Birds in Northumbria* and it didn't feature in the annual report's list of birding sites until the 2006 edition. It doesn't bristle with birds all the time – sometimes there's not much more than a few Moorhens. However, the records show that visits can be rewarding when waders are on the move and being grounded by adverse weather.

So-named because of the Beehive Inn, about 200 yards

south on the other side of Hartley Lane, the flash initially drew attention in 2005 through a series of wader reports, with a Temminck's Stint in late May and a Pectoral Sandpiper in early September particularly outstanding.

Other shorebirds that year included Little Ringed Plover, Little Stint, Ruff and Green and Wood Sandpipers.

Numbers were very small, mostly, but there were exceptions: up to 32 Black-tailed Godwits, 24 Dunlin and 16 Snipe in July and 87 Curlews in October. A few Garganey and Shovelers indicated at least limited potential for wildfowl too.

Most have been recorded since, some almost annually. The site may not have attracted a national rarity up to the time of writing, but Pectoral Sandpiper at least seems to favour it: another was recorded in September 2008, with further individuals reported in May and October 2009.

An arrival of Temminck's Stints in the North-East in May 2010 included one dropping in almost exactly five years after the site's first.

Curlew Sandpiper, Bar-tailed Godwit, Spotted Redshank and Greenshank are among other wader species logged, while Little Ringed Plover and Common Redshank have bred.

A Little Egret broadened the site's bird list in July 2010, and there was a BirdGuides Online report of a fly-over Osprey in May, 2006.

Yellow and White Wagtails are likely at the flash, particularly during the spring passage and Whinchats have been recorded too.

As well as feral Greylags, nearby fields may attract Pink-footed Geese (500 reported in January, 2009). Short-eared Owl is another winter possibility and the Hoopoe in September, 2008, shows the locality has scope for the unexpected.

Key points
(Beehive Flash)

• Space for two cars to pull off narrow Hartley Lane by flash (NZ 327 737).

• For safe parking patronise nearby Beehive pub (NZ 328 734) to justify using its car park.

• Short walk along Hartley Lane from Beehive pub is potentially dangerous as there is very little verge.

• Nearest public toilets at St Mary's Island car park on coast (four miles by road) to east.

• Beehive pub (0191 252 9352), serves meals up to 9pm. More extensive facilities at Cramlington and Whitley Bay.

How to get there
(Seven miles from Tyne Tunnel)

Turn off A19 four miles N of Tyne Tunnel on to A186 leading to Earsdon village (two miles).

Turn left at Earsdon roundabout on to A192 and then, after a short distance, right into Hartley Lane (B1325). Beehive pub is on right, a mile along lane, and the flash on left about 200 yards further (between a small plantation and a sharp right hand bend).

4. Backworth Pond (NZ 308 725)

Key points
(Backworth Pond)

• Park in obvious space by Holywest Kennels at east end of Backworth's Church Road (NZ 306 724).

• Cross stile onto public footpath running through Holywest Kennels site and then by pastureland. View pond from gaps in bushes or a small footbridge.

• Path may be muddy in places.

• Stiles make it unsuitable for wheelchair users.

• Nearest public toilets near A192/ A190 roundabout at Seaton Delaval (NZ 305 755), and St Mary's Island car park on coast (NZ 305 075).

• Pubs and shops in local villages. Sainsbury's supermarket off Earsdon Road (A186), Shiremoor.

LAND BETWEEN Backworth and Earsdon is prone to flooding during prolonged rainfall. That partly explains why the minor road between the two villages doesn't run directly across this area of rough pastures, but loops around its northern end.

Meanwhile, permanently wet areas have become established through subsidence resulting from deep coal mining, the main local industry from the early 1800s until 1980 when Backworth's last pit closed.

The combination of these circumstances has led to many passage waders breaking their journeys here over the decades. Inevitably, the smaller pools have become overgrown with reedmace and other dense marsh vegetation, but the main pond still has much open water and ponies occupying the adjacent field help to keep its south-western edges open and muddy. This can be reached by a public

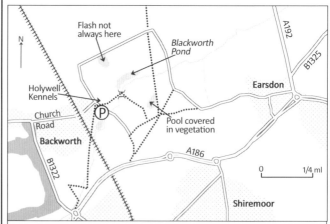

How to get there
(Five miles from Tyne Tunnel)

Turn off A19 four miles N of Tyne Tunnel onto A186 leading to Shiremoor and Earsdon villages. After half a mile, turn left (roundabout) at Shiremoor on to B1322 to Backworth village centre (one mile). On reaching mini-roundabout as B1322 bends sharply left, turn right into Church Road (signposted to West Holywell

and Earsdon). Cross railway after 0.25 mile and drive to Holywest Kennels at bend 200 yards further on. Area that may be flooded viewable from gateways and hedge gaps between a quarter and half a mile further along road to Earsdon.

Public transport: Buses to Backworth village. Pond is just over a mile, via lane from A186 and paths over fields, NW of Tyne-Wear Metro rail service's Shiremoor Station.

footpath from Holywest Kennels at the east end of Backworth's Church Road.

The local potential is increased if bad weather creates a temporary flash, especially during the spring or autumn migration. This can be viewed from the minor road between Backworth and Earsdon villages

Backworth doesn't seem to figure in early editions of *Birds in Northumbria* until 1974-78 ,during which there were visits by up to 20 Ruff and four Green Sandpipers, with Little Stints, Curlew Sandpipers and Wood Sandpipers turning up in ones and twos.

The next decade brought even more promise: it was the county's only site to produce Little Ringed Plover records in 1983 and its only Temminck's Stint of 1984. A Pectoral Sandpiper stayed for at least a week in October 1986, with up to seven Wood Sandpipers in May 1987 and nine more during an early return passage influx after mid-July.

I mention these old records because sightings over recent years compare reasonably well with that period. The past decade's highlights include a Temminck's Stint in June 2001, a Pectoral Sandpiper in May 2006, and a flock of 29 Black-tailed Godwits that landed on a flash present in April 2002.

Green Sandpipers occurred almost annually during 2002-12 and there has also been a succession of Little Ringed Plover and Wood Sandpiper reports, along with Ruff and Greenshank. In winter months you can expect Jack Snipe.

Other wetland species recorded include Water Rail, regularly during early and late months, and – less frequently – Kingfisher. Sometimes Common Terns make summer appearances.

While not a great source of wildfowl records, the site does pull in the occasional Garganey on spring passage. A few Shelduck,

Gadwall, Shoveler and Tufted Duck may linger and it can hold a small Teal flock in autumn and winter.

Pink-footed Geese may appear in the vicinity in winter; for example, 200 were reported in fields north of Backworth in December, 2009. There is potential for raptors on passage, with April reports of Marsh Harrier in both 2009 and 2010, while a ringtail Hen Harrier hunted over the area for more than a week in May, 2004.

Its production of occasional Hobby records goes back to at least the 1970s; as the species is being reported increasingly in the region, prospects of more in future are good.

What now seems like an amazing number of Short-eared Owls – up to 16 – was in the Backworth area during the 1987-88 winter. Such a concentration would be unusual anywhere in the region nowadays when one or two – none some winters – is the norm for this site.

With hawthorn scrub clumps reasonably plentiful, the area has potential for overwintering Long-eared Owl roost sites also; small numbers occurred in the past and though it seems none has been reported in recent years, this could be repeated in future. Little Owl was recorded annually, both during the breeding season and winter months, over 2004-08.

The passage bird range extends beyond wildfowl, waders and raptors. Cuckoos, Redstarts and Ring Ouzels were all reported after mid-April, 2010 and Wheatears are likely from late March, with birds showing Greenland race features later in the spring.

Yellow Wagtails – records include one of the continental Blue-headed race, a scarce passage visitor, in April, 2006 – and Whinchats may appear at migration times also. Lesser Whitethroats are among summer-visiting breeding birds and Reed

Warbler song has been heard almost annually over the past decade.

A Quail called for four days in June, 2006. In late summer many Swallows gather on telegraph wires at Holywest Kennels. Local year-round residents include Mistle Thrush (largish post-breeding flocks noted), Willow Tit and Tree Sparrow. Green Woodpecker was reported in early 2006.

Key points
(Arcot Pond)

• **Pull-off parking places on southern verge of Arcot Lane (NZ 252 751).**

• **View pond from hedge gaps in Arcot Lane. One certain viewpoint is a gate in the hedge.**

• **Two-mile circular walking route – allow a couple of hours for birding.**

• **Nearest public toilets (NZ 264 769) at Manor Walks shopping mall, Cramlington (about two miles by road from Arcot Pond).**

• **Toilets (including for disabled) at visitor centre at Plessey Woods Country Park (NZ 241 796) NW of Cramlington.**

5. Arcot Pond (NZ 251 753)

WHILE THIS attractive wetland is promising throughout the year, April 25 has become rather special in recent times. On that day in 2009, a Great White Egret was photographed stalking through its shallows. Remarkably, exactly 12 months later, there was another Great White Egret report from the site; on that occasion the bird flew over, heading north-west.

Named after nearby Arcot Hall (now the adjacent golf course's clubhouse), the pool is part of an SSSI covering almost 170 acres (68ha). The result of mining subsidence (several collieries used to be in the vicinity), Natural England's SSSI citation states that it is "believed to be fed by upwelling water."

The SSSI includes "probably the largest area of lowland species-rich unimproved grassland in North-East England" and also a surviving heathland fragment.

As well as an impressive array of plants and invertebrates of regional importance, one small moth, the least minor *Photedes captiuncula*, is nationally rare. The SSSI citation's only mention of birds is that the pond is "used by wintering waterfowl and passage migrants." However,

it is well known to birders and they are rightly concerned about the prospect of major housing development to the north. While the site itself may be protected, its capacity to attract birds could shrink if the new town of Cramlington – already uncomfortably close – sprawls even nearer.

It wasn't until July 2010 that Little Egret made its debut at the site, but considering the latter's increasing presence in the region, more can be expected. In contrast, Bittern has been recorded in the past, but not in recent years.

Whooper Swan and Goosander are among the pond's more prominent waterfowl species. March, which is when the swans start returning to Iceland after over-wintering in East Anglia, has been the best month for sightings, with records of around 20 on the water and fly-over flocks of up to 90. Smaller numbers may linger during the autumn southbound passage.

As for Goosander, up to 15 have been present in December, with smaller numbers over January-April. Of more frequently recorded ducks, only Teal and Mallard counts reach the 40-100

How to get there

(Ten miles from Tyne Tunnel)

At roundabout on A19 eight miles north of Tyne Tunnel, take fourth exit onto B1505, then immediately turn left at small roundabout onto A1171.

After half-a-mile, A1171 goes right at a roundabout but you head straight ahead into Arcot Lane. Cross main East Coast railway and drive to a double bend. Arcot Pond is on right after another quarter of a mile (watch for a gate on right and a few obvious spaces for off-road parking on left). The hedge hides the pond – if Arcot Hall (local golf course clubhouse) appears on right, you need to turn back.

From A1, turn onto A19 six miles north of Newcastle centre. After just 200 yards, turn left from A190 onto A1068 and then after a quarter of a mile turn right into Arcot Lane. Head east along lane for a mile and after passing Arcot Hall (local golf course clubhouse) on left, pond is a further quarter of a mile on left.

Public transport: Nearby Cramlington has bus links with Newcastle and Whitley Bay/Tynemouth; also local rail services from Newcastle (pond is about a mile SSW of Cramlington Station as crow flies – longer on foot via A1172 and Beacon Lane).

range; normally Pochard and Tufted Duck don't exceed 20. Meanwhile Shelduck, Gadwall, Shoveler and Goldeneye are seen usually in single figures.

Garganey, a scarce visitor, is possible at passage times and Mandarin Duck has occurred in late summer/autumn.

Little Grebe is a resident species and Great Crested Grebe may be present in the early months (nesting in 2004 produced a brood of three young). Red-necked and Black-necked Grebes are also on the site's list but neither has been seen in recent times.

The Black-necked Grebe's absence is perhaps due to habitat change; the species was recorded at the pond almost annually in the 1980s and continues to appear at Holywell Pond, less than five miles to the east.

Meanwhile, Water Rails are reported regularly but, inevitably, require patience due to their skulking nature; sightings tend to be during October-December, but there have also been April and September occurrences. Kingfishers tend to be recorded during the year's final months, but there are occasional breeding season sightings too.

Arcot's most outstanding wader was the Pectoral Sandpiper that turned up in late September 2006.

It was in the area for 13 days, spending parts of the first and second of them at the pond but, after being spooked by a fly-over Buzzard, returned to a flash near Seaton

259

**Key points
(Arcot Pond)**

• **As well as major stores (eg Asda and Sainsbury), Cramlington has pubs, restaurants and takeaways.**

Burn's Drift Inn, a mile to the south-west, for the rest of its stay.

Little Ringed Plover, Spotted Redshank and Green Sandpiper (up to eight) visited Arcot during July-October period also that year. Jack Snipe, Black-tailed Godwit, Greenshank and Wood Sandpiper have been reported in other years but not regularly.

As for terns, Commons may appear during late spring or summer, while a Black Tern is a passage possibility, though not seen for some time.

Short-eared Owls are likely mid-winter/ early spring attractions, with reports of generally one or two hunting over that period up to 2008. Long-eared Owl is reported less frequently but that may be due to its more nocturnal habits; one present for more than three weeks in early spring 2006 was seen hunting in daylight several times.

Both Barn and Tawny Owls have been recorded during April-August in recent years.

Grasshopper Warblers (seven were 'reeling' in late April, 2004), Sedge Warblers and Lesser Whitethroats are among more regular summer visitors; Reed Warbler song is heard occasionally also. Residents include Stock Doves, Green Woodpeckers, Long-tailed and Willow Tits, Jays, Bullfinches and Reed Buntings.

To appreciate the wider surroundings, take the public footpath running north from Arcot Lane (starts just E of hall), past woodland and across the golf course. After half-a-mile turn right on to a path heading east, past more woodland, to Beacon Lane – which brings you back to Arcot Lane (junction at double bend immediately W of railway crossing).

6. West Hartford (NZ 255 794)

INDUSTRIAL development plans threaten the long-term future of this other wetland on the fringes of Cramlington new town.

A well-established flash on former West Hartford farmland is earmarked for the construction of a prestige business park, though the continuing world-wide economic crisis appears to have delayed the start to the project.

Apart from a new community fire station and brigade headquarters at the entrance from the roundabout at the A192/A1171 junction, the only indication of growth was the thigh-high vegetation over the adjacent large acreage. Until buildings do begin rising, there is hope of a continuing flow of notable bird reports from the flash on the site's western side and the surrounding grassland.

The business park's access road continues north and then veers to the left (ignore a right turning just after bend as it just leads to an electricity sub-station).

When the road comes to an abrupt end there's a discernible path through long grass and low scrub to the west. Walk along this until the flash comes into view after a short distance.

The shallow acre or two of

**Key points
(West Hartford)**

• **Flash only 0.5 miles from A192/ A1171 junction roundabout. Allow two hours for a normal visit.**

• **Pay-and-display car park at Plessey Woods Country Park.**

Key points
(West Hartford)

- **Full circuit is about 1.5 miles and includes some steep steps. Surfaced paths suitable for wheelchairs run from visitor centre through woods to river.**

- **CP visitor centre (Tel: 01670 824 793) and cafe open 11am-4pm on Saturdays, Sundays, bank holidays (apart from Dec 25 & 26) and during school holidays.**

- **Public toilets (NZ 264 769) at Manor Walks shopping mall, Cramlington. Also available (dawn to dusk daily) at Plessey Woods Country Park.**

- **Shops, pubs, restaurants and takeaways at Cramlington.**

water has yet to be visited by a wader more unusual than the Temminck's Stint reported in late May 2010 but there has been a broad selection of more regular spring and autumn callers. The list includes Little Ringed Plover, Little Stint, Ruff, Black-tailed Godwit, Greenshank and Green and Wood Sandpipers.

Snipe can be prominent in mid to late autumn (eg 58 counted in October 2008) and there have been occasional winter records of Jack Snipe.

As for other marshland birds, it's perhaps a measure of the pool's comparative infancy that Water Rail was not recorded until December, 2008.

Wildfowl numbers are generally low and 308 Teal in early 2004 was most exceptional. The following year produced no more than 60-plus in March and counts during the same periods of 2006-08 were below 50.

The species' 2004 prominence may well have influenced the appearance of the flash's most scarce duck to date, a male Green-winged Teal present for ten days in March.

Normally a few Shelduck are seen during the first half of the year and this was among just 11 Northumberland sites where successful breeding by the species was recorded in 2008.

Very small numbers of Gadwall, Pintail and Shoveler have been logged and Garganey was

reported during 2010's spring passage. A male Mandarin Duck was reported in May 2010.

Short-eared Owl is something of a speciality, occurring annually during 2004-2012, though numbers vary from one to four. There have been occasional Long-eared Owl and Barn Owl sightings during April-August and Little Owls nest locally, with fledged juveniles noted during at least 2004.

Scarce raptor appearances have been sporadic; a juvenile Marsh Harrier was around for most of August, 2004, but apparently no more was seen of the species until a report of one in late May, 2010.

In the case of Hobby, one reported hunting over the area for two hours in July 2010, was seemingly the first noted there since a fly-over bird in June, 2003.

Residents of the rank grassland and low scrub around the flash include Reed Buntings, while Grasshopper Warblers may be present in spring and summer, with 'reeling' heard during most recent April-July periods.

Calls of Quail – a much scarcer and more irregular summer visitor to the region – were reported in June, 2010.

Autumn passage migrants may include Whinchat (at least four in September, 2004 and August, 2010).

To the north-west of Cramlington (about a mile from

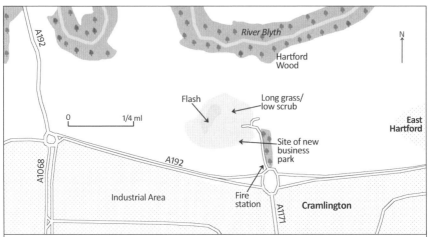

How to get there

(11 miles from Tyne Tunnel)

At big roundabout on A19 eight miles N of Tyne Tunnel, take fifth exit onto B1505, and then immediately turn left at a further small roundabout on to A1171.

On reaching a roundabout after half-a-mile, stay on A1171 as it turns right. Carry on north along A1171 for 2.5 miles until it joins A192 at a roundabout. Go onto access road into business park development site on north side of roundabout. Path leading to the flash starts from end of access road.

From A1, turn on to A19 six miles N of Newcastle centre. After just 200 yards, turn left from A190 on to A1068 and drive north for about three miles

until, at second roundabout along this stretch, it joins the A192. Turn right, heading east along A192 for a mile until it reaches roundabout at the junction with the A1171. Turn left there into the business park access road (rest as above).

Plessey Woods Country Park is just beyond Hartford Bridge over the River Blyth. This is more than half a mile north along the A192 from the above-mentioned roundabout at the junction with the A1068 (a mile west along the A192 from the roundabout at its junction with the A171 on the north edge of Cramlington).

Public transport: Cramlington has bus links with Newcastle and Whitley Bay/Tynemouth; also local rail services from Newcastle (Cramlington Station is a mile north along A1171).

West Hartford) is the Plessey Woods Country Park (NZ 241 796) off the A192 just north of the Hartford Bridge over the River Blyth.

The park covers 100 acres (40ha) providing much potential for woodland birds, including Marsh Tits, Nuthatches, Treecreepers, Lesser Redpolls and Bullfinches while Kingfishers and Dippers are among riverside possibilities. There are links with footpaths covering a much wider area.

DOMINATED by its huge castle, one of Northumberland's best known landmarks, Bamburgh is a beautiful area for finding spring and autumn migrants and for watching seabirds. It is close to the huge seabird colonies of the Farne Islands, while in winter it attracts divers, grebes, seaduck and waders. It is one of the region's most reliable sites for Slavonian Grebe and Purple Sandpiper.

Target birds *Summer* – Eider, Fulmar, Sandwich, Common and Arctic Terns (all 90%), Guillemot (70%), Puffin (70%), Rock Pipit (50%). *Autumn/winter* – Purple Sandpiper (90%), Slavonian Grebe (70%), Long-tailed Duck (60%), Red-breasted Merganser (60%).

Other possible bird species

All year	Great Northern Diver	Whinchat
Eider	Kestrel	Wheatear
Fulmar	Merlin	Yellow Wagtail
Cormorant	Peregrine	Tree Pipit
Shag	Ringed Plover	Brambling
Oystercatcher	Golden Plover	Siskin
Redshank	Grey Plover	Lesser Redpoll
Turnstone	Lapwing	*Occasional species*
Regular gull species	Knot	Cory's Shearwater
Skylark	Sanderling	Balearic Shearwater
Meadow Pipit	Dunlin	Storm Petrel
Rock Pipit	Bar-tailed Godwit	Red-necked Grebe
Stonechat	Curlew	Marsh Harrier
Linnet	*Passage seabirds*	Hen Harrier
Summer	Manx Shearwater	Hobby
Gannet	Sooty Shearwater	Curlew Sandpiper
Swift	Arctic Skua	Grey Phalarope
Swallow	Great Skua	Pomarine Skua
House Martin	Kittiwake	Long-tailed Skua
Willow Warbler	Little Gull	Sabine's Gull
Whitethroat	Little Auk	Iceland Gull
Sedge Warbler	*Passage migrants*	Glaucous Gull
Winter	Pink-footed Goose	Black Tern
Shelduck	Barnacle Goose	Roseate Tern
Wigeon	Greenshank	Little Tern
Scaup	Goldcrest	Red-backed Shrike
Long-tailed Duck	Chiffchaff	Great Grey Shrike
Common Scoter	Blackcap	Firecrest
Velvet Scoter	Ring Ouzel	Yellow-browed Warbler
Goldeneye	Fieldfare	Barred Warbler
Red-breasted Merganser	Redwing	Waxwing
Red-throated Diver	Black Redstart	Red-breasted Flycatcher
Black-throated Diver	Redstart	Mealy Redpoll
		Crossbill

Key points

- Area of Outstanding Natural Beauty.

- Historic castle and village.

- Good spring and autumn migration spot.

- Good seawatching.

- Scenic walks but steep slopes so not suitable for wheelchairs.

- Wheelchair viewing possible from flat roadside area above Stag Rocks.

- Pubs/hotels in Bamburgh village and Seahouses. Toilets in village centre.

- Village busy in summer but no parking problems in autumn and winter.

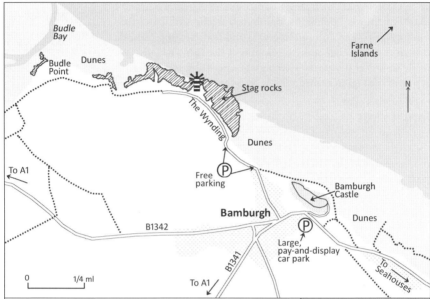

How to get there

(20 miles NE of Alnwick)

From the south, turn east off A1 at the large garage/motel 13 miles north of Alnwick and follow B1341 for seven miles to Bamburgh. From the north, an alternative is to leave the A1 just south of Belford and use the B1342 past Budle Bay to Bamburgh. Any other route from the A1 and sign-posted Seahouses can also be used. Bamburgh is three miles north along the B1340 from Seahouses.

There is a large pay and display car park on the south side of the village opposite the entrance to the castle. Alternatively, free parking is available by the dunes towards Stag Rocks and gives better access to the beach. Stag Rocks is reached from the village along a minor road, the Wynding, opposite the Lord Crew Arms.

Background information and birding tips

BAMBURGH is a very good birding area that over the years has produced some extreme rarities. There are extensive dunes with some bush and shrub cover, attractive to tired and hungry migrants, both north and south of the village. These are always worth searching during spring and autumn 'falls', as are the areas of woodland near the castle.

The beach faces the Farne Islands so offers the opportunity to see fishing terns between April and September, while to the north is the more rugged area of Stag Rocks (NU 178 359) which provides a good elevated seawatching point.

264

The castle rock has breeding Fulmars and in summer parties of Guillemots, Razorbills and Puffins diving for sand-eels are often offshore. A feature of local sheltered rocky areas in June and July are large 'creches' of Eider ducklings, closely guarded by several females after being escorted from breeding sites on the islands.

Cormorants and Shags moving to and from the islands are in view most of the time and Gannets from the Bass Rock colony in the Firth of Forth are regular, either diving offshore or passing to more distant fishing grounds.

The woodland's common breeding species are eclipsed in late summer and autumn by more unusual birds, especially during northerly and easterly weather which produces classic conditions for small migrants.

Just about anything is possible at Bamburgh. Rarities include Black Scoter (first Northumberland record), Surf Scoter, Bee-eater, Lesser Grey Shrike, Greenish, Blyth's Reed, Marsh and Pallas's Warblers, Thrush Nightingale, Nightingale, Isabelline Wheatear (another county first), Desert Wheatear, Arctic Warbler and Pine Bunting.

Stag Rocks, with its small white lighthouse, is a must for all visiting birders but you won't find it on the OS map! Officially it is Harkess Rocks but for decades it has been referred to by its common name because of the small white stag painted on the rock face which is regularly renovated by workmen maintaining the lighthouse.

This rocky outcrop provides a grandstand view in summer for terns, auks and other local seabirds. In late summer and autumn it is a good spot for passing shearwaters and skuas. In winter it is one of the best sites in Northumberland for Purple Sandpipers, with often up to 200 present.

The rocks overlook a stretch of sea rich in wintering species. Slavonian Grebes are usually present as are large feeding and 'crooning' parties of Eider. Large flocks of Common Scoters often attract Velvet Scoters. The Black Scoter mentioned above was with one of these big gatherings in spring 2011.

Parties of Long-tailed Duck, excitedly diving and often flying and calling, are usually present. Red-throated Divers are regular, along with occasional Black-throated and Great Northern Divers. Large numbers of Little Auks can occur, being blasted southwards during northerly gales or speeding northwards again when the weather improves.

The beach between the castle and Stag Rocks is well used by visitors and dog-walkers throughout the year but at quiet periods can hold Ring Plovers, Sanderlings and Bar-tailed Godwits.

There is a public right of way from Stag Rocks that skirts Bamburgh golf course to Budle Point and then along the side of Budle Bay, the southernmost section of Lindisfarne NNR. If time is available it is highly recommended. It gives panoramic seas views towards Holy Island and usually provides more good birding. Budle Bay holds large numbers of waders and wildfowl in autumn and winter (see page 233).

Contacts

Tourist Information 01665 510 665;
www.visitnorthumberland.com

GOING BIRDING?

If you are heading to Cumbria or the Borders, don't travel without this invaluable book....

This highly-acclaimed book in the *Best Birdwatching Sites* stable offers:

- Detailed maps and information for 49 bird sites in Cumbria and 47 sites in Dumfries & Galloway

- A monthly guide to the birds you'll see

- Expert seawatching advice

- Top tips for working each site

- Wheelchair access and public transport information for each site

THIS SMALL rocky tidal island with its landmark lighthouse and hinterland of grassland, scrub and a small wetland, provides the main birding attraction of North Tyneside. A hide on the seaward side of the lighthouse, now a visitor centre, provides a prime seawatching location.

Target birds *Spring/summer* – Eider, Gannet, Sandwich Tern, Kittiwake, Fulmar (all 100%), Wheatear, Whinchat, Sand Martin (all 80%), Sedge Warbler (50%). *Autumn* – Arctic Skua, Guillemot, Razorbill (all 70%), Manx Shearwater (50%), Roseate Tern (50%), Redstart (30%), Spotted Flycatcher (30%), Pied Flycatcher (20%). *Winter* – Eider (100%), Golden Plover (100%), Red-throated Diver, Ringed Plover, Knot (all 70%), Rock Pipit (50%).

Other possible bird species

All year	Skylark	Goldcrest
Teal	Wren	Chiffchaff
Mallard	Stonechat	Willow Warbler
Shag	Pied Wagtail	Blackcap
Oystercatcher	Meadow Pipit	Blackbird
Dunlin	Common finches	Song Thrush
Curlew	Linnet	Winter thrushes
Redshank	Reed Bunting	Robin
Turnstone		Brambling
Corvids	*Autumn/winter*	Siskin
	Purple Sandpiper	

Background information and birding tips

ST MARY'S ISLAND is a very popular destination for thousands of visitors throughout the year. The causeway is clear at low tide and safe crossing times are prominently displayed.

It is an extremely well-watched location (some local birders are there almost every day) and so has provided a long succession of good birds and many rarities.

The headland leading to the island is Curry's Point, named after Michael Curry, hanged in Newcastle in 1739 for the murder of a local publican. The Point has a small wetland which attracts a wide range of common species

and has also hosted Blue-winged Teal, White-rumped Sandpiper and wintering Lapland Buntings. The wetland is enclosed but there are several good viewing points with information boards.

The main attraction on the mainland lies north of the wetland where thick, high bushes and wet flushes with scrub and rough coastal grassland, provide a magnet for migrants.

Common warblers, flycatchers, pipits and finches abound in the right conditions and many rarities include Nightjar, Wryneck, Red-backed and Great Grey Shrikes, Firecrest, Greenish,

Key points
- Pay/display car parks include disabled toilets.
- Safe crossing times posted in car park and on www. whitleybayonline.
- Island and hide wheelchair accessible.
- Good track alongside wetland to prime migrant site/coastal grassland/fields.
- Lighthouse visitor centre open full-time (April-Sept) and at weekends, bank holidays (Oct-March only while the causeway is open.
- Many pubs, restaurants, cafes in Whitley Bay and Tynemouth.

Contacts
Friends of St Mary's Island: www.friendsof stmarysisland.co.uk

Visitor centre 0191 2008 650

Tourist information, (Whitley Bay Library) 0191 200 8535

Pallas's, Yellow-browed, Dusky, Barred, Blyth's Reed and Marsh Warblers, white-spotted Bluethroat, Red-breasted Flycatcher, Tawny, Olive-backed and Red-throated Pipits and Ortolan Bunting.

Northumberland's first Red-flanked Bluetail was seen by few folk in October 1960, so it was with great relief for local 'patch' devotees when another showed well in October 2010.

The local fields attract waders, pipits and larks and have held wintering Siberian Stonechat. A few pairs of Fulmars frequently nest on the cliffs between the island and Hartley. The island is rocky and along with rocks at the Point attracts large numbers of gulls, waders and occasional rarities.

The hide provides shelter in easterly or northerly winds when rough seas can provide some spectacular autumn passage with large numbers of Fulmars, Manx Shearwaters, Gannets, Kittiwakes, Arctic Skuas and various terns and auks.

Borrow a key for the hide from the lighthouse visitor centre. In bad weather when the hide is not available, local birders recommend seawatching from your vehicle in the car park.

During autumn wildfowl move past en route to Lindisfarne. Barnacle Geese are also regular in autumn. These periods can be enlivened occasionally by Cory's, Sooty and Balearic Shearwaters

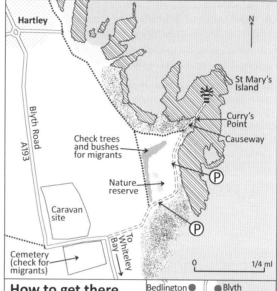

How to get there

(11 mile E of Newcastle)

From Newcastle take A1058 eastwards for 10 miles to Tynemouth seafront, then head north through Cullercoats on A193 Whitley Bay-Blyth road. Island, signposted one mile north from Whitley Bay. Look for Whitley Bay cemetery on left just before the island turn-off.

Public transport: Tyne and Wear Metro from Newcastle

to Whitley Bay. Arriva Northumbria 308 and Go-North East 309 buses from Park Avenue, Whitley Bay town centre to Blyth along A193 pass island turn-off.

and Pomarine and Long-tailed Skuas. Rarer species have included Gull-billed and White-winged Black Terns. A Zino's/Fea's Petrel flew north in November 1999. A county record total of 121 Storm Petrels passed St Mary's on July 26, 2011.

The town cemetery's cover attracts considerable numbers of migrants. They are always worth checking, as was demonstrated in September 1995 when Britain's second Eastern Bonelli's Warbler was present for nine days.

268

WILDLIFE FLOURISHES in the Rising Sun Country Park, despite its grim backdrop of 19th Century heavy industry. The main birding spot is Swallow Pond, which offers an impressive species range for a location just four miles from Newcastle city centre.

Target birds *All Year* – Willow Tit (50%), Water Rail (30%).
Spring to early autumn – Osprey (30%), Garganey (20%), Black Tern (20%), Black-necked Grebe (10%). *Spring/summer* – Grasshopper Warbler (40%), Little Gull (10%). *Winter* – Short-eared Owl (40%), Mediterranean Gull (40%), Tree Sparrow (40%), Iceland Gull (30%).

Other possible bird species

All year
Familiar waterfowl/gulls
Common farmland/
woodland birds
Gadwall
Teal
Shoveler
Pochard
Grey Partridge
Sparrowhawk
Kestrel
Lapwing
Stock Dove
Little Owl
Tawny Owl
Long-eared Owl
Skylark
Meadow Pipit
Pied Wagtail
Mistle Thrush
Goldcrest

Long-tailed Tit
Coal Tit
Greenfinch
Goldfinch
Linnet
Bullfinch
Yellowhammer
Reed Bunting

Spring to early autumn
Shelduck
Great Crested Grebe
Oystercatcher
Ruff
Black-tailed Godwit
Redshank
Greenshank
Green Sandpiper
Common Sandpiper
Common Tern
Swift
Hirundines

Whinchat
Wheatear
Sedge Warbler
Lesser Whitethroat
Whitethroat
Garden Warbler
Blackcap
Chiffchaff
Willow Warbler

Late autumn/winter
Wigeon
Goldeneye
Snipe
Curlew
Waxwing
Fieldfare
Redwing
Brambling
Siskin
Lesser Redpoll
Crossbill

Background information and birding tips

SWALLOW POND'S southern hide lies by the jogger and cyclist-haunted Wagonway, a former mineral line on which early 19th Century rail pioneer George Stephenson trialled his famous steam engines.

Thankfully this area of Wallsend is now a lot greener than at its low point during the Industrial Revolution when nine collieries,

a brickworks and a lime kiln were operating.

There was also a cokeworks that belched fumes so sulphurous that Rising Sun Farm workers choked while harvesting and the owner was sued for crop damage. The start of the 20th Century brought the sinking of a new pit – named, ironically, after the farm – which became one of Europe's biggest.

Key points
• Park (free) at visitor centre (NZ 303 696) or, when closed, in lane outside.

• Country Park always open. Visitor centre, with toilets and restaurant, open daily (times vary with seasons). Tel: 0191 200 7841

• Path around Swallow Pond less than a mile. With stops at hides and elsewhere, allow at least 2hrs.

• Paths network mainly flat and firm. Can be muddy in places (eg trail around pond's west side).

• Screen hide on pond's west side (NZ301693). Larger hide, with roof and seating on Wagonway (NZ 302 691) should be suitable for wheelchair-users.

269

Now the farm practises organic agriculture in a 400-acre (160ha) country park where 60,000 trees have been planted since 1973. The park's highest point is the hill landscaped from the pitheap of the Rising Sun Colliery which closed in 1969.

Swallow Pond, covering 35 acres (14ha), dates from 1953 when water gathered in a depression caused by underground operations. By 1956 it had already produced two Northumberland 'firsts' – Black-winged Stilt and Marsh Sandpiper – adding Lesser Yellowlegs to the county list in 1977.

However, after sightings of a further Black-winged Stilt and a White-rumped Sandpiper in the 1980s, problems with maintaining the water level have prevailed.

Black-tailed Godwit, Greenshank and Green and Common Sandpipers have occurred since 2000, but it is now well down the shorebird location league table. However, it can still surprise in other ways.

The 2008 star was a Pallas's Warbler which, as well as being four miles inland, appeared, unusually, in April and was a singing male. It attracted much attention over nine days as it associated with Goldcrests and tits. Remarkably, it was the site's second Siberian stray in a fortnight; its predecessor was a Yellow-browed Warbler,

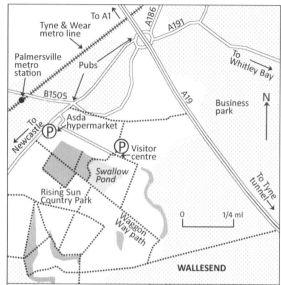

How to get there

(Seven miles from Newcastle city centre)

Country Park lies just off the A191 running between Newcastle and A19 (second left north of tunnel, fifth turning south from A1).

Key landmark to look for is an Asda hypermarket because the turning into a narrow lane to Rising Sun Visitor Centre (half a mile) is just 200 yards east of the roundabout outside it.

Public transport: Swallow Pond is 20-mins from Metro rail service's Palmersville

Station. From here walk east along B1505 Great Lime Road for quarter-of-a-mile to roundabout and then, after turning right onto A191, 200 yards to visitor centre lane turning).

Buses stop at Asda (walk to Swallow Pond along Wagonway starting from A191 near store).

also typical of autumn and coastal locations.

An Osprey, a Red-crested Pochard and a Red-rumped Swallow provided further April highlights. Late August

was marked by a Spotted Crake and a passage Marsh Harrier was logged in mid-September. Up to 18 Crossbills moved around the park's conifer belts from October.

Visitors to the site in winter may be lucky enough to encounter Short-eared Owls hunting over grassland areas.

Typically, Iceland and Mediterranean Gulls were logged during the preceding and subsequent winter months.

Swallow's wildfowl presence tends to be strongest between October and March. There was a site record count of 328 Wigeon in October 2005 (the normal figure is usually in the 50-150 range).

Another example was up to 62 Pochards during the 2007-08 winter; no other Northumberland water held more in those years. Around 100 Teal and 20-30 Shovelers may be present over this time of year, along with perhaps one or two Pintails.

Occasionally an autumn passage Whooper Swan party appears; up to 17 were reported in October 2010. More offbeat visitors in the past have included Green-winged Teals and Scaup.

Though Water Rail is present during the breeding season, it is seen mostly in winter when Short-eared Owls may be hunting over park grasslands. Long-eared Owl is another possibility, having roosted in park woodland or scrub in the past (also an adult and two juveniles during the 2009 summer indicated local breeding).

Look out for Willow Tits, which are year-round residents, and Tree Sparrows, while there may be Siskin and Lesser Redpoll parties too (also occasionally scarcer Mealy Redpolls as in December 2010).

Waxwings can show up during irruptions, possibly linked to larger flocks in the vicinity (Longbenton, two miles to the west, is a favourite stop-over).

Black-necked Grebes are spring regulars and there are always prospects of Garganey and Ospreys but in the latter case, the hard bit is being there at the right time.

Little Gulls and Black Terns can occur during spring or autumn passage and the two White-winged Black Terns (1977 and 1996) were both June birds. A Roseate Tern that arrived with mist drifting inland from the coast in June 2009 was a first for the site.

Northumberland's upsurge of Little Egret reports in 2010 included one at Swallow Pond in July, perhaps the precursor of more visits in future. Very occasional Hobby appearances tend to be in summer or early autumn. Breeding species since 2000 have included Pochard, Tufted Duck, Great Crested Grebe and Common Tern.

Key points

- Pay/display car parks include disabled parking/toilets.
- Tynemouth Haven accessible to wheelchairs but help needed on steeper paths. Pier, estuary path, fish quay all accessible.
- Telescope useful for scanning estuary birds.
- Food & drink: many pubs, restaurants, cafes in Tynemouth. Pubs/cafes around fish quay. Local fish and chips have a wonderful reputation.

THESE TWO SITES on the northern bank of the River Tyne may only be a mile apart, but their birding characters are very different. The steep, well-vegetated south-facing slopes of Tynemouth Haven attracts many migrants, while the Tyne estuary can hold significant numbers of birds – the Swinhoe's Storm Petrels located from the town's pier created ornithological history. Upriver, North Shields Fish Quay is one of the region's most important areas for wintering gulls.

Target birds *Spring/summer* – Eider, Gannet, Sandwich Tern, Kittiwake, Fulmar (all 100%), Wheatear, Whinchat, Sand Martin (80%), Sedge Warbler (50%). *Autumn* – Arctic Skua, Guillemot, Razorbill (all 70%), Manx Shearwater (50%), Roseate Tern (50%), Redstart, Spotted Flycatcher, Pied Flycatcher (all 30%), Black Redstart (15%). *Winter* – Eider (100%), Golden Plover (100%), Red-throated Diver, Ringed Plover, Knot (all 70%), Purple Sandpiper (60%) Rock Pipit (50%).

Other possible bird species

All year		
Teal	Skylark	Red-breasted Merganser
Mallard	Wren	Goosander
Cormorant	Stonechat	Goldcrest
Shag	Pied Wagtail	Chiffchaff
Oystercatcher	Meadow Pipit	Willow Warbler
Dunlin	Chaffinch	Blackcap
Curlew	Greenfinch	Blackbird
Redshank	Goldfinch	Fieldfare
Turnstone	Linnet	Song Thrush
Jackdaw	Reed Bunting	Redwing
Carrion Crow	*Autumn/winter*	Robin
	Goldeneye	Brambling

1. Tynemouth Haven (NZ 375 694)

THE HAVEN comprises a small popular boating venue under the steep rocky slopes of Tynemouth Priory. These banks are sheltered and south-facing, so provide birds with good hatches of insects, while many berried bushes provide autumn food for other tired new arrivals.

Chiffchaffs, Willow Warblers, Blackcaps and other common warblers find it attractive, as do Spotted and Pied Flycatchers and Black and Common Redstarts.

The site has produced many rarities including Wryneck, Pallas's, Yellow-browed, Radde's, Dusky, Barred and Great Reed Warblers and Red-breasted Flycatcher. The beach held an immature female Pied Wheatear for a week in December 1998.

The short grassy areas around the upper car park, which provide panoramic views of the estuary prove attractive to migrating pipits and finches and has held Shore Lark.

The North Tyne pier provides good views of the local cliffs which have around 30 breeding pairs of Fulmar and 100 pairs of Kittiwake. The pier is famous for producing the only British records of a Pacific species, Swinhoe's Storm Petrel. During tape-luring sessions to trap and ring Storm Petrels, three of these super-rarities were netted between 1989 and 1994, one of them in three successive years.

The trapping of the first two dark petrels lacking white rumps in July 1989 caused amazement in the birding community but it was several years before the mystery was finally solved.

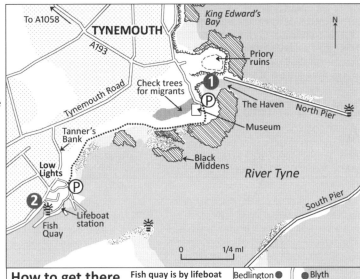

How to get there

(10 miles E of Newcastle)

Take A1058 from Newcastle to Tynemouth seafront. Turn south after 0.5m to Tynemouth village. For the Haven bear left down the hill just past Gibraltar Rock pub/Priory entrance.

For Fish Quay continue right along Front Street, turn left into Tynemouth Road. After 0.5m turn left to Fish Quay opposite Tynemouth Lodge pub.

Fish quay is by lifeboat station. Quay can also be reached on foot from Haven along riverside path and from North Shields town centre.

Public transport: North Shields town centre and Tynemouth village both served by Tyne & Wear Metro.

Buses: Arriva Northumbria 306 (Newcastle Haymarket-Tynemouth); Go North East 1 (Newcastle St James-Tynemouth); Go North East 301 (Newcastle Haymarket-North Shields town centre); Arriva Northumbria 306 (Newcastle St James-North Shields).

It took extensive physical examination, blood sampling, DNA testing and sound recording to finally confirm their identities and for this new species to be added to the British list.

The pier, which can be closed to the public during bad weather, provides a vantage point for watching passing seabirds and birds using the estuary. Purple Sandpipers and Rock Pipits are regular while the estuary attracts feeding parties of Eiders, Goldeneyes and occasionally Goosanders.

A short distance inland from the haven the trees around

273

the car park between Prior's Park and the Collingwood monument are worth checking for large numbers of migrants during autumn 'falls.' The monument commemorates the Northumbrian admiral who was Nelson's second-in-command at Trafalgar.

Prior's Park itself is private but its bordering trees are viewable from the car park. The park produced Northumberland's first Lanceolated Warbler in November 1984. Others rarities include Lesser Grey Shrike, Western Bonelli's and Blyth's Reed warblers.

2. North Shields Fish Quay (NZ 365 687)

A BROAD PATH runs almost a mile from the Haven along the side of the estuary to the quay This route can be excellent for birds, both on the grassy and shrubby slopes and on the water.

One of the best sites is the Black Middens, a patch of treacherous rocks just hidden at high water and on which many a ship has floundered. At low tide it has good numbers of commoner gulls and waders including Purple Sandpipers.

In late summer, the Black Middens are also popular for migrating common tern species. It is also a very regular site in late July-August for Roseate Terns on their way south from their breeding site on Coquet Island. Small parties make it a site to be checked regularly by local birders.

North Shields, in common with other ports, has suffered badly from the decline of fishing and now attracts far fewer boats. This has led to a reduction in fish waste and less food for birds. A long programme to clean up the Tyne, now restored as one of England's most important salmon rivers, has included the closure of sewerage outfalls, again reducing feeding for gulls and other scavengers.

Nevertheless, the quay continues to attract large concentrations of wintering gulls with the roofs and ridges of its sheds and other buildings lined with ever-watchful birds.

All of the regular gull species frequent the quay but the prizes for birders are the sought-

after 'white' gulls. One or two Glaucous Gulls are usually present and the area also attracts Iceland Gulls.

The big rise in Northumberland's population of Mediterranean Gulls has meant that sightings are becoming more frequent. Rarities have included Sabine's Gull. Ross's Gulls were present in January 1993 and May 1997, further proof of the need to always check this area.

Large numbers of Cormorants use the old wooden pilings near the lifeboat station as handy places to 'hang' out their wings to dry between fishing expeditions.

During the breeding season many Kittiwakes are present with a few pairs breeding at the ferry landing just upstream. Many more commute from the big breeding colony on the Tyne Bridge ten miles upriver, and in local riverside buildings, including the Baltic Arts Centre, Gateshead, and the purpose-built Kittiwake nesting tower now permanently located on the south bank of the River Tyne at Saltmeadows. The Baltic Centre has a camera on Kittiwake nests to give visitors the closest possible views.

In 2011 the tower was home to more than 100 pairs of breeding Kittiwakes and recently underwent a major facelift to renew the all-important ledges on which the birds build their distinctive nests. The Newcastle/ Gateshead colony is reputed to be the world's most inland site for the species.

THIS COMPLEX of five main lakes and two smaller reservoirs was created in 1848 to provide the first safe and reliable water supply for the rapidly expanding city of Newcastle and for Gateshead on the south bank of the Tyne. Despite regular disturbance because of coarse fishing and the fact that its banks are kept short-mown, the area has a very respectable bird species list of just over 200, with Little Egret and Common Crane being recent additions.

Target birds *Spring/summer* – Great Crested Grebe, Common Sandpiper, Common Tern, Yellow Wagtail (all 90%), Oystercatcher, Ringed Plover (both 80%), Osprey (10%). *Autumn/winter* – Whooper Swan, Goldeneye, Goosander (all 90%), Smew, Green Sandpiper, Merlin, Peregrine (all 50%), Kingfisher (10%).

Other possible bird species

Breeding birds	Greenfinch	Snipe
Tufted Duck	Goldfinch	Curlew
Great Crested Grebe	Linnet	Greenshank
Lapwing	Yellowhammer	Redshank
Common Sandpiper	Reed Bunting	Black-headed Gull
Tawny Owl	*Spring/autumn (regular*	Common Gull
Skylark	*migrants)*	Lesser Black-backed Gull
Whitethroat	Pink-footed Goose	Herring Gull
Sedge Warbler	Barnacle Goose	Swift
Yellow Wagtail	Wigeon	Sand Martin
Grey Wagtail	Marsh Harrier	Swallow
Pied Wagtail	Golden Plover	Whinchat
Meadow Pipit	Dunlin	Wheatear
Chaffinch	Ruff	White Wagtail

Background information and birding tips

AT FIRST SIGHT Whittle Dene (NZ 067 684) appears a typically rather bleak and open reservoir complex with little bank-side vegetation, reedbeds or emergent plant cover to provide nesting sites and feeding for birds.

The bare, high-walled concrete channels and sluices linking the different waters also look unpromising. Because of this, and disturbance from fishing and management methods, breeding numbers are low. Consequently, the area is much more attractive to birdwatchers as a spring and autumn migration stop-over site and as a winter habitat.

The only public access is to the Great Northern Reservoir (NZ 067 684) alongside the busy Military Road between Heddon-on-the-Wall and Chollerford and the Roman Wall country beyond. It is on the route of the Hadrian's

Key points

- Only Great Northern Reservoir accessible to public.

- View other waters from B6309 verges.

- GNR Hide access is via small gate at lay-by, along gravelled path 200 yards east. No wheelchair access to hide.

- Nearest food and drink in Heddon pubs and Corbridge pubs/cafes. Robin Hood pub on right on main road mile west of reservoirs. Vallum tea rooms/ farm shop short distance further on left at East Wallhouses.

Contacts
Northumbrian Water
0845 155 0236
www.nwl.co.uk

Wall Trail, which runs for 84 miles from Wallsend to Bowness-on-Solway and used by thousands of walkers annually. Fortunately, the trail is hidden below the high, steep embankment so there is no disturbance.

Other stretches of the reservoirs complex can easily be checked from the minor road which runs southwards at the crossroads just below and to the west of the Great Northern Reservoir. Northumbrian Water has designated the area as a nature reserve and provided a comfortable hide and picnic area in its south-east corner, overlooking a lake which is undisturbed by anglers and therefore much more attractive to birds.

The shoreline to the west of the hide is exposed when water levels drop and proves particularly attractive to both breeding Common Sandpipers, passage waders and, particularly, to foraging wagtails and pipits. Spring passage rarities such as Blue-headed Wagtail have occurred.

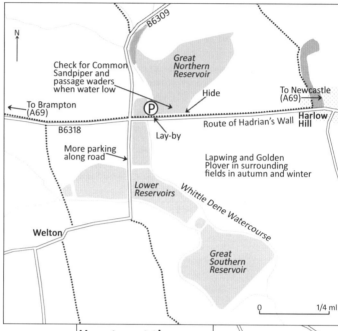

How to get there

(12 miles W of Newcastle)

From Newcastle take A69 west and turn left on the A6085 towards Throckley. At the roundabout, turn right onto the B6528.

Continue to Heddon-on-the-Wall, bearing right to join the B6318 (which crosses the A69). Look for a rough lay-by on the right, with parking room for four-five vehicles between

Harlow Hill and the crossroads with B6309.

Other space is available along road to reservoir houses.

In years when the water levels are low both Little Ringed Plovers and Ringed Plovers can breed. Great Crested Grebes and Tufted Ducks breed in the north-east corner, where there is some reedbed cover. A nesting raft has also been provided near the hide for Common Terns.

Migrant Ospreys are regular in both spring and autumn, attracted by stocks of roach, perch, dace, gudgeon, bream and carp. Ospreys habitually use the bare trees along the field edge behind the north-east corner as resting and feeding places. In some years immature Ospreys can remain into summer, often fishing in front of the hide.

The hedges near the hide attract singing and breeding Whitethroats, Sedge Warblers, Yellowhammers and Reed Buntings. Buzzards from nearby woodland and plantations are often in view, joined by the occasional Red Kite from the re-introduced population in the Derwent Valley, Gateshead, ten miles away. Kites frequently prospect the area for possible nest sites.

Less common autumn passage wader species include Little Stint, Curlew Sandpiper, Black-tailed Godwit, Whimbrel and Wood Sandpiper. Rarities, including Red-crested Pochard, Ferruginous Duck, Temminck's Stint, White-rumped Sandpiper, Pectoral Sandpiper and Buff-breasted Sandpiper, have also occurred.

Species more associated with coastal areas including Scaup, Eider, Knot, Sanderling, Purple Sandpiper, Turnstone, Arctic Skua, Kittiwake, Glaucous Gull, Black Tern, White-winged Black Tern and even Little Auk are also on the list but cannot be considered regulars.

During autumn and winter the reservoirs and surrounding farmland attract large gatherings of common geese and smaller groups of Whooper Swans. These concentrations have also attracted passing Bewick's Swans, White-fronted Geese of both Eurasian and Greenland races and Shelduck.

The reservoirs hold reasonable numbers of common duck including Mallards, Pochards, Tufted Ducks and Teal. Goldeneyes and Cormorants are usually present, as are Grey Herons.

Parties of Goosanders regular commute between Whittle Dene and the River Tyne at Wylam, taking advantage of rich fishing provided by both localities. Red-throated, Black-throated and Great Northern Divers have also been recorded.

The reservoirs are one of Northumberland's most reliable sites for Smew, with one or two usually present, often for long periods, in most winters. Most are 'redhead' females or immatures but beautiful marbled white adult drakes have graced the area in some years.

During winter Whittle Dene is also a reliable site for Green Sandpipers, which often find food in shallow water along the concrete channels. Kingfishers also like these areas, particularly where water cascades down into the deeper areas of the reservoirs. Grey and Pied Wagtails find good feeding in the same areas.

The local fields are also attractive in winter to large flocks of Lapwings and Golden Plovers, as well as parties of common finches and other farmland birds. These gatherings in turn bring in hunting Sparrowhawks, Kestrels and Peregrines. Hen Harriers can frequent the area in some winters.

THE PUBLISHERS are extremely grateful to Ian Kerr for creating this Checklist of Birds based on records collated by the region's bird clubs. Though many of the records concern rarities, including the recent Eastern Crowned Warbler (a first for Britain) and Glaucous-winged Gull (second UK sighting), the full list will provide an idea of how frequently individual species have turned up and the locations where they appeared.

Please use columns 1 and 2 to record your own sightings. For instance, one might be utilised to record a life list, while the other might be deployed to record birds seen in one of the individual counties that make up the region. It's your choice....

Categories

Very Common	Occurs in large numbers and is usually very widespread
Common	Occurs in fairly large numbers or is widely distributed in suitable areas
Fairly common	Occurs in moderate numbers in suitable areas and season
Locally common	Occurs in reasonable numbers but is restricted to certain areas
Uncommon	Occurs in small numbers
Scarce	Usually one to five records annually
Rare	Recorded less than annually
Very rare	Recorded between 6-25 times since 1950
Accidental	Recorded five times or less since 1950

A Quick Guide to North-East England's Birds
What are your chances of seeing .....?

Two blank columns have been added to allow you to record your own sightings. The third column contains a scoring system that will give you an idea of what you might see and the likelihood of seeing them [sightings will depend on time of year, the sites visited and how long you spend in the field].

1 = should see
2 = a good chance of seeing
3 = possible, but scarce/irregular

blank = unlikely, sub-rarities /rarities
# = feral birds

			British Name	Scientific Name	Status and Key Locations
		1	Mute Swan	*Cygnus olor*	Common breeding resident
		3	Bewick's (Tundra) Swan	*Cygnus columbianus*	Scarce passage and winter visitor
		2	Whooper Swan	*Cygnus cygnus*	Locally common on passage and in winter
		3	Bean Goose	*Anser fabalis*	Usually scarce but periodic influxes
		1	Pink-footed Goose	*Anser brachyrhynchus*	Common winter visitor
		3	White-fronted Goose	*Anser albifrons*	Usually scarce but periodic influxes. Greenland race scarce –Grindon Lough only regular site
			Lesser White-fronted Goose	*Anser erythropus*	Accidental: 2 in Budle Bay February 1978
		1	Greylag Goose	*Anser anser*	Locally common breeding resident and winter visitor
		#	Snow Goose	*Anser caerulescens*	Scarce/birds of dubious origin
		#	Canada Goose	*Branta canadensis*	Locally common breeding resident

			British Name	Scientific Name	Status and Key Locations
			Lesser Canada (Cackling) Goose	*Branta hutchinsii*	Rare winter visitor, usually with other geese species.
		2	Barnacle Goose	*Branta leucopsis*	Locally common passage migrant
		1	Brent Goose	*Branta bernicla*	Dark-bellied race uncommon winter visitors, usually c200 at Lindisfarne.
		1	Brent Goose	*Branta bernicla hrota*	Pale-bellied Svalbard race common at Lindisfarne (c3,000 most winters)
			Ross's Goose	*Anser rossi*	Accidental: Spittal 2009, Wooler 2011. Arriving with Pinkfeet and Barnacles suggests wild origins
	#		Red-breasted Goose	*Branta ruficollis*	Rare/birds of dubious origin
	#		Egyptian Goose	*Alopochen aegyptiaca*	Rare/birds of dubious origin
	#		Bar-headed Goose	*Anser indicus*	Scarce but regarded as escapes
	#		Ruddy Shelduck	*Tadorna ferruginea*	Rare/birds of dubious origin
		1	Shelduck	*Tadorna tadorna*	Uncommon breeder/winter visitor
	#		Mandarin	*Aix galericulata*	Rare resident. Small breeding population in North Tyne valley resulting from escapes.
		1	Wigeon	*Anas penelope*	Rare breeder/common winter visitor
			American Wigeon	*Anas americana*	Rare winter visitor
		2	Gadwall	*Anas strepera*	Uncommon breeder
		1	Teal	*Anas crecca*	Uncommon breeder/very common winter
			Green-winged Teal	*Anas carolinensis*	Rare winter visitor, usually associating with Teal flocks
		1	Mallard	*Anas platyrhynchos*	Common breeder/winter visitor
		3	Pintail	*Anas acuta*	Uncommon passage and winter visitor – Lindisfarne is prime site
			Garganey	*Anas querquedula*	Scarce breeder/passage migrant
			Blue-winged Teal*	*Anas discors*	Very rare winter visitor.
		2	Shoveler	*Anas clypeata*	Scarce breeder/increases in winter
	#		Red-crested Pochard	*Netta rufina*	Rare/birds of dubious origin
		2	Pochard	*Aythya ferina*	Scarce breeder/increases in winter
			Ring-necked Duck	*Aythya collaris*	Scarce winter visitor
			Ferruginous Duck	*Aythya nyroca*	Very rare
		1	Tufted Duck	*Aythya fuligula*	Uncommon breeding resident and winter visitor
			Scaup	*Aythya marila*	Uncommon, mainly offshore but occasionally coastal ponds
			Lesser Scaup*	*Aythya affinis*	Accidental: Saltholme 1999, Bishop Middleham 2003, Cleveland 2006, Liddleham 2003, Cleveland 2006, Linton 2007, Whitley Bay 2011-12

			British Name	Scientific Name	Status and Key Locations
		1	Eider	*Somateria mollissima*	Common island breeder, most in Northumberland
			King Eider*	*Somateria spectabilis*	Very rare
		3	Long-tailed Duck	*Clangula hyemalis*	Locally common in north Northumberland.
		1	Common Scoter	*Melanitta nigra*	Fairly common, particlarly winter
			Black Scoter	*Melanitta americana*	Accidental: Bamburgh, Goswick 2011
			Surf Scoter	*Melanitta perspicillata*	Rare visitor
			Velvet Scoter	*Melanitta fusca*	Uncommon visitor, usually with Common Scoter flocks.
		1	Goldeneye	*Bucephala clangula*	Locally common winter visitor. One pair bred in Northumberland in 2010 and 2011.
		#	Hooded Merganser	*Lophodytes cucullatus*	Accidental: Woodhorn Flash 1992/unknown origin
		1	Smew	*Mergellus albellus*	Uncommon winter visitor at reservoirs etc
		3	Red-breasted Merganser	*Mergus serrator*	Rare breeder/uncommon winter visitor
		3	Goosander	*Mergus merganser*	Uncommon breeder/winter visitor
			Ruddy Duck	*Oxyura jamaicensis*	Faded out in recent years after culling programme
		1	Red Grouse	*Lagopus lagopus*	Common, moorland areas only
		3	Black Grouse	*Tetrao tetrix*	Now uncommon except Durham dales
		3	Red-legged Partridge	*Alectoris rufa*	Fairly common from releases
		3	Grey Partridge	*Perdix perdix*	Now uncommon
			Quail	*Coturnix coturnix*	Usually scarce but light influxes some years
		1	Pheasant	*Phasianus colchicus*	Common breeding resident/also game releases
		3	Red-throated Diver	*Gavia stellata*	Fairly common winter visitor
		1	Black-throated Diver	*Gavia arctica*	Uncommon winter visitor
		1	Great Northern Diver	*Gavia immer*	Uncommon winter visitor
			Yellow-billed Diver*	*Gavia adamsii*	Rare winter visitor
			Albatros sp.	*Diomedea/ Thalassarches*	Accidental: St. Mary's Island, May 1970
		1	Fulmar	*Fulmarus glacialis*	Fairly common, mainly Northumberland
			Fea's/Zino's Petrel	*Pterodroma feae/ madeira*	Rare passage visitor
			Cory's Shearwater	*Calonectris diomedea*	Scarce passage visitor
			Great Shearwater	*Puffinus gravis*	Rare passage visitor
			Sooty Shearwater	*Puffinus griseus*	Usually uncommon passage visitor
		3	Manx Shearwater	*Puffinus puffinus*	Locally common passage migrant
			Balearic Shearwater	*Puffinus mauretanicus*	Rare passage visitor

			British Name	Scientific Name	Status and Key Locations
			Macaronesian Shearwater	*Puffinus baroli*	Accidental: Tynemouth 1986, Whitburn 1989, Seaton Sluice 1989.
			Wilson's Petrel	*Oceanites oceanicus*	Accidental. Off Blyth 2002, Hartlepool Headland 2006.
			European Storm-petrel	*Hydrobates pelagicus*	Uncommon summer passage visitor
			Swinhoe's Storm-petrel	*Oceanodroma monorhis*	Accidental: 3 trapped Tynemouth between 1989-94, first UK records
			Leach's Storm-petrel	*Oceanodroma leucorhoa*	Scarce passage migrant
		1	Gannet	*Morus bassanus*	Common offshore March-November
		1	Cormorant	*Phalacrocorax carbo*	Fairly common breeding resident
			Double-crested Cormorant*	*Phalacrocorax auritus*	Accidental: Billingham 1989.
		1	Shag	*Phalacrocorax aristotelis*	Fairly common breeding resident and winter visitor
			Bittern	*Botaurus stellaris*	Scarce but increasing winter visitor
			Little Bittern*	*Ixobrychus minutus*	Accidental: Hurworth Burn 1973, Witton-le-Wear 1976, St Mary's Island 2000
			Black-crowned Night Heron	*Nycticorax nycticorax*	Very rare
			Squacco Heron	*Ardeola ralloides*	Accidental: Blagdon 1979, East Chevington 2004.
			Cattle Egret*	*Bubulcus ibis*	Accidental: Witton-le-Wear 1979, Barrasford 1986, Longnewton, 1986, Barrasford and Longnewton 1986, Saltholme 2008.
		3	Little Egret	*Egretta garzetta*	Uncommon but increasing
			Great Egret	*Ardea alba*	Rare visitor
		1	Grey Heron	*Ardea cinerea*	Locally common resident and winter visitor
			Purple Heron	*Ardea purpurea*	Rare visitor
			Black Stork*	*Ciconia nigra*	Very rare
			White Stork	*Ciconia ciconia*	Scarce visitor
			Glossy Ibis*	*Plegadis falcinellus*	Very rare
			Spoonbill	*Platalea leucorodia*	Scarce but slowly increasing
		3	Little Grebe	*Tachybaptus ruficollis*	Uncommon breeding resident.
			Pied-billed Grebe	*Podilymbus podiceps*	Accidental: 1 Druridge Bay waters, 1992-94
			Great Crested Grebe	*Podiceps cristatus*	Uncommon breeding resident.
		3	Red-necked Grebe	*Podiceps grisegena*	Uncommon winter visitor, mainly north Northumberland
		3	Slavonian Grebe	*Podiceps auritus*	Uncommon winter visitor, mainly north Northumberland
			Black-necked Grebe	*Podiceps nigricollis*	Scarce resident breeder

		British Name	Scientific Name	Status and Key Locations
		Honey-buzzard	*Pernis apivorus*	Scarce passage visitor
		Black Kite	*Milvus migrans*	Scarce passage visitor
3		Red Kite	*Milvus milvus*	Locally common but only in Derwent Valley
		White-tailed Sea Eagle	*Haliaeetus albicilla*	Rare visitor
		Marsh Harrier	*Circus aeruginosus*	Uncommon passage visitor. Breeding resumed at Druridge Bay in 2009 after a gap of more than a century
		Hen Harrier	*Circus cyaneus*	Uncommon, occasional breeder in Northumberland
		Pallid Harrier	*Circus macrourus*	Accidental: Saltholme area 2011
		Montagu's Harrier	*Circus pygargus*	Rare passage visitor which has bred
3		Goshawk	*Accipiter gentilis*	Uncommon resident – mainly Kielder, Harwood and Hamsterley.
1		Sparrowhawk	*Accipiter nisus*	Fairly common throughout region
1		Common Buzzard	*Buteo buteo*	Fairly common resident
		Rough-legged Buzzard	*Buteo lagopus*	Uncommon winter visitor, mainly Cleveland
		Golden Eagle	*Aquila chrysaetos*	Rare winter visitor and occasional breeder in Northumberland
		Greater Spotted Eagle	*Aquila clanga*	Accidental: 1 Cresswell 1885
3		Osprey	*Pandion haliaetus*	Uncommon passage visitor, breeding at Kielder since 2009
		Lesser Kestrel	*Falco naumanni*	Accidental: Hauxley 1963
1		Kestrel	*Falco tinnunculus*	Locally common resident and winter visitor
		Red-footed Falcon	*Falco vespertinus*	Rare passage visitor
3		Merlin	*Falco columbarius*	Uncommon breeder and winter visitor, mainly on coast
		Hobby	*Falco subbuteo*	Scarce passage visitor and occasional breeder
		Eleonora's Falcon	*Falco eleonorae*	Accidental: Otterburn Training Area 2006
		Gyr Falcon*	*Falco rusticolus*	Accidental: Singles Pikestone Fell 1987, Eggleston 1991, Hunstanworth Moor 1995, Barnard Castle 2006
3		Peregrine Falcon	*Falco peregrinus*	Uncommon resident breeder/winter visitor
3		Water Rail	*Rallus aquaticus*	Uncommon resident breeder, more usual in winter
		Spotted Crake	*Porzana porzana*	Scarce passage and winter visitor
		Baillon's Crake*	*Porzana pusilla*	Accidental: Sunderland 1989
		Corncrake	*Crex crex*	Scarce migrant which formerly bred widely
1		Moorhen	*Gallinula chloropus*	Common resident breeder
1		Coot	*Fulica atra*	Fairly common breeder and winter visitor.

		British Name	Scientific Name	Status and Key Locations
		Common Crane	*Grus grus*	Scarce visitor
		Sandhill Crane	*Grus canadensis*	Accidental: 1 flew south in Sept 2011 at Newbiggin, Whitley Bay, South Shields, Hartlepool, entering 3 county lists in three hours!
		Great Bustard	*Otis tarda*	Accidental: Chillingham, Lindisfarne 1870-71
		Little Bustard*	*Tetrax tetrax*	Accidental: Amble 1906, Holy Island 1920, Craster 1937
	1	Oystercatcher	*Haematopus ostralegus*	Very common
		Black-winged Stilt*	*Himantopus himantopus*	Accidental: Beal 1986, Coatham Marsh 1986, Wallsend 1987, Hurworth Burn 1993, Wallsend 1987, Hurworth Burn 1993, Druridge Pools 1993 and Shibdon Pool 2012.
	3	Avocet	*Recurvirostra avosetta*	Uncommon/breeding Greatham Creek, Washington WWT, Cresswell
		Stone-curlew	*Burhinus oedicnemus*	Scarce visitor
		Cream-coloured Courser	*Cursorious cursor*	Accidental: Cheswick 1846, Goswick 1870
		Collared Pratincole*	*Glareola pratincola*	Accidental: Holywell 1960, Beadnell 1983
		Little Ringed Plover	*Charadrius dubius*	Uncommon breeder
	1	Ringed Plover	*Charadrius hiaticula*	Common
		Killdeer*	*Charadrius vociferus*	Accidental: East Boldon 1976, Cronkley 1990
		Kentish Plover	*Charadrius alexandrinus*	Very rare
		Dotterel	*Charadrius morinellus*	Uncommon migrant
		American Golden Plover	*Pluvialis dominica*	Rare passage visitor
		Pacific Golden Plover*	*Pluvialis fulva*	Accidental: Druridge Pools 1991, Whitburn 2002, Newbiggin 2005
	1	European Golden Plover	*Pluvialis apricaria*	Uncommon upland breeder and common winter visitor.
	2	Grey Plover	*Pluvialis squatarola*	Locally common winter visitor
		Sociable Plover	*Vanellus gregarius*	Accidental: Stamfordham 1971
		White-tailed Lapwing*	*Vanellus leucurus*	Accidental: Cleadon 1984
	1	Lapwing	*Vanellus vanellus*	Fairly common/very common in winter
		Great Knot*	*Calidris tenuirostris*	Accidental: Seal Sands 1996
	1	Red Knot	*Calidris canutus*	Locally common winter visitor
	1	Sanderling	*Calidris alba*	Locally common winter visitor
		Semipalmated Sandpiper*	*Calidris pusilla*	Accidental: Dorman's Pool 1989, Farne Islands 1992, Dorman's Pool 2002, Saltholme 2006 and Seal Sands 2011
		Red-necked Stint*	*Calidris ruficollis*	Accidental: Wansbeck Estuary 1995
	3	Little Stint	*Calidris minuta*	Uncommon passage visitor
		Temminck's Stint	*Calidris temminckii*	Scarce passage visitor

			British Name	Scientific Name	Status and Key Locations
			Long-toed Stint*	*Calidris subminuta*	Accidental: Saltholme 1982
			White-rumped Sandpiper	*Calidris fuscicollis*	Scarce passage visitor
			Baird's Sandpiper*	*Calidris bairdii*	Very rare passage visitor.
			Pectoral Sandpiper	*Calidris melanotos*	Uncommon passage visitor
			Sharp-tailed Sandpiper*	*Calidris acuminata*	Accidental: Cowpen Marsh 1963, Seal Sands 1977, Long Drag Pool 1997 and Greatham Creek 2010-11.
			Curlew Sandpiper	*Calidris ferruginea*	Uncommon late summer-autumn passage visitor most frequently to coastal sites
	3		Purple Sandpiper	*Calidris maritima*	Uncommon winter visitor/Bamburgh is prime site
	1		Dunlin	*Calidris alpina*	Very common passage and winter visitor, breeds in very small numbers on high moorland.
			Broad-billed Sandpiper*	*Limicola falcinellus*	Very rare passage visitor.
			Buff-breasted Sandpiper	*Tryngites subruficollis*	Scarce passage visitor
	3		Ruff	*Philomachus pugnax*	Uncommon passage visitor
			Jack Snipe	*Lymnocryptes minimus*	Uncommon passage visitor
	1		Snipe	*Gallinago gallinago*	Fairly common resident and winter visitor
			Great Snipe*	*Gallinago media*	Very rare visitor
			Long-billed Dowitcher	*Limnodromus scolopaceus*	Accidental: Cresswell 1964, East Chevington 1998, Bothal Pond 2004, Seal Sands 2007, Saltholme 2012.
			Short-billed Dowitcher*	*Limnodromus griseus*	Very rare
	3		Woodcock	*Scolopax rusticola*	Uncommon resident/fairly common passage visitor
	3		Black-tailed Godwit	*Limosa limosa*	Uncommon passage and winter visitor
	1		Bar-tailed Godwit	*Limosa lapponica*	Fairly common/Lindisfarne is best area
	3		Whimbrel	*Numenius phaeopus*	Locally common passage visitor
	1		Curlew	*Numenius arquata*	Common upland resident/very common in winter
	3		Spotted Redshank	*Tringa erythropus*	Uncommon passage visitor
	1		Redshank	*Tringa totanus*	Fairly common resident/common winter visitor
			Greater Yellowlegs	*Tringa melanoleuca*	Accidental: Druridge Bay 2011
			Marsh Sandpiper*	*Tringa stagnatilis*	Very rare passage visitor
	3		Greenshank	*Tringa nebularia*	Uncommon passage visitor
			Lesser Yellowlegs*	*Tringa flavipes*	Rare passage visitor
	3		Green Sandpiper	*Tringa ochropus*	Uncommon passage and rare winter visitor
			Wood Sandpiper	*Tringa glareola*	Uncommon passage visitor

			British Name	Scientific Name	Status and Key Locations
			Terek Sandpiper*	*Xenus cinereus*	Rare passage visitor
	2		Common Sandpiper	*Actitis hypoleucos*	Locally common breeding summer visitor, mainland upland streams
			Spotted Sandpiper*	*Actitis macularius*	Very rare passage visitor
	2		Turnstone	*Arenaria interpres*	Common winter visitor
			Wilson's Phalarope*	*Phalaropus tricolor*	Rare passage visitor
			Red-necked Phalarope	*Phalaropus lobatus*	Very rare passage visitor
			Grey Phalarope	*Phalaropus fulicarius*	Uncommon autumn and winter visitor
			Pomarine Skua	*Stercorarius pomarinus*	Uncommon passage visitor, usually autumn/ early winter
	2		Arctic Skua	*Stercorarius parasiticus*	Locally common late summer/autumn
			Long-tailed Skua	*Stercorarius longicaudus*	Uncommon passage visitor
			Great Skua	*Stercorarius skua*	Uncommon autumn passage visitor.
			Ivory Gull*	*Pagophila eburnea*	Accidental: Tyne Estuary 1970, Seahouses 1979, Saltburn 1986
			Sabine's Gull	*Larus sabini*	Uncommon passage visitor
	1		Kittiwake	*Rissa tridactyla*	Common breeding species
			Bonaparte's Gull*	*Larus philadelphia*	Very rare passage visitor.
	1		Black-headed Gull	*Larus ridibundus*	Very common winter visitor, locally common breeder
	3		Little Gull	*Larus minutus*	Uncommon summer visitor with occasional influxes
			Ross's Gull*	*Rhodostethia rosea*	Very rare passage/winter visitor.
			Laughing Gull*	*Larus atricilla*	Very rare winter visitor.
			Franklin's Gull*	*Larus pipixcan*	Accidental: North Gare 1977, Reclamation Pond 1991, Woodhorn 2005
	3		Mediterranean Gull	*Larus melanocephalus*	Uncommon – Newbiggin is best area
			Ring-billed Gull	*Larus delawarensis*	Very rare passage/winter visitor.
	1		Common (Mew) Gull	*Larus canus*	Very common winter visitor, very small breeding population
	1		Lesser Black-backed Gull	*Larus fuscus*	Fairly common summer visitor
			Yellow-legged Gull	*Larus michahellis*	Uncommon visitor, usually in winter
			Caspian Gull	*Larus cachinnans*	Very rare visitor visitor.
	1		Herring Gull	*Larus argentatus*	Common breeding resident/winter visitor
			Iceland Gull	*Larus glaucoides*	Uncommon winter visitor, mainly to harbours/fishing docks etc
			Kumlien's Gull	*Larus glaucoides kumliemi*	Scarce winter visitor
			Glaucous-winged Gull	*Larus glaucescens*	Accidental: Saltholme area 2008
			Glaucous Gull	*Larus hyperboreus*	Uncommon winter visitor

285

			British Name	Scientific Name	Status and Key Locations
		1	Great Black-backed Gull	*Larus marinus*	Very common, mainly winter visitor.
			Aleutian Tern	*Onychoprion aleutica*	Accidental: Farne Islands 1979
			Sooty Tern	*Sterna fuscata*	Accidental: Farne Islands 1966
			Bridled Tern*	*Onychoprion anaethetus*	Accidental: Hauxley 1989, Coquet Island 1992, East Chevington 2010
		3	Little Tern	*Sternula albifrons*	Uncommon summer visitor breeding Crimdon, Long Nanny Burn, Lindisfarne
			Gull-billed Tern*	*Gelochelidon nilotica*	Very rare visitor
			Caspian Tern*	*Sterna casia*	Very rare visitor
			Whiskered Tern	*Chilodonias hyrida*	Accidental: Budle Bay 1938, Linton 1969, Cresswell/Ashington 1970, Gosforth Park 1977
			Black Tern	*Chlidonias niger A*	Uncommon passage visitor
			White-winged Tern	*Chlidonias leucopterus*	Scarce passage visitor
		1	Sandwich Tern	*Sterna sandvicensis*	Common summer visitor, breeding Farne Islands
			Lesser Crested Tern*	*Sterna bengalensis*	Accidental: 1 regular Farne Islands 1984-1997.
		1	Common Tern	*Sterna hirundo*	Common in summer/ breeding Farne Islands, Coquet Island, Long Nanny Burn, Lindisfarne
		3	Roseate Tern	*Sterna dougallii*	Uncommon – Coquet Island is prime site
		1	Arctic Tern	*Sterna paradisaea*	Common summer visitor breeding Farne Islands, Coquet Island, Long Nanny Burn, Lindisfarne
		1	Guillemot	*Uria aalge*	Common – mainly Farne Islands
			Brunnich's Guillemot	*Uria lomvia*	Accidental: Farne Islands 1977
		1	Razorbill	*Alca torda*	Locally common – mainly Farne Islands
			Black Guillemot	*Cepphus grylle*	Scarce winter visitor – mainly Farne Island
		3	Little Auk	*Alle alle*	Usually uncommon but periodic influxes
		1	Puffin	*Fratercula arctica*	Common – mainly Farne Islands/Coquet Island
			Pallas's Sandgrouse*	*Syrrhaptes paradoxus*	Accidental: Holy Island 1899, Cleveland 1908, Elwick and Seahouses 1969
			Rock Dove	*Columba livia AC*	Now extinct, replaced by feral pigeons
		2	Stock Dove	*Columba oenas*	Locally common
		1	Woodpigeon	*Columba palumbus*	Very common
		1	Collared Dove	*Streptopelia decaocto*	Very common
			Turtle Dove	*Streptopelia turtur*	Scarce summer visitor
		#	Rose-ringed Parakeet	*Psittacula krameri*	Very rare, presumed to be escapes
			Great Spotted Cuckoo*	*Clamator glandarius*	Accidental: Wark Forest 1870, Greenabella Marsh 1995

			British Name	Scientific Name	Status and Key Locations
		3	Cuckoo	Cuculus canorus	Uncommon summer visitor, mainly to uplands
			Yellow-billed Cuckoo	Coccyzus americanus	Accidental: Morpeth 1995
		3	Barn Owl	Tyto alba	Uncommon/upland birds depleted by winters 2009-10, 2010-11
			Snowy Owl*	Bubo scandiaca	Accidental: Low Hauxley 1965, Bellingham 1973, Woolsingham 1981
			Little Owl	Athene noctua	Uncommon resident
		3	Tawny Owl	Strix aluco	Fairly common breeder, particularly forested areas
			Long-eared Owl	Asio otus	Uncommon breeder/winter visitor
		3	Short-eared Owl	Asio flammeus	Uncommon breeder/winter visitor
			Tengmalm's Owl*	Aegolius funereus	Accidental: Holywell Dene 1911, North Hylton 1929, Fishburn 1981 (leg only but bearing Norwegian ring)
			Nightjar	Caprimulgus europaeus	Uncommon breeder in new or clear-fell forest areas
			Red-necked Nightjar	Caprimulgus ruficollis	Accidental: Killingworth 1856
			Common Nighthawk	Chordeiles minor	Horden 2010
			Chimney Swift	Chaetura pelagica	Accidental: Holy Island 2005
		1	Swift	Apus apus	Common summer visitor
			Pallid Swift*	Apus pallidus	Very rare visitor
			Alpine Swift	Apus melba	Scarce migrant
			Kingfisher	Alcedo atthis	Uncommon resident
			Bee-eater	Merops apiaster	Rare visitor but a pair fledged young at Bishop Middleham quarry 2002.
			Roller*	Coracias garrulus	Accidental: Arcot 1950, South Gare 1993, East Boldon 2000, South Gare 2006, Holy Island/Beal 2006
			Hoopoe	Upupa epops	Scarce passage visitor
			Wryneck	Jynx torquilla	Scarce passage migrant, usually in spring
		1	Green Woodpecker	Picus viridis	Uncommon – mainly higher wooded valleys
		2	Great Spotted Woodpecker	Dendrocopos major	Locally common in deciduous woodland
			Lesser Spotted Woodpecker	Dendrocopos minor	Scarce resident breeder
			Red-eyed Vireo*	Vireo olivaceus	Accidental: Holy Island 1988, Seaburn 1990, North Gare 1991, Marsden Quarry 2004
			Golden Oriole	Oriolus oriolus	Very rare visitor
			Isabelline Shrike*	Lanius isabellinus	Very rare visitor

		British Name	Scientific Name	Status and Key Locations
		Red-backed Shrike	Lanius collurio	Uncommon passage visitor/spring and autumn
		Lesser Grey Shrike*	Lanius minor	Very rare visitor
		Great Grey Shrike	Lanius excubitor	Uncommon passage and winter visitor
		Woodchat Shrike	Lanius senator	Very rare visitor
		Chough	Pyrrhocorax pyrrhocorax	Accidental: Farne Islands 1976
	1	Magpie	Pica pica	Fairly common breeding throughout region
	3	Jay	Garrulus glandarius	Uncommon – confined mainly to deciduous woodland
		Nutcracker	Nucifraga caryocatactes	Accidental: Fenham (Lindisfarne) 1958
	1	Jackdaw	Corvus monedula	Common breeding resident
	1	Rook	Corvus frugilegus	Common breeding resident
	1	Carrion Crow	Corvus corone	Common breeding resident
		Hooded Crow	Corvus cornix	Scarce winter visitor
		Raven	Corvus corax	Uncommon upland resident
	1	Goldcrest	Regulus regulus	Locally common forest areas/passage migrant
		Firecrest	Regulus ignicapilla	Scarce autumn/winter visitor
		Penduline Tit*	Remiz pendulinus	Very rare visitor
		Bearded Tit	Panurus biarmicus	Scarce visitor, usually in winter
	1	Blue Tit	Cyanistes caeruleus	Common breeding resident
	1	Great Tit	Parus major	Common breeding resident
		Crested Tit	Lophophanes cristatus	Accidental: Low Hauxley 1984
	3	Coal Tit	Periparus ater	Locally common in forest breeding areas
		Willow Tit	Poecile montanus	Uncommon resident breeder
		Marsh Tit	Poecile palustris	Uncommon resident breeder, damp woodlands
		Calandra Lark	Melanocoryypha calandra	Accidental: Farne Islands 1999
		Greater Short-toed Lark	Calandrella brachydactyla	Very rare visitor, usually in winter
		Woodlark	Lullula arborea	Rare pasage visitor
	1	Skylark	Alauda arvensis	Fairly common, particularly marginal grasslands/moors
		Shore (Horned) Lark	Eremophila alpestris	usually scarce winter visitor
	1	Sand Martin	Riparia riparia	Common breeding summer visitor
	1	(Barn) Swallow	Hirundo rustica	Very common summer visitor
	1	House Martin	Delichon urbica	Common breeding summer visitor
		Red-rumped Swallow	Cecropis daurica	Scarce passage visitor

			British Name	Scientific Name	Status and Key Locations
			Cliff Swallow	*Petrochelidon pyrrhonota*	Accidental: 2nd British record, South Gare 1988
			Cetti's Warbler	*Cettia cetti*	Scarce but now breeding Cleveland
		3	Long-tailed Tit	*Aegithalos caudatus*	Fairly common resident
			Greenish Warbler	*Phylloscopus trochiloides*	Scarce late summer passage visitor
			Arctic Warbler*	*Phylloscopus borealis*	Very rare autumn visitor on coast
			Pallas's Leaf Warbler	*Phylloscopus proregulus*	Scarce autumn visitor on coast
			Yellow-browed Warbler	*Phylloscopus inornatus*	Uncommon autumn visitor on coast, Holy Island is prime area
			Hume's Leaf Warbler*	*Phylloscopus humei*	Scarce autumn visitor on coast
			Radde's Warbler	*Phylloscopus schwarzi*	Rare autumn visitor along coast
			Dusky Warbler	*Phylloscopus fuscatus*	Rare autumn visitor along coast
			Western Bonelli's Warbler	*Phylloscopus bonelli*	Very rare passage visitor
			Eastern Bonelli's Warbler	*Phylloscopus orientalis*	Accidental: Whitley Bay 1995
			Wood Warbler	*Phylloscopus sibilatrix*	Uncommon summer visitor in deciduous woodlands – Allen Banks is good area
		1	Chiffchaff	*Phylloscopus collybita*	Common breeding summer visitor
			Iberian Chiffchaff	*Phylloscopus ibericus*	Accidental: Woodhorn 2004
			Siberian Chiffchaff	*P.c. tristis*	Scarce passage visitor, October-November
			Scandinavian Chiffchaff	*P.c. albietinus*	Scarce autumn/early winter passage visitor
		1	Willow Warbler	*Phylloscopus trochilus*	Common breeding summer visitor
		1	Blackcap	*Sylvia atricapilla*	Fairly common breeding summer visitor
		2	Garden Warbler	*Sylvia borin*	Locally common in deciduous woodland
			Barred Warbler	*Sylvia nisoria*	Scarce autumn visitor on coast
		3	Lesser Whitethroat	*Sylvia curruca*	Uncommon breeding summer visitor
			Orphean Warbler*	*Sylvia hortensis*	Accidental: Hartlepool Headland 2012
		1	Whitethroat	*Sylvia communis*	Fairly common breeder in lowland and moorland habitats
			Subalpine Warbler	*Sylvia cantillans*	Rare migrant, usually in spring
			Lanceolated Warbler	*Locustella lanceolata*	Very rare autumn visitor.
		3	Grasshopper Warbler	*Locustella naevia*	Locally common, mainly in wetter habitats
			River Warbler	*Locustella fluviatilis*	Accidental: Bellingham, Seaton Burn, both 1996
			Savi's Warbler*	*Locustella luscinioides*	Rare passage visitor – 1 pair bred Long Drag 1994
			Aquatic Warbler	*Acrocephalus paludicola*	Accidental: Holywell Pond 1958
		1	Sedge Warbler	*Acrocephalus schoenobaenus A*	Locally common in wetter areas

			British Name	Scientific Name	Status and Key Locations
			Paddyfield Warbler*	*Acrocephalus agricola*	Very rare pasage visitor
			Blyth's Reed Warbler	*Acrocephalus*	Very rare visitor
			Marsh Warbler	*Acrocephalus palustris*	Very rare visitor
			Reed Warbler	*Acrocephalus scirpaceus*	Uncommon summer breeder – East Chevington is northern nesting limit
			Great Reed Warbler*	*Acrocephalus arundinaceus*	Very rare visitor, occasionally singing
			Booted Warbler*	*Hippolais caligata*	Very rare visitor
			Sykes's Warbler	*Hippolais rama*	Accidental: Druridge Bay Country Park 2010
			Icterine Warbler	*Hippolais icterina*	Scarce passage visitor
			Melodious Warbler	*Hippolais polyglotta*	Very rare visitor
3			Waxwing	*Bombycilla garrulus*	Uncommon in most winters but occasional big influxes
3			Nuthatch	*Sitta europaea*	Uncommon but increasing northwards in deciduous woodlands
3			Treecreeper	*Certhia familiaris*	Locally common in most woodlands
1			Wren	*Troglodytes troglodytes*	Common resident breeding species
1			Starling	*Sturnus vulgaris*	Common resident breeder/winter visitor
			Rosy Starling*	*Sturnus roseus*	Rare passage visitor
2			Dipper	*Cinclus cinclus*	Uncommon resident along suitable rivers/streams, particularly in uplands
			White's Thrush*	*Zoothera dauma*	Accidental: Castle Eden Dene 1872, Holy Island 1914, South Shields 1959
			Grey-cheeked Thrush*	*Catharus minimus*	Accidental: Horden 1968 (found dead)
3			Ring Ouzel	*Turdus torquatus*	Uncommon summer visitor, mainly to higher valleys/uplands
1			Blackbird	*Turdus merula*	Common resident/common winter visitor
			Dusky Thrush*	*Turdus naumanni*	Accidental: Hartlepool 1959
			Black-throated Thrush	*Turdus ruficollis*	Accidental: Holy Island 1979, Riding Mill 2005
1			Fieldfare	*Turdus pilaris*	Very common autumn migrant
1			Song Thrush	*Turdus philomelos*	Locally common breeding resident
1			Redwing	*Turdus iliacus*	Very common autumn migrant
2			Mistle Thrush	*Turdus viscivorus*	Uncommon resident breeder
1			Robin	*Erithacus rubecula*	Locally common resident/autumn passage migrant
			White-throated Robin	*Irania gutturalis*	Accidental: Hartlepool Headland 2011.
			Thrush Nightingale*	*Luscinia luscinia*	Very rare passage visitor – birds sang at Hartlepool Headland in 1979 and Bamburgh in 1983
			Nightingale	*Luscinia megarhynchos*	Scarce passage visitor, usually in autumn

		British Name	Scientific Name	Status and Key Locations
		Bluethroat	*Luscinia svecica*	Scarce passage visitor, usually in spring. Numbers have declined sharply in recent years.
		Siberian Rubythroat	*Luscinia calliope*	Accidental: Fulwell (Sunderland) 2006
		Red-flanked Bluetail*	*Tarsiger cyanurus*	Scarce autumn visitor but numbers increasing recently. i.e. 3 at Whitburn in autumn 2011.
		Black Redstart	*Phoenicurus ochruros*	Uncommon visitor, spring and autumn
		Eastern Black Redstart*	*P o phoenicuroides*	Accidental. Holy Island 2011
	3	Redstart	*Phoenicurus phoenicurus*	Uncommon breeding summer visitor/more plentiful as autumn migrant
	3	Whinchat	*Saxicola rubetra*	Uncommon summer visitor, mainly to higher valleys/moors
		Siberian Stonechat	*Saxicola maurus*	Very rare winter visitor
	2	Stonechat	*Saxicola rubicola*	Uncommon resident breeder, mainly on coast after harsh winters
		Isabelline Wheatear	*Oenanthe isabellina*	Accidental: Bamburgh 1980.
	1	Northern Wheatear	*Oenanthe oenanthe*	Locally common upland breeder, Greenland race birds often prominent on coast in May
		Pied Wheatear*	*Oenanthe pleschanka*	Accidental: Boulmer 1979, Seaton Snook 1984, Seahouses 1997, Tynemouth 1998, Newbiggin 2004
		Desert Wheatear*	*Oenanthe deserti*	Scarce autumn and winter visitor
	3	Spotted Flycatcher	*Muscicapa striata*	Uncommon breeding visitor/passage migrant
		Red-breasted Flycatcher	*Ficedula parva*	Scarce autumn visitor at coastal sites
	3	Pied Flycatcher	*Ficedula hypoleuca*	Uncommon breeding visitor to deciduous, particularly Oak woodlands
	1	Dunnock (Hedge Accentor)	*Prunella modularis*	Fairly common throughout region
	1	House Sparrow	*Passer domesticus*	Common but declining in some areas
	2	Tree Sparrow	*Passer montanus*	Uncommon but increasing resident breeder
	3	Yellow Wagtail	*Motacilla flava*	Uncommon and declining summer visitor
		Blue-headed Wagtail	*M f flava*	Uncommon passage visitor, usually spring
		Ashy-headed Wagtail	*M f cinereocapilla*	Very rare visitor
		Grey-headed Wagtail	*M f thunbergi*	Very rare visitor
		Black-headed Wagtail	*M f feldegg*	Accidental: Cresswell 1985, Holy Island 2009
		Sykes Wagtail	*M f beema*	Accidental: Farne Islands 1992
		Amur Wagtail	*M.a. leucopsis*	Accidental: Seaham 2005
		Citrine Wagtail*	*Motacilla citreola*	Very rare passage visitor
	3	Grey Wagtail	*Motacilla cinerea*	Uncommon breeder, mainly on higher rivers/ streams

			British Name	Scientific Name	Status and Key Locations
		1	White / Pied Wagtail	*Motacilla alba*	Fairly common breeding resident/passage migrant
			Richard's Pipit	*Anthus novaeseelandiae*	Scarce autumn visitor
			Tawny Pipit	*Anthus campestris*	Very rare passage visitor
			Olive-backed Pipit*	*Anthus hodgsoni*	Very rare passage autumn passage visitor
		3	Tree Pipit	*Anthus trivialis*	Locally common only in upland breeding areas
		1	Meadow Pipit	*Anthus pratensis*	Common breeding resident but uplands birds disappear in winter
			Red-throated Pipit	*Anthus cervinus*	Very rare passage visitor
		3	Rock Pipit	*Anthus petrosus*	Uncommon breeder along rocky coastlines
			Water Pipit	*Anthus spinoletta*	Scarce autumn and winter visitor
		1	Chaffinch	*Fringilla coelebs*	Common breeding resident and autumn migrant
		3	Brambling	*Fringilla montifringilla*	Locally common autumn migrant and winter visitor
			Serin	*Serinus serinus*	Very rare passage visitor
		1	Greenfinch	*Carduelis chloris*	Fairly common resident breeder
		1	Goldfinch	*Carduelis carduelis*	Common breeding resident
		1	Siskin	*Carduelis spinus*	Common forest breeding species and spring/autumn migrant
		1	Linnet	*Carduelis cannabina*	Locally common breeding resident
		3	Twite	*Carduelis flavirostris*	Uncommon autumn/winter visitor
		1	Lesser Redpoll	*Carduelis cabaret*	Common breeding resident mainly in conifer forest areas
			Common Redpoll	*Carduelis flammea*	Uncommon autumn and winter visitor
			Arctic Redpoll	*Carduelis hornemanni*	Very rare autumn and winter visitor
			Hornemann's Arctic Redpoll	*C.h. hornemanni*	Accidental: Farne Islands 2010
			Coue's Arctic Redpoll	*C.h. exilipes*	Very rare winter visitor
			Two-barred Crossbill*	*Loxia leucoptera*	Very rare autumn and winter visitor to forest areas
		3	Common Crossbill	*Loxia curvirostra*	Locally common breeder in forest areas/occasional influxes occur
			Parrot Crossbill*	*Loxia pytyopsittacus*	Very rare autumn and winter visitor
			Trumpeter Finch	*Bucanetes githagineus*	Accidental: Holy Island 1987
			Common Rosefinch	*Carpodacus erythrinus*	Uncommon passage migrant.
			Pine Grosbeak*	*Pinicola enucleator*	Accidental: Pelaw pre-1831 (year uncertain), Holy Island 1975
		3	Bullfinch	*Pyrrhula pyrrhula*	Uncommon breeding resident

		British Name	Scientific Name	Status and Key Locations
		Hawfinch	Coccothraustes coccothraustes	Uncommon breeding resident in deciduous woodlands
3		Lapland Bunting (Longspur)	Calcarius lapponicus	Uncommon autumn/winter visitor – Holy Island is prime area
3		Snow Bunting	Plectrophenax nivalis	Winter visitor, mainly to coastal areas, but annual numbers fluctuate considerably.
		Pine Bunting*	Emberiza leucocephalos	Accidental: Seaton Burn and Bamburgh 1990, Cresswell Pond 1992, Langley Moor 1998
2		Yellowhammer	Emberiza citrinella	Locally common breeding resident on lowland farmland
		Cirl Bunting	Emberiza cirlus	Very rare passage visitor
		Ortolan Bunting	Emberiza hortulana	Rare passage visitor, usually in spring
		Rustic Bunting	Emberiza rustica	Very rare passage visitor
		Little Bunting	Emberiza pusilla	Rare autumn passage migrant
		Yellow-breasted Bunting*	Emberiza aureola	Very rare, ten records from 1972, all but one from Farne Islands
		Black-faced Bunting	Emberiza spodocephala	Accidental: Newbiggin 1999
3		Reed Bunting	Emberiza schoeniclus	Locally common breeding resident in dunes, marshes and wet moorlands
		Black-headed Bunting	Emberiza melanocephala	Accidental: Low Hauxley 1977, Farne Islands 1971, 1999, 2004, 2009
		Corn Bunting	Emberiza calandra	Uncommon, increasingly scarce resident breeder
		Brown-headed Cowbird	Molothrus ater	Accidental: Belford 2010
		White-throated Sparrow	Zonotrichia albicollis	Accidental: Farne Islands 2007
		Eastern Crowned Warbler	Phylloscopus coronatus	Accidental: Trow Quarry, South Shields, 2009 – first British record

Still under review: Slender-billed Curlew (*Numerius tenuirostris*), Druridge Pools, 1998. Accepted by Northumberland Records Committee but still being considered at national level.

COUNTY BIRD RECORDERS

Cleveland: Tom Francis, 108 Ashton Road, Glebe Estate, Norton, Stockton-on-Tees TS20 1RE. E-mail: mot.francis@ntlworld.com

Co Durham: Mark Newsome, 69 Cedar Drive, Jarrow, South Tyneside, NE32 4BF. 07834 978 255. E-mail: munewsome@hotmail.com

Northumberland: Tim Dean, 2 Knocklaw Park, Rothbury, Northumberland, NE65 7PW. 01669 621 460.
E-mail: t.r.dean@btopenworld.com

BIRDS & WILDLIFE GROUPS

Butterfly Conservation
North East Regional Office, Low Barnes, Witton-le-Wear, Bishop Auckland, Co Durham, DL14 0AG. 01388 488 428. E-mail: dwainwright@butterfly-conservation.org

Durham Bird Club (DBC)
Secretary: Richard Cowan. 07882 780 825. E-mail: richardcowan2002@yahoo.co.uk
www.durhambirdclub

Durham Wildlife Trust (DWT)
Rainton Meadows, Chilton Moor, Houghton-le-Spring, Co Durham, DH4 6PU. 0191 5843 112. www.durhamwt.co.uk

Natural England
North East Regional Office, The Quadrant, Newburn Riverside, Newcastle upon Tyne, NE15 8NZ. 0300 0602 219. www.naturalengland.org.uk

Natural England Reserves
Lindisfarne – 01289 381 470.
Moor House – Upper Teesdale, 01833 622 374.
Teesmouth – 01429 853 325.

Natural History Society of Northumbria
Hancock Museum, Great North Road, Newcastle upon Tyne, NE2 4PT. 0191 2326 386. E-mail: nhsn.ncl.as.uk

Northumberland & Tyneside Bird Club (NTBC)
Sec. Alan Timouth, 12 Stowe Gardens, Pegswood, Morpeth, Northumberland, NE61 6 TH. 01670 512 013.
E-mail: ntb.org@gmail.com

Northumberland Wildlife Trust (NWT)
St Nicholas Park, Jubilee Road, Gosforth, Newcastle upon Tyne, NE3 3XT. 0191 2840 884. www.nwt.org.uk

North Northumberland Bird Club
Sec. Richard Narraway. 01668 214 759. www.northnorthumberlandbirdclub.co.uk

RSPB North East Regional Office
Sirus House, Amethyst Road, Newcastle Business Park, Newcastle upon Tyne, NE4 7YL. 0191 2334 300. www.rspb.org/northeast

RSPB Saltholme Reserve
Seaton Carew, Stockton-on-Tees. 01642 546 625.

Teesmouth Bird Club (TBC)
Hon sec: Chris Sharp, 45 Endeavor Close, Seaton Carew, Hartlepool, TS25 1EY. 01429 865 163. www.teesmouthbc.com

BIRDS & WILDLIFE GROUPS (REST OF UK)

Birding For All (formerly Disabled Birders Association)
Bo Boelens, 18 St Mildreds Road, Margate, Kent CT9 2LT.
www.disabledbirdersassociation.org.uk

British Dragonfly Society
Lynn Curry, BDS Membership Office, 23 Bowker Way, Whittlesey, Peterborough PE7 1PY. 01733 204 286. www.british-dragonflies.org.uk

British Trust for Ornithology (BTO)
The Nunnery, Thetford, Norfolk IP24 2PU
Tel: 01842 750 050. www.bto.org

Butterfly Conservation
Manor Yard, East Lulworth, Wareham BH20 5QP. 01929 400 209.
www.butterfly-conservation.org

Joint Nature Conservation Committee (JNCC)
Monkstone House, City Road, Peterborough PE1 1JY. www.jncc.gov.uk

Natural England
Head Office, 1 East Parade, Sheffield S1 2ET 0300 060 6000. www.naturalengland.org.uk

Royal Society for the Protection of Birds (RSPB)
Headquarters, The Lodge, Potton Road, Sandy, Bedfordshire SG19 2DL. 01967 680 551. www.rspb.org.uk

The Woodland Trust
Headquarters, Kempton Way, Grantham NG31 6LL. 01476 581 111. www.woodlandtrust.org.uk

OTHER USEFUL CONTACTS

Birdline North East
09068 700 246 (premium rate 60p per minute) 07626 983 963 (to report news).

English Heritage Regional Office
Bessie Surtees House, 41-44 Sandhill, Newcastle upon Tyne, NE1 3JF. 0191 2691 200.

Forest Enterprise North England
Eals Burn, Bellingham, Hexham, Northumberland, NE48 2HP. 01434 220 242. E-mail: enquires.kielder@forestry.gsi.gov.uk

National Trust Regional Office
Scots Gap, Morpeth, Northumberland, NE61 4EG. 01670 774 961.

Northumberland National Park
Headquarters: South Park, Hexham, Northumberland, NE46 1 BS. 01434 605 555. www.northumberlandnationalpark.org.uk

TOURIST INFORMATION CENTRES

Alnwick: 01665 511 333
Amble: 01665 712 313
Bellingham: 01432 220 616
Barnard Castle: 03000 262 626
Durham City: 03000 262 626

Durham Dales: 03000 262 626
Gateshead: 0191 4338 420
Middleton-in-Teesdale: 03000 262 626
Middlesbrough: 01642 243 425
Newcastle: 0191 2778 000
Saltburn: 01287 - 622422
Stockton: 01642-528130
Wooler: 01668-282123

LOCAL AUTHORITIES

Durham County Council
0300 0260 000.
www.durham.gov.uk

Hartlepool Borough Council
01429 266 522.
www.hartlepool.gov.uk

Gateshead Borough Council
Tel. 0191 4333 000.
www.gateshead.gov.uk

Newcastle City Council
0191 2328 520.
www.newcastle.gov.uk

North Tyneside Borough Council
0345 2000 101.
www.northtyneside.gov.uk

Northumberland County Council
01670 533 000.
www.northumberland.gov.uk

Redcar and Cleveland Borough Council
01287 622 422.

South Tyneside Borough Council
0191 4271 717.
www.southtyneside.gov.uk

Sunderland City Council
0191 5205 555.
www.sunderland.gov.uk

Stockton Borough Council
01642 393 939.
www.stockton.gov.uk

295

BIBLIOGRAPHY

THE REGION'S three main bird clubs all produce annual reports covering their relevant areas and back numbers are usually available via their websites. I have also selected a small number of other publications which may be of interest to both resident and visiting birders. Some are now out of print but may be available on the second hand market.

BIRDS

A Summer Atlas of the Breeding Birds of County Durham.
Editors: Steve Westerberg & Keith Bowey (Pub: DBC 2000).

The Atlas of Breeding Birds in Northumbria.
Editors: John C. Day, Mike S Hodgson & B Nick Rossiter (Pub: NTBC 1995).

The Atlas of Wintering Birds in Northumbria.
Editors: John C Day & Mike S Hodgson (Pub: NTBC 2003).

The Birds of Durham
Editors: Keith Bowey and Mark Newsome (Pub: DBC 2012).

The Birds of Holy Island & Lindisfarne NNR by Ian Kerr (Pub: author 2007).

The Birds of Kielder by Brian Little, David Jardine & Chris Probert (Pub: Forest Enterprise 1993).

Blyth's Birds by Steve Holliday (Pub: author 2000).

The Breeding Birds of Cleveland by Graeme Joynt, Ted Parker and Vic Fairbrother (Pub: TBC 2008).

Hadrian's Birds by John Miles (Pub: Miles and Miles of Countryside 1992).

History of the Birds of Durham by George.W. Temperley (Pub: NHSN 1951).

A Naturalist on Lindisfarne by Richard Perry (Pub: Lindsay Drummond Ltd 1945).

Northumbrian Birds – their history and status up to the 21st Century by Ian Kerr (Pub: NTBC 2001).

Northumberland's Birds by Bryan Galloway & Eric R. Meek (Pub: NHSN 1983).

Birds of Gateshead by Keith Bowey, Steve Rutherford & Steve Westerberg (Pub: Gateshead Council 1993).

Where to Watch Birds in Durham Editor Keith Bowey (DBC 1992).

OTHER TOPICS

Butterfly Summary, annual report North East branch Butterfly Conservation.

Flora of Northumberland by George.A. Swan (Pub: NHSN 1993).

MAPS

The site accounts give map references but some readers may wish to also explore surrounding areas using the following 1:25 000 OS Explorer maps which give greater detail for such visits:

304 Darlington
305 Bishop Auckland
306 Hartlepool/Teesmouth/local coast
307 Consett
308 Durham/Peterlee/local coast
316 Newcastle/Gateshead/local coast
325 Ashington/Morpeth/Druridge Bay
332 Alnwick/Amble/local coast
340 Bamburgh/Lindisfarne/Farne Islands/ local coast
OL 16 Cheviot Hills
OL 42 Otterburn/Kielder
OL 43 Hexham

BEST SITES WITH DISABLED ACCESS

THE SITES which I consider to have reasonable access for wheelchair users are listed. However, please bear in mind that some will be more difficult than others because of slopes or distances involved and that is indicated in the brief summaries.

I would recommend that readers with mobility issues should use the relevant telephone numbers where listed on the Site Guide page to get up-to-date advice about local ground conditions at the time of visits. A path which is good after a dry summer or autumn may be very different after winter rain or snow.

I am grateful to Paul Anderson of the Durham Bird Club for advice about sites in his county and to John Walton of the National Trust about access to the Farne Islands.

CLEVELAND

Cowpen Bewley
Good tracks around the area make it suitable for wheelchairs.

Coatham Marsh
The track suitable for wheelchairs is reached via the Kirkleatham Lane access.

Cowpen Marsh
Wheelchair access is possible along the grassy track quarter of a mile south of NNR car park on the A178.

Greatham Creek
A firm track runs along the south bank giving good viewing of surrounding area. The NNR car park is just south of the creek. The Avocet colony can be easily watched from the viewpoint 100 yards south of the creek on the east side of the A178. Please take care crossing from the car park as this a very busy road.

Hartlepool Headland
There is good wheelchair access as virtually all birding is from paved/tarmac areas.

Locke Park
Hard tracks around park make it accessible for disabled visitors.

Saltholme RSPB Reserve
The whole reserve has very good facilities for disabled visitors. The Discovery Centre, hides and various paths are all wheelchair-friendly.

Scaling Dam
There is good wheelchair access to the hide along the firm path from the sailing club car park.

Seal Sands
The track along the south bank of Greatham Creek leads to the hide which is accessible. The track is good and gates are wheelchair friendly.

Sleddale
As most viewing is from parking areas there are no problems for disabled visitors.

Seaton Snook
Soft sand rules out wheelchair access to Snook but users can view the area from the road crossing Seaton Common.

South Gare
Good hard surfaces and parking make it very suitable for wheelchair users wanting to seawatch or look for migrants in roadside scrub areas.

COUNTY DURHAM

Baldersdale
The reservoir and surrounding area can be viewed from the car park but local tracks are unsuitable for wheelchairs.

Blackhall
The coastal path is suitable for wheelchairs.

Bishop Middleham
Parts of site are viewable from tracks but Castle Lake hide is accessed via a stile and impossible for wheelchair access.

Chopwell Woods
There are many miles of accessible tracks but please enter from Chopwell village or Hookergate. The Lintzford access track is unsuitable for wheelchairs because of soft surfaces and steep gradients.

Croxdale
There are good firm paths around Hall and grounds suitable for disabled visitors.

Dawdon Blast Beach
The coastal path above this site is suitable for wheelchairs.

Derwent Reservoir
Hard tracks suitable for wheelchair users lead from the car park to the dam viewing areas.

Hamsterley Forest
This area has many miles of accessible forest tracks suitable for wheelchair users.

Greta River Walks
Only the Brignall Lane and Moorhouse Lane sections are suitable for wheelchair-users.

Langdon Beck
Viewing of the Black Grouse lekking area is from roadside parking so there are no problems for disabled visitors

Low Barns
Tracks around the reserve and hide are accessible for wheelchairs.

Widdybank Fell
The track from Cow Green Reservoir to Cauldron Snout (almost 2 miles) is wheelchair accessible.

TYNE & WEAR

Beehive Flash
The only viewing point is a small roadside lay-by that can be used by all birdwatchers.

Far Pasture Reserve
The hide is fully wheelchair accessible and is just 50 yards from the parking area.

Holywell Dene
There are good firm tracks through the dene but some steep slopes could be a problem.

Marsden Quarry & Whitburn Coastal Park
Good firm track into quarry area and good smooth paths through park.

Prestwick Carr
Good firm tracks past the best birding areas are

suitable for wheelchairs but can be bumpy in places. The rougher track running north from Mayfield House is not recommended except in dry weather.

Shibdon Pond
The hide is wheelchair accessible but grassed areas leading to it are often soft and could prove difficult.

St Mary's Island
The island is fully accessible via the stone causeway from car park. The seawatching hide also wheelchair accessible.

Swallow Pond
A good firm track runs southwards from the ASDA supermarket along the old colliery wagon-way to the pond and viewing areas.

Thornley Woodland Centre
The visitor centre is fully accessible with disabled facilities but paths down into the Derwent Valley Walk are steep with steps in places and impossible for wheelchair users. However, the Walk can be accessed along flat paths from Winlaton Mill car park, half a mile north of the centre at the village traffic lights.

Tynemouth Haven and North Shields Fish Quay
The Haven and North Pier are fully accessible but down a reasonably gentle slope. The Estuary path is smooth and very good. The Fish Quay area is also fully accessible

WWT Washington
The whole area has very good access and facilities for wheelchair users.

NORTHUMBERLAND

Allen Banks
Good access only on path along west side of river from parking area. Other areas inaccessible because of a footbridge and some steep slopes.

Amble
The harbour and pier are fully accessible but unfortunately there are no facilities for getting wheelchairs on boats for Coquet Island visits.

Alwinton
Good access only in Alwin Valley, quarter of a mile south of village along minor road to Clennel and Kidlandlee. You can drive a couple of miles up this road and then use the firm flat track along the Alwin Burn leading into Kidland Forest.

Bamburgh
The sea can be viewed easily from various parking areas along Wynding. The Stag Rocks area can be watched from the parking area above but it is impossible to get a wheelchair down to beach.

Beadnell Bay/ Long Nanny Burn
The track behind the dunes from the main Beadnell Harbour parking area to the burn is usually good but a footbridge with steps is a barrier to wheelchairs.

Cresswell Pond
The hide is fully accessible with a wheelchair ramp but the short path from farm is often soft.

Druridge Pools
Only the main hide is wheelchair accessible along the main track where boardwalks have been built over soft patches. Unfortunately the other hides have steps.

Druridge Bay Country Park
The visitor centre and the lake are fully accessible with good tracks. In poor weather, the lake can also be easily viewed from various parking areas.

East Chevington
The southern-most hide of the North Pool is best for wheelchairs as it is only 100 yards from the parking area. The two viewpoints for South Pool are unsuitable because of steps. There are good hard tracks around the reserve which give easy access to the more distant hides.

Grindon Lough
The only viewing is from the roadside above the lough, so no problems for disabled visitors.

Harthope Valley
Only the valley bottom roads and tracks are suitable for wheelchairs.

Harwood Forest
Many miles of firm flat tracks give good access. The forest and distant Simonside Hills can also be viewed well from small parking area at Winter's Gibbet (good in spring for scoping Goshawks).

Hauxley Reserve
The hides are accessible with good firm tracks. The only problem might be the slope to west side of the reserve.

Holy Island (see also Lindisfarne NNR)
Most of the village (churchyard, Rocket Field, harbour etc.) is fully accessible. The Heugh can only be reached from the harbour via a fairly steep slope which could require help. The Watchtower is not accessible because of stairs but panoramic views of the flats and sea can be obtained from this high point of the island. The southern end of the Straight Lonnen and west end of the Crooked Lonnen (the best birding areas of both) have firm paths but further on both can be muddy. The Lough hide has a wheelchair ramp but the old wagon-way from the castle (almost 1 mile) can often be soft and muddy. Blue badge holders can drive along the road to the Castle field gates but please don't obstruct the shuttle bus turning area.

Kielder Forest
Good firm tracks run for many miles through forest and around reservoir.

Linton Pond
The hides are accessible but the tracks from parking area can be soft.

Maiden's Hall
Viewing is from roadside parking area but future plans include tracks around lake.

Newton Pool
There is a reasonably good track with boardwalks from the village to the scrape and pond.

Newton Point
Access is along a hard track from the 'tin church' midway between High and Low Newton villages towards former radar station at point.

Lindisfarne NNR (see also Holy Island)
Budle Bay is easily viewable from roadside parking on south side. Fields north of bay (good for winter geese) can be viewed from Harper's Heugh parking area a further mile along B1342. The bottom deck of the Lowmoor hide is fully accessible for wheelchairs with parking outside. The flats are also viewable from lay-bys on Holy Island causeway and alongside the Snook. The Snook itself is not suitable for wheelchairs because of boggy ground and soft sand.

Newbiggin
Church Point seawatching spot is accessible from main car park (100 yards) on path around south side of church. Newbiggin Mound is difficult and not recommended for wheelchairs because of rough and often very muddy paths.

Queen Elizabeth Country Park
The park and its lake have good hard tracks suitable for wheelchairs.

Seahouses (for Farne Islands)
The harbour and pier are fully accessible for wheelchairs. Some boats can take wheelchairs and there are facilities for disabled visitors on Inner Farne, though users will need help from a friend/family etc. Wheelchair users should seek advice from boat operators in advance as getting aboard can be a problem at low water.

IN COMMON with many areas of the United Kingdom, using public transport to reach birdwatching sites in North-East England has its limitations and challenges. Sadly, many remote upland areas have no bus services at all and, at a time of public spending cuts, other routes heavily subsidised by local authorities were under threat at the time of writing.

I have listed the sites which are reasonably practical to reach by public transport from the region's main centres, Middlesbrough, Hartlepool, Durham, Sunderland, South Shields, Newcastle, Alnwick and Berwick, all of them easily accessible by either bus, rail or Metro.

The information has been taken from the most recent timetables prior to the publication of this book but please bear in mind that routes and services can change without warning. All the services listed take the traveller to within one mile of their required birding site.

Please bear in mind that in rural areas in particular some services only operate from spring to autumn or at reduced frequencies in winter. The sole service to the prime birding site of Holy Island also has to take account of the tides. Each bus and train company publishes its own timetable on websites or in leaflet form. Most can also be obtained from local Tourist Information Centres with contact details given in the various site accounts.

Because of the uncertainties about the future the golden rule for any visitor must be: please check before you make your travel plans!

Traveline is an invaluable service:
www.travelinenortheast.info or 0871 200 2233

SITES ACCESSIBLE BY PUBLIC TRANSPORT

GENERAL TRAVEL INFORMATION

BUS COMPANIES

Arriva North East - www.arrivabus.co.uk
0871 200 2233

Arriva Northumbria- www.arrivabus.co.uk
01670 363 300

Go North East - www.simplygo.com
0845 6060 260

Stagecoach - www.stagecoachbus.com

Stagecoach North east 0191 5675251

Stagecoach Hartlepool 01429 267082

Stagecoach South Shields 0191 4277119

Perrymans Buses, Berwick (for Holy Island)
enquiries@perrymansbuses.com
01289 308717

Rothbury Motors, Rothbury 01665 606616
www.rothburymotors.co.uk

Snaiths Travel, Otterburn 01830 520 609.
www.howardsnaith.co.uk

The county councils of Durham and Northumberland both have the latest bus service details on their websites. The sites are www.durham.org.uk and www.northumberland.org.uk

RAIL COMPANIES

East Coast (mainline operator London-Edinburgh via Darlington, Durham, Newcastle, Berwick.

www.nationalrail.co.uk
08457 4849 50

Northern Rail (operator Newcastle, Sunderland, Seaham, Seaton Carew, Hartlepool, Middlesbrough etc)
www.northernrail.org

Tyne & Wear Metro (Newcastle, North Tyneside, South Tyneside, Sunderland etc)
www.nexus.org.uk - 0191 2020 747.

THE SITES

CLEVELAND

Cowpen Bewley Country Park
Stagecoach service 34 from Middlesbrough bus station-Billingham serves this area.

Cowpen Marsh, Greatham Creek, Seal Sands, Long Drag and Greenabella Marsh
Sites close together and served by Stagecoach bus 1 from Hartlepool York Road-Port Clarence. The best place to start a visit is at Greatham Creek bridge.

Hartlepool Headland
Stagecoach Hartlepool service 7 runs from town centre to Headland. The town centre is also linked with Newcastle, Sunderland and Middlesbrough by Northern Rail.

Locke Park
Services X3, X4 and 22 from Middlesbrough bus station stop near the park. Redcar railway station on Middlesbrough-Saltburn route is half a mile east of the park.

Saltburn-Hummersea Coast
Arriva North East service X4 from Middlesbrough bus station to Saltburn. X5 runs from Middlesbrough to Staines. Middlesbrough-Whitby Northern Rail trains also serve Saltburn.

Scaling Dam
Arriva North East service 93 from Middlesbrough bus station to Scarborough calls at Scaling Dam Sailing Club, close to reservoir hide etc.

Sleddale
Middlesbrough-Whitby Northern Rail service calls at Commondale Station. In summer a ramblers Moors Bus operates from Middlesbrough daily during school holidays. More info www.northyorkstravel.

Seaton Snook-Zinc Works Road
Also served by Stagecoach service 1 from Hartlepool York Road-Port Clarence. Local rail details as above.

Seaton Carew
Also served by Stagecoach service 1 from Hartlepool York Road and Newcastle-Middlesbrough trains.

Teesmouth (North-East) – Coatham Marsh
Arriva North East Middlesbrough bus station-Redcar-Loftus services X3, X4 and 22 stop at Coatham roundabout close to marsh. This is the closest stop to South Gare (3 miles away) but unfortunately there is no public transport link to this prime spot.

Teesmouth (North-West) – North Gare-Seaton Common
Hartlepool York Road-Port Clarence service 1 by Stagecoach goes along main A178 route with stop near this site. Also Newcastle-Middlesbrough trains serve Hartlepool and Seaton Carew stations.

Teesmouth (South-West) – RSPB Saltholme
Hartlepool York Road-Port Clarence Stagecoach service 1 stops near reserve entrance.

COUNTY DURHAM

Blackhall
Sunderland City Centre interchange-Hartlepool Arriva North East service 23 to Blackhall Rocks, about one mile from coast.

Bishop Middleham
Durham City-Bishop Auckland Arriva North East services 56 and 33 call at village.

Castle Eden Dene
Sunderland City Centre interchange-Hartlepool Arriva North East 31A to Peterlee and then Go North East 206 to Castle Eden School, about one mile to coast.

Chopwell Wood
Newcastle St James-Consett Go North East services 45 and 46 stop at Lintzford near forest's southern end track, the most convenient access point of entry for bus travellers.

Dawdon Blast Beach-Hawthorn Dene
Sunderland city centre-Dawdon Go North East service 60.

Crimdon Dene-Hart Dunes
Hartlepool York Road-Durham City Arriva North East service 24 to Crimdon.

Croxdale Hall
Durham City-Bishop Auckland Go North East 20 stops at Hall.

Low Barns
Bishop Auckland-Barnard Castle Arriva North East service 88 stops at Witton-le-Wear, 15 minutes walk from reserve.

Marsden Quarry and Whitburn Country Park
South Shields-Sunderland Stagecoach North East services E1 and E2 pass these coastal sites. Metro also runs from Newcastle to South Shields and Sunderland.

Shibdon Pond
Newcastle Newgate Street-Winlaton Go North East service 31 to Shibdon Road.

Thornley Woodlands Centre and Far Pasture
Newcastle-Consett services 45 and 46 stop at centre and also at Rowlands Gill traffic lights, close to access lane down to Lockhaugh and Far Pasture.

WWT Washington
Sunderland Holmeside-Washington Arriva North East service 961 and Go North East service 50A call at Waterview Park, the government office buildings close to the reserve.

SITES ACCESSIBLE BY PUBLIC TRANSPORT

NORTHUMBERLAND

Allen Banks
Newcastle St James-Carlisle Stagecoach-in-Cumbria 685 stops at Ridley Road half a mile from site entrance.

Alwinton
Newcastle Haymarket-Rothbury Arriva Northumbria X14 to Rothbury. Then Rothbury Motors service to Alwinton but please check before setting out (contact details given in introduction) for dates and timings.

Amble (for Coquet Island)
Newcastle Haymarket-Amble-Alnwick Arriva Northumbria 518 to town centre.

Bamburgh
Newcastle Haymarket-Bamburgh Arriva Northumbria service 501 (travel time two and a half hours).

Beadnell Bay and Long Nanny Burn
Newcastle Haymarket-Berwick Arriva Northumbria 501 calls at Beadnell April-October. Long Nanny is one mile south along coastal path behind dunes or along beach.

Cresswell Pond
Newcastle Haymarket-Newbiggin Arriva Northumbria X21 and then Arriva Northumbria service 1 to Cresswell village. Pond is half a mile north along coast road.

Druridge Bay Country Park and East Chevington
Newcastle Haymarket-Amble-Alnwick Arriva Northumbria 518 stops at Red Row, about one mile from these adjoining sites.

Holy Island
Berwick Railway Station-Holy Island Perrymans service 477 operates to fit in with tides and seasons, so it's essential to check in advance to see if trip is possible. From March-October when the island is accessible by road the Lindisfarne Castle shuttle bus links island car parks, village and castle. It's useful for folk with limited time.

Holywell Dene
Whitley Bay Park Avenue-Blyth Arriva Northumbria 308 and Go North East 309 stops at Hartley. The dene is half a mile inland along B1325.

Kielder Forest and reservoir
Newcastle St James-Carlisle Go North East 10 or Stagecoach-in-Cumbria 615 to Hexham and then Snaiths 880 to Kielder (travel time almost 3 hours). Please check in advance for timings etc.

Newbiggin
Newcastle Haymarket-Newbiggin Arriva Northumbria X21. Terminates five minutes walk from Church Point seawatching spot. Newbiggin Mound is half a mile NW on other side of golf course.

Prestwick Carr
Newcastle Haymarket-Morpeth Arriva Northumbria X44 calls at Dinnington. The Carr is half a mile west along road signposted Prestwick, past the White Swan pub.

Seahouses(for Farne Islands)
Newcastle Haymarket-Bamburgh Arriva Northumbria service 501 (travel time two and a half hours).

St Mary's Island
Whitley Bay Park Avenue-Blyth Arriva Northumbria 308 and Go North East 309 both pass island turn-off. Whitley Bay is also served by Metro from Newcastle.

Swallow Pond
Newcastle Haymarket-Whitley Bay Go North East 53 and Arriva Northumbria X8 stop at ASDA Benton store. The pond is along the wagonway running south on the west side of the store. The site is also about 20 minutes walk from Metro station at Palmersville.

Tynemouth Haven and North Shields Fish Quay
Newcastle Haymarket-Tynemouth Arriva Northumbria 306 and Newcastle St James-Tynemouth service 1 go to both. North Shields and Tynemouth also served by Metro from Newcastle

Birds mentioned in the index are generally those that are featured as Target Birds in the site reports. Commonly occuring species are omitted to keep the index to a manageable size.

INDEX

CLEVELAND & COUNTY DURHAM SITES

COUNTY DURHAM AREA

1 **Backstone Bank Wood**

2 **Baldersdale**

3 **Bishop Middleham**

4 **Blackton Beck & Middle End**

5 **Bollihope Burn**

6 **Castle Eden Dene**

7 **Crimdon Dene & Hart Warren Dunes**

8 **Croxdale Hall**

9 **Dawdon Blast/Hawthorn Dene**

10 **Deepdale Wood**

11 **Derwent Reservoir**

12 **Easington-Blackhall Coast**

13 **Greta River Walks**

14 **Hamsterley Forest/ Bedburn**
(Hamsterley Forest, Adder Wood/Bedburn Beck, Dryderdale, Hamsterley Common/Pikeston Fell, Harthope Wood)

15 **Low Barns**

16 **Lower Derwent Valley, Gateshead**
(Chopwell Wood, Far Pasture Nature Reserve, Shibdon Pond Nature Reserve, Thornley Woodlands Centre)

17 **River Derwent (Coalgate Burn Gorges)**

18 **Tyne & Wear Coast**
(South Shields, Marsden Quarry, Whitburn, Sunderland (Harbour, Roker Park and Seaburn))

19 **Uppermost Teesdale**
(Bowlees to High Force, Langdon Beck, Widdybank Fell)

20 **Washington Wetland Centre & Barmston Pond**

CLEVELAND AREA

1 **Hartlepool Headland**

2 **Saltburn-Hummersea Coast**

3 **Scaling Dam Reservoir**

4 **Sleddale**

5 **Teesmouth NE Sites**
(South Gare, Coatham Marsh, Locke Park, Redcar)

6 **Teesmouth NW Sites**
(North Gare/Seaton Common, Seaton Carew, Seaton Snook/Zinc Works Road)

7 **Teesmouth SW Sites**
(Saltholme RSPB
Reserve, Cowpen Bewley Woodland CP, Cowpen Marsh, Greatham Creek, Greenabella Marsh, (The) Long Drag, Seal Sands)